# The Sounds Of Music: Perception And Notation

Gerald R. Eskelin, DME

Stage 3 Publishing

Woodland Hills, California

# THE SOUNDS OF MUSIC:
# PERCEPTION AND NOTATION

**Gerald Eskelin, DME**

Stage 3 Publishing
5759 Wallis Lane
Woodland Hills CA
91367 U.S.A

Manufactured in the United States of America

Library of Congress Catalog Card Number: 98-060321
ISBN 1-886209-13-8: $37.50 Softcover with CD

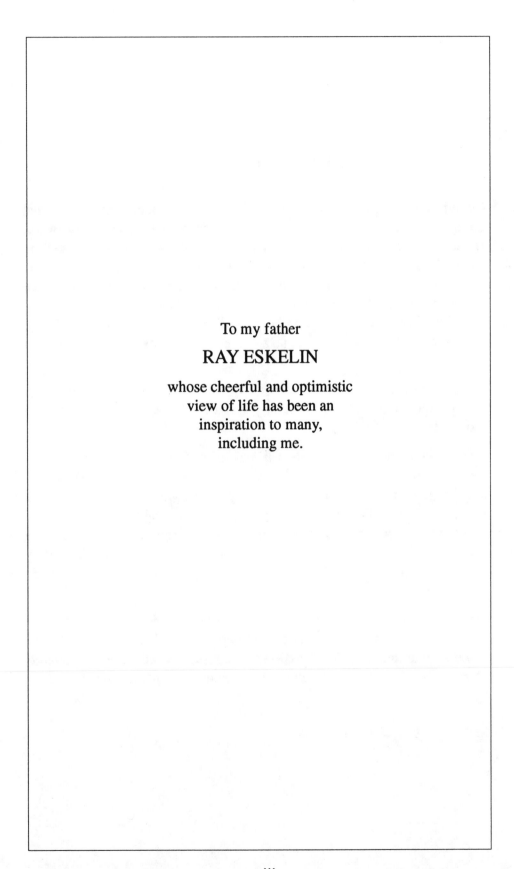

To my father

RAY ESKELIN

whose cheerful and optimistic
view of life has been an
inspiration to many,
including me.

# ABOUT THE AUTHOR

Gerald Eskelin has been making music for more than four decades. His vocal group, the L.A. Jazz Choir, has been nominated twice for a Grammy award. Having also been a college music teacher for thirty five years, including tenures at the University of Southern California, California Institute of the Arts and Pierce College in Los Angeles, he has had considerable experience in both commercial and academic music. His conducting experience ranges from symphony orchestra to marching band and master chorale to pop choir. He has sung opera, show music, jazz, barbershop and even a bit of southern gospel.

His academic credits include a Doctor of Music Education and Master of Arts degrees from Indiana University and a Bachelor of Arts degree from Florida Southern College.

The legal community frequently requests his expertise on musical matters. He has testified in court on behalf of such well-known composer/performers as John Fogerty, Stevie Wonder, Allen Sylvestri, Michael Jackson, Ronald Isley, and the Spin Doctors, and has given musicological opinions regarding songs by dozens of others, including Tom Petty, Ray Parker Jr., Madonna and Kenny Loggins / Guy Thomas. His corporate clients include Disney Studios, Warner Brothers Studios, Warner Chappel Music and EMI Music Publishers.

Dr. Eskelin's book *Lies My Music Teacher Told Me* is nearing its third printing. The success and popularity of that book has evidenced the need for a wider and more thorough discussion of the issues raised there. *The Sounds Of Music:Perception And Notation* was written in response to that need.

# Prelude

Why launch another music fundamentals book into an already flooded market? The reason is that this one bears little resemblance to others dealing with basic musical concepts. Most start out with "this is a quarter note" and end with "this is a ninth chord." Many use a simplistic connect-the-dots approach and never deal systematically with the musical perceptions and concepts that notation represents. Also, the fact that pianos and other keyboards produce compromised pitches is consistently ignored, which limits understanding of the true nature of music. This book is aimed at correcting these significant omissions.

*The Sounds Of Music: Perception and Notation* first deals with the physical nature of music, then with the perception and conception of its separate and combined elements, and finally with systems of representing music on paper or computer screen. The early chapters address elemental musical sounds and explore the perceptual experiences that lead to the development of practical musical concepts, not just theoretical constructs. Middle chapters show how these elements combine in simple and understandable ways to create "harmony," "melody," "rhythm," "form" and other perceptual/conceptual elements of music. Later chapters trace the development of music notation and explore both the strengths and weaknesses of our standard systems.

A possible reason that college music textbooks consistently begin with discussions of notation is that authors and educators assume that students already have experience making music and they simply want to know how to read and write it. In the past, when college students came from flourishing high school choral, band and orchestral programs, that approach may have been reasonable. Today, however, young people entering college have a completely different experience base. The recent explosion of recorded music has produced a generation of listeners. There are now more people familiar with more music than the world has ever seen.

Fascinated by music and wanting to know more, scores of college students register for "beginning" music classes. More often than not, they are confronted with and quickly frustrated by empty notational constructs and drills. Frequently, the music offered for study has little relation to the music that inspired their interest.

Nevertheless, some students intuitively figure out how music works and are successful, while others study long and hard and never discover it. This undoubtedly contributes to the popular view that certain people are talented and others simply are not.

Commonly, children who develop musical skills are considered "special." In contrast, consider our expectations regarding language skills. To no one's great surprise, most children learn to speak, then *later* learn to read and write. In college music education, we tend to operate in reverse. We attempt to teach adult students to read and write in a medium in which they have little or no functional skills. Under these circumstances, one would never really know what an "untalented" student might accomplish if provided with structured experiences in the *real* language of music—sounds—before dealing with "notes" and "staves."

An idea widely held is that some people are simply tone-deaf and thus have little chance of joining the "talented." That view is seldom held, however, in regard to language learning. While it is well known that children learn language more efficiently than adults, we normally don't reject the idea that adults can learn languages. Yet, many teachers abandon hope for the adult musical "ear." Sadly, many potentially musical people accept this idea and give up their dreams.

Why must this be so? Most adults have an advantage that most children do not—logical thought. Careful use of language can help adults focus on the correct perceptual information. What remains is to translate that basic information into concepts and then systematically attach appropriate labels to the results.

Once experiential concepts are secure, learning musical notation is more meaningful. Notation becomes an imaging of aural musical constructs, just as written language is an imaging of ideas. Music reading becomes more than merely naming notes on a page or pushing the right buttons on an instrument. Symbol combinations then evoke images of real sounds in real musical relationships.

The discussions of perception and conception in this book are not intended to be taken clinically, although reference to formal studies are occasionally made. Much of what is offered is the result of practical experience combined with logic. There is no intent to prove any particular psychological theory of music perception. The concern here is only for what the human ear can hear and how experienced musicians commonly organize that information.

The value of this book will be realized when the ideas offered here make practical sense to the reader. The ultimate goal of this effort will be attained whenever this book helps someone achieve musical success after believing it was beyond his or her reach.

Although much of the discussion focuses on Western music, the basic principles presented relate to any musical tradition—old or new, Western or exotic, classical or popular. Since the emphasis is on perception and conception of sound patterns in a temporal setting, these principles can be applied to most any musical style.

There is a very healthy trend in college classes toward universality and away from provincial views of the world. Some universities no longer accept transfer of traditional notation-based "fundamentals of music" classes for general-education and/or humanities credit. Hopefully, *Sounds Of Music: Perception and Notation*, in addition to providing information of interest to the general reader, will also provide a much-needed college textbook. It would be gratifying to have assisted teachers in developing classes that more effectively teach students how music works and how to apply that information to a much wider musical world.

# Contents

# Contents continued

# Acknowledgements

Persons who contributed to this project include a great many more individuals than those who deliberately and directly helped to bring it into existence. The thousands of students and singers in my classes and choirs who, over the decades, provided the exchange of ideas and the opportunity to hone teaching techniques are, without question, most responsible for development of the ideas contained in this book. To be sure, my own teachers influenced this writing—those who inspired and challenged as well as those who seemed satisfied to dutifully and unquestioningly pass along what they themselves were taught. In fact, it is probably the latter that demonstrated the urgent need for this book.

Closer to the project are those who seem to find value in ideas I have been sharing in recent years regarding choral performance and music teaching in general. When my recent book, *Lies My Music Teacher Told Me*, was enthusiastically received by both teachers and students, by both professionals and amateurs, I knew I had to write this book. The positive reinforcement from those who agreed to read early drafts indicated to me that my decision was a good one.

Dr. Frank Ventimiglia, scientist at the University of California at Davis and avid saxophone player, had read "Lies" and expressed such enthusiasm that I asked him to provide feedback on the early drafts of this book. That, too, proved to be a good decision. Frank's detailed comments have contributed greatly to the clarity of writing in this book. Other readers who have provided valuable feedback on various chapters are Ken Emmer, of Fresno, California, who also had read "Lies"; Lionel Greenberg and David Pinto, my faculty colleagues at Pierce College; Scott Guy, musician and TV writer/producer; and most important, my wife Marlene, who checked every page before it left the office.

The final editing was done by Stephanie Vitale, who thoughtfully pruned my unnecessary words and rearranged others, allowing the meanings to emerge more efficiently and clearly. Thanks to Stephanie's skilled eye, logical thinking and sensitivity to what I was attempting to say, you will find this book much more understandable and enjoyable than would otherwise have been the case.

I invited Dr. Patrice Madura, assistant professor of music education at the University of Southern California, and Jerry Luedders, music department chairperson at California State University at Northridge, to read a late draft and, if they found it appropriate, to offer their comments. This proved to be another good decision. Their generous "reviews" exceeded anything I could have imagined. Also, thanks to Steve Allen for his continued support and encouragement.

The recorded audio illustrations that accompany this book were created and/ or compiled by a number of talented and knowledgable people. The orchestral items were selected by Dr. Allan E. Green, music faculty member of Union College, Barbourville, Kentucky. Scott Guy researched the licensing of these items and negotiated the contract with Delta Music.

Dr. John Schneider, my colleague at Pierce College and celebrated guitarist, created several of the electronic illustrations. The assistance of Elin Carlson, L.A. Jazz Choir singer and rising opera star, was very helpful in selecting vocal solo examples. The piano excerpts were performed by my friend and long-time accompanist, Dwight Elrich.

The vocal solos and some choral excerpts are performed by members of the L.A. Jazz Choir. Soloists are Cindy Bourquin, Elin Carlson, Rick Kasper, John Hendricks, Brad McMurray, John Revheim, Patricia Tollett and Alison Wedding. Other singers who participated in the choral recordings are Cindy O'Conner, Scott Guy, Ron Harris, Sandy Howell, Eric Seppala and Heidi Summers. Additional choral examples are excerpts from recordings by the L.A. Jazz Choir, the Valley Master Choral, the Pierce College Choir, all directed by the author, and the Los Angeles Chamber Singers, directed by Peter Rutenberg.

Recording engineer, James Mooney, retired soon after this session following many years of recording some of the most well-known names in jazz. Jim was the recording engineer for all the L.A. Jazz Choir albums.

The attractive and appropriate cover was designed by Paul Haven, of San Clemente, Californina. Thanks to Gabe Watts and Tim Wertheimer of Data Reproductions, and Bonnie Bonhivert and Earl Gordon of Vision Disk International for efficiently facilitating the manufacture of the book and CD.

Most importantly, I would like to thank my wife, partner and friend Marlene for her dilligent attention to every detail in coordinating the production of this book. Her "taking care of business" allowed me to concentrate on writing.

Finally, I want to thank you for reading it. I hope you find it of value.

Gerald Eskelin

# Finding the "Sounds"

In the spirit of this book's main premise—that one should acquire an understanding of the *sounds* of music before studying methods of notating it—a CD containing audio illustrations is affixed inside the back cover. As you read, you will frequently encounter the symbol shown here, along with a reference number. The number will direct you to a specific item recorded on the CD which illustrates the discussion. The number before the hyphen refers to a chapter; the number after the hyphen refers to an item within the chapter.

9-12

As there are more than a hundred audio illustrations on this CD, it is not practical to number them consecutively since most CD index systems are limited to 99 numbers. Instead, the CD index system will be used only to locate the chapter. The individual items within each chapter are slated aurally on the CD.

Some illustrations contain more than one example, so do not assume that the item is completed when you reach the first silence. A clicking sound will signal the end of each item. When you hear the click, push the PAUSE button on your CD player. (Don't push the STOP button unless you are finished reading, since that would put you back at the beginning of the CD.) When you are ready to hear the next item, push PLAY. Listen to the new item number and make sure it corresponds to the illustration you are expecting to hear.

To easily locate the beginning of an example you want to hear again, just note the time display on your machine as you push PLAY. You then can quickly find the beginning of that item using the rewind scanning button. Pushing the button that gets you back to the previous index mark will put you back to the beginning of the present chapter.

It is also important to have a keyboard available while reading this book. If you have the choice, use an electronic keyboard or organ. While a piano will do the job, it is much better to hear sustained sounds, particularly while listening for accurate tuning. Lack of experience with the keyboard will not present a problem here since it is not expected or required. We will be using the keyboard only as an illustrative tool and as a means of establishing specific pitches.

Are you ready? Let's go.

Orchestral examples are licensed through
**Delta Music, Inc., Los Angeles, California**.

World music examples are licensed through
**Multicultural Media, Barre, Vermont**

# I

# Introduction

What are your interests in music? Are you a listener, a performer, a teacher, a student? What are your expectations in reading this book? Do you want to increase your perception of meaningful elements in the music you hear? Are you hoping to elevate your performances to a more insightful level by expanding your understanding of music's inner workings? Would you like to improve your ability to communicate musical principles and characteristics more clearly to others by gaining clearer insights into music itself? Are you exploring a subject you have always wanted to know more about and are finally getting around to it?

If you answered "Yes" to any of these questions, you will find this book helpful in moving you toward your goal. Regardless of your present level of musical understanding, you will find much to provoke your *own* thinking on the subject. While the discussions are basic enough for the novice to understand, many topics are approached from a fresh point of view offering opportunities for those more experienced in music to reevaluate currently held ideas.

While it is certainly possible to simply absorb the information contained here and mechanically memorize it, that is not the book's purpose. Each chapter is written with the idea of helping you understand the background and historical events that led to practices and conventions we use today. Some of our current popular notions are "right on the money," but others leave much to be desired. In each case, we consider reasons for either supporting or challenging these ideas and conventions. The important thing is that *you* will have thought about them.

Early chapters describe music without using standard notation. This may be bothersome to some of you who already read notation and may feel that some discussions would be more efficiently demonstrated by using it. On the other hand, many of you not yet proficient with notation will probably appreciate the opportunity to acquire basic concepts without having to deal with it. Tolerance aside, it might be beneficial to notationally literate readers to view musical constructs expressed in spacial graphics. It never hurts to consider a different way of looking at things.

In that regard, we all tend to deal with music mostly in terms of our own direct experience with it. As a means of broadening our concepts of what music is, it will be helpful to look at it from a universal point of view before we deal with its details in a particular style or tradition. So, let's move a few paces back from our own personal experience, widen our field of vision, and consider music as a world-wide means of human expression.

# 1

# A World View Of Music

As communications systems improve, the world seems smaller somehow. Travel is becoming more accessible, making it easier to come in close contact with people from all parts of the globe. As a result, our concepts of the similarities and differences among cultures move toward reality and away from hearsay. As we learn more about others, it sometimes is startling to discover that all people do not see the world the same way, and often gratifying to find that we all have some important values in common.

However, there are some things we have always had in common, such as the way our eyes, ears, legs, fingers and other body parts work. Two plus two equals four everywhere on earth. Gravity causes apples to fall toward the ground no matter on whose tree they grow. Although our interpretation of what we hear and say may differ, the dynamics of *how* we hear and say things is based on principles of conception that are universally the same.

With that in mind, we will begin our exploration into the wide world of music. Realizing the world's musical traditions are as varied as the many cultures and subcultures that exist, we will seek out common elements to give us insight into how music works, not just in our own cultures, but in all. Although it is a fascinating study, we will not address the various ways different people use music. Our focus will be on the perception of music's basic elements.

# Clear Thinking and Definitions

As we explore the world of music, we should agree on our use of important words to ensure that we are talking about the same things. In our everyday conversation, we frequently say things that are not very precise. Consider, for example, the interviewee on the TV dance show who says, "I like that song because it has a good beat." What is a "beat"? Are there "good" ones and "bad" ones? Is a piece of music good simply because "I like it"? What makes music "good" or "not so good"?

The terminology commonly used today to describe music, both in and out of academia, is disturbingly imprecise. For that reason, a brief review of the logical nature of *defining* might provide helpful preventative medicine and encourage insight into the nature of the musical experience rather than adding further confusion.

**the art of defining**  In simple terms, a definition specifies the essential characteristics of a concept. It does this by combining other words that represent related concepts. By carefully selecting these related words, a definition also cuts away, or excludes, all the things in the world that the concept is not. It is critically important to exclude concepts that are unessential and do not apply to all instances of the concept. For example, a definition of "man" should not include "big," since not all men are big.

Let's practice. One might define the word "chair" as "something to sit on." But a sofa, as well, is "something to sit on" so the definition needs the words "for one person." One person could also sit on a rock, but a rock normally is not thought of as a chair, so the term "furniture" is needed to make that distinction. One might wish to include "four legs" in the definition, but pedestal chairs don't have four legs, so that should not be included. So, what about "stool"? How do we cut that out of the definition of "chair"? By adding "with a back support"? By specifying the height of the seat?

As you can see, definitions can be rather illusive. But this is merely an illusion. A concept, for the person using it, is an "in" or "out" matter. As one applies the concept, things either fit the concept or *don't fit* the concept. If something doesn't quite fit, the user combines the main concept with other simple concepts to clarify and add precision to the meaning. If the "new" concept becomes a permanent part of the main definition and causes it to change, the revised concept still works on that same "in" or "out" basis. Things encountered in experience either fit and are included, or don't fit and are excluded.

This may seem rather odd, since we are continually faced with "shades of gray" in real life. Nevertheless, this "in or out" juggling goes on behind the scenes and usually works adequately well in our day-to-day thinking. Much of our confusion comes from coexisting concepts that conflict. For example, when we are taught something about life that doesn't match our own experience we have to sort out our own "reality" for the sake of our emotional peace of mind. Sometimes this process can get rather complicated.

However, the basic mechanics of clear thinking are rather simple. A good analogy can be found in the workings of a computer. Although storage disks are filled with complex data, every little piece of information depends on patterns of little "in" and "out" signals, or more specifically, zeros and ones. When the computer does a search and finds the right pattern of signals, it projects the image to the screen with amazing speed. Similarly, when the human mind encounters experiences it recognizes, the corresponding concepts (with or without a name tag) are brought to some level of awareness. To a large extent, education is a matter of naming and cataloging these experiences.

While most of the terms commonly used to describe music will be defined throughout this book, it will be helpful to establish a definition of "music" at this point. Since we will be sampling a variety of musical styles in this chapter, this definition will provide a basis upon which to conduct our observations.

**music defined**

A definition of "music" quite obviously should include the word "sound," but most probably not all sound. So, we need another word, or words, that specify sounds that constitute music and exclude sounds that don't. It might be tempting to consider "sounds I like," but that would certainly be too self-serving a definition for music in a universal sense.

So, what makes the sounds of music different from other sounds? The answer is "organization." When sounds are ordered in a way that is different from the random sounds of our everyday existence, we tend to notice the difference. Therefore, **music** is "organized sound." The experience can take on special significance ranging from "nice" to "profound," from "enjoyable" to "annoying," from "satisfying" to "strange." But, in all cases, we can tell there is something unique about our experiences of these sounds. However, our definition should avoid such words as "good," "enjoyable," or "satisfying." These personal emotion-based judgments don't apply to all music. In order to keep our definition precise, we will leave them out.

On the other hand, who is to say whether any given collection of sounds is "organized"? One listener might hear "music" in a cat thumping across the roof while another hears it simply as "a cat thumping across the roof." Does this mean that each individual is the judge of what music is and what it is not? If we are going to be intellectually honest, we're stuck with that fact.

Just as beauty is "in the eye of the beholder," music is "in the ear of the listener."

So, if some fellow says "The compositions of J. S. Bach are just a lot of noise," is he right? Well... sort of...but not exactly. If he means "Bach's music is noise for everyone," he is clearly mistaken. If he means he personally finds no meaning in the music he may be telling the truth. However, he is likely saying more about the condition of his musical ear than about the music of Bach.

## Musical Traditions

At a wedding party in Los Angeles, a band was playing Egyptian music. A Caucasian guest was overheard to say, "I don't get this music; it has no melody." The ironic thing about this remark is that Middle Eastern music, including the music heard at this wedding, consists almost entirely of melody (and rhythm, of course). A more accurate "translation" of the remark perhaps would be "This music is new to me and I don't have a vocabulary of experience to help me understand and appreciate it."

One of the distinguishing characteristics of an intellectually honest person is the acknowledgment that one's own experience *automatically* is inadequate to support accurate and meaningful perceptions from a novel encounter. Once that understanding is secure, one is ready to begin following where curiosity leads. Rather than suffering the limitations of naive judgments, one's intellectual doors to new worlds of meaning are flung wide open.

In the paragraphs that follow, we will take a whirlwind tour of some of the musical styles heard around the world and also take a quick look at some traditions from the past. As you can imagine, this survey can only provide a peek into the world's limitless diversity of music. To explore it with meaningful depth would require vast libraries of books and recordings.

Nevertheless, our brief trip will remind us that the music we grew up with is not the only tradition that exists, neither is it necessarily the most highly developed, nor is it the least. Also, all traditions change to some extent through the ages, some more than others, so it is a mistake to assume the music of our own few decades is intrinsically better than the music of another time—past or yet to come.

As you listen to the recorded selections, you will notice things that are unique about each of them. For our purposes, it will be more helpful if you concentrate on what these styles and traditions have in common. Also, try to seek out "organization" in these excerpts. Some basic principles of music perception are universal, even when cultural meanings of various musical products are quite different.

We know that music was an important ingredient in ancient Greek culture, one of the earliest known musical traditions (eighth century B.C.). Written descriptions of early Greek music have helped provide a general idea of how this music was made and how various human emotions were believed to be evoked by listening to it. However, we don't know exactly how it sounded. Unfortunately, Hollywood Records did not have a branch office in Athens at that time. **Ancient Greece**

At least three principle instruments were used during this period. The kithara, a small harp, was used by all classes of Greeks to perform songs of love and hate, politics and sports. The syrinx, or pan-pipes, provided the peaceful mood of the shepherd. The aulos was a double-reed wind instrument with unstable and flexible tuning, making it particularly appropriate to express emotional and ecstatic moods. Much of the music was improvised according to musical formulas.

While we don't know much about the actual music of this period (only a few songs are known), we do know quite a bit about its music theory. This is largely due to the writings of the famous early Greek philosopher and scientist Pythagoras, whose ideas we will have more to say about later. Greek musical style, which reached its highest point of classicism in the fifth century BC, died out after the fall of Athens in 404 BC. Greek music is believed to have had little or no direct influence on Western culture, but appears to have exerted considerable influence on the musical direction of many Eastern cultures.

In contrast, much is known about the music of the European Medieval period (c. 300 to 1450 AD), also referred to as the Middle Ages. Because of the development of music notation during this time and the preservation of extensive descriptions of performance styles, modern performers have been able to recreate the music of this period with considerable accuracy. **Europe**

Sacred music (having to do with the church) and secular music (not having to do with the church) were not always different during this long period. The selections provided here, however, are representative of music distinctly sacred and distinctly secular. One is a portion of a chant, as it might have been heard in a first millennium cathedral. The other is a dance that may very well have delighted the nobility attending a party at a royal palace. 1-1

It was during this period in Europe that the revolutionary idea was born to sound more than one pitch at the same time. This development caused music in the Western world to take a completely different direction than music in nearly every other world culture. 1-2

To a considerable extent, traditional European music can be viewed as two distinct entities: art music and folk music. While art music has been largely international in its development, folk music generally belongs to one tradition or another. Many folk songs in western European countries are based on the seven-pitch medieval modes of the first millennium. Although originally created for solo performance, many melodies have since been harmonized for group singing.

1-3

Folk music in eastern Europe reflects many characteristics of Middle Eastern music. Hungarian gypsy music, for example, is often based on exotic scales as well as complex rhythmic patterns. Folk instruments include the accordion, the bagpipe and the hammered dulcimer, as well as various fiddles, flutes and plucked stringed instruments.

1-4

**Middle East**  Little was written about Middle Eastern music in the first millennium BC, largely because Islamic attitudes discouraged musical expression. Since then, however, rich musical traditions have flowered, based somewhat on ancient Greek practices, but with indigenous flavors decidedly unique to various regions.

Middle Eastern musical traditions share a number of common characteristics. All are based on melodic systems that include some pitches that are "in the cracks" (compared to the scales of Western music). All employ drums of various sizes with which to play rhythms that are at times rather complex, particularly when played by a soloist. Most music is performed by soloists or small groups.

1-5

Instruments include a vertical flute called the nay, a violin or fiddle, a vase-shaped drum and a tambourine. In groups having more than a few players, a larger drum is usually added to the ensemble. An important instrument in Persian music is the dulcimer, usually played solo.

**Asia**  Traditional music in many Far Eastern countries exists today side by side with music from the West. The musical fare available on any day in Tokyo, for example, might include a symphony orchestra concert, a jazz performance, a rock music extravaganza, and a Kabuki theater performance. This was not always the case, of course, and before the modernization of Japan beginning in the mid-nineteenth century, musical art in this country was largely isolated from the rest of the world.

During the first millennium A.D., while European music was emerging from the chants of the Roman Catholic church, traditional music of Japan was emerging from the Buddhist chants. Traditional Japanese music is to be "seen" as well as heard, in that the sounds are intended to be experienced in connection with dance and/or theater.

In contrast to the tightly packed pitches of Middle Eastern music, Far Eastern music is largely based on a simple five-pitch scale. The music is restrained and refined and musicians are not concerned with exploring new territory, as in much Western music, but rather with expressing established musical ideas in an elegant manner. Improvisation is rare.

*1-6*

An important instrument of Japan is the genteel koto, a thirteen-stringed zither-like instrument that would be present in the household of every well-bred family. The music played on a koto is taught by rote, as opposed to being written. The traditional Japanese Kabuki orchestra contains about a dozen musicians, including three drummers, a flutist, several shamisen (a three-stringed instrument) players, and singers.

A unique tradition in the Far East is the gamelan orchestra of Indonesia. A large ensemble may include up to thirty musicians, playing end-blown flutes, a rebak (fiddle), several gongs, and various metal drums tuned in different ways. In spite of the large number of players, most "compositions" are based on a single melody, sometimes quite complex and requiring meticulous rehearsal. Sudden changes in loudness frequently contribute to the music's dramatic effect.

**Africa**

When speaking of African music, one is usually referring to traditions south of the Sahara, since the music of the Mediterranean countries reflects Islamic and Arabic traditions. Because Africa is so large and contains many cultures, it is a mistake to assume that all African music is the same. Nevertheless, some generalizations are possible.

For the most part, African music is not performed for an audience. It is a part of everyday life, and almost always performed in conjunction with dance or ceremony. It is utilitarian in that songs are used in the context of some specific activity or event, such as a religious service, marriage, birth, death, hunting, war, work or social gatherings. It is repetitive, frequently employing a "call and response" form in which one singer sings a phrase and the other singers respond to it.

*1-7*

There is an enormous variety of instruments used in traditional African music. Besides the ever-present drums, other instruments include rattles, one-string fiddles, xylophones, natural (valveless) trumpets and flutes. Hand clapping often accompanies singing. While most ensembles consist of two or three musicians, large drum orchestras numbering in the hundreds are common.

Due to extensive missionary influence from the West during the nineteenth and early twentieth centuries, African music now contains many crossover elements. For example, songs are frequently sung in harmony, often without instrumental accompaniment. Western influence continues today as African-American popular music is increasingly heard in African urban centers.

**Latin America**    As Cortez led his Spanish armies against the ancient civilizations in the New World, native musical traditions were systematically replaced by European art music. As a result, we know very little about early indigenous music in the Latin American countries.

In the early nineteenth century, as the Spaniards were expelled, the music we now recognize as distinctly Latin American began to emerge. We can identify a number of discrete styles from Latin-American traditions: salsa, an Afro-Cuban style influenced by jazz; Tex-Mex, the music of the border regions between Mexico and Texas; mariachi, a Mexican folk style; bossa nova, a jazz-based music from Brazil. A Jamaican musical tradition based on African rhythms mixed with Latin elements, called Reggae, is generally thought to belong to this general group.

1-8    All of these styles contain interesting rhythmic elements contrasted to an underlying steady rhythmic flow. All employ simple harmonies similar to those of European and American folk music. Small groups of musicians, usually from four to six, are common, and include vocalists as well as instrumentalists. Most frequently, the players also do the singing. This excerpt is from Peru.

Instruments include guitars, a string bass or guitarrón, and various percussion instruments. Violins, trumpets and other instruments are common, particularly in salsa and mariachi music.

**Native American**    Although Native Americans have assimilated into American society and frequently listen to and perform rock and country music, a concentrated effort continues to preserve traditional "Indian" music. While its supernatural and ritualistic associations have been largely abandoned, the celebration of the culture itself has taken the form of annual inter-tribal ceremonies and pow-wows.

1-9    This music is extremely simple, consisting of songs having limited vocal range and accompanied by a large drum, occasionally with a flute or a single-stringed fiddle. The drum pattern, in bold contrast to the intricate rhythms in African and Latin American music, almost always consists of steady even strokes in sets of four. The flute or fiddle plays alone or duplicates the vocal melody.

Native American songs frequently consist of a mixture of meaningful lyrics and vocables (nonsense syllables). The melodies often are composed on a simple five-pitch scale, as is the traditional music of many cultures around the world. Like African music, songs are associated with specific activities or ceremonies; however, this has changed somewhat in recent years in that music is sometimes performed purely for entertainment.

Folk music traditions in the United States can be identified by a number of **United States** separate as well as interwoven threads. Besides the music of Native Americans, other traditions include the Cajun music of southern Louisiana, various "hillbilly" styles of the Appalachian mountains, cowboy songs from 1-10 the plains of the western states, and the jazz of New Orleans. This bluegrass southern gospel song is typical of the style.

Until the middle of the twentieth century, concert goers in the United States were largely a satellite audience for the art music of Europe. In the first half of the twentieth century, composers began to write music that was decidedly "American." George Gershwin not only wrote many popular songs, but 1-11 composed "classical" music with a distinctly jazz flavor. Today, European and American art music finds audiences in nearly every civilized country in the world.

To varying degrees, these early traditions have influenced contemporary popular music today. Country music combines elements of mountain music and cowboy songs. Pure swamp blues has merged with jazz to produce a number of styles that have become popular during the past few decades, including early rock-and-roll, the Motown sound, and rhythm and blues. Other kinds of "fusion" have produced jazz-rock, classical-jazz, rap music, black gospel, contemporary gospel, and a host of others.

Imported styles merging with American homegrown styles has resulted in **a mixture of** the wide variety of music available today. The sophisticated English influ- **world styles** ence of the Beatles combined with the raw rock-and-roll energy of Bill Haley, Elvis Presley, Jerry Lee Lewis and others has had a profound influence on rock and other popular music in the last third of the twentieth century. Latin American and African styles have already had a significant impact on mainstream popular music. While rock-and-roll elements have mixed with Middle Eastern and Asian styles to produce popular music in those cultures, the reverse is also true. It is not uncommon to hear an East Indian sitar, for example, in a performance of Western popular music.

With increased speed of communication and the explosion of mass media, it is inevitable that changes in music will accelerate in the decades to come. Hopefully, that process will not diminish efforts to preserve the rich musical heritage of our diverse pasts.

## Hearing Musical Significance

As you listened to the musical excerpts in this section, did you find that our definition of music as "organized sound" applied to all of them? To what extent were you able to find organization in each example? If you were not able to discover organization in a particular excerpt, did you assume it was the fault of the music or perhaps due to your unfamiliarity with the style?

Were you able to identify characteristics or elements common to all of them? What kinds of perceptions did you employ as you listened? Were you aware of a sense of flow in time? Was the time organized? If so, how was the time organized? Did you hear "shapes" in all of the excerpts? If so, how were the shapes defined perceptually? What elements contributed to the sense of shape in each?

In the remaining pages, we will examine the basic elements of music—hopefully, of all music—that form the basis for human perception of "organized sound." During this process, we will look at the terminology commonly used to refer to and describe those elements. We will find that some traditional notions fit the observable facts better than others, so we may want to discard certain preconceptions and replace them with more accurate and effectual concepts. Our goal in this regard will be to arrive at a reasonably accurate picture of the nature of musical expression and to acquire appropriate terminology with which to refer to its various characteristics.

# II

# Musical Sound

Much of the information we absorb from our environment has to do with "either/or" categories—for example, time and space. While philosophers may encourage us to believe that time/space is a single physical phenomenon, the fact is we perceive each one as a separate mode of experience. As we view a painting, assuming the light is steady and we sense no movement around it, we contemplate its static spacial relationships. While it takes time to enjoy the experience, our focus is not so much on the "dynamics" of our own thoughts and eye movements, but on the painting itself, which simply hangs there, motionless. We are seeing "space."

Although we tend to think of space perception as a visual thing, we can also *hear* space. Sounds in a small room appear different from sounds in a large one. If we only hear, but can't see, the automobile driving past our house, we frequently know the direction from which it approaches and to which it departs. When we both see and hear an event happening in space, the two senses collaborate to reinforce the experience. The development of "surround sound" in cinema production greatly enhances our enjoyment of a good movie.

Similarly, we can experience "time" in more than one perceptual mode. The sense of time passing, however, seems to require some active modification of the aural environment. Hearing and/or seeing an unchanging stimulus offers no sense of temporal "motion." Only the flow of our own thoughts provides temporal awareness in such a circumstance.

The art of music exists primarily in the temporal mode where meaning is created by our perception of significant sound modifications within a duration of time. We normally don't think of the actual modifications themselves as having to do with time, even though sound itself depends on the passage of time in order to contain enough dimension to be perceived.  For example, changes in "loudness" have to do with the concept "amount of sound," an abstract idea. It doesn't take time to contemplate "loudness" once we have formed the concept. The same is true of a number of other physical aspects of sound used to create musical meaning.

The kinds of perceptual modifications used to create meaningful experiences in sound have changed during the historical development of music. Very likely, the earliest means of creating contrast was simply to make patterns of sounds and silences. Sustaining and modifying the aspect of sound we call "pitch" must certainly have become a means of creating musical meaning at a very early stage of human experience. As our predecessors learned more about the possibilities for modifying sound, other physical attributes of sound began to contribute to the art of music as we know it today.

Since perception of "time" is impossible until it contains "events" created by contrast, we will begin our discussion of musical perception by looking at the attributes of sound that make contrast possible, and which thereby contribute to the creation of meaningful temporal patterns. Once those concepts are in place, they will provide a foundation from which to discuss the nature of musical rhythm.

2

# Attributes
# Of Sound

Earlier, we looked at how definitions work and noted that the process of basic thinking is rather simple, using "in or out" judgments to formulate concepts and bringing the right ones to action when needed. Perception, also an important part of the thinking process, employs previously formed concepts to access and deliver important information for use in making both trivial and critical life decisions.

During any waking moment, our senses are bombarded with data. Much of this we ignore, largely because it doesn't fit a concept (named or unnamed) that we "recognize." The more concepts we form, the more data is potentially usable. By deliberate selection, we decide, consciously or subconsciously, what deserves our attention. As we go through life, adding new concepts and improving old ones, our perceptions become more plentiful as well as more precise.

One way to think about the dynamics of learning is to think of perception as the process and conception as the product. As perception collects meaningful data, it is stored in "containers" called concepts. Using these concepts as a basis for sorting experience, perception then goes out and brings in new data. All of this appears to be done by those little "in or out" signals we talked about earlier. Also, once a concept is formed, it can be used to *think* about something without really experiencing it at that moment. For example, we don't need to *see* a piece of apple pie in order to think about one.

Interestingly, our minds can collect concepts without consciously naming them. It's like recognizing a face but not being able to come up with a name. The perception and conception of musical experience is very much like that. If we had to name every concept used in receiving perceptual data while listening to a Beethoven symphony, we would become buried in frustration.

**unnamed concepts**

We simply absorb from the experience whatever our present state of musicality allows, and the rest just floats past us because it doesn't fit any present concept. That's why a third-grader might classify such an experience as "strange," a teenager might think it "cool," a college student might find it "interesting," someone middle aged might regard it as "moving," and a senior citizen might deem it "profound." All or most of this can happen without naming anything.

However, our goal here is to improve musical perceptions and conceptions, and a good way to do that is to *name* things, logically and carefully, at least the basic things. This will make it easier to identify and discuss them with some precision. That's what definitions are for. They help assure us that our own concepts are reasonably similar to those that other people have formed. Therefore, we will want to construct our definitions in a very orderly and systematic way. This will help ensure that each term we use is carefully attached to a clear concept that fits logically within our total conceptual picture of what music is and how it works.

**misnamed concepts** Picking up music terminology that is not attached to appropriate conceptual data is a major obstacle to creating an accurate music vocabulary. This condition is a natural outcome of studying music using the vocabulary of music notation before concepts of musical sound are well established. That being the case, we may need to root out some "clinkers" and either replace them or revise their name tags to prevent them from jamming the system.

It is critical to start our exploration with music itself, the *sounds* of music, thereby minimizing the collection of empty (unattached) and/or erroneous (misattached) terminology. You will find that by methodically examining the simple elements of music, you can reap a rich harvest of fresh practical concepts that will provide you with meaningful and practical ways of thinking about music—what it is, how it works, how to enjoy it and how to communicate it to others by means of the printed page.

## Hearing Musical Sounds

Developing an "ear" for music, like most learning, is a matter of focusing attention on the right bits of perceptual data. That, of course, depends on first *having* clear and logical concepts with which to perceive musical data accurately. If clear concepts are not present with which to interpret certain data, that data is simply ignored. Attempting to assign terminology to "undefined" experience obviously is hazardous.

**fuzzy thinking, fuzzy perception** Thinking in terms of unclear concepts is the most common cause of perceptual confusion in any field. Music is no exception. Failing to realize that sound has a number of distinct and easily recognizable characteristics often imprisons musical hopefuls in a frustrating whirl of perceptual mystery.

It is not uncommon for college students to mistake one characteristic for another, or to use the wrong word for what may be an accurate perception. For example, when hearing a passage that grows louder, some students describe the music as "rising in pitch." The error might simply be caused by a lack of focused listening, resulting in unclear concepts of "pitch" and "loudness." On the other hand, the perceptions might be accurate, but the terms may not be properly assigned. Possibly, a class discussion in which "pitch" was said to go "up and down" was confused with changes in "loudness," which, in a way, also goes "up and down." (Actually, neither one goes "up or down" in the usual sense, but we'll deal with that later.)

**clear thinking, clear perception**

The means of escaping this frustration is the same in music as it is in any other field of intellectual pursuit, that is, (1) to experience the subject in terms of its simplest components, (2) being careful to observe how the components relate to each other logically, and (3) being sure that name tags are properly attached to each concept. Here's an example. "Sound," the basic stuff of music, can be categorized as "noise" or "tone." Both have the attributes of "loudness" and "timbre." "Tone," which has to do with regularity of sound waves, gives rise to an additional attribute called "pitch." Pitch, thanks to a human capacity for perceiving small-number ratios of frequencies, gives rise to the perception of "harmonic" relationships. (We'll discuss each of these concepts later.)

A systematic way to focus awareness on the "right thing" in musical sound is to vary one characteristic while holding the others steady. The listener can then more easily focus on the characteristic that is "moving." This is the same technique that researchers use to isolate single factors in a complex situation. They call it the *scientific method*. If it works well for scientists, it should work well for us.

With that in mind, we will begin now to break down musical perception into its basic and separate concepts. As you probably realize, this process is largely a matter of discovering "reality," in that the process of musical perception, in the physical sense, is essentially fixed by nature.

**sound**

In order to cover all our bases, and before isolating the separate characteristics of sound, we should include a definition of sound itself. Physically, **sound** consists of vibrations moving through the air. More specifically, it is the movement of air particles that, upon reaching an ear, cause corresponding activity in the moveable ear parts. Since this "ear sensation" is different from all other human experience, sound (in the physical sense) eventually becomes "sound" (in the psychological sense), a concept we can then name.

Does that mean that whenever our ears are stimulated by these air movements, the concept "sound" kicks in? The answer is "No, not necessarily." The process of hearing largely goes on without our thinking about it. We only use the concept consciously when we *think* about sound. Concepts are *thinking* tools; they aren't directly connected to, or necessarily triggered by, the things or experiences that brought them into existence. A concept is an "abstraction," or "mental picture," and as we know, pictures don't always represent something physically real. "Horses" are real, and "unicorns" are not. If one doesn't know that, either or both might be considered real or not real; yet either or both can give rise to concepts.

So, whether sound is actually happening at any given moment, it still can be thought about simply by focusing on the concept "sound." However, in order to imagine an *experience* of sound, you will need the help of other concepts in order to make it seem real. Let's experiment. Imagine that you are hearing an airplane fly overhead. How close is it? Is it a large air liner? A roaring fighter jet? Is it annoyingly loud, or just a faint hum? You see, your imagination used a *combination* of concepts in order to make the imaginary perception possible. Remember, it was not "airplane" alone that you were imagining. It was the *sound* of an airplane. But even the imaginary sound could not "exist" without a combination of concepts.

Careful definitions of *each* of the basic perceptual data streams, or concepts, which make up a sound experience are important. It also is important to realize that we relate individual concepts to physical sounds only in terms of our past experience with them. Additionally, when we attach a word (in any language), we do so with a bit of faith that our own use of that word reasonably and accurately matches other people's use of the word.

To recap: Sound has a few vital characteristics that must be isolated in experience in order to ensure that we are (1) focusing on a "correct" data stream, (2) forming vivid and logical concepts, and (3) connecting the right word. In the sections following, we will look at the individual perceptual characteristics of sound that can be isolated and named. We'll start with a fairly easy one.

**loudness**    Loudness is sometimes referred to as "volume," but this term is imprecise and probably should be avoided when discussing sound. "Loudness" specifically refers to "an amount of sound," while "volume" is commonly used to refer to "an amount of cubic space." This metaphorical transfer of the term from spacial to aural application is not particularly difficult to understand, but in the interest of clear thinking and precise terminology, **loudness** is the better term.

All sound has some degree of loudness. Without sufficient stimulation, ears hear nothing. In physical terms, loudness, or *amplitude*, is measured in decibels. At the quiet end of the hearing range, sounds at -10 decibels can be heard but changes in loudness in this neighborhood usually can't be discriminated. At the loud end of the range, sounds reaching 100 decibels can cause damage to human ears, to which some factory workers, jet mechanics and rock-band performers can attest.

The significance of loudness in creating musical meaning has to do with *variation* in loudness, called **dynamics**. The word *dynamic* is simply the opposite of *static*, or "motionless." Since meaning in art requires contrast, music in which there are no *changes* in loudness is not using this attribute artistically. "Loudness," in that case, would be simply a matter of making sure the music can be heard.

The terms "soft" and "quiet" are variously used to indicate the opposite of "loud." Since "soft" has other meanings, "quiet" is probably the better word to use. Yet, the phrase "loud and soft" is heard more frequently than "loud and quiet," so this represents a bit of awkward logic. Also, there is no generic term, like "amplitude" (which refers to a mechanical measurement), that names the perceptual concept "loud/soft" other than the word "loudness." Sorry about that.

This recorded example illustrates the concept "loudness" by varying that perceptual attribute of sound. All other perceptual attributes are held constant. 2-1

Dynamics, or *changes* in loudness, has not always been a significant element in western music. It became an important musical component in the seventeenth century when large and small groups of performers were used to vary the amount of sound generated in various parts of a composition. Also, nineteenth century "romantic" composers used loudness very effectively, creating enormous emotional swings between tender quiet moments and thundering climaxes. Listen to this excerpt from Handel's *Water Music* and notice how loudness is used to shape the music. 2-2

Physically, **timbre** (pronounced tam-ber or tim-ber) is the configuration of **timbre** simultaneous frequencies of varying strengths that cause a sound to take on "bright," "dark," "hollow," "brassy," or other qualities that we may or may not recognize as concepts. A trumpet, for example, sounds quite different than a flute; however, even an experienced listener might have trouble distinguishing a soprano saxophone from a bassoon playing in a high register. Whether the sound source is recognizable is irrelevant. The important thing is hearing *contrasts* in timbre when this aspect of sound is artfully used in a composition.

"Timbre" is to the ear what "color" is to the eye. Just as we can't see anything that doesn't contain some color, we can't experience sound without some kind of "timbre." (Although black is said to be the absence of color, we do have a name for it—therefore we see it as a "color.") Although sound engineers use the term *sine wave* to describe simple sound having no timbral character, this is not logically possible in psychological terms. When we hear a sound having "no timbre," that *is* its timbre. Perceptually, it is something like "white" sound, but carrying that metaphor into physical analogies is problematic.

Perhaps this will help. "Silence" means the absence of sound. Ordinarily, silence has no perceptual significance. If we're hearing nothing, there is no particular reason to pay attention to it. But when we *expect* to hear something, a silence is significant. It is a *perception*, if you will, of the absence of sound. The concept "sound" is used to provide a contextual meaning for this particular silence. Composers use this principle to create wonderful effects in music. Sometimes an emotionally charged silence can be more effective than a thundering din. So, a silence is not always a "nothing." Likewise, a sine wave also is not a "nothing." It offers its "characterlessness" as a contrast to the kaleidoscope of possible "sound colors" available to human ears.

Practical use of timbre is not limited to music. For example, we tend to recognize the sounds of our friends' voices. Having had many perceptual experiences with those sounds, we have formed vivid concepts of their "timbre." A common definition of timbre is "tone quality" or "sound quality." Since "sound" has at least three basic qualities, or characteristics, that definition is vague and really doesn't help us much. Also, the word "quality" has connotations of "good" or "bad," which is misleading, since it is used here with no intention of evaluating the sound in question.

2-3  Here are some sound examples to help isolate the characteristic of sound we call "timbre." What is important here is to focus on what timbre *is*, or more specifically, what the *concept* of "timbre" is.

2-4  The modern symphony orchestra uses many timbres to convey musical messages to the ear. Sometimes a single timbre is presented in contrast to other accompanying sounds. At other times individual timbres are mixed to create new "colors" of sound. Note that not all timbres have names. In fact, not all timbres have concepts. In other words, we don't have to remember having heard a particular timbre in order to notice that it is different from the timbres around it.

**tone**  When sound vibrations are received in regular waves, the result is said to be **tone**. When vibrations are irregular, the result is said to be **noise**. Any sound that isn't "tone," then, is "noise," and vice versa.

Logically and conceptually, that is a simple truth. What is also true, however, is that each person evaluates what to them is "tone" or "noise." To one listener, the thud of a bass drum may be nothing but "noise," while an experienced percussionist may hear the same sound as "tone." To a third listener, the sound may *almost* approach "tone." Most "tone versus noise" perceptions are not this problematic, however. All three of those listeners would be *more* likely to agree that a timpani produces tone, and *very* likely to agree that a chime produces tone. As with many other perceptual experiences, it is up to the individual to decide which concept—noise or tone—a perceptual data stream of sound appears to fit.

Listen to these sounds and make your own judgment as to noise and/or tone. Are there any you are reluctant to place in either category? To what extent do you think hearing a sound in context with other sounds would help you make a decision?

2-5

So, while the *concept* "tone/noise" is a simple either/or matter, a given perceptual judgment might not be obvious. But this needn't cause us to confuse conception with perception. A concept may be perfectly clear even when perception of it is quite elusive. Understanding this can help avoid unnecessary frustration while developing one's listening skills. It will even help after one has achieved considerable experience.

**pitch**

The percussionist referred to above who claims to be hearing tone from a bass drum, could support that claim by stating that he was hearing its "pitch." You see, pitch can only exist when vibrations are regular. So, does that mean that "tone" and "pitch" mean the same thing? No, it doesn't (although loose usage of these two words is fairly common). Strictly speaking, *tone* refers to the concept of regular vibrations, while **pitch** has to do with the highness/lowness of a tone. In physical terms, tone specifies that vibrations are traveling in regular waves and pitch indicates the frequency, or speed, of the waves.

The term "speed" will be used here somewhat metaphorically in regard to pitch. On the one hand, both speed and pitch are measured in units occurring within a given time period. On the other hand, we perceive speed as motion against a static background and perceive pitch as being more or less motionless. Also, in this context, our use of the terms "fast" and "slow" in the following paragraphs refers to the physical nature of pitch, not to its perceivable nature.

For lack of better terms, we commonly describe fast pitches as "high," and slow pitches as "low." When the speed of the waves gradually increases, we say the pitch is going "up," and when the speed slows, we say the pitch is going "down." However, these expressions do not mean that high pitches are farther from the center of the earth, nor that low pitches closer. On the other hand, we all have noticed more than a few tenors straining and stretching their necks to "reach" a high note. Do they know something the rest of us don't? And what about pianists, who reach to the right for "high" pitches and to the left for "low" ones. What is going on here?

Perhaps there is some subconscious perceptual justification for using this terminology. When the roadrunner in the popular cartoon veers quickly, hurtling the pursuing coyote over the cliff, we would tend to agree that the sound effect should go "down" in pitch, in keeping with this gravitational event (regardless of the Doppler effect). It would seem wrong, somehow, for the pitch to go "up." For whatever psychological reason, the impression that pitches move "up and down" is firmly, and perhaps hopelessly, reflected in our music vocabulary.

2-6

At this point, we are not concerned about naming individual pitches or hearing their relationships to each other. We just want to make sure we can hear *changes* in pitch, indicating that the concept is clear, perception is accurately focused, and the correct word is attached to the experience. In these audio examples, the only perceptual characteristic that changes is pitch.

**"perfect" pitch**
A relatively small percentage of people apparently have an innate ability to perceive specific pitches and can produce them vocally without the help of an instrument. This ability is popularly called "perfect pitch," but is more accurately described as "pitch recognition." Although there have been attempts to teach and/or learn pitch recognition, the results are inconclusive. Some experienced singers, however, seem to develop a "muscle memory" for pitches. These folks apparently remember how pitches feel in the vocal mechanism, particularly in the extreme high and low registers. A sore throat, however, can render this technique quite useless.

One reason to judge the term "perfect pitch" a misnomer is that many people who don't have pitch recognition often produce pitches more accurately (relative to other pitches) than those who do have it. Also, as we shall see later, pitch names only approximately refer to specific sound wave frequencies (apparently the basis for the recognition).

**relative pitch**
Knowledge about how pitches relate to each other has been extant for thousands of years. Pythagoras, the ancient Greek mathematician, demonstrated that pitch relationships, like many of our cosmic systems, are linked to mathematics. However, mathematics skills are not required in order to perceive pitch relations. Somehow, our perceptual mechanism does the "math" for us and translates the experience into concepts we can easily grasp.

Knowledge of the numbers only helps to clarify *why* music takes the shape it does. The numbers also explain why certain pitch relationships are easier to hear (and therefore, conceive), and why composers use certain pitch combinations to create tension and other pitch combinations to provide resolution. Incidentally, the numbers we are talking about here are not complex and should present no problem for those who are not gifted in that regard.

You may be surprised to learn that the most closely related pitches, and therefore the easiest to conceptualize, are not pitches next to each other in a row, but are pitches a considerable distance apart. Likewise, pitches close to each other are more difficult to capture as usable and repeatable relational concepts. The reason for this can be seen in the numbers.

Here's how it works. When certain pitches are sounded simultaneously, the combination of their frequencies creates a quality that can be heard and identified. Furthermore, that same quality can be heard when a different set of pitches is sounded, provided these pitches are in the same relationship as the first set. So, it really is the *relationship* between the pitches that can be identified, not the pitches themselves. Somehow, our brain hears the pitches, compares the frequencies, and sends our consciousness an abstraction, or image, of the physical relationship. Quite incredible, don't you think?

Let's get back to the numbers. One of the things Pythagoras observed was that a plucked string not only vibrates as a whole, creating a basic pitch called the **fundamental**, but it also vibrates in halves, thirds, quarters, etc., creating other related pitches, called **partials**. These are the "little pitches within a big pitch" we mentioned earlier in relation to timbre. We don't actually hear the little pitches individually, but rather the patterns created by the varying strengths of the partials which creates the perception we hear as timbre.

Here are the first sixteen partials extracted electronically. Following that, six partials are combined to create a timbre which is then used in a short melodic phrase. Notice that when the melody is played we hear the blended partials as "one sound." (See sidebar "The Harmonic Partials Series," p. 25.)  2-7

Let's take a closer look. When plucked, a string not only vibrates as a whole but also in simple proportional segments. Every time a whole string moves

back and forth one time, each half of the string moves back and forth twice. In other words, the half string is moving twice as fast as the whole string. This means that not only is the pitch of the half string

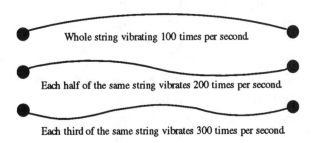

Whole string vibrating 100 times per second

Each half of the same string vibrates 200 times per second

Each third of the same string vibrates 300 times per second

higher than the pitch of the whole string, but it is related in a simple way to the pitch of the whole string. We can express the relationship of the two pitches as a ratio of one to two (or 1:2). Similarly, each third of the string vibrates three times as fast as the fundamental, creating a pitch vibrating three times as fast as the fundamental. Each fourth of the string vibrates four times as fast, each fifth five times as fast, and so on, to the fringes of perception.

Wind instruments are constructed on the same principle in regard to the length of their wind columns. The vibrating air inside the instrument is shaped into patterns that create nodes at the halfway point, the one-third point, the one-fourth point, and so on. Similar principles apply to percussion instruments.

The factor that defines the sound character of various instruments has to do with the relative strengths (loudness) of the individual partials. Each instrument (or other sound source) has its own characteristic configuration of partial strengths, and this configuration remains relatively constant as the instrument travels up and down its pitch range. Sound communicates this mathematical data to our ears, but in the process perception translates the "little pitches" into "timbre," while delivering the fundamental as "pitch." We can't count or measure the vibrations, yet we can tell when we're hearing an oboe and when the oboe's pitch moves up and down. Incredible!

## Pitches in Combination

**harmony**    Nature not only structures *timbre* on the basis of small-number ratios, but also uses small-number ratios to help us perceive *combinations* of fundamental pitches, which we call **harmony**. In fact, the "partials" of timbre are often called "harmonics," which offers a convenient transition to this new topic. In short, these two concepts—"timbre" and "harmony"—are physically made of the same stuff, namely, vibrations in small-number ratios, but they manifest themselves perceptually in different ways.

It is important to note that neither timbre nor harmony requires conscious mathematical calculations in order to function. Our perception mechanism does all that automatically and "out of sight." We can't hear the individual partials in timbre (at least most of us can't) much less compare their individual amplitudes. Nor can we hear the individual waves (vibrations) within a pitch, much less count the number in a given time period. Even if pitches came with their frequencies clearly marked, a mathematical genius couldn't figure their harmonic ratios "on the spot." Yet, with modest effort, we can learn to hear instantly basic harmonic relationships.

# The Harmonic Partials Series

When "Pythagoras's string" (or any sound source) vibrates with many partials sounding, the lower partials (larger segments represented by smaller numbers) represent pitches that are farther apart than the upper partials (smaller segments represented by larger numbers). For example, the difference between half the string and a third of the string is a sixth of the string; while the difference between an eighth of the string and a ninth of the string is one seventy-second of the string.

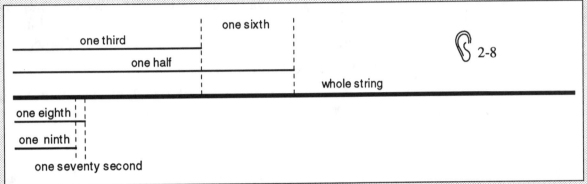

Therefore, pitches represented by lower neighboring partials are farther apart than are pitches represented by higher neighboring partials.

In the graphic to the right, 1 represents the frequency of the whole string, or fundamental pitch, 2 represents the frequency of half the string, 3 represents a third of the string, and so on. The bold lines are all multiples of 1:2 ratios and are heard as the "same pitch" (see p. 26). Notice that the space between the bold lines is much more crowded with partials nearer the top than the bottom.

The partials series provides two important perceptual functions. First, it provides for the sense of timbre, the discrimination of different "tone colors," in that the configuration of loudness among partials varies from one sound to another. It is not within the province of this book to go into detail here, although the topic is certainly interesting, particularly for anyone focusing on orchestration or electronic music.

The other important perceptual function of the partials series is to enable recognition of consonance and dissonance. When two pitches are sounded in a ratio corresponding to smaller numbers in this series, the harmonic result is considered a consonance. When two pitches are sounded in a ratio corresponding to larger numbers in this series (or to *no* numbers in the series), the harmonic result is considered dissonant. This principle functions in "shades of gray" and the judgement, to some extent, is made in terms of musical style and personal taste.

In this section and in some later chapters, we will be using ratios to describe the physical relationship between pitches. While this discussion will not venture very far from the basics, it will be helpful to notice a few principles of musical acoustics. For example, ratios using the numbers 1, 2, 4, 8, 16, and so on, are essentially representing the "same" pitch.

In other words, comparing the pitch corresponding to the third partial (represented by 3) to the whole string (represented by 1) is essentially the same as comparing it to the half string (represented by 2), or the quarter string (represented by 4), etc. For reasons that will later become clear, it is more practical to refer to this relationship by using the numbers 2:3 instead of 1:3. Similarly, 1:5 and 2:5 are essentially the same as 4:5, the latter being the practical ratio for general reference.

Also, the sound of 2:3 is very similar to 3:4. Again, this has to do with 2 being in a 1:2 relationship with 4. Simply keep in mind that doubling a number does not drastically change the perceptual harmonic quality of a combination of pitches.

**consonance**   What all of this means is that we not only hear single pitches, but we also hear a *relationship* between two pitches when their frequencies are related in small-number ratios. To illustrate, let's again borrow Pythagoras' string. We will combine a pitch corresponding to the whole string and a pitch corresponding to half the string. How can we tell when the half-string pitch is vibrating twice as fast as the whole-string pitch? Certainly not by counting the vibrations. Some people believe that it has to do with the distance, or number of scale steps, between the two pitches. However, humans are not very good at precisely measuring distances without mechanical devices—not in space, not in time, and also not in matters of pitch. What we *do* have is the ability to hear **consonance**, which is what we call a harmonic relationship in which individual pitches seem to fuse together, or "agree" with each other. So, even though we can't hear or count vibrations, we can tell when one pitch is vibrating twice as fast as another. Amazing!

2-9 〔ear icon〕   This sound example contains a demonstration of consonance. It consists of two simultaneous sound sources, or *voices*, one holding a pitch constant while the other slides upward very slowly. The sliding voice begins at the same frequency of the steady voice and continues upward to a point at which it is vibrating twice as fast, or in a ratio of 1:2. At two places along the way, the ascent lingers to give you opportunity to hear the voices in small-number ratios.

As the sliding voice ascends, the first lingering moment is when the voices are in the 4:5 ratio. Of the distance travelled up to that point, there has not been a ratio of numbers that small, therefore this "event" stands out in contrast to anything since the 1:1 ratio heard before the moving voice began to separate from the steady voice.

Continuing, the next time the ascending voice lingers is at the 2:3 ratio point. Because these numbers are smaller than the 4:5 ratio, this relationship is perceived as more consonant. Eventually, the sliding voice reaches the 1:2 point and fuses with the steady voice as if they were producing the same pitch. In fact, pitches in this relationship are commonly said to be the "same pitch."

If your ear is experienced in hearing harmony, you may have identified other places along the ascent in which the two voices fused into consonances of varying degrees. We passed ratios of 3:4, 5:6 and 6:7, any of which may have caught your ear. Each of these has a role to play in structuring the perception of music.

In the following pages, we will focus on each of these and a few other harmonic relationships, showing how they relate to music with which you may already be familiar. By associating these ratios to sounds you already know, and by giving them names that relate to our common systems of music, you will probably find that you can identify them by sound. Of course, the more experience you acquire, the more secure your identifications will be.

The relationship between two pitches in a 2:1 ratio, as in the demonstration above, is a very easy one to hear. In Western music, it is named "octave," because it spans eight scale steps. But it might have been called by other names, perhaps "pentave" in a five-note system, or "duave" by virtue of its 1:2 physical relationship. In any case, it is an easily perceived and conceived relationship that is virtually universal in any music system.     **"same" pitch**

A common example of the "octave" relationship usually occurs when men and women sing the same melody at the same time. In general, women's voices are higher in pitch than men's in about this same 1:2 relationship. Therefore, when singing the same melody together, women's pitches vibrate twice as fast as men's pitches. Yet, we have no problem with the notion that they are singing the "same" pitches even though we know they are not. The  2-10 impression of "sameness" is perceived because the simultaneous pitches of men's and women's voices are related in a simple 1:2 ratio. Another description would be to say that the voices are in the most consonant relationship possible other than singing identical pitches.

The next most consonant harmonic relationship consists of pitches in a 1:3 (or 2:3) ratio, one pitch corresponding to the whole (or half) string, the other corresponding to a third of the string. Pitches in this relationship are less likely to be described as "the same," as were those in the 1:2 examples above.

2-11

Nevertheless, there have been, and still are, musical styles and compositional practices in which two voices (or groups of voices) perform "the same song" using this 2:3 pitch relationship. Although less consonant than the 1:2 relationship, the two sounds tend to fuse rather readily into a harmonic "concept" that one likely would recognize when heard again.

2-12

Since 3:4 is simply a variation of 2:3 (more later), we will skip here to 4:5. This is the relationship we first noticed in the sliding pitch demonstration. The sound here is less consonant than either the 1:2 or the 2:3 relationships; however, it is still rather secure in its quality of "agreement." Using this relationship with two voices singing the "same" melody is uncommon (for reasons that will eventually become clear), therefore, the audio example here simply contains sustained voices in this relationship.

You may have recognized these three sounds—1:2, 2:3 and 4:5—to be the components of the most common harmonic structure in Western music—the major chord. But we're getting ahead of our story. We will leave this thread now and pick it up again soon.

**dissonance**    Consonance, as with many perceptions based on clear concepts, sometimes depends on a shades-of-gray judgment. When a listener feels that pitches tend to disagree rather than agree, the word he or she would use for that perception is **dissonance**. Needless to say, one listener's "consonance" is another's "dissonance." Interestingly, the judgment has tended to move through history toward greater tolerance of "disagreement." Many sounds previously considered dissonant have now moved into the consonant zone.

It is not particularly important to designate any given pitch combination as either consonant or dissonant. What is more important is to realize that some sounds are more or less consonant than other sounds. Composers use the principle of consonance/dissonance to create moments of unrest and resolution. Eventually, as with any concept, these "sounds" can exist purely in the composer's imagination. Beethoven didn't have to stop composing after he became deaf. He already knew what various pitch combinations sound like. In other words, he had developed a "vocabulary" of pitch relationships, including their consonance/dissonance characteristics.

The main point to remember from this discussion is that we don't need to know the names of individual pitches in order to experience them. Most of us can't identify frequencies anyway. What we *can* perceive and recreate are the *relationships* between pitches, and with a bit of practice and experience we can learn to recognize, identify and reproduce those relationships. We refer to these relationships as **intervals**.

Before we leave this section, let's do a safety check on definitions of concepts we've been discussing. *Timbre* is "tonal color" and is based on patterns of strength among partials. *Pitch* is the "highness/lowness characteristic of tone" and is based on speed, or frequency, of sound waves. *Harmony* is the "perception of relationships between two or more pitches" and appears to be based (to some extent) on small-number mathematical ratios between and among the frequencies of the pitches. *Consonance* and *dissonance* have to do with the extent to which pitches seem to agree or disagree.

**vocabulary recap**

## Intonation

The forgoing discussion has considerable impact on the concept of singing or playing "in tune." Many people, including some musicians, think of tuning as maintaining a standard pitch, for example "A" equaling 440 vibrations per second (vps). This view assumes that once an instrument is tuned to a mechanical (or electronic) device sounding that pitch, all that remains is to play the other pitches in relation to that standard. The trouble with that idea is that those of us who can't recognize 440 vps can't recognize any other frequency either, so that is probably not the best way to think of tuning. One reason student bands sound amateurish is that players believe that once they have tuned up before the concert, all they have to do is push down the right fingers and blow.

The seasoned professional knows that a performer must listen to the total sound, continuously adjusting pitches to agree with the prevailing harmonic context. You see, the right pitch is not necessarily the one that agrees with the tuning device, but is the one that agrees with other pitches sounding at that moment.

Perhaps a bit of historical background might help clarify this. Through the centuries, musicologists have described a number of mathematical "systems" they believed would explain how pitches work together harmoniously. The Pythagorean scale is composed of pitches derived from an extended series of perfect fifths (2:3 ratios) and then reduced by the "same pitch" principle to "pitches in a row." Ancient Chinese music theorists similarly explained their five-pitch scale as a series of ascending fifths and descending fourths (3:4 ratios). However, these methods produce some scale steps that are far too high in pitch for practical use.

**tuning systems**

In the sixteenth century, the "mean tone" system was introduced, which squeezed the perfect fifths (moved the pitches closer together) to the extent that a more practical tuning resulted. This system not only depended on compromised pitches to achieve its goal, but created considerable problems in regard to the tuning of some pitches. A number of eighteenth and nineteenth century scholars developed the system known as "just tuning," which derives the major scale from the "pure" tuning of the partials series. But this system did not account for all of the scale steps used in European music.

**flexible tuning**   All these theories ignore the possibility that the human ear may not handle pitch relations in the static way scientists have tended to describe them on paper (or papyrus). It has been observed that some of the pitches we prefer to hear are not the same ones that show up on the scientists' graphs. For example, singers and string players tend to tune certain pitches differently when certain other pitches are also sounding. This demonstrates that well-tuned pitches *move* according to context. (We will hear a demonstration soon.) This evidence should lead to the conclusion that, on one hand, we likely hear pitches quite simply (one to one, in small-number ratios) and, on the other, more complexly (as pitches adjust tuning to accommodate relationships to multiple pitches).

Practical experience demonstrates that the ear intuitively tries to put together the "best" combination of pitches it can hear. If that is true, musicologists' traditional arguments over *which* tuning theory is correct—Pythagorean, mean tone or just—are somewhat irrelevant. The practical answer is "all of them are in error," simply because they are all fixed-pitch systems. The ear seems to prefer flexible pitches that seek a "best possible tuning," always striving to minimize dissonance. In simple harmonies, these adjustments are quite easy to make. As more pitches are added, more experience is required to develop the sensitivity to achieve the best tuning.

This need not suggest that developing sensitivity to fine tuning is a difficult skill to achieve and is reserved for those who are formally trained. On the contrary, the world has many examples of "uneducated" musical people who are stunning performers. Once the basic concept "in tune" is experienced and understood, one can progress rather quickly to applying that concept to some fairly complex harmonies, regardless whether one understands the theories on which they are based.

Children who grow up around music tend to absorb tuning information easily without formal study. This is particularly true when youngsters participate in singing. Apparently, when pitch relations are experienced physically as well as aurally, tuning concepts seem to be more intuitively understood and skills are developed quite effortlessly.

This is not to imply that adults cannot learn tuning skills. Often, the most difficult aspect of adult learning in this area is breaking through the crust of self doubt that has formed over the years. Learning to hear and perform music with a good sense of intonation can be developed at any age.

# Can The Human Ear Hear Ratios?

Some musicologists argue that we do not hear pitch relations by means of simple-number ratios. Their arguments are usually based, in part, on the observation that musicians do not always seem to prefer simple acoustical tunings. While this is true, it is also true that we *can* hear the "in tune" consonance that results when two pitches are adjusted to correspond to what appears to be nature's simple ratios.

Experience offers these observations:

- Acousticians from Pythagoras to Helmholtz and beyond have demonstrated the existence of the harmonic series and its relationship to small-number ratios.

- Some authorities have referred to the harmonic series as a "cognitive template." (While this has no implications toward derivations of tonal systems, it does imply that perception in terms of this "template" may be part of the basis for such theoretical constructs.)

- When pitches are adjusted to correspond (apparently) to small-number ratios, they appear to be more consonant, or "in tune." This phenomenon can be heard by anyone with normal hearing. These adjusted pitches do not correspond to those of the keyboard.

- The smaller the numbers in an interval's ratio of vibrations (for example, 1:2, 2:3, 3:4, etc.), the easier to hear, recognize and reproduce it vocally.

- The more "in tune" an interval, the easier it is to perceive its unique sound quality. In contrast, one poorly-tuned interval doesn't sound significantly different from any other poorly-tuned interval. Recognizing intervals purely in terms of their "size" is unlikely.

- When pitches in a chord are flexibly tuned, allowing the ear to seek the "best possible" adjustment, the individual pitches tend to disappear into the sonority. This occurs in fairly dissonant chords as well as in simple consonant ones.

While we may not yet understand everything there is to know about the perception of harmonic relations, it seems appropriate to act on what we *do* know and can observe in practical experience. Whether we really perceive and conceive pitch relations in some manner that corresponds to small-number ratios, the notion that we probably do is certainly on the right track. There is too much empirical evidence supporting that idea to ignore it in teaching ear training. It seems responsible to proceed with educational efforts based on the experience we already have instead of teaching nothing in this regard while arguing psychological theory.

*Preference* in tuning, then, is another matter. We are told that the eminent cellist Pablo Casals believed that:

> Raised accidentals should lean toward their upper neighbors in pitch, lowered accidentals toward lower.... In general, we are obliged to keep the half-tones close together.... Expressive intonation, when observed continuously throughout a composition, becomes a foremost factor in the communication of emotional content. (*Casals and the Art of Interpretation*, David Blum, 1977, pp. 102-8.)

If Casals' view can be understood as "expressive deviations from a norm," it follows that the norm itself must first be established. The most likely "norm" would seem to be the pitch relationships heard in the natural harmonic partials series, particularly since we apparently have the ability to hear them. It would seem wise, then, to first learn to recognize the norm in order to benefit from expressive deviation.

Whether one is attempting to match the same pitch or attempting to cause one's own pitch to fit well with different but related pitches, the method is more or less the same. It is the perception of "consonance" that leads to success here. Intonation skills are developed not so much by thinking "up" or "down" but by listening for the adjustment that minimizes acoustical conflict and produces the "best possible" agreement for those pitches. During the early stages of developing tuning skills, one must be ready to move considerable "distances" to find consonance. As experience is gained, success becomes a matter of making very small adjustments to reach a satisfying result. Again, successful perception is a matter of paying attention to the right concept.

# 3

# Harmonic Systems

Although **melody**, the organization of single pitches in a series, is more prevalent in the history of world music than **harmony**, the organization of pitches sounded simultaneously, we will discuss harmony first. There is good reason to believe that melody, even without simultaneously sounded pitches, is largely based on harmonic concepts. In other words, the pitches that ancient and modern composers have used for their melodies seem to be selected largely because of their acoustical relationships to a unifying pitch.

In some styles and traditions, composers have tended to select pitches that are easily heard as consonant. In other styles, composers have favored pitch relationships that are more dissonant and therefore more challenging and interesting to experienced listeners. In both cases, harmonic considerations are essential in making artistic pitch decisions.

The unifying pitch, referred to above, is called a **tonal center**. Music constructed on this principle is referred to as **tonal music**. Nearly all of the world's musical traditions are based on the perception of **tonality**. Those that are not are sometimes referred to as "artificial scales," because they are based on arbitrary sets of pitches rather than on the perceptual principles of nature.

**tonality**

The earliest known use of simultaneous pitches is the **drone**. This consists of a single sustained pitch, usually a low one, with the melody's changing pitches sounding above it. The drone serves as a tonal reference, by which to more easily perceive the consonance/dissonance qualities of melodic pitches performed along with it. This is similar to the sliding-pitch demonstration of consonance presented earlier; however, in this case, pitches are selected by a composer, to a large extent *because* of their consonance/dissonance characteristics.

3-1

Sounding an audible drone appears to be more prevalent in musical traditions in which melodies are very complex and highly decorative. This makes sense, since an audible drone assists the listener in evaluating the harmonic significance of melodic pitches. Listen to this example from India.

This is not entirely unlike the perception of a melody *without* an audible drone. An experienced listener usually hears a melody, at least a tonally constructed one, in terms of its tonal orientation. In a sense, he or she is imagining a kind of silent "drone" by which to harmonically evaluate and/or select melodic pitches. The difference, then, is simply the physical sounding or the imagined "sounding" of a drone.

3-2

Simple melodies need no drone because tonality is generally implied by the harmonic relationships of the melodic pitches themselves. Here are some melodies performed without a drone. Can you determine the central pitch implied by the melodies themselves?

**the birth of polyphony**

Before the ninth century, all the world's music was essentially **monophonic**, meaning music consisting of a single line of pitches. The term implies that music was performed as "one sound," or in "one voice." When people sang and/or played instruments together, they all performed the same pitches, more or less, at the same time. Of course, the actual pitches sung by women (and children) likely sounded higher than those sung by men, as described earlier. Also, some instruments may have sounded higher or lower pitches than others. But, all participants sounded pitches in a 1:2 harmonic ratio, resulting in a "same pitch" perception.

About the eighth or ninth century, one of the most significant developments in music history occurred in Europe. Musical chant was sometimes performed in churches and monasteries with *more* than one line of pitches. Some of the monks and priests sang one line of pitches while others sang a different line of pitches with harmonic relationships that were *not* 1:2.

Thus, **polyphonic** music made its entrance and added a whole new dimension to composition. By sounding two or more melodies at the same time, music became "many voiced." While most of the world continued to create monophonic music, this turn of events significantly altered the way music would be made in Europe during the centuries that followed.

At first, the two **voices** (so called, even though many people might be singing each line of pitches) clung somewhat firmly to each other harmonically. Not surprisingly, the voices related in very consonant ratios of 2:3 or 3:4. Both voices often followed a similar contour, turning up and down together in **parallel motion**, which helped to secure the harmonic connection. This simple type of polyphonic composition was called **organum**. Evidently, the early musicologists who named it would have agreed with our use of the word "organized" in forming a definition of music.

Eventually, the relationship between the voices became more and more independent, yet never giving up a rather firm connection of consonant harmonic relationships. Early ventures into independence allowed the voices to move in **contrary motion**, one voice moving up while the other moved down, as well as **oblique motion**, one voice moving while the other held the same pitch. Eventually, the voices flowed in different rhythmic patterns, contributing significantly to the perception of independent melody lines. Nevertheless, this independence was never "freedom." To maintain its status as "organum," the composition had to maintain a harmonic connection among its voices.

3-3

During the Gothic period (roughly the twelfth and thirteenth centuries), an interesting application of compositional "rules" occurred. The Gothic mind was a very religious one, and life was full of regulations that one was expected to follow without question. What apparently happened is that composers followed the principles of consonance between the main voice and each of two added voices, but neglected the harmonic relationship between the two added voices themselves. In addition, they often used a different set of words for each line of music. The resulting sound was not especially pleasing, but then "pleasant" was not particularly high on the priority list of values in that society. They were focusing more on the "next world" than on communicating to each other in this one.

3-4

Things changed dramatically in the Renaissance (late fifteenth and sixteenth centuries), when attention turned toward human values and aesthetic pleasure. Composers made sure all the voices fit together in a harmonically satisfying way. Dissonance was used specifically and artistically to create moments of tension, particularly with lyrics that expressed pain or other unpleasantries. They were always careful to resolve dissonances by moving "offending" pitches melodically to more agreeable ones within the total harmonic context of the composition.

3-5

By the end of the sixteenth century, composition shifted from polyphony, with its emphasis on individual melodic lines, toward **homophony**, in which the composer focused primarily on the harmonic relationships of all the voices at important rhythmic points. This change involved more than having the voices agree harmonically; composers had been doing that for several hundred years. Now, many people felt polyphonic music was becoming outdated and that its complexities tended to obscure lyrics.

**homophony**

But even *more* importantly, musicians began to notice that when certain combinations of simultaneous pitches moved to other combinations, an interesting *new* thing happened. The pitches seemed to work together in little acoustical "families." They didn't called them **chords**, as we do today, but that is essentially what they were. For about a hundred years, they simply specified the individual pitches to be played by the keyboardist above each bass note.

Then, in the early eighteenth century, a music theorist and composer named Phillipe Rameau published a book entitled "Functional Harmony." In this landmark publication, Rameau systematically described what composers of that time already seemed to realize intuitively: that certain groups of pitches, the ones usually selected by composers to be sounded together, relate to a fundamental pitch. Also, he showed that chords are not just isolated families of pitches, but that chords relate in specific ways to *other* chords. Thus, the remarkable musical machinery we now call the **major/minor system** was described for the first time.

It is important to understand that the emergence of the major/minor system was not merely a new invention with which to make music. It was more like a *discovery* of additional natural acoustical and perceptual realities. No one "constructed" the major/minor system. It was always there, waiting for musicians to become aware of its possibilities.

In the early Baroque period, the first half of the seventeenth century, this new way of thinking about music got off to a very conservative start. Although composers began thinking in terms of harmonic structures, their harmonies didn't stray very far from where a composition began. One reason was that music in the late Renaissance tended to use some rather bizarre and challenging harmonies, to which early Baroque composers responded with a determined move toward simplicity.

**the mysterious tritone unmasked** Another reason, and perhaps a more significant one, was that an important acoustical element nicknamed the "tritone" was still not fully understood. The tritone consists of two pitches in a ratio of 5:7. (We'll discuss its nickname later.) Medieval composers called it *musicus diabolicus*, or "devil in music," because of its harmonic instability. They were instructed to avoid using it. The more worldly and bold Renaissance composers attempted to "fix" it. Their term for the repair was *musica ficta*, or "false music," evidencing their reluctance to fiddle around with natural sounds. They probably had no idea their efforts would expose the true nature of this enigmatic ingredient in nature's gift of music.

In the late seventeenth century, about the time the violin was invented, composers began to understand the tritone and its important role in directing harmonic focus from one tonal destination to another. Instrumental music was flourishing at this time and composers took full advantage of this new insight. Chamber groups and orchestras were everywhere, playing music with harmonic abandon, taking tonal excursions never before heard. All of this was a direct result of discovering the tritone's influence on tonal perception.

3-6

Unfortunately, the emergence of the major/minor system conflicted with practical technology. In order for the tritone to function effectively, considerable tuning adjustments were required as the music moved through various tonalities. While vocalists, string players and wind players could readily make these pitch adjustments, keyboard players could not. In the early baroque years, a harpsichordist would simply tune his instrument to the tonality of a particular piece. This usually worked, since any changes in tonality during that period were not harmonically distant. Later, however, when composition ventured to any key the composer designated, the keyboardist had no hope of playing in tune.

**trouble in paradise**

Many attempts were made to add extra digitals (levers) to keyboard instruments to accommodate abrupt key changes, but these were cumbersome at best, and even with the added mechanisms, keyboards were not up to the task. So, what to do? Abandon the harpsichord and organ? Forget about inventing the piano and the modern synthesizer? Clearly, those would have been poor choices. As it turns out, a new system of tuning was developed in which pitches were compromised sufficiently to enable keyboard instruments to play in any key without retuning. Musical practice in the western world, for better or worse, went with the new "tempered-tuning." While it was basically the right decision, it was not made without a price (see sidebar "The Keyboard: The Good News and the Bad News," p. 38).

As you play the examples in this book, remember that keyboards can only *approximate* true harmonic relationships. Where possible, play only one pitch at a time on the keyboard and sing the others, tuning carefully, listening for "consonance," in order to hear clearly the item under consideration.

Most of the discussion of harmonic systems in the following pages has to do with the major/minor system. This should not necessarily be taken to mean that it is the most important or most widely-used system in today's music. However, since it appears to be based on natural acoustical phenomena, it is probably the best one to focus on in regard to developing a musical "ear." The sound vocabulary presented by the major/minor system can provide a basis from which to perceive and understand any other harmonic system (to the extent perception of its harmonic characteristics is practical).

# The Keyboard: The Good News and the Bad News

One of the most important musical instruments in the world, historically and currently, is the keyboard. With a keyboard, a single musician can create multi-pitch sounds. Ten fingers on two hands can actualize music that otherwise would require an ensemble of performers. For centuries, keyboards have provided harmonic accompaniments for solo singers and instrumentalists who by themselves cannot perform more than one pitch at a time. Composers use the keyboard as a tool to "try out" their creations. Music students with various specialties find the keyboard of significant help in understanding music theory and harmony. Piano virtuosos thrill us with their dexterity and artistry. That's the good news.

The bad news is that modern keyboards and human ears do not operate on the same system of pitch relations. Because acoustically tuned music (that's the kind ears hear naturally) does not travel well from one tonality (fundamental pitch center) to another without significant adjustments. A keyboard tuned to play accurately in one tonality sounds quite awful when playing in another. In the eighteenth century, an imperfect solution was adopted in which the pitches of the keyboard are adjusted from acoustic tuning to a system in which all twelve pitches within each octave are the same distance apart. This tuning system, appropriately called *equal-tempered*, makes it possible to play keyboards in any tonality without retuning, a very practical advance in music technology. The adjustment of pitches, it was believed, was so slight that the human ear would not be sensitive to the difference. This, it turns out, is not true. A modern keyboard cannot deliver the pitch relations described in this book.

The *very* bad news is that this information is not widely known and most music students today (as well as many music teachers) believe that listening to a keyboard will lead to the development of a musical ear. Instead, using a keyboard as a sound model actually *interferes* with accurate perception of harmonic relationships. Not only does this practice result in faulty and misleading perceptual data, it gives the impression that "this is as good as it gets." Therefore, many music students (guided, in turn, by misguided teachers) flounder in mistuned "interval drills" and other keyboard-based "ear training" devices, and never develop a vivid and meaningful sense of pitch relations, harmonic structures and harmonic functions.

A research paper published in Spring 1995 in *Music Perception* notes that in a controlled experiment in which experienced violinist and pianists were asked to discriminate among major scales using various tunings, the "violinists rarely failed to detect differences between scales, whereas pianists frequently failed." Although this was not the major focus of the study, it seems to indicate that musicians who are not highly exposed to equal-tempered tuning tend to develop a keener sense of tuning.

The point here is not to criticize keyboards or keyboard players. In fact, we will use the keyboard throughout this book as a reference while describing pitch relations. The keyboard, although imperfect, is a convenient tool for visualizing the harmonic systems we will be discussing in the next chapter. The important thing to keep in mind is that the keyboard should *not* be used for developing a sense of accurate tuning and harmonic relationships.

# 4

# The Major Mode

The inner workings of the major mode are quite remarkable. In fact, this harmonic system is unique among musical traditions in that its components balance symmetrically and logically. What is most interesting about the major mode is that its physical structures and musical functions appear to correspond with our natural perception of acoustical phenomena.

Like most of the world's music systems, the major mode is a *tonal* system. As you may remember, this simply means that the collection of pitches in its system relate to a tonal center, a central pitch. As noted earlier, pitches related in a 1:2 ratio are so basic that we loosely refer to them as the "same pitch." Therefore, when we designate a tonic pitch, we are also applying that designation to pitches that relate to it in multiples of 1:2 (1:4, 1:8, 1:16, etc.).

4-1

Some readers having previous musical experience may be anxious at this point for a connection to a keyboard or to letter names. It will be much better to avoid the keyboard connection for the moment in order to focus on the acoustical relationship of pitches instead of mechanical ones. Also, once the concepts of basic harmonic relationships are in place, assigning letter names will be fairly easy. Of course, both topics will be covered in upcoming chapters. For now, it will be more helpful to concentrate on the pure acoustical sounds of these examples and to avoid playing them on the keyboard.

In the following paragraphs, the basic and consonant harmonic ratios will be applied to songs that you probably already know. Even if you don't, the song fragments are demonstrated in audio examples for your convenience. Either way, it would be a good idea to sing along with the demonstration in order to get a physical feeling for the sound concepts being discussed.

4-2 👂 If you have not yet learned to match your voice to a given pitch, you might like to practice with the help of this audio example. Most people new to pitch matching tend to start out below the given pitch. The idea is to get your voice sliding upward (or downward), something like a siren, until you hear and feel your voice "locking in" with the given pitch.

Once you get the idea, you will be able to do it more quickly, and eventually you will be able to begin your own sound immediately in tune with a given pitch. You might find it helpful to imagine the pitch before you begin to sing it. Think about how it will feel in your own voice, and then actualize your image of the sound by singing it.

The graphic illustrations here will use letters to designate the tonal functions of the pitches used in each demonstration. For example, the tonic pitch will be represented by "T." As each new function is introduced, focus on connecting its sound relationship with its name. Remember, this book is intended to help you become more familiar with the *sounds* of music, not just provide information *about* music.

**tonic**    It was mentioned earlier that the most closely related pitches are not next to each other, in terms of frequency, but are a considerable "distance" apart. As you know, the simplest relationship between two pitches is the octave, having a 1:2 ratio. This relationship occurs in the song "Somewhere Over The Rainbow" in which the second pitch (on the second syllable "-where") vibrates twice as fast as the first pitch (on the first syllable "some"). "The Christmas Song" also begins with a 4-3 👂 1:2 melodic skip (on the syllables "chest-" and "-nuts." In both songs, these pitches function tonally as **tonic**.

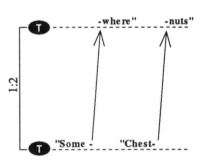

If you have difficulty singing these pitches accurately, you might play a pitch on a keyboard (any pitch will do provided it is in the lower part of your singing range) and sustain it while you move your voice to the higher pitch. The sliding technique will help. When you hear it "lock" into the octave relationship with your keyboard pitch you will know that you are correct. Listen to the audio demonstration again to make sure that your performance sounds similar to it.

The next simplest harmonic relationship is the 2:3 ratio. Again, we will designate the pitch represented by the number 2 as tonic. The pitch represented by the 3 in this 2:3 ratio is called call the **dominant** pitch. In terms of frequency, or "up and down" perception, the dominant pitch is positioned slightly higher than halfway between two tonic pitches. Therefore, the melodic distance is larger from dominant *down* to tonic (2:3) than from dominant *up* to tonic (3:4).

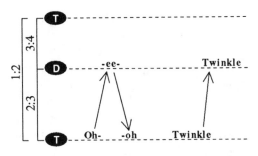

The 2:3 relationship occurs melodically in the "March Of The Winkies," in which the melody consists of movement up and down between the tonic pitch and the dominant pitch. "Twinkle, Twinkle Little Star" also begins with this 2:3 relationship.

4-4

Since the pitch ratio of 3:4 also consists of a tonic/dominant relationship, it sounds very much like the 2:3 ratio except that in this case the tonic pitch is the higher one. Since the difference in "distance" between the 2:3 and 3:4 relationship is not easily perceived, it is better to focus on the sense of tonality here. The songs "Here Comes The Bride" and "Auld Lang Syne" both begin on the dominant pitch (partial 3) and then move *upward* to the tonic pitch (partial 4).

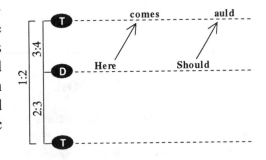

4-5

In a melodic or harmonic fragment containing the tonic and dominant pitches, if the lower pitch sounds like tonic it is the 2:3 relationship and if the upper pitch sounds like tonic it is the 3:4 relationship. Again, the more experience you have with these sounds, the more accurate your perceptions will be. Again, attempting to identify these sounds in terms of their difference in "distance" will probably lead more to frustration than to success. Our perceptual sense of distance (in any mode) is not at all precise.

**mediant**

The next most consonant ratio is 4:5. Designating the pitch represented by 4 as tonic, the pitch represented by 5 falls slightly higher than halfway between tonic and the dominant above it. Its name, somewhat appropriately, is **mediant**. The sound of this ratio is somewhat less consonant than the tonic/ dominant relationship, but in the larger context of all of the ratios commonly used in music, this one is decidedly more "agreeable" than "disagreeable."

4-6

In fact, the mediant brings a quality to music that one might describe as "pretty." While the tonic and dominant pitches sounding alone tend to sound "empty," the addition of the mediant seems to fill in the emptiness and provide a distinctive "color" to the sound. In this example, the tonic and dominant pitches are sounded, then the mediant is added.

4-7

**combining consonant pitches**

A great many melodies use the tonic, mediant and dominant pitches in series, both up and down. Some well-known examples are: "The Marines' Hymn" (up from tonic on the

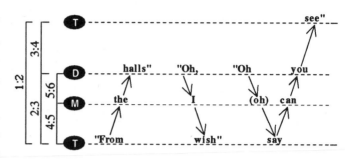

4-8

syllables "From the halls"), "Dixie" (down from dominant on the syllables "Oh I wish"), and "The Star Spangled Banner" (down from dominant then up to the high tonic on the syllables "Oh say can you see").

Notice that the next most consonant ratio, 5:6, appears between the mediant and the dominant pitches. Like the sound of the 4:5 ratio, the sound of the 5:6 ratio is relatively "agreeable."

# Tradition

It is rather surprising that it took such a long time for musicians to discover the major mode's delightful benefits. But then it took almost as long to discover that the world was a sphere and not flat, and that it revolves around the sun and not vice versa. In both cases, tradition offered strong resistance toward more accurate insights. Novel ideas, it seems, no matter how valid, often must wait until the intellectual climate is "ready" for them in order to impact established points of view.

In our own day, tradition defines the major mode as a configuration of "whole steps" and "half steps." This view is based, at least in part, on two assumptions, both of which are perceptually suspect. The first assumption is that the equal "steps" of a piano configure to the same pitches that a well-tuned musical ear hears while performing music. The second assumption is that melody is most easily perceived, pitch after pitch, in a linear way, connecting one pitch to the next without regard for their harmonic relationships. Regarding the first, there is no question that keyboards have been compromised. Even if the modification were slight (which it is not), the fixed equal steps on a keyboard cannot provide insight into the flexible nature of tuning needed to maximize harmonic import in a musical performance. Regarding the second, the pitch relationships that are easiest to conceive and perceive are those having small-number ratios (acoustically 1:2, 2:3, 3:4, 4:5); whole steps and half steps (acoustically 8:9 and 15:16) are among the most difficult to conceive and perceive and continually are the most problematic in developing a musical ear.

Considerable research indicates that tuning preferences are influenced by one's exposure to a particular tuning method. There is no challenge here to that conclusion. However, using that conclusion to cast doubt on the idea that our ears do not hear pitch relations in terms of small-number ratios is a leap in logic. It also ignores simple observable phenomena. Tuning adjustments that produce the *most consonant* result seldom leave room for preference differences. That intervals in small-number ratios appear to "lock" when they arrive at the best possible agreement is an observable phenomena. These judgments are not a matter of preference, they are a matter of paying attention to specific sensations.

At this point it will be helpful to add some vocabulary. First, let's define **chord** as "three or more pitches sounded simultaneously." This concept applies to *any* pitches sounded together, not just ones in small-number relationships. The term **triad**, however, specifically refers to three pitches related in a combination of 4:5 and/or 5:6 ratios. The term applies whether the pitches are sounded simultaneously or one after the other. Thus, a triad is a specific type of chord.

**some useful terms**

The three pitches of a triad need not always be sounded in upward order from a fundamental pitch. A triad can be sounded with its pitches in any order or any distance apart, using the "same pitch" principle to move any member up or down an octave. Remember, the concept "triad" is only an idea. As with most ideas, a triad can be expressed in many different ways.

4-9

When a triad has the relational configuration that occurs when tonic and dominant pitches are sounded along with a mediant pitch in a 4:5 ratio, as

Music educators have relied on the keyboard as an ear-training tool and have taught music theory based on its equally spaced pitches for a very long time, probably since the advent of equal-tempered tuning. In the nineteenth century, Hermann Helmholz, an eminent scientist and acoustition, observed that music educators were missing the mark by relying on the keyboard for musical training. He writes:

> It is impossible not to acknowledge that at the present day few even of our opera singers are able to execute a little piece for several voices, when either totally unaccompanied, or at most accompanied by occasional chords...in a manner suited to give the hearer a full enjoyment of its perfect harmony.... But where are our singers to learn just intonation and make their ears sensitive for perfect chords? They are from the first taught to sing to the equally-tempered piano–forte.... The singer who practises to a tempered instrument has no principle at all for exactly and certainly determining the pitch of his voice.

> On the other hand, we often hear four musical amateurs who have practised much together, singing quartetts in perfectly just intonation. Indeed, my own experience leads me almost to affirm that quartetts are more frequently heard with just intonation when sung by young men who scarcely sing anything else, and often and regularly practise them, than when sung by instructed solo singers who are accustomed to the accompaniment of the pianoforte or the orchestra. (*On The Sensation Of Tone*, 1863. English translation, Ellis, 1875, p. 326)

The observation that Helmholz made more than a hundred years ago still applies today. Amateur singing groups, such as barbershop quartets and choruses and street doo-wop groups, tend to sing more in pure tuning than "trained" singers who tend to "learn their notes" by means of a piano. Clearly, nature is fully prepared to supply accurate perceptions of pitch relations. The piano is not.

Over the centuries, an enormous investment of time and money has gone into the propagation of music theory based on an artificial construct. Its proponents will not likely abandon such a well-established position lightly. Nor should they. The only intellectually honest reason to change one's ideas is when a more logical and practical view is found which seems to better explain how the real world works.

The evidence suggests that there is a better way to train our musical sensibilities. We should simply listen to what nature has to say on the subject instead of unquestioningly clinging to the fuzzy tonal conceptions offered by a mechanical and synthetic system.

above, the triad is said to be **major**. Since this same configuration can be constructed on pitches other than tonic, we refer to the one that appears on a tonic pitch as a **tonic triad**. The tonic is the **fundamental** pitch of this triad.

How do the other pitches in the major mode relate? Are they simply slipped in between these three to fill out the scale? The answer is that other pitches do, in fact, relate to the tonic pitch, but most frequently they do so by means of other chords which are closely related.

**the dominant triad**

The dominant pitch, functioning as a fundamental, generates its own family of related pitches, just as the tonic pitch does. To place this in perspective, remember that the dominant pitch is related directly to the tonic in a very basic way—a 2:3 ratio. Also, in case you wondered about it, the dominant is more closely related harmonically to the tonic than to the mediant, even though it is closer to the mediant in frequency.

4-10

The **dominant triad** is quite aptly named in that it delivers most of the musical energy that drives the major/minor system, making it unique among the world's musical styles and traditions. Before describing its details, let's hear what it sounds like in action.

4-11

As you listened to the music, did you hear some melodic pitches that didn't seem to relate directly to your sense of tonic? Listen to the same melody again sounded with a continuous tonic pitch. Notice the dissonance that is created when some melodic pitches disagree with the tonic.

4-12

As you might suspect, the pitches that don't agree with the tonic are generated from a different fundamental pitch. In this melody, the pitches that are dissonant to the tonic are generated from the dominant fundamental. When the accompaniment changes to a dominant chord where the "offending" pitches occur, the result is more consonant.

The use of this contrasting harmony introduces a new and different kind of energy. By shifting the focus of the pitch relationships to the dominant triad, a sense of restlessness is experienced. This creates an expectation to return to the tonic triad before quitting the music in order to make it feel complete and resolved.

4-13

Significantly, the dominant pitch itself is the only member of its own chord that is also a member of the tonic chord. The others are not. That is what helps dominant harmony create tension. The pitch that relates to the dominant in a 2:3 ratio (in effect, a dominant of the dominant), is located scalewise just

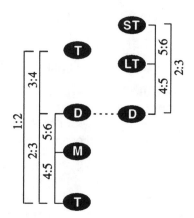

above the tonic pitch. Appropriately, it is called the **supertonic** (ST). The pitch that relates to the dominant in a 4:5 ratio (like a mediant of the dominant) falls just below the tonic. It is called the **leading tone** (LT) because of its strong tendency to "lead" a melodic line to the tonic pitch. These three pitches—dominant, leading tone, and supertonic— constitute the dominant triad.

Composers commonly include an additional member in the dominant chord. This added ingredient contributes greatly to the dominant chord's tension and restless nature. Even the simplest major/minor music often includes this

pitch. In addition to the 4:5 leading tone and the 2:3 supertonic (4:6 in this graphic), the pitch corresponding to the seventh partial (1:7, or 4:7 here) is frequently added.

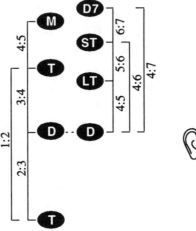

 4-14

Unfortunately, the 4:7 pitch doesn't have a traditional name of its own, probably for a couple of reasons. First, it is so far out of tune with the tempered keyboard that it has been deemed "unusable" by many teachers and theorists. Also, because it shares the same keyboard digital (in tempered tuning) with another scale member, it was evidently deemed expedient to use the other member's name for both functions. But neither the name nor the namesake's pitch matches the chord member generated by the dominant fundamental. There is another traditional name we can use for this discussion, although introducing it in this context will not be totally systematic. We will call it the **dominant seventh pitch**. This seventh harmonic of the dominant falls into place in the major scale just above the mediant.

Because most of the music we hear today is created on tempered-tuned instruments, we don't often hear the the dominant seventh pitch in its pure tuning. Listen to this pitch in three musical cultures in which it is tuned (in relation to a tonic fundamental) "as nature intended." Does it sound "flat" to you? If so, tempered tuning has probably influenced (and limited) your judgement. You might like to experiment by sounding a fundamental pitch and sliding your voice in the area of the dominant seventh pitch until you hear it lock in tune.

4-15

The importance of the dominant seventh pitch in the major/minor system cannot be overstated. This pitch is a member of the mysterious "tritone" that was so misunderstood in the Middle Ages. Its collaboration with the leading tone to create harmonic thrust in major/minor music is of paramount importance. The way it works will be much easier to understand after we have covered a number of other matters, so we will leave it for the time being.

**the subdominant triad**

Similar to the relationship of the fundamental dominant pitch to the tonic in a 2:3 ratio *above* tonic, another important member of the major/minor system is found at a 2:3 ratio *below* tonic. Logically, it is called the **subdominant**, and like both the tonic and dominant, the pitches it generates form a major triad. The pitch above the subdominant in a 2:3 ratio is, of course, the tonic pitch itself, so it is somewhat debatable as to "which generated what." In any case, the pitch in the 4:5 ratio falls between the subdominant and the tonic above. Its name is **submediant**, since it is positioned between tonic and subdominant.

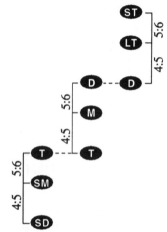

The terms *subdominant* and *submediant* —indicating relationships below tonic— logically mirror the terms *dominant* and *mediant*—relationships above tonic. However, it should be noted that while the dominant and subdominant relationships to tonic mirror each other in ratios of 2:3, the mediant and submediant ratios from tonic are *not* mirrored. The ratio from tonic up to mediant is 4:5, and from tonic down to submediant is 5:6, a smaller distance in terms of frequency.

**functional harmony**

It is this shifting of harmonic focus from a tonic triad to other related chords that Rameau described many years ago as **functional harmony**. These events not only can be perceived as harmonic shifts in the general sense, but with a bit of listening experience, one can learn to identify them specifically.

The three harmonies—subdominant, tonic and dominant—acoustically supply all the basic pitches used in the major mode. The tonic pitch seems to serve as a pivot to the subdominant and the dominant pitch seems to serve as a pivot to the dominant. One might conclude from the graphic above that the dominant and subdominant harmonies are more or less equal in their functional relationship to tonic harmony.

This is not the case, however, and the different roles of these two "alternatives" can be better seen in this graphic. By moving the dominant seventh chord down one octave, we can see how its members relate individually to the members of the tonic and subdominant triads.

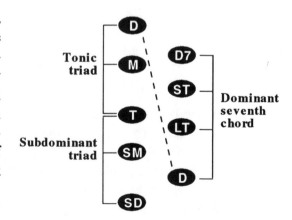

Two pitches in the dominant seventh chord are positioned more or less equally between their tonic/subdominant neighbors and two are positioned more closely to one neighbor than the other. Specifically, the leading tone and the dominant seventh pitch are closer to the tonic and mediant pitches (respectively) than the dominant and supertonic pitches are to either of their neighbors. This is one of the most significant characteristics in the major/minor system. The harmonic importance of this feature will become clearer as we proceed. At this point, simply noticing this configuration of major mode scale members is sufficient.

It will be valuable to remember the chord or chords to which each member belongs. It is also important to note its neighboring members and to which chords they belong. Every pitch in the major mode has its own special position and role in the major/minor system, making it possible to recognize each one by its unique "personality." Let's do a rundown.

**home pitch**

The **tonic** pitch is central to the major mode. It acoustically generates the mediant and the dominant pitches. Melodies tend to gravitate to the tonic and its chord members as places of rest. This is particularly true of the tonic pitch itself at the end of a composition. Composers almost always begin their works by establishing tonic harmony, the melody starting on one of the tonic chord members.

**restless neighbors**

The tonic pitch is neighbored above by the **supertonic** and below by the **leading tone**, both of which belong only to the dominant chord. These two pitches, being near the tonic melodically, are dissonant to it. This creates a restless feeling that is said to "resolve" when a melody moves from these pitches to the tonic. The supertonic has approximately an 8:9 ratio to tonic, a relatively dissonant relationship. However, the leading tone, being closer to tonic in actual pitch, has approximately a 15:16 ratio to tonic, a much more dissonant harmonic sound. In general, the more dissonant the harmonic ratio, the stronger the restlessness.

**pretty pitches**

The **mediant**, belonging only to the tonic chord, normally implies tonic harmony. Its neighbors, the supertonic and dominant seventh, are dissonant to it, particularly the upper one, which is very close in frequency. The **submediant**, belonging only to the subdominant chord, normally implies subdominant harmony. Its lower neighbor is the dominant pitch, to which it frequently resolves when the harmony moves to either a tonic or dominant chord. Its upper neighbor is the leading tone, which seldom moves down to it. This is partly due to the leading tone's strong attraction to the tonic and also because the dominant chord usually is not followed by subdominant harmony. When the leading tone does move down to the submediant, it usually does so in a "just passing through" manner or because other harmonic elements are affecting its basic melodic tendencies.

**sturdy pitches**    The **dominant** pitch is easily the second most frequently used pitch in virtually every tonal music system in the world. In the major/minor system, the dominant pitch is both the 2:3 member of the tonic chord, as well as the fundamental, or parent pitch, of its own chord. Ironically, it is both the second most stable pitch, as well as the generator of the most restless family of pitches. These combined factors provide the energetic "dominant function" in the major/minor system and also focus that energy toward tonic.

The **subdominant** pitch is also very stable, having the tonic pitch in its family in a 2:3 ratio. The subdominant pitch, along with its chord members, provides an alternative to dominant harmony, supplying the "subdominant function." This completes the set of three principal harmonic functions basic to the major/minor system.

**the power source**    The **dominant seventh pitch** is the most dissonant chord member in the basic major/minor system, and therefore the most restless. It relates to its parent pitch, the dominant, in a 4:7 (1:7 reduced) ratio, to the leading tone in a 5:7 ratio, and to the supertonic, its other chord mate, in a 6:7 ratio. Its tritone relationship to the leading tone is paramount to understanding how the major/minor system works, and we will focus on that very shortly. It *always* (either in fact or in perception, if that makes sense) resolves downward to the mediant when moving to tonic harmony.

These relational characteristics remain the same no matter what actual pitch is assigned the role of tonic. As mentioned earlier, most of us are not able to identify specific pitches in terms of their vibrational frequency, and relational concepts are the only organizational ones available to us. On the other hand, those who *do* have the innate ability to identify pitches will be perceptually and musically enriched by developing a vocabulary of sound concepts regarding the unique functional characteristics of the various ingredients of the major/minor system.

**pitches in a row**    Now let's configure the major mode pitch members in a more conventional way. In the illustration on the facing page, they are arranged, by means of the "same pitch" principle, in order of their frequency from a tonic pitch up to the next higher tonic pitch. To help you remember their individual "personalities," each pitch is presented within a graphic shape that characterizes its role. Membership in the three principal harmonies is indicated by brackets, showing acoustical ratios between neighboring chord members. Because the dominant seventh pitch and the subdominant pitch are traditionally played on the keyboard using the same digital and represented by the same notational symbol, these pitches are represented by a compound graphic shape that shows their different roles and personalities.

# Major Scale Members In Pitch Order

(The 2:3 ratios between scale steps 1-5, 4-1, and 5-2
are omitted here to minimize visual confusion.)

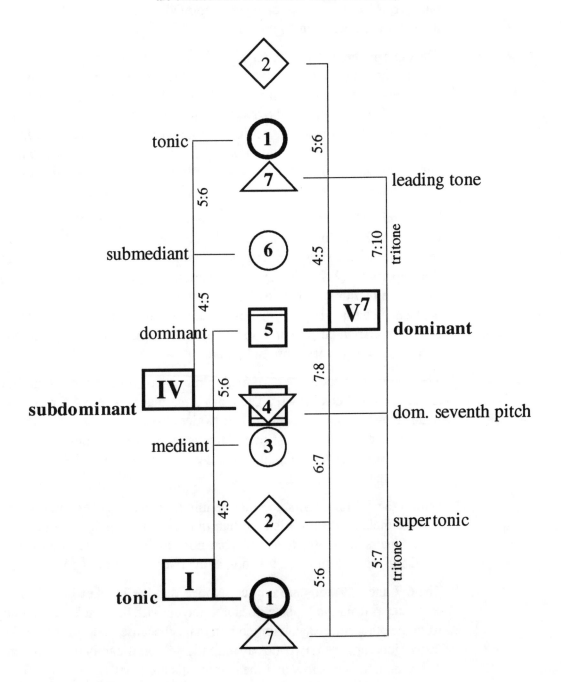

The names of the scale members introduced above are important in that they tell us something about their unique functions. However, since multisyllabic names are somewhat cumbersome, scale steps are commonly referred to as numbers or solfege syllables (do, re, mi, etc.). Since syllables would add another new element for some readers to memorize, we have opted for numbers. Chords, as well, can be represented as numbers, and are identified here by traditional Roman numerals.

The tonic pitches (1) are shown here within bold circles, the lower one bracketed as the fundamental of the tonic triad (I) and the upper one as the 2:3 member of the subdominant triad (IV). The dominant (5) and subdominant pitches (4) are set in bold boxes, one with an added line below the number (indicating its 2:3 position below tonic), and the other with an added line above the number (indicating its 2:3 position above tonic). The mediant (3) and submediant (6) pitches are encased in fine-line circles indicating their lighter harmonic weight and their relatively restful nature.

The dominant fundamental firmly anchors its family members to the tonic by its own 2:3 ratio to the tonic pitch. The other members of the dominant seventh chord are shown in figures that indicate their active melodic nature. The supertonic (2) is seen here in a diamond shape, indicating its tendency to move either up or down to a more restful scale step. The leading tone (7) is placed in a triangle pointing upward and the dominant seventh pitch (4) is placed in a triangle pointing downward, showing their strong "magnetic" attraction to their very close neighbors.

The diagram offers an opportunity to reinforce some information that we already know. Let's browse. There are three places where 4:5 ratios occur: scale steps 1 to 3, 4 to 6 and 5 to 7. Notice that in all three pairs, the lower member is a fundamental of one of the three main harmonies (I, IV, and V). In each case, the intervening scale step is equally spaced (more or less) between the two members.

Within the 5:6 ratio pairs, the intervening scale step is off center, verifying that the melodic distance is less than in the 4:5 ratio pairs. In other words, the 5:6 pairs are closer together. That information will become even more vivid and significant when we look at the major scale on the keyboard.

The 6:7 and 7:8 ratios are unique. Notice that the bracket line pointing to scale step 4 from the $V^7$ side does not line up with the bracket line pointing from the other side. As you remember, that is because scale step 4 is asked to do two jobs, and these two jobs use slightly yet significantly different pitches. The ratio numbers show that these intervals are smaller, and therefore less consonant, than any others shown here.

Notice again that scale step 4 (in its dominant role) works with scale step 7, the leading tone, to provide the most energetic activity in the whole system. The two pitches relate harmonically in a 5:7 (or 7:10) ratio, creating that very restless pitch combination called the "tritone." Both members of the pair are very close to their respective resolution pitches. Notice also that these two members are in the *only* locations in the major mode where scale members are that close together. In one case, it is the upper of the two pitches (4-3) that is the tritone member and in the other case it is the lower of the two pitches (7-1) that is the tritone member.

The more you can digest the characteristics and configurations in this chart, the more meaningful the upcoming discussions will be. If something doesn't fit well into your logical overview of these constructs, go back and think through the fuzzy parts again. You needn't feel uneasy about not being able to apply these constructs to all the musical pieces you know. That isn't necessary at this time. If you are studying this material with a teacher, this might be a good time to engage in constructive dialogue to ensure that everything is in place. But, if you feel that the ideas discussed up to this point are fairly clear, you are ready to proceed.

The chart on the following page entitled "Major Scale As Primary Chords" **ear-training drill** contains two octaves of pitches shown in terms of their membership in the three primary chords discussed in this chapter. Accompanying the chart are suggested ear-training exercises that will help you negotiate your way around the sounds of the major mode.

If you are not used to hearing and producing finely-tuned pitches, employing a drone pitch will help you tune chord members to their respective fundamentals. If you are drilling with others, as in a class situation, one or more can sing a drone while others sing chord-member pitches represented on the chart. By pointing to each scale member as it is sung, all following the exercise will be able to visualize the harmonic shift when moving from one chord to another. It is much easier to hear fine tuning when timbres are similar. Therefore, instead of singing numbers, *think* numbers while you sing a consistent vowel sound, such as "ooh," "oh" or "ah."

If you are practicing alone, you can provide a drone using a keyboard. Although the fundamental pitches you play will be slightly out of tune to each other, this is of far less consequence than the benefit you will derive from tuning to a sustained pitch. Since the sound of a piano decays and constantly needs to be resounded, it is preferable to use an electronic keyboard. Turn off any vibrato or stereo effects and choose a simple flutelike or stringlike timbre. As you sing pitches try to match the keyboard's timbre with your voice. It is easier to accurately tune when timbres are similar.

# MAJOR SCALE AS PRIMARY CHORDS

IV          I          V⁷

# Suggestions For Ear-Training Drill

The ear-training charts in this book show the function of scale steps as they appear in basic harmonic contexts. They will protect your drills from wandering around in an "endless sea of possibilities." Instead of simply practicing scales like eggs in a row, you will experience pitches as chords members. This provides an added dimension to your aural experience, not only showing which pitches appear in which chords, but also demonstrating that a given pitch can sound different when heard in a different harmonic context.

Using these charts to direct your practice will help you visualize the harmonic relations of pitches as you sing them. By pointing to scale numbers in a given chord while you sing them, you will begin to recognize their unique qualities. You will also learn to hear the harmony shift as you move your pointer from one chord to another.

A keyboard can be used with early drills to help maintain a sense of tonic and to hear chord changes, however, a keyboard should *not* be used to guide the voice through a drill by playing the pitches to be sung. Not only does the keyboard not play pitches in pure acoustic tuning, but you need to learn to create musical structures *without* the help of an instrument. Singing with a keyboard will result in a clouded sense of pitch relations and will only delay success. Your ear *can* hear pure tuning when given the opportunity. A keyboard should be used with these drills mainly to sound fundamental pitches.

Graphic figures appear on scale numbers that are a member of that chord. This shows what the chord tones are while imaging (or hearing) a particular harmony. The root of each chord is marked with a small arrowhead to help you quickly identify it.

Drill 1: Without referring to the chart, sound a fundamental pitch (on a keyboard or by other singers) in your low singing register. Name it "1" (tonic) and sing it. Tune and blend it until your voice causes no disturbance when the two sounds are combined. Then sing the next higher "1" (1:2 ratio) and listen to the relationship between the keyboard and your voice. Then find the 2:3 ratio pitch (scale step 5) and tune it. Do the same for the 4:5 ratio (scale step 3). When you are confident that you have mastered these skills, go on to Drill 2.

Drill 2: Play and sustain any low pitch, name it tonic and point on the chart to the low scale step 1 in the center column, identified by the Roman numeral I (tonic chord). Sing it, then move your voice and pointer to the other chord members (3 and 5). Move up and down among the chord members, first in narrow leaps, then larger ones. Stay in this column and restrict your drill to tonic chord members (1,3, and 5). Proceed carefully, moving your pitches slightly up or down until you hear them "lock in" with the sustained fundamental pitch. Repeat this drill starting on various pitches. When you have mastered this drill, move to the next.

Drill 3: Begin as in Drill 2. After you have established a strong sense of tonic harmony, move your pointer to chord tones in the IV chord (4, 6 and 1). Sound the new fundamental pitch when you move to pitches in the IV chord, and back to the tonic fundamental when you return. As you move from chord to chord, sing smoothly from a member of the chord you are leaving to a nearby member of the new chord, such as 3 to 4 or vice versa. As you go back and forth between the IV and I chord, you will hear the harmony shift. Tune all pitches carefully and notice how much or how little the pitch moves as you change from scale steps in one chord to scale steps in the other.

Drill 5: Now include the $V^7$ chord in your drill. The $V^7$ chord has four chord tones, two of which are very particular about where they want to go when moving to the I chord. If you are singing step 4 as you change to the tonic chord, you must follow the arrow to step 3. If you are singing 7 when changing to tonic, you must follow the arrow to 1. Incidentally, the $V^7$ chord almost never goes to IV. But IV often goes to $V^7$ in major-minor music, and you should include this progression in subsequent drills.

If you need a hint to find a pitch you want to sing, tap it on the keyboard (if you know which one to play), but don't sustain it while you sing. Singing all the scale members with the keyboard's tuning will prevent you from hearing nature's simple tuning. Instead of improving your ear, singing with the keyboard will prevent such insights. The argument that tuning to a keyboard is better than no tuning at all assumes that hearing acoustic tuning is more difficult than imitating pitches on a keyboard. It is not. Try it.

As you drill, listen to the distinctive sound of each chord member in relation to its fundamental pitch—the "same pitch" 1:2 ratio quality of the tonic pitch, the "warm" sound of the 4:5 ratio and the "structural" sound of the 2:3 ratio. Also notice that when the fundamental changes, these same relationships and qualities can be heard on different scale steps, however, they take on a slightly different tonal flavor in each context. This demonstrates that the perception of musical elements is always influenced to some degree by the context in which they are heard. Knowing this will help you avoid aural confusion as you explore the sounds of music.

What is especially important in this regard is the perceptual difference of scale step 4 as heard in the subdominant chord and in the dominant chord. As you know, the tuning of scale step 4 is considerably different in these two contexts. To practice hearing the difference, sing scale step 3 over a tonic fundamental and then alternately sing scale step 4 over each of the other fundamentals. Notice how little the pitch moves when going to dominant harmony in comparison to going to subdominant harmony.

(You will find other ear-training charts throughout this book. All of these can be purchased as a set from the publisher. Laminated charts for convenient individual drill are available as well as overhead projector transparencies for classroom use. See p. 336 for ordering information.)

5

# The
# Keyboard

It will be helpful at this point to become acquainted with the keyboard and to notice how the major mode fits its configuration of black and white **digitals**, the levers used to activate the sound. Although these levers are commonly called "keys," we will use the term *digital* (pertaining to finger, as opposed to *pedal,* pertaining to foot), to avoid confusion with the term **key**, meaning "pitch location of a tonal center."

At first glance, one notices that the white digitals are evenly spaced and the black digitals are not, and that the black digitals are grouped in sets of twos and threes. It is the pattern of alternating sets of two and three black digitals that enables quick perception of specific locations. In fact, this configuration makes it easy to play the keyboard without looking at it. It is quite easy to learn to feel one's way around the keyboard by means of the black digitals.

The sets of two and three black digitals help visually as well as tactually. You see, the white digitals are assigned names by virtue of their physical relationship to the black ones. The black ones don't have names of their own, but are identified in terms of the nearest white ones. If that sounds a bit confusing, don't be concerned. It will clear up presently. For the moment, however, we'll be concerned only with naming the white ones.

The English system of naming the white digitals uses the first seven letters **abcdefg** of the English alphabet, and assigns the letters in order from low (in pitch) to high. On the keyboard, "lower" means "to the left" and "higher" means "to the right." You may be surprised that only seven letters are needed to name all the white digitals spread across the instrument, but by applying the "same pitch" principle we observed earlier, the pattern of white-digital names is repeated up the keyboard after every seventh step.

Notice that this distance corresponds perfectly with the repeated pattern of five black digitals. On a real keyboard, put your finger on any white digital, call it "one," move to the next and call it "two," and so on, until you get to eight. When you arrive, your finger will be on a digital that is in the same relation to a pattern of five black digitals as the one you started on. It works in either direction.

**"same pitch" principle revisited**  The reason we only need seven letters, and not eight, is because the eighth digital gets the same name as the first one, since it is in the same position relative to the pattern of five black digitals. In fact, all of the digitals on the entire keyboard having this relative position to its own set of five black digitals will have this same name. So, you see, seven letters works just fine. We have other means of referencing specific digitals having the same name, but we'll save that for later.

Deciding on which digital to begin the seven-letter sequence was somewhat arbitrary. The decision was made in the Middle Ages when early keyboards were developed. Any digital probably would have worked fine. In any case, this is where "A" and the other six letters were assigned.

The distance from any letter to the same letter above or below is in a 1:2 ratio, or a multiple of it, thus the "same pitch" principle applies to any digitals having the same name. Since the distance from any letter name to the same letter name *next* above or below involves 8 digitals, that distance is called an **octave**.

## The Major Mode on the Keyboard

The keyboard's white digitals, being evenly spaced, are useless in regard to demonstrating how the major scale fits into its configuration of digitals. In fact, these evenly spaced white digitals actually provide misleading information, and focusing on that feature may in fact prevent, or at least delay, the formation of accurate concepts. So let us make it very clear that the *pitches* produced by playing a consecutive series of white digitals are not evenly spaced.

However, when black and white digitals are considered *together* they do produce sounds that are equally spaced. This was accomplished by translating vibration rates to "cents" (100 cents from any digital to its neighbor) by means of mathematical calculations called logarithms, resulting in twelve equally-spaced pitches between each set of 1:2 ratio "same note" pitches. This method of tuning is appropriately called **equal-tempered**.

The result, incidentally, is that the octave (1:2 ratio) is the only true small-number ratio on the keyboard. All the others are "out of tune" to varying degrees. These tuning discrepancies were not considered serious enough for concern (see sidebar "Now Hear This," p. 58). Some music educators, however, are beginning to realize that this is not true, and are cautioning their students in this regard.

Since all of the keyboard's digitals, black and white together, are evenly spaced in terms of the sounds they produce, it logically follows that pitches produced by some of the white digitals are actually closer together because there is no black digital between them. That is, in fact, true. Notice there are two places within each octave where no black digital appears between two white ones—between E and F and between B and C.

The terminology used to describe this digital placement is **whole step** and **half step**. From any digital, black or white, to its neighboring digital, black or white, is a half step. Therefore, the distance between two white digitals having a black digital between them is a whole step; and the distance between two white digitals having no black digital between them is a half step. Whole steps can also occur between two neighboring black digitals or between black

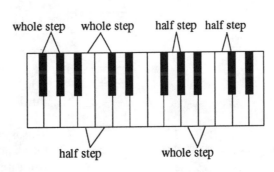

and white digitals, provided there is one digital between them (which, logically, will be white).

The pattern of black and white digitals not only provides tactile orientation to the keyboard, it also provides a visual representation of the major scale. To make the transition from the acoustic view of the major mode to the keyboard view, we will translate the major triad's acoustical *ratios* to keyboard *steps*. The 4:5 ratio (tonic to mediant, for example) translates to 2 whole steps. The 5:6 ratio (mediant to dominant) translates to a step and a half. (Keep in mind that these translations are approximations since they are not acoustical equivalents.)

**"steps," a keyboard concept**

# Now Hear This!

Most of the approximate pitches of the major scale appear within the fourth octave of the partials series—between partials 8 and 16 (see graphic). The term "approximate" is appropriate in that not only do the keyboard's scale steps (shown on the left) not tune exactly to nature's tuning (shown on the right), but pitch-sensitive musicians tend to tune some scale steps differently when the harmonic context changes. Therefore, even the pure tuning of the acoustic series presents only part of the story.

The *Harvard Dictionary of Music* has this to say about acoustic and keyboard tuning discrepancies:

> The deviation of the fifth (2 cents) is too small to be perceived. With the thirds, the difference is considerably greater, the well-tempered third (400 cents) being 14 cents (one-eighth semitone) larger than the pure third (386 cents). However, the modern ear has become completely accustomed to the "error," and the advantages of the system far outweigh its flaws.

In regard to "fifths" (2:3), simple auditory experience demonstrates that the "2 cents" difference between the keyboard's version and the ear's perception-of-consonance version *can* be perceived. Helmholtz observed and commented on this a century ago, and not all "modern ears" have "become accustomed." Even beginning music students can easily hear that when tonic and dominant pitches are well-tuned by ear, the result is not duplicated when sounded on the keyboard. Incidentally, there is no question about the advantages of tempered tuning; however, those advantages have nothing to do with the development of musical "ears."

Regarding "thirds" (4:5), sensitive choral singers usually agree on a third which is actually *higher* than the tempered third when the perfect fifth is also sounding. When the fifth is not sounding, singers usually agree on the "pure" third, which is *lower* than the tempered third (see graphic).

This is evidence that pure acoustic pitch ratios are only part of the total picture. Additional research is needed in order to solve the "mystery of the elusive third" as well as other interesting tuning preferences. In the meantime, it is clear that the keyboard is not a source of truth in regard to accurate tuning.

5-1

To keep things simple, we will look for places on the keyboard where these patterns fit on white digitals. Since the 4:5 ratio fits two whole steps, we'll look for places where there are two black digitals within three white ones. The most obvious place is the set of two black digitals between C and E.

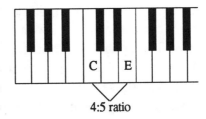

Let's see if the step-and-a-half 5:6 part of the major triad fits next to it. To the right of our C-E interval is a half step and a whole step. This is what we are looking for. Add the G and play the resulting triad. It sounds like the pitches in "The Marines' Hymn" and "The Star Spangled Banner," so we evidently have located one place

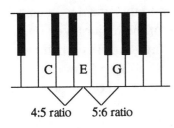

where a major triad fits (roughly) the white digitals.

Now, let's find others. There are only two more places where there are two black digitals between three white ones—between F and A and between G and B. Both locations, then, will accommodate the 4:5 part of a major triad.

Let's check to see if the 5:6 part will fit on the white digitals to the right of each 4:5 part. In both cases, it does. Play them to check out the sound. Both of these triads sound like the one on C-E-G (although on different digitals). Now we have three.

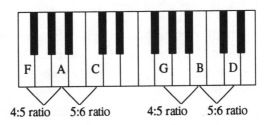

Are there any more? No, there is no other place (except octave duplications) where a major triad occurs on white digitals. Is that significant? Yes, it is.

As you probably realized, we have just located the three primary triads of the major mode. The tonic triad fundamental is on C, the dominant triad fundamental is on G, and the subdominant triad fundamental is on F. Since the tonic pitch is C, this configuration of pitches is called **the key of C major**. A major key can be constructed on any pitch, but the key of C is the only one having all of its members on white digitals. Every other major key must include some black digitals to properly configure the three primary major triads around its tonic pitch.

**the key of C major**

As you can see, the keyboard provides a helpful means of viewing major-mode characteristics and relationships. It is even more helpful for viewing the scale in a linear configuration. When we assemble the pitches in the key of C in ascending order from one tonic to the next higher tonic, we can see

**half steps in C major**

the two places where no black digital appears between two white ones—between steps 3 and 4 and between steps 7 and 1. This corresponds to our earlier observation that those scale steps are closer together than any others in the major scale.

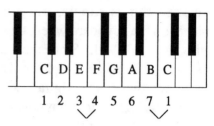

Compare this graphic to the one on p. 49. Review the relational and functional characteristics in that graphic and apply them to this one. Do you see that the white digitals of the keyboard fit the shape of the major mode quite well when C is the tonic? Did you notice that leading-tone B is a half step from tonic C, and that dominant seventh pitch F is a half step from its resolution pitch E? As we noted earlier, all the other pairs of neighboring members are a whole step apart.

Keep in mind that the concept of steps and half steps is a keyboard idea, and that all of the scale members (other than tonic) depend on acoustical relationships to their sponsoring fundamentals for accurate tuning. Therefore, acoustic "whole" steps are not exactly equal. Also, well-tuned "half" steps are more accurate when the two pitches are tuned to their respective fundamentals than when tuned to each other.

As mentioned earlier, there is only one digital available (F in the key of C) to express both the subdominant and the dominant seventh pitch. As we noticed then, these two scale members do not actually share the same pitch acoustically. While using the digital on scale step four to play the dominant seventh pitch is certainly very convenient, doing so creates the most significant distortion of the well-tuned major-mode.

If this distortion applied merely to an insignificant and rarely used element in the major mode, it would not deserve much concern. However, the dominant seventh pitch and the leading tone working together to create the dynamic "tritone" constitutes the very heart of what the major/minor system is all about. Therefore, this element warrants considerable attention.

## Significance of the "Tritone"

Try this experiment. Using your right hand, place your thumb on the tonic (C) and then place your four remaining fingers on the next four digitals in order. This will locate your little finger on the dominant (G). Now, holding your thumb and little finger in a rigid position, use them to play C and G at the same time so you can hear them together. This is the keyboard's version of the 2:3 ratio. We refer to it as a perfect fifth. The "fifth" part of the name describes the number of scale steps contained within this "distance." Discussion of the "perfect" part will have to wait until later.

Now move your locked hand position one whole step to the right, to the pitches D and A. Notice that it sounds exactly like the C-G pair you just played (except higher, of course). Move up to each new pair of white-digital pitches in order: E-B, F-C, G-D, A-E, B-F, C-G. You are now an octave higher than the pitches on which you began. Did all the combinations sound alike?

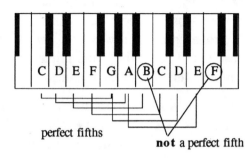

perfect fifths

**not** a perfect fifth

Did you notice that B-F did not sound like the others? If you didn't notice the difference, play the series again. B-F is much more dissonant than the others. Notice that between the two pitches in all the other pairs there are three black digitals, and between B and F there are only two. Therefore, the pitch distance from B to F is not the same size as the others.

**a unique fifth**

Remember that *both* B and F are only a half step away from their *inside* white-digital neighbors. (We observed that feature when we examined the scale members in the linear charts above.) In none of the other pitch combinations we played does that occur. The point here is that this interval is unique among the fifths in *any* major key. Also, this specific B-F pitch combination is unique to the key of C, in that C is the only major key that has this specific pitch combination in its scale. Is that significant? Very!

Now let's do another experiment. Play F, and then go up in whole steps to B. How many whole steps are there between F and B? If you counted three, you were correct. Now, play B and go up in whole steps until you come to F. (Clue: You will use some black digitals.) If you counted three, you were correct. This means that the distance from F up to B and the distance from B up to F is the same. Because the distance is *three* whole steps whether you are going up or down, from either pitch to the other, this relationship reflects its special nickname—the **tritone**.

**the invertible tritone**

This relationship is unique among two-pitch pairs on the keyboard in that it is the only one that remains the same size when its lower pitch is moved up an octave. You may remember that the dominant pitch is farther from the lower tonic (2:3) than from the upper tonic (3:4). This same "off-center" relationship is true of the other pitch pairs in the major mode. Since one member of the tritone is exactly in the middle of its upper and lower tritone partner, the distance (on the keyboard) is the same either way. This is most easily seen by viewing the tritone that occurs between C and the black digital between F and G. If you count the half steps, you will find that it is the same number whether you count up or down from the black digital to C. (Now, forget that number. It is no longer important.)

The name *tritone* is only a description of the *shape* of this relationship. The prefix "tri" is logical, since it has to do with the concept of "three" (three whole steps) but the other syllable, "tone," is not as logical since it requires *two* tones, specifically two *pitches*, in order for this relationship to exist. (In case you thought the name might imply something that has to do with the tritone's function in the major/minor system, it doesn't.)

The keyboard's compromised tuning of the tritone allows it to be heard either way. This, of course, is in keeping with the whole idea of tempered tuning, enabling the keyboard to move freely from key to key. Composers have taken full advantage of the ambiguity of the tempered tritone, substituting one of the two possible destination harmonies for the other (particularly in jazz). The important point here is to realize that the invertible concept of a "tritone," being equidistant either way, applies only to the keyboard. Is the tritone a valuable concept? Yes. Is the concept of a tritone somewhat misleading? Yes. Read on.

**the acoustical "tritone"**  The concept of an invertible tritone is strictly a keyboard idea. When a tritone is well-tuned, as scale steps 7 and 4 in a **dominant seventh chord** (the triad plus the dominant seventh pitch), its unique and dissonant prime number ratio of 5:7 provides the strongest tonality-determining energy music has ever known. Once the two pitches join forces with accurate tuning, tonality is determined. Whether this is due to nature or to nurture is beside the point. Practical experience verifies that one can hear the tritone's locked-in tuning and feel its harmonic tug.

The reason for this unambiguous determination is that the pitch distance is smaller from 7 up to 4 than from 4 up to 7 when these combinations are well tuned. Since the dominant seventh pitch actually tunes lower than the keyboard's digital plays it, it is closer to the leading tone below it and farther from the leading tone above it. Stated another way, when the tritone's leading tone is on the bottom, the pitch distance between the two pitches is smaller than when it is on the top. Therefore, if the tuning of B and 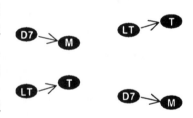 F is stretched out of its C major allegiance and tuned the other way, the two pitches would swap roles and belong to another key.

This is not to suggest that we necessarily *perceive* one as larger than the other. We don't have accurate perception of "distance" in any perceptual mode. The way experienced musicians perceive the difference is to focus on the different functional qualities of the two pitches. The leading tone has a tendency to move up to the tonic and the dominant seventh pitch has a tendency to move down to the mediant. If the top member sounds like it wants to move upward, that pitch is probably the leading tone. If the upper member sounds like it wants to move downward, that is probably the dominant seventh pitch. The point here is that we can *hear* the difference.

The most important fact surrounding the well-tuned relationship between the leading tone and the dominant seventh pitch (in contrast to the invertible tritone of the keyboard) is that, when considered together, these two pitches are fully capable of perceptually determining (or defining) a tonal center. Even the tonic pitch itself is less conclusive. The reason is that the harmonic combination of these two pitches is unique in the major mode. There is *only one* per key. Therefore sounding any two pitches having this relationship automatically defines the tonic to which they belong, even out of context.

Perceptual discrimination of the functional tendencies of a tritone is not as difficult as one might think. Considering that much of our aural experience with tritones has been with the ambiguous version offered by the keyboard, where leading tones and dominant seventh pitches are perceptually indistinguishable, it is not surprising that music students and teachers might consider this a difficult perception to acquire. Actually, when its pitches are well tuned, a tritone's tonal orientation is vividly clear. The main problem in learning to make the discrimination, then, would seem to be in finding well-tuned tritones with which to practice.

**hearing "tritones"**

Here are some. In these examples, the leading tone is sometimes the bottom pitch and sometimes the top pitch. See if you can predict the direction of the top and/or bottom pitch of each "tritone" before its resolution is heard. In other words, which sets of pitch pairs sound like they will contract (move closer together) and which sound like they will expand (move farther apart)? Can you can tell the difference? If so, you can appreciate the value of hearing and producing acoustically tuned sounds while developing a musical ear.  5-2

## Major Mode Wrap-Up

The major mode consists of pitches organized in systematic acoustical relationships around a single pitch. The central pitch, called *tonic*, is flanked equidistantly above and below by two pitches related to the tonic in a 2:3 ratio, the *dominant* above and the *subdominant* below. Each of those three *primary* pitches acoustically generates additional pitches in 4:5 acoustical ratios, the tonic producing the *mediant*, the dominant producing the *leading tone*, and the subdominant producing the *submediant*. The dominant pitch also generates two additional pitches—the *supertonic* and the *dominant seventh pitch*. These names also apply to pitches related to these members in a 1:2 ratio, both above and below, since the ear tends to hear those pitches as "the same."

The collective pitches in the major mode relate to the overall system in two ways: (1) *harmonically*, in relation to the principal pitch that generated it, and (2) *melodically*, in relation to the sequence of pitches in order of frequency, modified and described on a keyboard as *steps* and *half-steps*.

The most dynamic element in the major mode is the pitch relationship nicknamed the "tritone," wherein the leading tone and the dominant seventh pitch, both members of the dominant family, relate in a unique and dissonant way, impelling musical energy toward the tonic pitch.

The major mode can be generated from any pitch, and can be moved to any other pitch provided the internal harmonic relationships remain intact. When the tonic is designated as the pitch C, all of its individual members can be played (with some compromise of pitch) on the white digitals of the keyboard, named C, D, E, F, G, A and B.

# 6

# The Minor Mode

The functional workings of the minor mode are essentially the same as those of the major mode. The minor mode is based on the same three primary pitches and their harmonic families: tonic, dominant and subdominant. The difference between the major and minor modes is principally a matter of harmonic color, manifested largely in the tonic and subdominant harmonies. The dominant chord uses the same configuration in both modes, thus maintaining its dynamic function as controller of the music's tonal focus.

The transformation from the major to the minor mode is accomplished by a very simple acoustic adjustment in the tonic and the subdominant triads. Here's how it works. The relationship of the tonic pitch to the dominant

**mirrored triads**

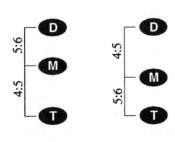

pitch, a sturdy 2:3 ratio, is unchanged in the transformation to minor mode. It is the mediant that accomplishes the task. By moving the mediant downward in pitch to a point where its 4:5 ratio to the tonic pitch is transferred to the dominant pitch and its 5:6 ratio to the dominant is transferred to the tonic, the ratios, in effect, flip upside down.

As with many perceptual concepts, this is an either/or matter. Logically, there are only two positions the mediant pitch can assume where the ear will hear three pitches having 2:3, 4:5 and 5:6 ratios. The major triad is one, the minor triad is the other. There are no other possibilities. This is an example of a logically *closed system*. As a well-tuned mediant in a major triad slides down in pitch, there is a place, and only one place, where it will "lock" into the configuration we have named **minor triad**.

Listen to this demonstration in which a major triad is gradually transformed into a minor triad. Notice that the place where the the mediant descent should

 6-1

stop is made clear by its arrival at a place of consonance, or "agreement." You might like to explore this principle for yourself by singing back and forth between major and minor mediants tuned to a sustained tonic pitch (and dominant pitch, if other singers are available). Incidentally, singing this exercise to both tonic and dominant pitches played on keyboard will not produce a well-tuned acoustic result and probably should be avoided.

This transformation also occurs in the minor sub-dominant triad. The submediant pitch moves down to the other locked-in position, changing what was a major triad in the major mode to a minor one in the minor mode.

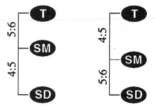

If the same treatment were applied to dominant harmony, the leading tone would no longer be a "half step" from the tonic, and therefore would lose its name and function. The pitch a whole step below tonic is called **subtonic**. This is not a case of "a rose by any other name smelling as sweet" because when lowered to become a subtonic, the leading tone loses its purpose as well. Moving scale step 7 down to a minor-triad position also destroys its tritone relationship to the dominant seventh pitch. The change seems to produce a perfect fifth, but this may depend on other considerations. Losing its unique acoustical ability to define tonal allegiance would take the domi-

**minor dominant
"blows a fuse"**

6-2

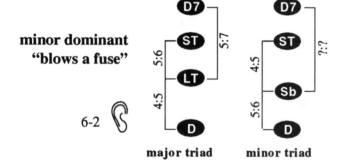

major triad          minor triad

nant chord right out of the major/minor system. Without the tritone, the dominant chord lacks its essential function, and without the functional dominant we are back in the Middle Ages.

Therefore, the dominant team of pitches, particularly the tritone members, must not change from one mode to the other. The essential difference between the major mode and the minor mode is simply that the mediant and the submediant pitches are lowered, making the tonic and subdominant triads minor rather than major. Basically, that's it.

## The Minor Mode on the Keyboard

The keyboard, of course, cannot acoustically tune the pitches of the minor mode any better than it can the pitches of the major mode. Nevertheless, it continues to provide an excellent means of viewing the structural modifications in the minor mode resulting from lowering the mediant and submediant pitches.

In the key of C minor, the digitals E and A are not used. Instead, they are replaced by the black digitals immediately to their left. Earlier, we mentioned that black digitals do not have names of their own. Instead, they are identified in terms of the white digitals near them. The term **flat** is applied to any digital (black or white) when it is named in terms of the digital just above it (to its right). The music notation symbol for *flat* is "♭." The mediant in C minor is named E♭, signifying that it is a half step lower than E. The same is true of the submediant in the key of C minor, which occurs on A♭, a half step lower than A.

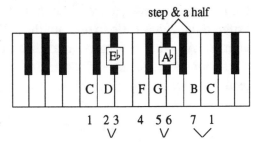

As you can see, lowering these two scale members changes the pattern of whole and half steps characteristic of the major mode. Two new half steps result from the changes, but neither is a functional half step like those in the tritone resolution we noted above. The mediant (E♭) is now a half step above the supertonic (D), and the submediant (A♭) is now a half step above the dominant (G). These two half steps, plus the one between the leading tone and tonic, make a total of three half steps in the minor scale.

Lowering the submediant creates an awkwardness in the minor scale that the major scale does not have. The distance from the lowered submediant (A♭) to the leading tone (B) in the minor mode is a step and a half, a feature that composers have had little trouble overcoming, but which seems to have caused considerable confusion among music theorists. The awkwardness of this feature is principally a melodic one, so we will describe the composers' solution later when we discuss melody.

Since the dominant chord in the minor mode is the same as in the major mode, the half step between the leading tone (B) and the tonic (C) remains intact. However, the half step below the dominant seventh pitch (F) is no longer there. This means that when the tritone resolves in the minor mode, the dominant seventh pitch must move down a whole step to the minor mediant pitch (E♭).

Another feature created by lowering the submediant is an apparent tritone between the supertonic (D) and the submediant (A♭). The piano shows these pitches to be three whole steps apart. However, this is generally not a functional tritone since the supertonic belongs to the dominant family and the submediant belongs to the subdominant family. Under these circumstances, the tunings would not likely cause these pitches to be heard as a real tritone.

**another tritone?**

In equal temperament, however, this relationship sounds exactly like the functional tritone, so composers traditionally have taken considerable care to avoid simultaneous use of these pitches, preventing this "false tritone" from tearing the harmonic allegiance away from the real tonic and sending it off into another key.

(Some experienced readers may be wondering about the use of the submediant pitch in an extended dominant harmony, as a "dominant ninth." In that case, the pitches in question *are* likely a functional tritone, but that tuning of the "submediant" has little to do with the submediant as tuned in a subdominant context. As with any perceptual discrimination of functional tritones, the confusion exists primarily because of equal-tempered tuning, which in turn results in equal-tempered thinking.)

## Minor Mode Wrap-Up

The harmonic elements and functions in the minor mode are essentially the same as those in the major mode. The difference is primarily a matter of modal "color" created by lowering the mediant (scale step 3) and submediant (scale step 6) by a half step. These modifications change the tonic and subdominant triads from major to minor. The dominant chord does not change in the minor mode, but rather retains its normal configuration in order to perform its dynamic function of determining tonality.

Lowering the mediant and submediant causes whole steps and half steps to appear in different places than they do in the major mode. It also creates a step and a half between the leading tone and the lowered submediant, which requires special care when composing melodies in that vicinity.

The apparent "tritone" created between the supertonic and the lowered submediant is not a functional tritone, largely because these pitches belong to different harmonic families. Composers generally have been careful to avoid prominence of this pitch combination.

Explore and compare the sounds of the major and minor modes by playing their primary harmonies on the keyboard. Incidentally, keyboard examples generally are not included in the recorded audio illustrations accompanying this book, since you can readily play them yourself.

**ear-training drill**  On the following page you will find an ear-training chart to help you explore the sounds of the primary chords in the minor mode. As before, sing chord members while hearing sustained fundamental pitches sounded in a low register. Tune all pitches carefully so you can hear them in their pure consonant relationships. Also, listen to the changes in sound as familiar ratios appear in new places in the minor mode. The 5:6 ratio in this context will

# MINOR SCALE AS PRIMARY CHORDS

sound different than it did in the major mode. We'll have more to say about that when we discuss intervals later.

Pay particular attention to where the new half steps occur—between steps 2 and 3 and between 5 and 6. Also, notice that when resolving the dominant seventh pitch (scale step 4 in the V7 chord), your voice must now move down farther to the lowered mediant (♭3) in the tonic chord.

Tune all these new features carefully as you change back and forth from one chord to the other. Patience and care in exploring these sound relationships will pay off greatly in the development of your musical awareness.

# 7

# Secondary Triads

The terms *tonic*, *dominant* and *subdominant*, in addition to referring to the three primary triads, can be expanded to include the concept of **harmonic function** within the major/minor system. Each function includes a primary triad, described earlier, and also a **secondary** triad, which can be used in place of its related primary triad, bringing harmonic and melodic variety to a composition without disturbing its overall harmonic structure. Each pair of chords has two pitches in common and one pitch that is different.

## Secondary Triads in the Major Mode

The three primary triads in the major mode are all major, having a major third (4:5 ratio) from the root of the chord to the third of the chord and a perfect fifth (2:3 ratio) from root to fifth. Each of these triads is related to a secondary triad, consisting of the lower part of the primary triad (4:5 ratio) plus a pitch a minor third (5:6 ratio) below the root. The result in all three harmonic functions is a minor triad.

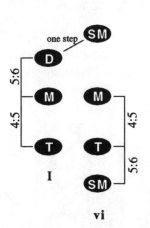

**submediant triad**

The tonic triad and the submediant triad cover the tonic function. The tonic triad, being major, is symbolized by an upper case Roman numeral. The submediant triad, being minor, is symbolized by a lower case Roman numeral. A higher submediant pitch is included here to show that the difference between these chords is merely a matter of replacing the fifth of the principle triad with the scale step above it.

Composers generally use the submediant triad (vi) as an alternate to the tonic chord (I) once the tonality of a piece has been established. The minor flavor of the secondary triad brings a refreshing change to the music without disturbing the tonal function—in this case, tonic. When both chords are used consecutively, the tonic chord normally comes first.

**supertonic triad**

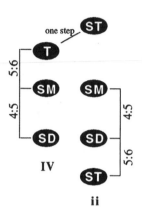

The subdominant triad and the supertonic triad perform the subdominant function. Both triads, one major and one minor, move gracefully to the dominant chord. Like the tonic function pair above, these chords are somewhat interchangeable, the primary chord (IV, in this case) relating directly to the tonic in a perfect fifth relationship, and the secondary chord (ii, in this case) relating to the dominant chord in a perfect fifth relationship. (Check this out on the keyboard.) When both are used consecutively, the IV chord normally comes first.

**mediant triad**

The dominant triad and the mediant triad have the same relationship as the pairs above. However, the iii chord is not exclusive to the dominant harmonic area. Because the iii chord also shares two pitches with the tonic triad, it frequently serves as a tonic function as well. To determine which role it is playing, one must examine its harmonic context. When the mediant triad is serving its dominant master, the dominant pitch is usually sounded in the bass, emphasizing that function. When serving as a tonic substitute, the mediant pitch is usually in the bass, emphasizing the tonic harmonic function.

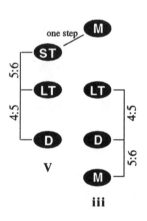

The dominant function also includes the leading tone triad, which will be discussed shortly. Presentation of "vii" was omitted here because it generally is not considered a secondary triad in the sense described above.

**keyboard view**

Here are each of the functional pairs of triads on the keyboard in the key of C major. In each case, secondary triads are shown with the **root** pitch (the one by which it is named) as the lowest pitch, called **root position**, and also with the root moved to a higher position, called an **inversion**.

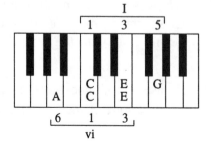

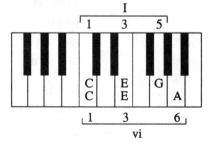

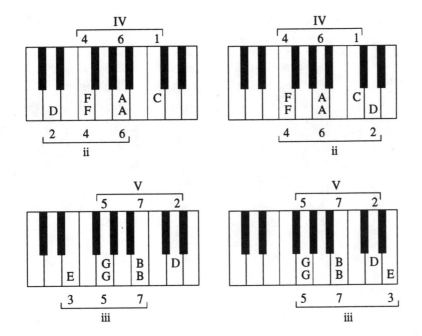

This symmetrical pattern between major primary triads and their secondary minor triads is just one more remarkable feature of the major mode. Noticing and understanding these relationships offers significant insight into how the overall system works.

The right side of the chart "Major Mode - Diatonic" on p. 74 contains the secondary triads in the major mode. Notice that they are arranged here in a fourth/fifth root relationship to each other and to the dominant chord. In other words, the root of the ii chord is a fourth/fifth from the root of the dominant chord, the vi chord is a fourth/fifth from the root of the ii chord, and the iii chord is a fourth/fifth from the vi chord. (The vii chord is included here in the pattern, but since it has no real acoustical root of its own, it does not function similarly in relationship to the iii chord.)

**ear-training drill**

This arrangement makes it possible to practice hearing these chords connecting in the fourth/fifth relationship, the one most frequently used in the major/minor system. Notice that each pair of neighboring chords shares one scale member in common and that the other two members are one scale step apart. To hear these chords in their tonal context, establish a tonal center by improvising on the primary chords, then move (from any primary chord) to a secondary chord. Establish that chord by singing its chord tones, then proceed to the chord on its left, moving either stepwise or by common tone. Going to a chord whose root is a perfect fifth lower (perfect fourth higher) is commonly described as "root movement *toward* the tonic." Continue through the chords to the left, establishing each one, until you reach the tonic chord.

# MAJOR MODE - DIATONIC

As with all these drills, play (or have others sing) the fundamental (root) of the chord you are singing to ensure that you are hearing its pitches accurately tuned. When you are confident that tuning is secure, you might like to try a drill without sounding the fundamental. If you still "hear" the fundamental in your imagination, you have reached an important milestone in the development of your musical sound concepts.

## Secondary Triads in the Minor Mode

Because considerable changes in scale configuration are caused by lowering the mediants in the minor mode, the secondary triads in the minor mode are not as symmetrical as those in the major mode. The primary triads themselves are not symmetrical; the tonic and subdominant triads are minor and the dominant triad is major.

The supertonic triad in minor mode, the subdominant function's secondary triad, has an apparent tritone instead of a perfect fifth. (The pitch a perfect fifth above D is A, not Ab.) A triad having a minor third and a **diminished**

**supertonic triad in minor mode**

**fifth** (half step smaller than perfect) is called a **diminished triad**, and is signified by a superscript "o" beside a lower case numeral. Notice also that both the lower third (D to F) and upper third (F to Ab) are both **minor thirds** (step and a half on the keyboard).

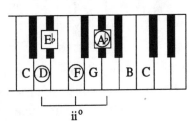

As mentioned earlier, to provide tonal stability, composers have tended to camouflage this feature and minimize any tritone influence by inverting the

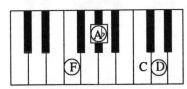

pitches and using the third of the chord (the subdominant pitch) as the lowest pitch. It properly can be thought of as a IV chord (F-Ab-C in C minor) with the supertonic pitch (D) substituted for the tonic pitch (C).

In contrast, the submediant triad, the tonic area's secondary triad, is very stable in the minor mode. Since its root (submediant) and fifth (mediant) are

**submediant triad in minor mode**

*both* lowered in the change to minor mode, the perfect fifth interval remains intact. As a result, the submediant triad in minor turns out to be a major triad. It is frequently used with its own root as the lowest pitch. Its strength

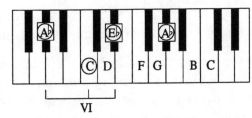

sometimes rivals the minor tonic for attention, therefore composers must decide to use or avoid this chord according to artistic purpose. Like the other secondary triads in both modes, its root (A♭ in the key of C minor) also appears just above the fifth (G) of its principle triad.

**mediant triad in minor mode**

The mediant triad in the minor mode, the dominant area's secondary triad, is unique in that it has neither a tritone nor a perfect fifth. The keyboard version might be described as two major thirds combined (E♭ to G and G to B in C minor). The interval from root (E♭) to fifth (B) is an **augmented fifth** (a half step larger than perfect). This chord, then, is called an **augmented triad**. It is designated by a plus sign following an upper case Roman numeral.

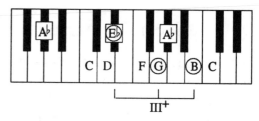

Acoustically, this chord is very difficult to tune. It is seldom used in this form with the root (mediant) as the lowest pitch. Like the ii° chord, this one

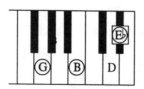

usually appears in an inversion with its third (the dominant pitch) on the bottom. In practical terms, it is probably best described as a dominant triad with the mediant pitch (E♭ in C minor) substituted for the supertonic pitch (D).

As we have seen, the mediant triad in both major and minor modes is sometimes used as a substitute for the tonic triad, with which it has two pitches in common. When this is done in the minor mode, the leading tone (B in C minor) is usually lowered a half step (since the leading tone function is not needed in tonic-function harmony) creating a major triad, a more stable chord. This lowered seventh scale step (B♭ in C minor) is called **subtonic**, a whole step below the tonic pitch.

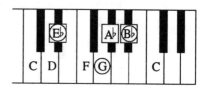

**leading-tone triad**

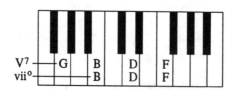

Although it is usually listed among the triads of the major and minor modes, the triad that spells out "in thirds" on the leading tone is not really an independent functional chord in its own right. Its pitches are entirely contained in the dominant seventh chord.

Even though the dominant pitch (G in C major and minor) appears not to be included in the vii triad, its presence is felt in that the three sounding pitches most likely are acoustically generated from the dominant fundamental. This view is supported by the common use of the leading tone triad as a dominant-function chord. Composers have used it that way almost exclusively,

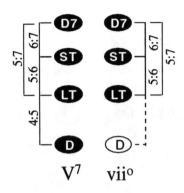

V⁷     vii°

and also consistently avoided placing the leading tone in the lowest voice, presumably to minimize the instability of the tritone.

Another reason the leading tone triad does not have independent status in the major/minor system, and perhaps the most important reason, is that the leading tone does not function as an acoustic fundamental pitch. It has no pitches (in this context) in a 2:3 ratio, as do major and minor triads. The supertonic chord in the minor mode, also a diminished triad, suffers from this same deficiency, thus its special treatment by composers.

**ear-training drill**

The right side of the chart "Minor Mode - Diatonic" on p. 78 contains the secondary triads in the minor mode. As in the major-mode chart, they are arranged here in a fourth/fifth relationship to each other and to the dominant chord. Don't forget, however, that in this mode the root of the VI chord does not have a perfect fifth relationship to the root of the ii° chord. Also, remember that the ii° chord does not contain a perfect fifth, therefore the sound of scale step 6 will not tune easily to a sounding root in that chord. Try tuning this chord to a subdominant pitch and you will see why composers favored using this arrangement of pitches in the ii° chord.

As in the major mode, each pair of neighboring chords shares one scale member in common and the other members are one scale step apart. As before, begin your drills by establishing a tonal center, then move (from any primary chord) to a secondary one. Moving from a primary triad to its own secondary "partner" is the best way to start. Establish the secondary chord in your "ear" by singing its chord tones, then move to the chord to its left, either by means of a common tone or stepwise movement, and establish that one. Continue this pattern toward the left until you reach the tonic chord.

# Chart 2 - MINOR MODE - DIATONIC

## Primary Chords

iv　　　i　　　V⁷

## Secondary Chords

ii°　　　VI　　　III(III+)　　　vii°

# 8

# Intervals And Chords

Most music dictionaries and textbooks define **interval** as "the distance between two pitches." That definition might be helpful if we had a perceptual ruler by which to measure the distances between pitches. As we noted before, humans do not perceive distances accurately in any mode of human experience. Just as we cannot trust our perceptual accuracy in measuring fifteen and three-quarter inches, we cannot trust "distance" in our sense of pitch.

Perhaps the definition above assumes that the keyboard will serve as the "ruler." However, playing intervals on a keyboard does not translate well to hearing them perceptually. In fact, learning to vocally reproduce intervals played on a keyboard can result in muddled concepts and out-of-tune singing, maladies that are already far too common.

While a keyboard cannot help you learn to hear intervals accurately, the keyboard is a very good tool for learning the vocabulary of intervals and for demonstrating how they work together. Later, we will discuss the systematic vocabulary of musical intervals. We will focus here only on the intervals contained in the primary chords of the major and minor modes. For now, the keyboard will only be used to demonstrate basic terminology.

Here is a caution. You will be wise to resist any temptation to count the half steps contained in intervals. Memorizing the number of half steps in larger musical intervals is not only a waste of time, but assumes that the information relates to musical concepts, which it does not. Attempting to learn intervals this way is to risk wandering into a dark forest of musical confusion.

On the other hand, there probably is some value in noticing the half-step/ whole-step configuration in intervals of one or two steps, which is more a matter of instantaneous visual perception than counting. The instantaneous visual perceptions of the larger keyboard intervals (other than octaves) are much harder, particularly when black digitals are included.

**feeling intervals**     A far more profitable way to use a keyboard for learning about intervals is to use one's hand as the "ruler." Placing five fingers on the keyboard, one finger per consecutive digital, helps to "measure" more than half of the basic intervals. Since intervals are named by the number of scale members included in the "distance," a second is measured by any two neighboring fingers. A third is measured by "every other" finger, for example the thumb and middle finger, or the index and ring fingers, or the middle and little finger. A **fourth** is measured by the thumb and ring finger or the index and little fingers. A **fifth** is the distance between the thumb and little finger.

Even though we are now out of fingers, the hand can still be helpful in identifying larger intervals in terms of distance. Muscle memory, the same tool that many experienced vocalists use to find specific pitches, can be used to "feel" the remaining intervals. A one step stretch of the hand provides the distance of a **sixth**. Stretching one and two more steps provides the **seventh** and the **octave**. Pianists with large hands can memorize the feeling of **ninths** and **tenths** as well.

Hand measuring intervals won't help you feel the difference between "large thirds" and "small thirds," however. The "two whole steps" third between C and E and the "step and a half" third between E and G will feel the same. Since all white digitals are equally spaced, it's knowing where you are on the keyboard that provides the sense of these differences. For example, being aware that there is only one black digital between two white ones translates to "small third."

**hearing intervals**     Of course, describing intervals as distances on a keyboard has little to do with how we perceive and conceive intervals in sound. We recognize intervals aurally by means of their perceptual quality of consonance/dissonance. By virtue of our perception of their small-number ratios (thanks to nature's translation), we are able to identify various intervals as octaves, fifths, thirds, etc. Once an interval's identifying characteristics are conceived as a unique experience, we can recognize and name experiences of that interval and learn to recreate it vocally.

We can conceive the unique qualities of intervals without naming them, just as we learn other practical things in life for which we have no labels. Children reared in musical families often develop the ability to "harmonize" vocally without knowing the vocabulary that describes what they are doing. Even the ability to sing a simple melody accurately depends on having conceived some sense of musical "intervals." Primitive music would not have even been possible without this human capacity. Certainly, people did not develop these skills "in the wild" by means of a keyboard!

Earlier, we looked briefly at another important perceptual skill that is help-ful, perhaps even essential, in identifying intervals. It is the ability to hear fundamental pitches. We noted that the 2:3 ratio, commonly referred to as a **perfect fifth**, and the 3:4 ratio, commonly referred to as a **perfect fourth**, are, in one sense, the "same" interval, in that they both can contain a fundamental pitch and its dominant pitch. These intervals appear consecutively in the series of acoustical partials, therefore they sound very similar as far as consonance/dissonance is concerned. Their essential difference is that in the perfect fifth, the 2:3 ratio, the lower pitch is the fundamental (actually, a multiple of it), and in the perfect fourth, the 3:4 ratio, the upper pitch is the fundamental (actually, a higher multiple of it).

**hearing fundamental pitches**

8-1

Since the perfect fifth and the perfect fourth contain the same scale steps "upside down," they are called **inversions**. While the perfect fifth and fourth are considerably different from thirds, seconds, sixths and sevenths, it is primarily the sense of "fundamental" that provides the perceptual difference between perfect fifths and perfect fourths.

A similar sense of "which pitch is the fundamental" helps distinguish some other intervals as well. The "large" third, the one having two whole steps, occurs in a major triad between a fundamental and its 4:5 ratio pitch, for example C and E. It is called a **major third**. The lower of the two pitches is the fundamental. Its inversion, E up to C, sounds similar, but the fundamental is now on top (in a ratio of 5:8). It is called a **minor sixth**. Distinguishing between these intervals is not as difficult as between the perfect fifth and perfect fourth in that the difference in pitch distance is more pronounced. Nevertheless, the conclusive perceptual difference is that in the major third the fun-damental is on the bottom and in the minor sixth the fundamental is on top.

8-2

Applying the terms "major" and "minor" to intervals is an unfortunate tradi-tion. In major and minor modes, and in major and minor triads, there is a perceptual sense of "color" or "flavor" in the difference that validates the use of the terms. Using these same terms to describe intervals implies that there is a distinctive flavor for major intervals and a different one for minor intervals. This simply isn't true. A major third sounds very much like a minor sixth in that they both involve the same scale steps, a tonic and a mediant, one interval with the fundamental on the bottom and one with the funda-mental on the top.

The remaining interval contained in the major tonic triad is the 5:6 interval, for example, the interval between the mediant (E) and the dominant (G) of the C major tonic triad. This "small" third is called a **minor third** and its inversion is the "large sixth," or **major sixth**). In these intervals, the fundamental (C) is not sounding.

**phantom fundamentals**

8-3

One might think the ear would select one of the sounding pitches as a fundamental, but experience indicates that this isn't the case. More often than not, when a minor third is sounded out of context, intermediate music students will identify it as a "major third." Apparently, this is not because they don't know the difference, but because they are partly hearing and partly imagining the sound of a major triad. The mediant pitch and the dominant pitch are heard and the fundamental is imagined.

Part of their misperception is caused by thinking that intervals have major and minor "flavors," as do chords and keys. The students' hearing a "major flavor" was a result of employing the concept "major triad" to perceive, partly in imagination, the sounds they were hearing. Recognizing that our perception can play these "tricks" is very helpful in avoiding aural confusion.

**minor-triad intervals**

The intervals discussed above are contained in all major triads, and therefore appear in all three primary triads in the major mode. These same intervals appear in the minor mode as well, but with the thirds and sixths in different places. Although they are the same intervals, they sound different in the context of the minor mode.

You may have noticed that the "minor third" between the supertonic and the dominant seventh pitch was not included in this discussion. The reason is that this interval is not the same "minor third" as the one described above. Even though the keyboard uses D and F to sound these pitches in the key of C major, the actual interval is smaller. The dominant seventh pitch relates to the supertonic acoustically in a 6:7 ratio, not 5:6. The keyboard, of course, cannot demonstrate the difference, but your ear can hear it. That is why you need to be aware of this information. We don't have a standard name for this interval, since its existence has been ignored and/or denied by musicologists.

**so, who's perfect?**

You also may be wondering why some intervals are "perfect" and others are "major" or "minor." That question will be easier to answer after we have discussed major and minor keys in other tonalities. At that time, we'll take a systematic look at intervals.

We have a very handy system for naming the individual members of triads and other chords. Instead of using the functional name ("tonic," "dominant," etc.) for each member, this terminology travels to any chord—major, minor or any other—and designates each member in terms of its keyboard-name relationship to the chord's "fundamental," or **root**. In the chord C-E-G, C is the called the **root,** E is called the **third** (since it relates to the root in the interval of a third) and G is called the **fifth** (since it relates to the root in the interval of a fifth).

**names for
chord members**

This terminology is blind to the function of the triad as well as to the function of the individual pitches. It doesn't care whether C-E-G is a tonic chord, a dominant chord, or any other function. It also doesn't care about the shape of the triad, even if the members don't fit a standard pattern—C, E♭, G♯, for example. All that is required is that the "spelling" of the chord use "every other" letter names in ascending order.

As mentioned earlier, it is not required that chord members be sounded in any particular order or configuration, only that they *can* be arranged in consecutive thirds. Once the pitches are so arranged, the lowest pitch is the root. All of these are C major chords:

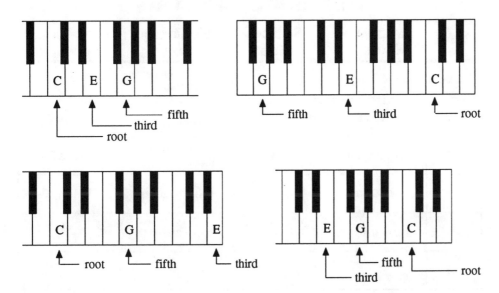

The use of these terms can be confusing, however. Such statements as "the interval between the third and the fifth is a third" can bewilder someone who doesn't realize that the same word is used to refer both to chord members *and* to intervals. It is usually wise to include clarifying phrases, such as "interval of a third" or "fifth of the chord." The system extends to include **sevenths** (as in "dominant seventh chord"), **ninths, elevenths,** and so on.

**ear-training**   Conduct your improvisational drills as you have before, but now think consciously about the size of intervals as you sing them. Use the charts on pp. 74 and 78, focusing your drill toward intervals in the primary chords of both modes. This drill will not only help you connect the sound of each intervals to its name, but it will also reinforce your awareness of the location of specific intervals in the major/minor system.

The following chart will help you firm up the connections among sound concepts, interval terminology and application. It includes only basic intervals contained in the major mode. You might want to construct a similar chart for the intervals in the minor mode, or at least to think through the modifications resulting from the differences in the two modes.

As you study this chart, keep in mind that it is far better to *experience* the relationships in musical constructs than simply to memorize descriptive words and numbers. Therefore, it will be extremely beneficial to play the items listed here on the keyboard. You also might find it interesting and helpful to sing and tune the intervals as sound ratios and compare those sounds to the keyboard's version of the same intervals.

# Harmonic Intervals

| RATIO | INTERVAL NAME | SCALE LOCATION | KEYBOARD SIZE | WHITE-DIGITAL LOCATION |
|-------|---------------|----------------|---------------|------------------------|
| 1:2 | octave | 1-1, 2-2, 3-3, etc. | thumb to little finger plus 3 | all |
| 2:3 | perfect fifth | all except 7-4 | thumb to little finger | all except B-F |
| 3:4 | perfect fourth | all except 4-7 | index to little, thumb to ring | all except F-B |
| 4:5 | major third | 1-3, 4-6, 5-7 | two whole steps | C-E, F-A, G-B |
| 5:6 | minor third | 3-5, 6-1, 7-2, 2-4 | step and a half | E-G, A-C, B-D, D-F |
| 6:7 | small "minor third" | 2-4 | none | none |
| 5:7, 7-10 | tritone | 4-7, 7-4 | three whole steps | F-B, B-F |

9

# The Major/Minor System

The language and practice surrounding Western music traditions may give the impression that the major and minor modes offer two different ways to compose music. We note titles such as "Symphony In C Minor" or "Sonata in A Major." It frequently is suggested that music in the minor mode is "sad" and music in the major mode is "happy." Books on music, including this one, contain separate chapters on the major and minor modes.

Actually, the lines between the modes are not clearly drawn. Virtually every symphony and sonata (as well as nearly every other compositional genre) contain passages in the "other" mode. Many quite jolly Eastern European folk songs are composed in the minor mode while the song "Melancholy Baby" is firmly in the major mode. As you have seen, the major scale contains major chords and the minor scale contains major chords. So, if you have picked up any simplistic overgeneralizations as to what is "minor" and what is "major," this will be a good time to dispose of them and take a fresh look at how the major and minor modes work together to create artistic meaning.

## Interchangeability of Modes

Here is a familiar song that is normally heard in the major mode. The chords are indicated by Roman numerals below the lyrics. As you remember, upper case Roman numerals indicate major chords.

 9-1

| O give me a home where the buffalo roam, where the deer and the antelope play |
|---|
| I                  IV           I           V7 |
| Where seldom is heard a discouraging word, and the skies are not cloudy all day. |
| I          IV         I   V7    I |

Here is the same song translated to the minor mode. The tonic and subdominant chords are minor, shown here by lower case Roman numerals. The dominant seventh chord is major, of course, to preserve the leading tone and the harmonic influence of the tritone.

9-2

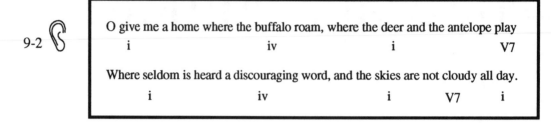

O give me a home where the buffalo roam, where the deer and the antelope play
i                              iv                         i                        V7

Where seldom is heard a discouraging word, and the skies are not cloudy all day.
i                              iv                         i            V7          i

The alternate "flavors" of major and minor can operate interchangeably around a given tonic pitch, composers making the artistic decision to choose one mode or the other at any point. A change can last for quite a long time, or might involve only one chord in an entire song (or arrangement), as it does here.

9-3

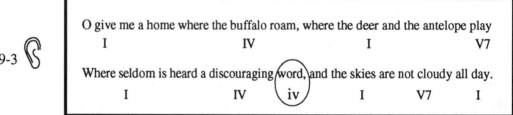

O give me a home where the buffalo roam, where the deer and the antelope play
I                              IV                        I                         V7

Where seldom is heard a discouraging word, and the skies are not cloudy all day.
I                              IV          iv             I            V7          I

The use of the minor triad on the lyric "word" is simply a matter of changing to the minor mode for that moment and then returning to the prevailing major mode. The tonality, or key center, does not change; only the mode changes, and only for the duration of the chord or chords affected. In effect, the composer has borrowed the chords in question from the "other" scale.

## Modulation

Most of the world's musical systems are based on a sense of tonality, and in almost all of them a single tonality is retained in a composition from beginning to end. The element that makes the major/minor system unique is the magnetic action of the leading tone, frequently working with its tritone partner, the dominant seventh pitch, to propel the tonal energy in a variety of directions. From the key of C major, a composer can change tonalities, either temporarily or permanently, by modifying the shape of the prevailing scale to create new tritone relationships. Changing from one key to another is called

**modulation**. The most frequently used modulation moves from a tonic key to the key of its dominant. We'll use the keyboard here to show how this is accomplished.

In the key of C major, the subdominant (F) is replaced by a pitch a half step higher, using the black digital to its right. The term **sharp** (♯) is applied to a digital (black or white) when it is named in relation to the digital just below it (to its left). So, we'll call this pitch "F-sharp." Notice that F♯ has a tritone relationship (three whole steps) to C, the original tonic. Usually, when a

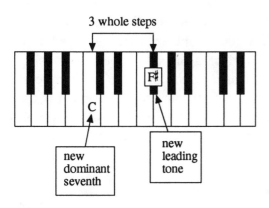

scale member is raised (more accurately, replaced) to create a new tritone, that new pitch is the leading tone and the other tritone member becomes the dominant seventh pitch. In this case, F♯ is the leading tone to the key of G. When the tritone resolves to the new tonic chord, the other member, C, moves down to B, the mediant of the G triad.

Notice that all the pitches other than F (or F♯) are the same in the keys of C major and G major. This single adjustment shifts the tonality from C major to G major (or vice versa). The F-B tritone in C major is "repaired" (made perfect, and therefore

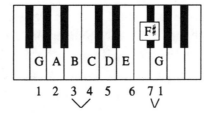

stable) and a new dynamic and restless tritone (F♯-C) is created that gravitates toward, indeed defines, the key of G major.

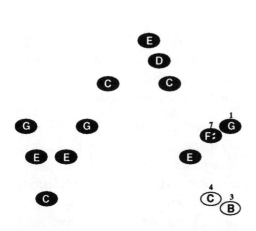

Here is an example using this change of tonal center. Read the graphic from left to right, sing or play the pitches and you will hear a familiar melody. (Or, if you prefer, play the audio example.) The white symbols represent the dominant seventh pitch and its resolution. This phrase begins in the key of C major and moves to G major when the F♯-C tritone appears.

 9-4

In this illustration, a new tritone is created by lowering the leading tone of the original key (C major), resulting in a modulation to its subdominant key (F major). This graphic shows the F major scale from dominant to dominant. Even though it doesn't "start" on F in this diagram, it *is* the F major scale because of the configuration of whole and half steps. If this disturbs you,

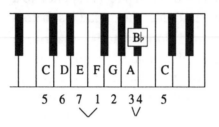

you might need to free yourself from the misconception that a scale must be confined to the space between two tonic pitches.

In this case, the leading tone (B) in the key of C is replaced by a pitch a half step lower, creating a tritone relationship between itself (B♭) and the original mediant (E). Usually, when a scale member is "lowered" (replaced) to create a new tritone, that new pitch is the dominant seventh pitch and the other member becomes the leading tone. In this case, E takes on the leading-tone role and moves the tonality to the key of F. Completing the resolution of the tritone, the B♭ will move down to A, the mediant of the tonic triad in F major.

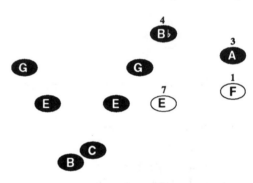

9-5 Here is a song that employs this change of tonality. Sing or play these pitches and see if you recognize the famous Broadway show melody. (Or play the audio example.)

9-6 Listen to this random bouquet of tritones resolving to their tonics. In each case, one of the tritone pitches is moving up a half step to a new tonic and the other is moving down a half step (or whole step in minor mode) to the mediant of that tonic.

Basically, that is how modulation, or changing the tonal center, is accomplished. By repositioning the tritone, the sense of tonal center is shifted. This is done by sounding either the leading tone or the dominant seventh pitch of the new key, which "repairs" the old tritone and creates a new one.

Incidentally, modulation frequently is achieved by sounding only the new leading tone without sounding the dominant seventh pitch at the moment of transition. However, the memory of the dominant seventh pitch (having been heard in previous chords) likely exerts its tritone influence in accomplishing the change of tonality. Remember, the sense of tonality is caused by a sense of the *overall* configuration of scale steps used, including the tritone members.

# Keys

As mentioned earlier, a major/minor tonality, or **key**, can be established on any pitch. It simply is a matter of having member pitches in the appropriate harmonic relationships to a specific pitch. Soon, we will demonstrate how major keys relate to each other, but for this exercise we will arbitrarily select a pitch and find its major scale members, by logic and by ear, applying harmonic ratios or intervals. Let's start by constructing the key of A major.

We know the tonic/dominant relationship, a perfect fifth interval, can be found on all the "white fifths" except B and F, so finding the dominant and subdominant will be easy. Placing the right thumb on A and the other four fingers on consecutive white digitals, we locate the dominant under the little

finger, on E. Play the tonic and dominant pitches together. Does it sound right? Yes, it does.

Likewise, placing the right little finger on A and the other four fingers on con-

secutive white digitals, we locate the subdominant under the thumb, on D. Play the tonic and subdominant together and check the sound.

Now let's find the mediant and submediant. They need to be located two whole steps (a major third) above the tonic and subdominant pitches. In both cases, we see that the white digital will not serve this purpose and must be

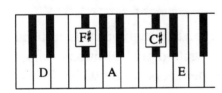

replaced by the black digital just above it. The mediant in this key, then, is C♯, and the submediant is F♯. Let's keep track of the number of adjustments we make while configuring the key of A major. Thus far, we have two members designated by sharps.

The supertonic and leading tone are easy to find. One is a whole step above tonic (B), and the other is a half step below tonic (G♯). Notice that we don't call that pitch A♭. We have already used the designation A for the tonic. We must use all seven

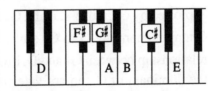

letters in every scale in order that each scale member has a unique designation. Since we haven't used G, it works out perfectly to call it G♯.

Now lets play these pitches in sequence from one tonic up to the next. We can see (and hear) that the relative placement of the whole steps and half

**key of A major**

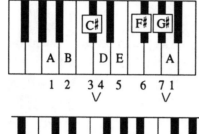

**key of C major**

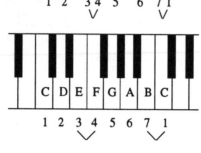

steps here are the same as they are in the key of C major. Of course, the physical spacing and tactile feeling is different, since C major uses all white digitals.

We have made a total of three adjustments in order to shape the key of A major. A song placed in this key is sometimes said to be "in three sharps" and musicians know that this likely means the key of A major. The word "likely" is appropriate here because, although A major is the only *major* key having three sharps, some keys in other modes may also have three sharps, so there is more to identifying a tonality than counting the number of sharps or flats.

**key of A minor**

Now let's make a minor key, again using A as the tonal center. The tonic, dominant and subdominant pitches (A, E, and D) will be the same as they are in A major. So will the supertonic and leading tone (B and G♯). The only members that will be different, as we noticed while comparing C major and C minor, are the mediant and the submediant. Instead of two whole steps above the tonic and subdominant, they will be a step and a half (a minor third) above them. So,

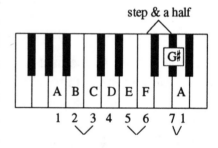

instead of using C♯ and F♯, we will lower these a half step each to C-**natural** and F-**natural** (a term specifying original white-digital positions, whose notational symbol is ♮). In A minor, all the members are on white digitals except the leading tone, G♯.

**relative major and minor keys**

It is this G♯, as a matter of fact, that makes the difference between C major and A minor. This intimate relationship between these two keys is frequently exploited by composers, using G♮ in C major, and using G♯ in A minor. From C major, changing G to G♯ shifts the tonal center to A by creating a tritone relationship between G♯ and D. From A minor, changing the G♯ to G♮ supplies the dominant of C and activates the B-F tritone, sending the tonality there. This relationship between a major and a minor key is called **relative major** and **relative minor**. In other words, the key of A minor is the relative minor of C major, and C major is the relative major of A minor.

9-7

Here are two examples of compositions in which the tonality is shifted—one to the dominant key and one to the relative minor key. Can you hear the modulation in each example?

That is how the major/minor system works. By using the previously misunderstood and mistrusted element, the tritone, seventeenth-century composers introduced this new dimension to music called **modulation,** the shifting of tonality within a composition. Although significant efforts were made in the early twentieth century to obliterate tonality in music, the major/minor system remains the one most widely used today, very likely because it closely corresponds with nature's way of perceiving pitch relationships.

## Major Keys in Relation to Each Other

We noted above that the opening phrase of "The Star Spangled Banner" includes a "raised" pitch near the end of the first phrase that briefly shifts the tonality from the key of C major to the key of G major. We know that the pitches C and G are closely related harmonically in a basic 2:3 ratio. As noted earlier, the major scales on these two pitches are also very closely related in that all of their scale members are the same except for one pitch—F (or F♯). Because the tonics C and G are related in a 2:3 ratio, a perfect fifth, and because their scale members are nearly the same, they are said to be **closely related keys.** While C major has no sharps, G major has only one.

key of C major

key of G major

The key of G major, of course, has its own set of related pitches. Its dominant is D, located a fifth higher than G. Its subdominant is C, located a fifth lower than G (and the pitch to which it relates as a dominant). Its mediant and submediant are B and E, and its supertonic is A. Its only black digital is the leading tone, F♯.

It is important to notice that the pitch change causing the shift to a next-related key takes place within the tritone. The effect of moving the F to F♯ "repairs" the B-F tritone, resulting in a perfect fifth between B and F♯. At the same time, this change creates a new tritone between F♯ and C. More specifically, the old dominant seventh pitch (F) is abandoned, having been replaced by the F♯, which becomes the leading tone pointing toward the new tonic, G.

Just as the key of C major relates to the key of G major, the key of G major, in turn, relates to its own dominant key, D major. The transformation from G major to D major is accomplished in the same way as from C major to G

**key of D major**

major. G major's dominant seventh pitch (C) is raised to become the leading tone (C♯) to D major. The F♯ used in the key of G as the leading tone is retained, becoming the mediant of D, giving the key of D major two sharps.

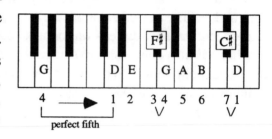

Remember that the key of A major has three sharps. Since D major has two, that is what we would expect in the key having a dominant relationship to D.

**key of E major**

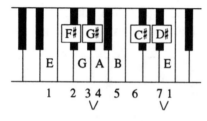

Logically, the dominant key of A major, namely E major, has four sharps.

This pattern continues, each tonic in turn sponsoring the next related key on its dominant pitch. It is important to note that the dominant pitch of B major is not F (its white-digital tritone partner), but is F♯, a perfect fifth above B. B major has five sharps.

**key of B major**

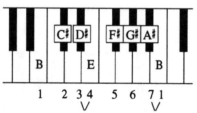

The next related key in turn is F♯, which has six sharps. (If you counted seven in the illustration, you likely didn't notice that the tonic is represented twice.) Next is C♯ major, which logically has all seven steps sharped since all its members would be a half step higher than the members of the key of C major.

**key of F♯ major**

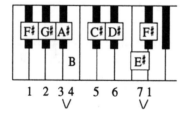

Notice that some of the sharps needed for the last two keys are on white digitals. For example, the leading tone of F♯ major, since it must use a different letter and be a half step from the tonic, is named E♯, even though it uses the white digital usually named F. Likewise, the leading tone in C♯

**key of C♯ major**

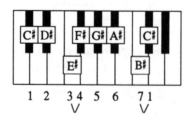

major is B♯, also a white digital. If you are startled by this information, it may be that you have been thinking about musical relationships only in keyboard terms.

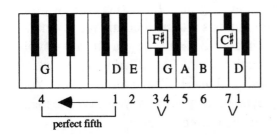

Now, let's look at the relationship of these keys in reverse. Let's take the key of D, for example. It's most closely related key having one *less* sharp is, of course, on its subdominant pitch, or the key of G major.

**key of D major**

To move from D major to the key of its subdominant, G major, the C♯ leading tone of D major is abandoned in favor of C♮, which provides not only the subdominant pitch (scale step 4) of the key of G but, more importantly, the dominant seventh pitch of G major. The two sharps of the key of D major changes to one in the key of G major.

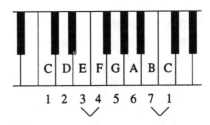

**key of G major**

To go from G major to C major, the same modification applies, replacing the F♯ leading tone in G with the F♮ dominant seventh pitch of C major.

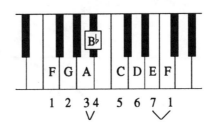

**key of C major**

Continuing this process from C major to its subdominant key, F major, we have to use a flat to accomplish the change. In order to go from C major to F major, the leading tone in C major (B) gives way to B♭, the dominant seventh of the key of F major. The tritone partner of the new B♭ is E,

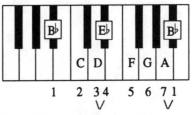

**key of F major**

already in place, which becomes the new leading tone. The key of F major, then, has one flat, this occurring on B♭, its fourth scale step.

In turn, the subdominant of F major is its fourth step, B♭, the pitch that just entered the system as we moved from C major to F major. (Notice that F's subdominant is not B natural, F's white-digital tritone partner.) The leading tone for B♭ major (A) is already in place, as expected, so it is the

**key of B♭ major**

other member of the tritone (E♭) that is needed. That is supplied, as above, by flatting the leading tone of the previous key (E in F major). B♭ major, then, has two flats: B♭ and E♭.

The process continues in this pattern, adding new flats to each new sub-dominant key by converting old leading tones into new dominant sevenths. The key of E♭, the next one in turn, will add an A♭; the key of A♭ in turn will add a D♭; the key of D♭ will add a G♭; the key of G♭ will add a C♭ (a white digital); and, finally, the key of C♭ will add an F♭. That's all there are. You may want to play each scale on the keyboard to make sure you have the idea. Be careful to call white-digital flats by the correct name.

In the interest of clarity, remember that the dominant seventh pitch uses the same digital and pitch name as the subdominant in any given key (for example, F in the key of C). We have correctly used the designation "dominant seventh pitch" here since the action that gets us out of one key and into the next related key takes place by modifying one or the other members of the tritone. Once a key is established, however, the pitch a perfect fifth below the tonic is properly called the subdominant, not the dominant seventh.

**the circle of fifths**     Perhaps one of the most popular (and useful) tools among music students is a chart which shows all the major keys in relation to each other. It is called a *circle of fifths* because it demonstrates that some keys having many sharps use the same digitals as some keys having many flats. Notice that F♯, for instance, uses the same digitals as G♭. In other words, the process of moving "up a perfect fifth" or "down a perfect fifth" can continue infinitely (theoretically, at least).

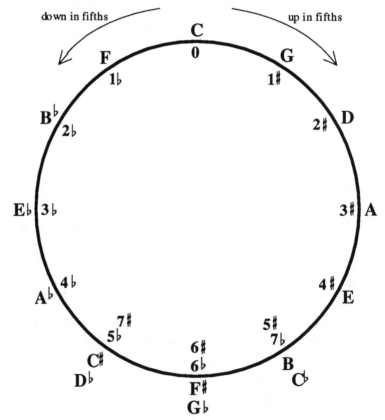

This is true only in terms of the keyboard, however. In acoustic tuning, 2:3 ratios are larger than tempered "perfect fifths." Therefore, in moving *acoustically* around the circle of fifths, the keys having many sharps are considerably higher in terms of absolute pitch than the "corresponding" ones having many flats. But this is not a practical problem. Not only are keys having many flats or sharps not frequently used, but seldom does a composition in the major/minor system modulate to more than a few related keys.

Nevertheless, the chart not only demonstrates the relationships of major keys, but also serves as a handy reference to the number of sharps and flats in each one. Hopefully, this chart will quickly fall into disuse, since anyone even slightly interested in how music works would want to memorize this information. (Enough said?)

**transposition**

The phrase "change keys" is ambiguous. It doesn't differentiate among (1) modulation (changing the tonal center *during* a musical composition), (2) mode changes (alternating between major and minor modes) and (3) moving an entire composition intact to a different pitch level.

The latter is called **transposition** and is most frequently used to raise or lower the pitch of a song, unchanged in any other way, into a key that is more comfortable for the singer. Transposition is also used in orchestration, creating music notation for instruments built in various keys, such as trumpets and clarinets (B♭), alto and baritone saxophones (E♭), french horns (F), etc. We will return to this topic later when we discuss music notation for instruments.

**ear-training drill**

The "Major Mode Chromatic" chart on p. 96 contains the dominant chords of closely related keys arranged in "circle of fifths" order. Each **chromatic** chord, so named because it contains pitches ("colors") out of the tonic key, resolves naturally to a chord whose root is a member of the tonic key. Thus, they are collectively referred to as "secondary dominants." Each can resolve either to the **diatonic** (non-chromatic) secondary triad to which it relates, or to the chromatic dominant seventh chord built on that root. In either case, the root movement is down a fifth (up a fourth), or toward tonic.

Therefore, the secondary chords are not shown on this chart since their roots are busy supporting secondary dominant chords. In a sense, each secondary triad is modified here by raising its third (making each triad major) and adding a dominant seventh pitch. For example, the ii chord is replaced here by the "V$^7$ of V," both of which use the same root. If this is still unclear, play the ii chord on the keyboard and then play the "V$^7$ of V" and compare. Remember, just as the ii chord progresses down a fifth to V, so does the "V$^7$ of V" progress down a fifth to V.

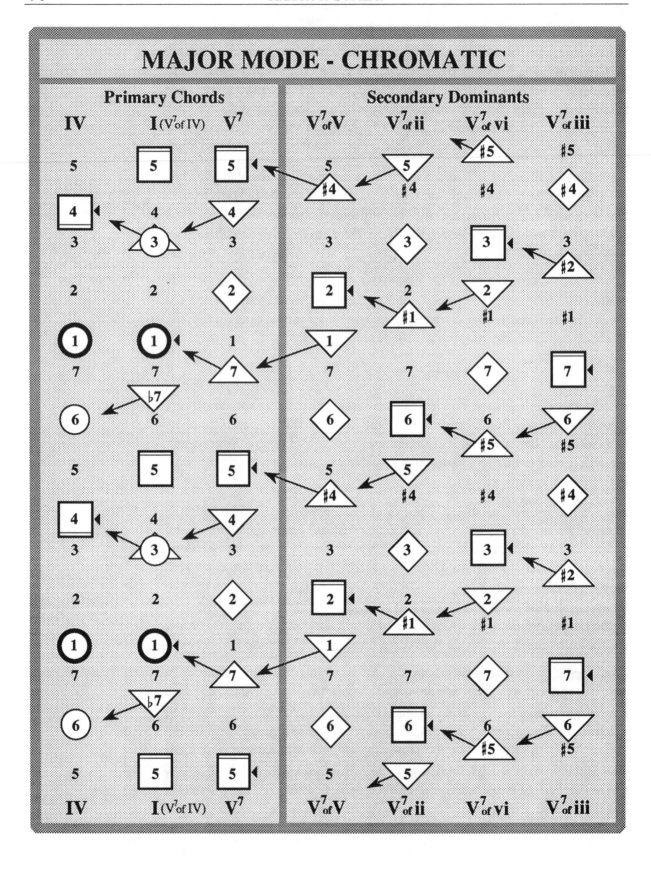

It is best not to perform drills with this chart until your diatonic skills are very secure. If you have not reached that proficiency, you should use this chart only to gain insights regarding the harmonic relationships illustrated there. You might find it helpful to play these chords on a keyboard in the key of C major, observing how "raised" pitches become leading tones creating tritones that impel the music toward their respective resolution chords.

If your sound concepts of diatonic tonal relations are secure, you may now apply those same concepts to the chromatic chords on this chart. After establishing a sense of tonal center, "raise" the root of the tonic chord a "half step" and tune it as a leading tone to scale step 2. This chord is shown on the chart as "V$^7$ of ii." To help tune it, play its root (scale step 6, marked by a small black arrowhead [◄] on the chart). When this leading tone is in clear focus, sing and tune the other members of this chord. Your ear will recognize the sound of the dominant seventh chord and you will feel the harmonic tug of the tritone (♯1 and 5) toward the ii chord.

Perform similar drills by raising the root of the other primary chords and transforming them to leading tones. The raised subdominant pitch is the leading tone in the "V$^7$ of V" chord and the raised dominant pitch is the leading tone in the "V$^7$ of vi" chord. The root of each chord is found, of course, a third lower and is marked on the chart by the small black arrowhead.

Notice that the tonic chord can be transformed into a secondary dominant by lowering its leading tone to become the dominant seventh pitch of the "V$^7$ of IV" chord. Since the subdominant root is a fifth lower than the tonic, this modified tonic chord relates to the subdominant chord as its secondary dominant.

Although this chart shows each secondary dominant resolving to the next secondary dominant in sequence, this is not always the case in practice. The chart is intended to provide direction for chromatic practice, not to demonstrate examples of every possible resolution. It is assumed that when you are able to navigate the changes in tonality represented here, you should have little difficulty handling the variations.

When chromatic resolution leads to a permanent shift in tonality, the result is called a **modulation**. The difference between a secondary dominant and a modulation is sometimes a judgement call, depending on the length of time the sense of tonality remains in the chord (or key) of resolution. The mechanics of "getting there" is the same in both cases, and that is what this chart is all about.

# Numbers and Syllables

Although we already have used much of the information contained in this section, the discussion here will systematize it and provide a review. As you probably realize, repetition is what makes ideas "stick," and seeing them in a logical context is what makes them clear.

**melodic use**    The two most frequently used means of supplying simple and handy references for melodic scale members, or scale "steps," are **numbers** and **syllables**. Numbers have the advantage of familiarity, and do not require the user to learn a new set of symbols, therefore, as you are aware, we have opted for numbers in this book.

Syllables have the advantage of a single syllable per pitch, eliminating the need to sing "se-ven" or "flat three" to signify a single pitch event. However, that becomes somewhat academic here since it is suggested that ear-training drills be performed using a tunable vowel sound while "thinking" names instead of orally naming scale steps while singing them. Therefore, this discussion is provided more for information than for oral use in performing drills. If you prefer to "think" syllables rather than numbers while performing drills, there is no reason not to do so.

In some languages, syllables are used for absolute pitch identification, similar to the English system of using letters. In these traditions, "do" (pronounced "doh") means "C," and "re" means "D," and so on. This is called a "fixed do" system. Syllables are also widely used to represent the members of the major and minor scales, where "do" means tonic, "re" means supertonic, etc. This is called a "moveable do" system.

In the following chart, syllable names are of the movable sort. Our interest here is in the *relationships* between pitches, which is what numbers and movable syllables are all about.

## Scale Step Designations

| Scale Function | Major, Numbers | Major, Syllables | Minor, Numbers | Minor, Syllables |
|---|---|---|---|---|
| Tonic | 1 | do | 1 | do |
| Supertonic | 2 | re | 2 | re |
| Mediant | 3 | mi | flat 3 | me |
| Subdom./Dom. 7th | 4 | fa | 4 | fa |
| Dominant | 5 | so | 5 | so |
| Submediant | 6 | la | flat 6 | le |
| Leading tone | 7 | ti | 7 | ti |

Some musical traditions use Arabic numbers to designate chords as well as single scale steps. However, the most common method for designating chords is to assign each one a Roman numeral, using upper case numerals for major chords and lower case numerals for minor chords. As described above, diminished triads (containing a minor third and a diminished fifth) are signified by lower case numerals with a superscript circle, and augmented triads (containing a major third and an augmented fifth) are signified by upper case numerals with a superscript plus sign. The inclusion of additional (more than three) chord members is signified by a superscript number (7, 9, 11, etc.). Primary-chord function names are shown in upper case letters here and secondary-chord function names are in lower case to help distinguish them. The leading tone triad, in parentheses, is usually included in such lists, and therefore is included here. **harmonic use**

## Chord Designations In Scale Order

| Chord Function | Major Mode | Minor Mode |
| --- | --- | --- |
| TONIC | I | i |
| supertonic | ii | ii$^\circ$ |
| mediant | iii | III$^+$, or III |
| SUBDOMINANT | IV | iv |
| DOMINANT | V, or V$^7$ | V, or V$^7$ |
| submediant | vi | VI |
| (leading tone) | (vii$^\circ$) | (vii$^\circ$) |

Here is the same information arranged by tonal function.

## Chord Designations By Tonal Function

| Tonal Function | Chord Function | Major Mode | Minor Mode |
| --- | --- | --- | --- |
| TONIC | TONIC | I | i |
| | submediant | vi | VI |
| | mediant | iii | III |
| SUBDOMINANT | SUBDOMINANT | IV | iv |
| | supertonic | ii | ii$^\circ$ |
| DOMINANT | DOMINANT | V, or V$^7$ | V, or V$^7$ |
| | mediant | iii | III$^+$ |
| | (leading tone) | (vii$^\circ$) | (vii$^\circ$) |

Needless to say, mastering these charts is quite worth the effort. Playing these chords on the keyboard is a good route to that goal.

**chord substitution**  Composers frequently use secondary chords as substitutes for a related principle triad. In this example, the first phrase consists entirely of primary triads, and the second phrase (essentially a repeat of the first phrase melodically) introduces secondary triads in both the tonic and subdominant functions.

9-8

> O give me a home where the buffalo roam, where the deer and the antelope play
> I                          IV                      I                    V7
>
> Where seldom is heard a discouraging word, and the skies are not cloudy all day.
> I        vi        IV        ii              I        V7        I

Using a secondary triad in place of or in addition to a primary one not only provides melodic variety in the bass line, but also changes the modal flavor of that moment.

# Chord Connections

The defining characteristic of the major/minor system is the functional use of harmony. Changing chords as music proceeds adds "color" to its artistic impact. Connecting chords in the major/minor system has been given much attention by composers. In general, the goal is to make the connections as smooth as possible (when this suits the artistic purpose), moving pitches in one chord to the nearest pitches in the next chord. In other words, a C major triad played from the root up (C-E-G) would not ordinarily leap to a G major triad played from the root up (G-B-D). Instead of picking up the hand from a C position and dropping it on a G position, the hand stays in the same neighborhood and moves appropriate individual fingers to play the nearest pitches in the second chord. Demonstrations are forthcoming.

After noting the many kinds of chords described above, you may be surprised to learn that there are only three basic ways to connect triads smoothly. (This is another example of a logically closed system.) No audio examples are provided here since it will be more beneficial for you to play them on your keyboard. Practicing these three types of connections will develop muscle habits (and thinking habits) that will form a solid base for establishing your keyboard (and theory ) skills.

**triads with roots a fifth/fourth apart**  The most frequently used connection is between two triads whose roots are a fifth apart, either up or down. The tonic triad and its root relationship to its dominant and subdominant triads is a good example. Let's take a closer look.

First, remember that a fifth away is the same as a fourth away in the other direction. From C up to G is a perfect fifth, and from C down to G is a

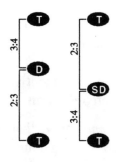

perfect fourth. From C up to F is a perfect fourth, and from C down to F is a perfect fifth. In harmonic terms, it doesn't matter in which direction you go; the result is the same.

Any two chords whose roots are a fifth or fourth apart will have certain relational characteristics. In this type of connection, the two chords will have one pitch in common and the remaining two pitches in each chord will be one scale step from the remaining two pitches in the other chord.

As you know, the tonic triad (1-3-5) contains the dominant pitch, which is in common with the dominant triad (5-7-2). The two remaining pitches in the tonic triad—tonic (1) and mediant (3)—are each one scale step away from the two remaining pitches in the dominant triad—leading tone (7) and supertonic (2). To play these on the keyboard, one finger stays put and two fingers move one scale step in the same direction, no matter what position the first triad is in. (The arrowheads indicate the root of the triad.)

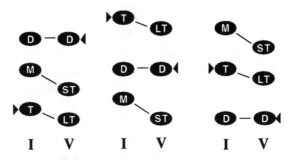

(Note: On the keyboard, it sometimes is more comfortable to exchange the index finger for the middle finger, and vice versa, instead of moving these fingers to a neighboring pitch.)

The same characteristics are found in the relationship of the tonic (1-3-5) and subdominant triad (4-6-1). Play these chords in various positions and notice that one pitch stays put while the other two move together to neighboring pitches.

These characteristics are also contained in any other triad connections whose fundamentals are five (or four) steps apart. Those remaining in the system are listed below. The pitches in common are shown in bold numbers. Play each pair and notice the similar connection they all share. (All triads are shown from the root up. Be sure to rearrange their pitches appropriately for smooth connection.)

Supertonic (**2**-4-6) to or from dominant (5-7-**2**)
Supertonic (2-4-**6**) to or from submediant (**6**-1-3)
Mediant (**3**-5-7) to or from submediant (6-1-**3**)
Mediant (minor ) (♭**3**-5-♭**7**) to or from subtonic (♭**7**-2-4)

**harmonic direction**

It seems the direction of harmonic progression established by dominant harmony's strong attraction to tonic is reflected throughout the major/minor system. When harmonic movement is toward a root a fifth lower (or fourth higher), the chord connection is called a **progression**. When movement is toward a root a fifth higher (or fourth lower), it is called a **retrogression**.

This does not mean that every chord connection of this type *must* move that way, but rather that it is the usual choice. This can be seen by moving counterclockwise around the "circle of fifths" (see p. 94). In musical practice, after leaping clockwise from tonic to some point on the circle, the root sequence *progresses* by fifths back toward tonic harmony. *Retrogression*, then, is moving the other way, or clockwise on the "circle of fifths," away from tonic.

The roots of two chords in "circle of fifth" connections in major mode are always related in perfect fifths, like the dominant-tonic relationship. However, in the minor mode, the submediant triad sometimes moves to the supertonic triad, even though their roots are in a tritone relationship. This weak "progression" usually occurs only when it is included in a sequential series of progression of more stable fourth/fifth connections.

**triads with roots a third/sixth apart**

Connecting triads whose fundamentals are a third apart is very simple. We saw it earlier when we demonstrated the relationship between a primary triad and its secondary partner. In fact, that is the most frequent use of this type of connection. As we noted, triads in this relationship have two pitches in common, and the remaining one is a scale step away from the remaining one in the other chord.

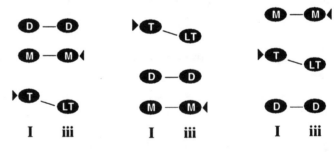

Like the connection by fifth/fourth, root movement in thirds is sometimes better in one direction than the other, particularly when the roots of both chords are the lowest sounding pitches. From primary triad to secondary triad seems to be the more satisfying direction. From secondary to principle seems not to advance the harmonic movement, and feels "backwards." In a sense, the secondary triad following its primary triad adds color to the harmony (as in "Home On The Range" above), but the primary triad following its secondary seems to "remove" color (perhaps because, in the major mode at least, a minor triad seems more dissonant than a major one).

In a connection from a primary triad to its related secondary triad, the movement of the root is, of course, down a third (or up a sixth). Movement *up* a third does seem to advance the harmony when a principle triad root moves up to someone else's secondary triad. For example, the tonic triad followed by the mediant triad clearly gives the impression of "going somewhere." The same is true of the subdominant triad moving to the submediant. (The dominant triad moving up a third to a leading tone triad is, of course, "going nowhere" root-wise, but is simply adding its own dominant seventh pitch to the sound.)

The third and last type of triad connection is between two chords whose roots are on consecutive scale steps, or a second (or seventh) apart. In this case, every pitch in one triad is one step away from a pitch in the other triad, therefore there are no pitches in common.

**triads with roots a second/seventh apart**

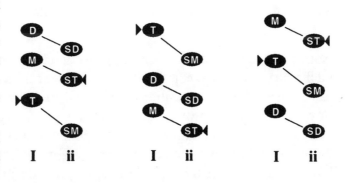

I    ii            I    ii            I    ii

The most obvious way to connect these triads smoothly is simply to move all the pitches in the first chord up (or down, as the case may be) one step to the pitches of the second chord. In some musical styles, this is a standard procedure—in rock and roll, for example. However, composers of major/minor music commonly have preferred to move the individual pitches contrary to movement of the roots, particularly when the independence of multiple melodic lines is important. When all the pitches move one step together in the same direction, this independence is lost. When the melodic movement goes against the stepwise root movement, one of the connections moves by third, in contrast to the other two connec- tions, which move by step. In this illustra- tion, the melodic third is from the tonic to the submediant).

I    ii            I    ii            I    ii

The art of **voice leading**, handling the internal melodic activities within chord progressions, is a topic beyond the scope of this book. However, the information above will give you a foundation upon which to undertake such a study in the future. The main purpose for including it is to demonstrate how chords flow melodically from one to the next, instead of jumping awkwardly from root position to root position. Practicing these connections on the keyboard until they feel comfortable will be a very worthwhile project, first on white digitals, then on mixed digitals in various keys.

## Major/Minor System Wrap-up

The major and minor modes are not simply two more scales to be added to those already in use. They are not merely different ways of configuring a set of seven pitches. The major/minor system is an integrated musical construct in which the minor mode provides an alternate "color" to the major mode. The functions and "personalities" of the various scale steps in the system are essentially the same in both modes.

The color difference of the two modes is due to the flexibility of the mediant and submediant scale steps, alternately rendering the tonic and subdominant triads either major or minor. Selecting one color or the other is a matter of artistic choice. Either mode can be emphasized throughout a composition, or both modes can be mixed, creating internal modal contrasts.

While a major/minor system composition might consist entirely of major harmonies, it cannot consist entirely of minor harmonies. The functional dominant chord is always based on a major triad, usually with the dominant seventh pitch added, which continually focuses tonal direction toward a tonal center. The active ingredient in the dominant seventh chord is the tritone, the unique interval that impels tonal direction toward specific pitches.

By introducing chromatic pitches in strategic locations, a composer is able to redirect tonal focus toward other keys, either temporarily or permanently. Usually, those new pitches are either the leading tone or the dominant seventh pitch of the destination key, working together with its tritone partner to create the new focus.

Normally, the connection of chords is accomplished by moving individual pitches in one chord to nearby pitches in the next chord. There are only three basic types of triad connections, which, when followed, creates a smooth flow in the music. However, there are many possible deviations from these basic patterns that add interest and adventure to a composition. Exploring those possibilities is the essence of creating meaningful musical art and is beyond the scope of this book. Hopefully, this discussion has helped you construct a firm "launching pad" for your exploration of the musical "space" we call the major/minor system.

# 10

# Other Harmonic Systems

Although the major/minor system has been an important influence in the direction of world music, it is not the only harmonic system in use. Before the dynamic value of the tritone was discovered, music was made of harmonies that purposely avoided it. Early in the twentieth century, many composers attempted to defeat the natural sense of tonality in music, and purposefully used the tritone (and other dissonant pitch combinations) in ways that would defy the tritone's tendency to define a tonal center. Of course, tempered tuning was (and is) an important ally to that cause.

Recently, in certain popular music, the functional use of the tritone has been considered "old fashioned," and therefore avoided. Instead of ending compositions using the traditional penultimate dominant seventh chord, a dominant eleventh chord (omitting the leading tone) is often used instead. This chord can be described as a subdominant chord sounding over a dominant bass pitch. This usage is likely a result of the influence of modal harmonies in popular music of the 1960s and 1970s. While this progression is firmly tonal, it does not reflect traditional major/minor practice.

## Modal Harmonies

Since chords as we know them today were not a part of modal music during its development in the Middle Ages (at least in practice), the discussion in this chapter should be understood to reflect the harmonic application of modal scales in recent use. The reappearance of modal scales in Western mainstream music occurred largely in the late nineteenth century and continues today.

According to a common use of the term **modal** music, the defining characteristic is that, instead of a leading tone (half step below tonic), a **subtonic** (whole step below tonic) is used. This, of course, eliminates the tritone between scale steps 7 and 4, replacing it with a perfect fifth (and fourth). The functional tritone is not an essential ingredient in modal music since modulation, in the major/minor sense, is not one of its important features.

The truth is that not all modes have a subtonic. However, modes that don't are not popular today. This information, admittedly, renders the term "modal" somewhat vague, but then, popular use of language is not always systematic.

Modes in popular use contain the same types of chord connections as those described above, having progression in fifth/fourths, third/sixths and second/sevenths. Parallel movement of chords and pitches is generally more prevalent and, since the tritone is not functional, considerably less attention is given to melodic tendencies of scale-member pitches. The sense of tonality is usually present in modal music. It is produced not so much by natural acoustics but by compositional pitch patterns, both harmonic and melodic, that tend to make one pitch appear more prominent than others.

All the traditional modes are **diatonic**, in that their scales are a mixture of *two* kinds of steps—whole steps and half steps. It is the arrangement of these steps that provides the individual characteristics of each mode. Like the major scale, all modal scales have five whole steps and two half steps. That being the case, it is practical to identify each scale simply by locating its half steps.

There are two convenient ways to view these defining half steps: one is to locate each mode on the keyboard's white digitals (they are all there), and the other is to compare each modal scale to a major or minor scale. We will do both.

Although the traditional modes were developed in the Middle Ages by Roman Catholic clergy, they have Greek names. The shapes of these modes have nothing to do with the way music was made in ancient Greece, nor were these names known during the Middle Ages. Glareanus, a sixteenth century musicologist, suggested the Greek names. During the Renaissance, using Greek names was considered a very "in" thing to do.

**modes on white digitals**     Modal scales are often referred to in terms of the position in which their configurations correspond to the keyboard's white digitals. Although some traditional modes were conceived before the keyboard was invented, their steps and half steps happen to fit the keyboard's steps and half steps. Other modes were conceived later, some perhaps *because* of the pattern of steps and half steps on the keyboard.

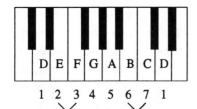

The "D mode," called **dorian**, has half steps between scale members 2 and 3 and between 6 and 7.

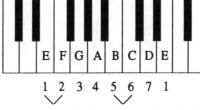

The "E mode," called **phrygian**, has half steps between members 1 & 2 and between 5 & 6.

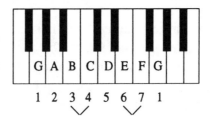

The "F mode," called **lydian**, has half steps between members 4 & 5 and between 7 & 1.

The "G mode," called **mixolydian**, has half steps between members 3 & 4 and between 6 & 7.

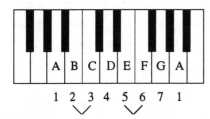

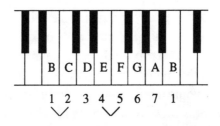

The "A mode," called **aeolian**, has half steps between members 2 & 3 and between 5 & 6.

The "B mode," called **locrian**, has half steps between members 1 & 2 and between 4 & 5.

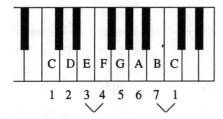

The "C mode," called **ionian**, has half steps between members 3 & 4 and between 7 & 1.

While we have used the white digitals to demonstrate the shapes of these scales, they are not limited to these tonalities. Like major and minor scales, the tonic of a modal scale can be located on any pitch.

Only the first four of these (D, E, F and G modes) were used in the Middle Ages. The others (A, B and C modes) were added later, perhaps from an urgency to "complete the system." Of the three added later, only the aeolian became popular. The locrian mode was rejected almost as soon as it was defined and named, undoubtedly because of the tritone relationship between its tonic and "dominant" members (B-F). The ionian, as you may have noticed, has the same shape as the major scale, at least the keyboard's version of it. Virtually no one thinks of the C mode as a "modal" scale, except perhaps those who feel the need to name everything imaginable, whether or not it is practical. To think of the C mode as just another configuration of whole steps and half steps is to miss the whole import of the major/minor system.

Since the shape of any mode is quickly available by imagining its position on the keyboard's white digitals, you might choose not to memorize the half steps in each mode unless you enjoy that sort of thing. It seems more efficient simply to memorize the letter name on which each occurs, then visualize its shape on the white digitals. Once visualized on the keyboard, the pattern can be transferred to any other tonality.

**modes on C**     A more practical and musical way to memorize the shapes of the modal scales is to compare each one to a major or minor scale, whichever seems more similar. That choice is best made by noting the interval between the tonic and third scale step of the mode: if it's a major third, use the major scale for the comparison; if it's a minor third, use the minor scale. All the illustrations in this section will use C as the tonic pitch. Although our emphasis is on harmony, the audio examples will provide the melodic perspective of each mode.

The most popular of the traditional modes in use today are the mixolydian and the dorian, so we'll look at those first. The **mixolydian** mode is the same as the major scale except for a lowered seventh step. Harmonically, the tonic and subdominant triads are the same as

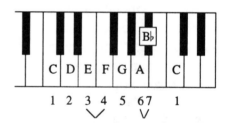

in major and the "dominant" triad (not in the major/minor sense) is characteristically minor. Although this scale resembles F major, there is little danger of mistaking one for the other as long as C and G are used prominently and the E-B♭ tritone is not emphasized melodically or harmonically.

The use of modes in popular music today is largely a result of the "British invasion" in the 1960s, led by the Beatles. The Beatles song "A Hard Day's Night" begins in the mixolydian mode. If you know the song, begin on E and pick out the melody that goes with the lyric "It's been a hard day's night and I've been workin' like a dog." You will find that B♭ occurs on "*workin'*." Here is a folk song in mixolydian mode.

10-2

The **dorian** mode is similar to the minor scale except for a "raised" sixth step and "lowered" seventh step. An attractive feature of this mode is that its tonic triad is minor and its subdominant triad is major, creating an interesting "tritone"

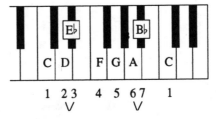

relationship between the thirds of these chords. The dominant chord, of course, is minor.

Among the many popular songs composed in the dorian mode is Michael Jacksons's mega hit, "Thriller." If you know it, try to pick out the title-hook phrase " 'cause this is thriller, thriller night." It begins on G and uses the pitches nearer the high tonic. Here is a folk song in the dorian mode.

 10-3

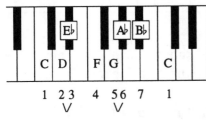

The **aeolian** mode is also quite popular. It is the same as the minor scale except for a subtonic instead of a leading tone. Both the tonic and subdominant chords are minor, and again the dominant chord is minor.

"Can't Buy Me Love" is a Beatles melody that suggests the aeolian mode. The first phrase of its verse, "I'll buy you a diamond ring my friend if it makes you feel all right," begins on G (with a C tonality). Pick it out on the keyboard and you will find it uses both E♭ and B♭ within that first phrase. Here is a well-known Christmas carol in the aeolian mode.

10-4

Those three modes are the only ones that have a whole step both above and below the tonic. As stated earlier, this characteristic seems to be the principle reason today why a composition is labeled "modal." Incidentally, a modal popular song does not necessarily continue in one mode throughout. Madonna's "Vogue" begins in mixolydian (natural 3 and "lowered" 7) in the lower end of the range of pitches. As the melody moves higher, the mode becomes aeolian or perhaps dorian (with lots of "lowered" 3 and 7 sprinkled with touches of natural 6). Significantly, there are no leading tones or suggestions of "out of fashion" dominant seventh chords.

The patterns of principal-triad chord quality in these three modes leaves out one logical possibility. None of the standard modes has a major tonic triad and a minor subdominant triad. That sound is not unfamiliar in the major/minor system, but would be unique when combined with a minor dominant triad. Very likely, composers have used this configuration, but in general conversation about music, this "mode" remains nameless.

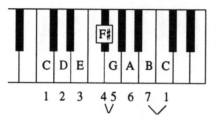

The two modes having a half step below tonic are the lydian and the ionian. The latter needs no discussion here, since it is identical to the major scale. The **lydian** is nearly identical to the major scale except for an F♯ instead of an F. This

10-5 pattern provides a "leading tone" to both the tonic and the dominant pitches, quite a delightful and musical effect. This improvisation expresses the lydian flavor.

The two modes having a half step above tonic are the phrygian and the locrian. The **phrygian** mode was one of the original medieval modes. It is like the minor scale with a "lowered" second step as well as the standard "lowered" seventh

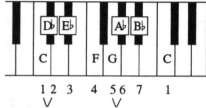

step. Like the aeolian mode, its tonic and subdominant triads are minor, however its dominant triad is more or less dysfunctional, not having a perfect fifth (G-D♭). This mode was quite popular among turn-of-the-century impressionist composers, likely due to its tonal ambiguity. Here is a Sephardic

10-6 chant based on the phrygian mode.

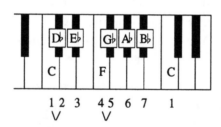

The **locrian** mode suffers harmonically even more acutely than the lydian by not having a perfect fifth in its tonic triad. Its "dominant" triad is minor, which also lacks a perfect-fifth root relationship to the tonic. Subdominant is the only "normal" primary triad, and is minor. As you would imagine, examples of this mode are not easy to locate. Perhaps the only compositions in existence are ones in which a composer expressly wished to try his or her hand at handling the ambiguity and awkwardness of this mode.

Although these more exotic modes are not extensively used in the wider world of music, they seem to have been used in esoteric jazz. Such notables as Miles Davis, John Coltrane and Dizzy Gillespie are said to have employed modal scale patterns to achieve sounds that were considered "far out" a few decades ago. It is not clear, however, which came first, the theory or the sounds. Were these artists simply experimenting with new sound possibilities, when they (or others) noticed the apparent modal orientation, or did they purposefully set out to improvise on predetermined modes? Jazz experts are divided on the question.

# Atonal Harmonies

The term **atonal**, meaning "without a tonal center," is a concept that took hold in the early twentieth century. Apparently, it was assumed that since music had been principally tonal for centuries, it was time to try something new. The stage had been set for this thinking long ago when the keyboard was set up in twelve equal intervals. It was a short step then to work out a system that would negate tonality and free music from the "bondage" of the major/minor system.

Arnold Schoenberg (1874-1951), an Austrian composer-theorist, developed the **twelve-tone system** of composition that was widely used in the early to middle decades of the twentieth century, and is still used to some extent today. Briefly, this compositional technique avoids structurally consonant sounds in order to prevent the impression that the music is centered around a single pitch. A general principle of the technique, stated in very simplified terms, is to use all twelve pitches before returning to a used pitch. To maintain the impression of atonality yet provide stability and form, a composer creates a **tone row**, accomplished by ordering the twelve pitches of the keyboard into a kind of random-sounding "scale" to be used in the process of composing a piece.

The **original** row is then manipulated by **retrograde** (reversing the order of pitches), **inversion**, (turning the row "upside down" by reversing the direction of its intervals), and by **retrograde inversion** (the combination of the two). These four versions can be transposed intact to the eleven other pitch levels, thus creating a large reservoir of raw materials available to the composer. Following is the tone row upon which Schoenberg composed his *Suite For Piano*, Opus 25. The original row can be heard in the first twelve pitches played in the upper voice.

10-7

| Row | Retrograde |
|---|---|
| E F G D♭ G♭ E♭ A♭ D B C A B♭ | B♭ A C B D A♭ E♭ G♭ D♭ G F E |
| Inversion | Retrograde-inversion |
| E E♭ D♭ G D F C F♯ A G♯ B B♭ | B♭ B G♯ A F♯ C F D G D♭ E♭ E |

From these pitch patterns, a composer selects "chunks" for use in the musical work. Any version of the row can be divided into halves, thirds or quarters, resulting in dozens of six-, four-, and three-pitch fragments to be used as chords or melodic elements. Yet, because the elements are drawn from an organized row, the composition maintains a sense of unity within an atonal context.

Quite a number of composers followed Schoenberg's lead. By mid century, most university music schools required their composition students to learn the twelve-tone system, also referred to as **serial** composition. Composers eventually expanded the serial concept to include systematic cycling of timbres, rhythms, dynamics, and other elements. Many compositions of major artistic import have been created using these compositional values, including a number of "classics" that will likely continue to be performed well into the future. Of particular importance are Alban Berg's opera *Wozzeck*, Anton Webern's *Symphony, Opus 21* and Stravinsky's ballet *Agon*.

Nevertheless, the general population of concert goers have not embraced atonal music with the passion and pleasure they continue to express for the music of other twentieth century composers whose music is more tonally oriented. A number of major twentieth century composers have expressed their musical artistry in styles that are well outside of traditional major/minor system values, yet unmistakably employ the principle of tonality. These include Aaron Copland, Bela Bartok, Dimitri Shostakovich, Igor Stravinsky and a host of others.

10-8  Of interest is Paul Hindemith's *Ludus Tonalis*, a set of preludes and fugues in twelve different tonalities. His work was created in the spirit of *The Well-Tempered Clavier*, J. S. Bach's eighteenth century celebration of the keyboard's ability to play in all the major and minor keys. In Hindemith's case, twelve pieces sufficed since his music doesn't differentiate between major and minor modes.

Part of the reason for a cool reception of atonal composition is that music perceived as going "up" and "down" in distances that seem unrelated harmonically feels "unsettling." Since by nature we hear pitches in simple harmonic relationships, it may follow that attempting to negate that basic instinct is like swimming upstream. Perhaps humans *need* to find some tonal orientation in music in order to perceive its organization. Whether that is true, people in general seem to respond with more immediate interest and enthusiasm to tonal music, even when its other aspects may be quite exotic and unfamiliar.

Perhaps the clearest body of evidence relating to this point is music composed for motion pictures. Scenes that are peaceful, exhilarating, triumphant, resolute, or in other positive dramatic moods, are usually enhanced with tonal music; while scenes that are mysterious, frightening, macabre, frustrating, disorienting, or in other negative dramatic moods, are frequently underscored with atonal music. (Having made this rather sweeping judgment, it will be interesting to watch for musical exceptions to that notion.)

# Electronic and Aleatory Music

Mid twentieth century advances in electronic technology produced the world's first music without natural vibrating bodies such as strings, lips, vocal cords, reeds, etc. Electrical impulses are now used to create sounds and to control their pitch, timbre, dynamics, and even "spacial" (stereo) characteristics as well. The only vibrating bodies here are membranes in speaker cabinets that send the perceptual data to the ear. Composers of **electronic music** can create timbres that imitate "real" instruments as well as manufacture sounds that humans have never heard before.

Music composed directly onto a recording medium—at one time a tape, now a computer disk—does not require a performer. Such music is not restricted by the technical, physical or musical limitations of voices or instruments. The whole spectrum of sound is available for use, and composers have taken advantage of this fact. Washes, flashes, and blips of strange sounds sweep across the audio field, mostly without regard for scales, tone rows or any other traditional pitch structure.

However, the knowledgeable composer of electronic music is not unaware of the nature of sound and its relation to human hearing. The shapes of sounds created electronically are governed by the same acoustic principles as was Pythagoras' string. The differences are of complexity, not of substance. Creating electronic sounds emphasizing small-number ratios, in pitch or timbre, will tend to produce a sense of tonality in a composition. Creating sounds with more complex acoustical ratios will tend to blur tonality. The nature of the "paint" is the same as it always has been, even though the "palette" may be larger.

Composers of **aleatory** music, sometimes called "chance music," utilize this increased sound spectrum by inviting performers to make artistic choices within parameters set out within a composition. A group of choral singers might receive such instructions as "sing loudly any medium pitch on any vowel in a strident manner; then, on cue, slide down slowly to any fairly low pitch while gradually changing the vowel to a mellow "ooh" and gradually diminishing loudness; then sustain the resulting sonority until cut off." A section of string players might be asked to "tap the bow quietly on the shoulders of the instrument at a fairly fast rate of speed." The sound resulting from these kinds of instructions would be different, to some degree, in every performance. The harmonic relationships between pitches is left to "chance."  10-9 Any impression of tonality likely depends on the performers' preferences, moods and experience.

The listener will have to make a judgment, of course, regarding whether any particular electronic composition or aleatory performance satisfies the logical requirement, discussed early in this book, that music be "organized." But then, a good listener will attempt to make that judgment in regard to any music.

## Harmony Wrap-Up

It is interesting to note that one era's "dissonance" becomes another era's "consonance." Early polyphonic style, around the end of the first millennium, required that all voices (musical lines) converge to the tonic pitch at the end of a composition in order to achieve resolution of musical unrest. A few hundred years later, the fifth above tonic was approved as a concluding pitch. By the sixteenth century, the third of the tonic chord was deemed consonant enough to be included in a final sonority. Today, compositions conclude with almost any pitch combination, and often include added sixths, ninths, and sometimes even a tritone. That a final sound offer a consonant release from preceding dissonant sounds is the norm in nearly all styles, but what constitutes "consonance" changes from age to age and from style to style.

No matter how complex the musical style, its harmonic elements are more easily perceived when they relate to each other in small-number ratios. The process of improving your perception of harmonic structures is best accomplished by establishing solid concepts of simple relationships, like those found in the primary harmonies of the major/minor system. Once these are in place, you can begin to master additional layers of tonal conception—secondary harmonies, chromatic inflections, modulation to other keys, and eventually hearing and performing atonal music.

# 11

# Melodic Systems

In general terms, **melody** refers to pitches sounded one after the other, in series, as opposed to harmony, which usually refers to pitches sounded simultaneously, as in chords. While these definitions sound reasonably logical and precise, applying them to specific examples can be /difficult, if not downright confusing.

Some of the difficulty is caused by failing to realize that *both* melody and harmony rely on the same natural acoustical principles. Although melody appears to predate harmony by many centuries, perhaps many millennia, examination of the world's early music shows a rather universal preference for sturdy acoustical small-number ratios as a basis for melodic structures. So, using the word *harmony* to mean "acoustical relationships between pitches," and the word *melody* to mean something other than that does not stand up.

Another usage problem occurs when *melody* in the general sense is confused with *melody* in the specific sense. For example, music today is commonly described as having "melody" and "harmony." In this sense, *melody* means "the part of the music a singer would sing" and *harmony* means "the part of the music the piano player would play." In fact, the pianist in this circumstance will likely perform many passages which invite the ear to follow series of pitches in melodic phrases, even though he or she may never play *the* melody.

Unfortunately, common terminology in this area is not always helpful and, like much language, often appears to be related to nebulous concepts. In our discussion of *melody*, we will use the term to mean "pitches considered in series," making no judgment regarding compositional prominence or formal role. The pitches C and E sounding at the same time, then, is a *harmonic* event, and the pitches C and E sounding one after the other is a *melodic* event.

In the following pages, we will look at a variety of pentatonic scales that have formed the basis of a number of primative and current musical cultures. Then we'll explore the impact of harmony on the construction of melody in the major/minor system. This section will conclude with a brief look at modal melodies, blues melodies, some ethnic scales and the role of melody in atonal, electronic and aleatory music.

12

# Pentatonic Melody

A great many ancient cultures seem to have developed a **pentatonic scale**, or five-pitch configuration, for composing music. What mysterious authority could force such conformity on all those different peoples? Clearly, geographic separation would suggest that there was no world-wide music symposium at which these divergent cultures met to discuss the shape of music. The answer appears to be that human ears more easily hear pitch relationships that are acoustically consonant, even when the pitches are not sounded simultaneously. So, that "mysterious authority" is probably nature.

There clearly is something universally attractive about experiencing pitches sounding in natural simplicity. Not all early cultures had a Pythagoras to explain the math involved. However, theory almost always comes after art, the artist blazing new paths by instinct and intuition and the scientist/philosopher later studying the artist's product to explain how and why it works.

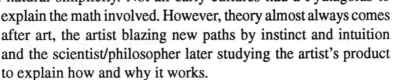

The ancient musician's universal preference for the same five pitches (relatively) was likely a result of noting which ones work well together. Inversely, of course, this also would have to do with avoiding pitches that seemed disquieting. Notice the pitches "missing" from the traditional pentatonic scale are none other than the troublesome tritone. Evidently, the misgivings medieval European musicians held for the tritone were experienced even earlier by the ancients.

**the missing tritone**

Of course, the pentatonic scale is usually considered a melodic structure, and certainly not a harmonic one in the same sense as the major mode. Therefore, this comparison should not be carried further than simply noticing the tritone's absence. Regardless whether all the pitches in the pentatonic scale are thought to generate from a single tonic pitch, the members of the major scale are not. As we observed earlier, the tritone pitches of the major mode are generated through the dominant fundamental, and the subdominant pitch does not appear at all as a partial of the tonic fundamental. All the more reason, one would think, that scale steps 4 and 7 would not appear in the primitive pentatonic scale.

**"major" pentatonic**

12-1

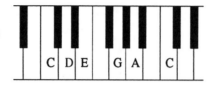

Through the ages, various pentatonic modes have been used, with each culture (or composer) selecting one of the five pitches to use as a tonic. A favorite mode in Eastern traditions is the "C" mode (which can be transposed to any pitch, of course), a major-sounding scale. Note how this traditional cowboy song uses the major pentatonic scale.

Commercial songs in Japan and China often reflect the cultural heritage of the major pentatonic scale. These are frequently a mix of Western rock and roll rhythms and Asian melodic traditions.

**"minor" pentatonic**

Many Appalachian melodies, as well as those from other cultures, are built on the "A" mode, a minor-sounding scale. Notice the same pitches are used here as in the C-mode scale, but the configuration of members around the tonic is different. Also, notice the "missing" pitches are still B and F, the tritone.

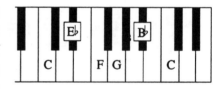

Here is the "minor" pentatonic transposed to a C tonic. It resembles the C minor scale, but without a leading tone, of course. An interesting feature here is that the top half of this scale (G-B♭-C) has the same intervalic configuration as the bottom half (C-E♭-F). That feature is heard prominently in this folksong, the middle section being sounded entirely in the top part of the scale.

12-2

This pentatonic configuration is not confined to Western culture, however. The Japanese *Yo* scale is similar, as are many others around the world.

**the blues**

Another pentatonic scale having identical halves is the popular melodic system known as **the blues**. Although its pitches appear (in keyboard terms) to be the same as those of the "minor" pentatonic scale, this is probably not the case. The so called "blue notes" in this style (very-flat 3 and very-flat 7) clearly tune lower than the corresponding pitches in the major/minor system.

In fact, performing these expressive elements with "standard" tunings denies the very flavor of the blues style.

Primitive blues melodies are commonly performed over an unchanging tonic harmony. This, combined with the blues practice of performing the tonic fundamental in repeated alternation with subtonic, suggests that the tuning of the blues subtonic pitch would naturally correspond to the seventh partial. It seems reasonable, then, that the "blue" seventh and the "blue" third are expressions of the 4:7 and 6:7 acoustic ratios.

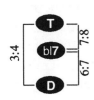

A prominent melodic feature of the blues style is to oscillate between tonic and the blue seventh, occasionally descending to "dominant," establishing a set of three pitches.  12-3

Blues-style melodies frequently move above the tonic as well, utilizing pitches that appear to duplicate the intervalic relationships of the lower set of three pitches, using the tonic as a pivot serving in both the low and high segments of the system. This duplication of upper and lower segments of a pentatonic scale was observed earlier. The new pitches are the "subdominant" pitch (to borrow a major/minor system term) and a blue third. These, then, are the five pitches that make up the blues scale. As in most scales, its pitches can be duplicated in octaves.

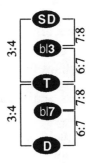

In general, scalewise melodic movement in the blues moves downward, in keeping with its melancholy mood. A standard melodic formula in this style is to perform a series of repeated tonic and subtonic pitches in high range and then, at the end of the phrase or section, descend, usually scalewise, to the low tonic.  12-4

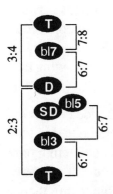

An additional "blue note" is frequently incorporated into the style, challenging the status of the blues as a purely pentatonic system. This added pitch appears to be another blue 6:7 interval above the one on tonic. It makes no musical sense to view this pitch as a 5:7 (tritone) ratio above the tonic. It is clearly not a *keyboard* tritone, nor is it a functional tritone as in the major/minor system. Its allegiance and tuning seem to lean toward the pitches below, not to the dominant above, and most likely directly to the blue third below it (♭3).  12-5

This simple melodic system, sometimes referred to as "folk" blues, or "swamp" blues, gave rise near the turn of the century to "New Orleans jazz," a mixture of melodic blues elements over a functional major/minor harmonic foundation. This expanded blues style goes beyond the current topic, and therefore will be described later.

**other pentatonic scales** Music traditions have produced other pentatonic scale patterns, as well. Here is another that appears to be constructed in identical halves, consisting of superimposed major thirds and perfect fourths. This scale has been called the **semitonal** pentatonic scale, as opposed to the **tonal** pentatonic scale described above. These terms relfect that one scale has whole steps between

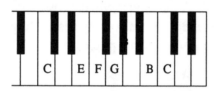

3-4 and 7-1 and the other has half steps in those same locations. However, those names are loaded with potential confusion. The term *tonal* usually means "having a central pitch," but here it means "whole step." Semitone, on the other hand, regularly means "half step." Since *both* scales are "tonal," in the sense of "having a tonal center," this terminology probably should be avoided. Perhaps future musicologists will develop clearer vocabulary.

This scale has been used by ancient Greeks as well as modern Japanese. It vaguely resembles the lydian scale with its apparent "leading tone" to two different pitches. It also resembles the major

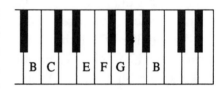

mode, however, the half-step interval is usually not used as a leading tone in this mode. Melodic usage seems to favor the lower of the semitone pitches (B and E, in this key) as the more stable of the two. While the Japanese *Yo* scale resembles the "minor" pentatonic scale, the *In* scale uses B (in this key) as tonic.

The Javanese **sléndro** is a pentatonic scale, sometimes called *pentaphonic*, which is of a completely different variety. It has five equidistant steps between its tonics. Javanese musicians are fond of creating synthetic (as opposed to acoustic) scales by dividing the octave into various numbers of equal parts. It should be noted that Javanese music is largely instrumental, allowing ears to enjoy this music without necessarily reproducing it vocally.

**why five?** It is not entirely clear why so many traditions focused on the idea of having five pitches in a scale. If piling up perfect fifths were, in fact, the basis of the early pentatonic scale, it seems strange to have stopped after collecting only five pitches (C-G-D-A-E) since the next fifth (E-B) would not yet have produced the troublesome tritone (B-F). But then, that is supposing theory influenced practice, which is not the way it appears to have worked out. Perhaps you have an idea on the matter.

# 13

# Melody In The Major/Minor System

Which comes first—melody or harmony? Regarding music conceived in major or minor modes, the answer to that question might very well be "both." The interrelationship of melody and harmony in the major/minor system is very intimate. Melody, by itself, almost always contains harmonic implications, and harmonic progressions almost always influence structural elements in melody. Therefore, to discuss melody in the major/minor system without regard to its relation to harmony is to omit one of melody's most important characteristics.

A popular concept of melody is "pitches in a series of steps and/or skips of various sizes." This thinking has led, almost universally, to musical ear-training methods which appear to assume that "steps" are more basic than "skips." These methods invariably begin with drills consisting of scale fragments in "whole steps" and "half steps." Later, "skips" and larger intervals are drilled. Such methods appear to be based on the idea that smaller intervals are easier to conceive than larger intervals.

This view ignores the evidence that melodic perception, like harmonic perception, is related to acoustics. It is a simple physical fact that certain larger intervals are acoustically simpler than steps. Therefore, it follows that these larger intervals are much easier to conceive clearly and precisely, particularly when the "steps" are based on synthetic values. Experience in teaching ear training from an acoustical starting point has clearly shown this to be true.

Since the facts are so clear, it almost seems foolish to suppose that drilling tempered-tuned scale fragments is a better way to train musical ears than drilling acoustic intervals (see sidebar "It Is Good To Listen To Mother Nature," p. 123).

Whether melody is even possible, in any style, without regard for harmony, musical practice during the past three or four centuries assures us this certainly is not the case in the major/minor system. This melodic style is always securely anchored to chords in rather specific ways. In the following discussion we will examine those ways.

**arpeggio**    Skipping from one chord tone to the next in a series of melodic pitches is called **arpeggiation**. Many songs begin with an arpeggio on tonic harmony. We have already seen this in "The Star Spangled Banner," "The Marines Hymn" and "Dixie" (p. 42). Below are a few more.

If you are beginning to develop your musical ear, you might play these phrases on a keyboard to get a sense of their contour. Then, sing along with your playing (temporarily) to get your voice involved. Finally, play only the tonic pitch and sing the melodies carefully, tuning each pitch by ear until you are satisfied that your tunings are the best possible. Play a tonic pitch at least an octave below the pitches you are singing; this causes the pitches you are singing to fit into the harmonic pitch series at a place that is easy to hear.

All the melodies in this section are in the key of C. The audio examples are also performed in C. Some examples are a bit high or low in this key, but these will help stretch your vocal range. Of course, it is always possible to sing a melody an octave higher or lower. You might find it interesting to sing and/or play these phrases in other keys as well.

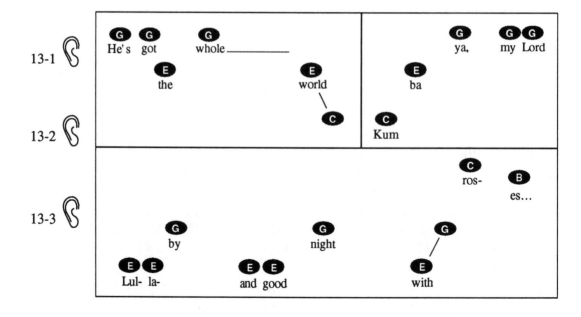

# "It Is Good To Listen To Mother Nature"

In our modern world of keyboard-generated sounds, nature (in regard to tonal relations) is not very easy to hear. That may explain, to some extent, why so many people feel they "can't carry a tune in a bucket." Restaurant renditions of *Happy Birthday* indicate, sadly, that most are telling the truth. Even formally trained singers rarely experience pure acoustic pitch relationships. Their ears have become dulled by years of practicing scales and chords with a tempered-tuned piano. Many swim through melodies with the hope that they are somewhere near the pitch. To exaggerate the problem, music educators commonly use keyboards to *train* ears.

Amateur choral singers almost universally "learn their notes" in tempered tuning. The altos practice their part by hearing it played on the piano, and so do the sopranos, tenors and basses. Because their concept of tuning is to "match the keyboard," when these piano-coached choirs perform *a cappella* (without instruments) they are tonally adrift.

Many modern ears have heard so much tempered tuning that it sounds "right." Veteran pianists sometimes report that acoustically-tuned intervals "sound sharp." String and wind players have a much better circumstance for learning accurate tuning simply because they do their practicing without a keyboard. Mother Nature is more likely to be heard when she doesn't have to shout through artificial tuning.

American culture is not totally without natural acoustical influences, however. Many youngsters grow up in families where informal singing,often in harmony, is a normal part of life. In the 1950s, a great many high schools and colleges supported a cappella choral singing. Unfortunately, such programs are rare today. On the other hand, popular recordings now include a cappella groups, both professional and amateur. Traditional "barbershop" singing, dating back to the late nineteenth century, is alive and well.

The only instrument in a barbershop rehearsal is a pitch pipe. A single pitch is given, each singer hums an assigned pitch in acoustic relation to the sounded tonic. As the song progresses, the singers listen to *each other*, tuning pitches by their relation to the overall sound. The aural result is often quite stunning. Musical academia could learn a great deal from barbershop tradition—if they were listening. The good news is that some are.

Those melodic phrases are firmly attached to the tonic chord of the key of C major. Although each melody begins on a different chord member, the tonal orientation is quite clear, even without an accompaniment.

Usually a melody not only outlines the tonic triad, but also outlines other triads as it continues. In most simple melodies, the triads used are the three primary ones. When secondary triads are included, they appear less often than primary ones, since they are used primarily for contrast. Incidentally, when a melody changes from one harmony to another, it usually moves by step or common pitch, making the transition smooth and solid.

As you sing the following melodies over a fundamental keyboard pitch, be sure to change the pitch when the chord changes. Here's a tip: If you place your five fingers on consecutive digitals, you will be able to *feel* the correct roots without looking at the keyboard. (That practice will speed up your music reading.)

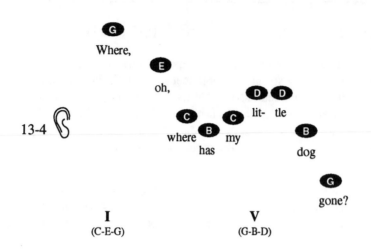

In this melody, the tonic triad is outlined from the dominant step down to tonic. The leading tone appears briefly to reverse the melodic direction. Then the dominant triad is outlined, moving from supertonic down to the dominant root. Both chords are sounded from fifth down to root, the second pattern serving compositionally as an "answer" to the first pattern.

This tune begins by climbing the tonic chord from root to root. Upon arrival at the higher tonic, that pitch becomes the fifth of the subdominant triad, which lingers as the melody moves down and then up on those chord members. The G (not a member of the F major triad) appears briefly between F and A at a relatively weak rhythmic moment. The **contour** (general shape) of this melody is quite different from the one above.

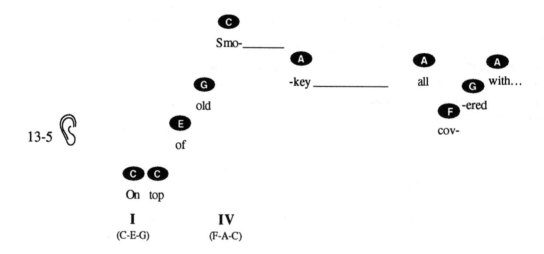

In the following melody, the tonic chord is outlined by moving upward from the dominant pitch, turning back at the mediant and returning to the original pitch. In the descending portion of the first phrase, D is included as a non-chord tone between E and C. The second phrase is an exact duplication of the first, but with each pitch sounding one scale step higher. The implied harmony of the second phrase, logically, is the supertonic triad. The non-chord tone in the second phrase is the E.

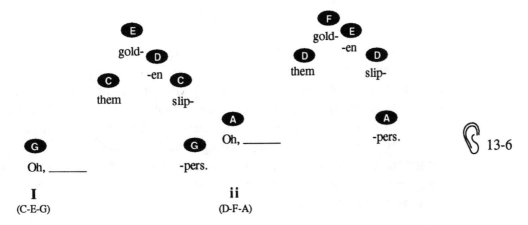

In all the above tunes, melodic movement proceeds stepwise as one chord changes to another. A variation on this principle occurs when a melody skips to a chord member in the new chord that was *recently* neighbored by a previous melodic pitch.

This type of melodic structure suggests that memory can retain a series of pitches (even when a melody is unfamiliar) while the reader perceives their melodic relationships, even when other melodic pitches intervene. This information reinforces the idea that melody is more than simply a string of pitches.

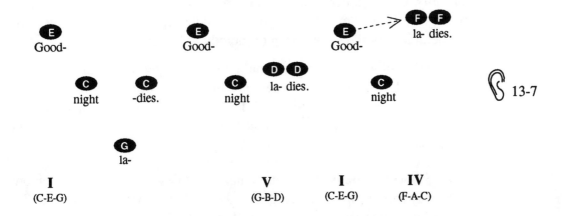

Using the chart "Major Mode Diatonic" (p. 74), sing melodic patterns based on the three primary chords. If you feel you are ready, you might like to venture into secondary chords. Singing over sounding fundamental pitches will help you check the accuracy of your tuning. Even if you are fairly experienced at singing melodies, practicing acoustic tuning will help you overcome any tendency you may have acquired toward singing with tempered tuning.

**ear-training drill**

# Non-chord Tones

Even though some pitches in the major scale are there by sponsorship of a harmonically related fundamental, they are not required to remain silent when their sponsor is not in command. When a pitch that is not a member of the prevailing harmony is sounded melodically, that pitch is called a **non-chord tone,** or **nonharmonic tone.** Over the years, descriptive terms have emerged which refer to the various ways composers have used non-chord tones. Although the terms are not thoroughly systematic, and there remains some disagreement among music theorists regarding their proper application, these terms work reasonably well.

The obvious benefit of non-chord tones is to enable a melody to express itself in a linear or flowing way instead of always proceeding in skips from one chord member to another. We saw this in the melodic examples above. Without non-chord tones, a melody composed of consecutive scale steps would have to change chords on each melodic tone, which would be cumbersome in fast-paced music.

The paragraphs that follow show various ways composers have handled pitches that do not belong to a prevailing harmony. A decision to memorize or not memorize these terms depends upon your goals. If you are going to pursue theoretical studies in music, you will want to study each concept very carefully. On the other hand, if you simply want to learn, in general, how melody works, you might prefer just to read through this discussion to form a general idea of the relationship of melody to harmony.

A great deal of wonderful melody has been written by composers who knew nothing of this terminology. Experience in the style of major/minor composition is far more important. Although learning these terms will not necessarily lead to the creation of great melodies, it will help improve one's melodic craftsmanship.

A **neighboring tone** is just what the name implies—a non-chord pitch one step away from a chord tone, either higher or lower. Also frequently called an **auxiliary,** it is used to embellish a chord tone during the time its chord is sounding. This melodic idea begins on a chord tone, moves up or down to a non-chord tone, then back to the original pitch. It doesn't matter if the chord changes as the melodic figure returns, but it must return to the same pitch to justify this name. Neighboring tones can be **diatonic** (pitches in the scale) or **chromatic** (pitches not in the scale). More than one pitch in a chord can simultaneously sponsor a neighboring tone.

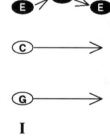

I

Another simple non-chord tone is the **passing tone**, which moves by step, or steps, from one chord tone to another chord tone. Usually, both the departure tone and the destination tone are in the same chord, but this is not a requirement, and composers often achieve interesting results by changing harmonies as a melodic passing tone arrives at its destination. Passing tones can be either diatonic or chromatic. It is possible to have more than one consecutive passing tone, for example, filling the gap between a chord's fifth up to its root ( **G-A-B-C**).

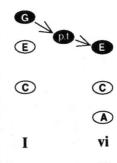

Leaping to a non-chord tone is permitted as long as the melody then moves by step to a chord tone. This is called an **appoggiatura**. If the leap is upward, the resolution to the chord tone is usually downward. Likewise, if the leap is downward, the resolution to the chord tone is usually upward. This "turning back" feature helps to maintain a melody's central balance, however, there are many exceptions to this very general principle. An appoggiatura usually (some say, always) occurs at a strong rhythmic moment. Both diatonic and chromatic appoggiaturas are possible, depending on the scale step and the availability of both diatonic and chromatic neighboring pitches.

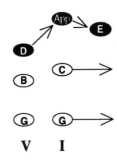

Composers of sixteenth-century vocal music were very fond of the **suspension**. It is accomplished by sustaining a pitch member of one chord into the

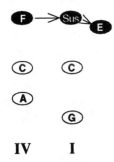

time-space of the next chord. Of course, this doesn't work if the selected pitch is common to both chords—for example, the dominant pitch in a I to V progression. There would be no non-chord tone created in that case. The pitch sustained must resolve by step, usually downward, to a pitch member of the second chord. Suspensions are usually diatonic. Also, they always occur at a strong rhythmic moment and resolve to the chord tone at a weaker moment, always after the chord to which it is resolving has been established.

Some music theorists use the term **ritardation** for suspensions that resolve upward, presumably because the word *suspension* connotes "holding up," and holding something down doesn't fit the term as well. But a suspension and a ritardation are basically the same thing— sustaining a chord tone, or tones, that become dissonant to the following chord and that resolve by step after the

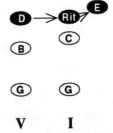

new chord has been established. Also, some theorists say the suspended or ritarded pitch can be re-articulated with the second chord, while others would call that an appoggiatura.

The opposite of the suspension and ritardation is the **anticipation**. Here a chord-member pitch leaves early, at a weak rhythmic moment, moving to a neighboring pitch, one that is dissonant to the prevailing harmony but will become a chord member in the following chord. It can go up or down without having a different name.

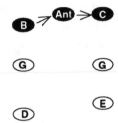

An **escape tone**, or **échappée** (ay-sh'-pay), is a non-chord tone in which a melody leaves a chord tone by step, then leaps in the other direction past that chord tone to a member pitch of a new harmony. It works in either direction, diatonically or chromatically.

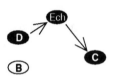

Here is the logical opposite of the escape tone. The **cambiata** is a non-chord tone in which a melody leaps from a chord tone in the first harmony past a chord tone in the second harmony, diatonically or chromatically, and then turns back to the new chord tone.

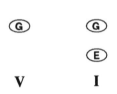

These standard (more or less) non-chord names don't cover all the possibilities, so the term **free tone** is sometimes used as a catch-all for any others. In actual practice, however, a free tone is rare. It seems that composers have taken care that pitches not belonging to prevailing harmonies maintain some perceiveable relationship to the overall flow of the music. Leaping capriciously from one non-chord tone to another would tend to disengage a melody from the music's harmonic flow. (Of course, if a composer *wants* that effect, this is the way to get it.)

**ear-training drill**

The "Major Mode Diatonic" chart (p. 74) can be used to drill melodic fragments containing simple non-chord tones, such as neighboring tones and passing tones. Playing fundamental pitches will not help you tune non-chord tones, but will help you secure "sponsoring" chord tones while executing melodic non-chord patterns. If you have difficulty finding accurate tunings for a non-chord tone, temporarily tune it to its own fundamental pitch, and then use your ear and your vocal "muscle memory" to sing it in its non-chord context.

The "Major Mode - Appoggiaturas" chart on the facing page provides a basis for drilling many of the other non-chord tones described above, including

# MAJOR MODE - APPOGGIATURAS

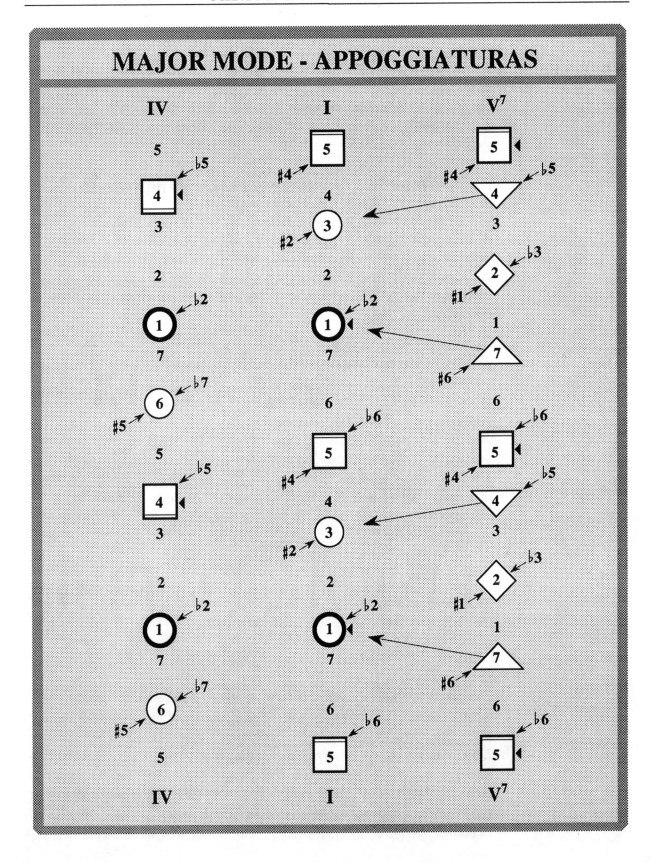

chromatic ones (those not belonging to the major scale). Concentrate on leaping to non-chord pitches by focusing on the chord tone to which it will resolve by step or half step. Hearing fundamental pitches may not help you hear and tune non-chord tones, especially chromatic ones, but will help you "hear" (in imagination) the chord tones to which they will resolve. In this drill you need not be concerned with the rhythmic characteristics of nonchord-tone melodic fragments.

## Melodic Adjustments in the Minor Mode

Composing a melody in the major mode is usually quite trouble-free, since all of its scale members are a whole or half step apart. Melodies based on a diatonic scale flow easily from step to step. The minor mode has a problematic feature that is not found in the major mode. The interval from the lowered submediant to the leading tone is a step and a half, creating a "pothole" in the melodic roadway.

Composers have easily solved this problem. To "repair" the step-and-a-half melodic gap, they either (1) move the submediant up a half step, forsaking its minor flavor and restoring this portion of the scale to a major mode configuration, or (2) move the leading tone down a half step, to a subtonic position, for-

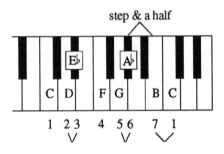

saking its leading-tone function. Making the choice is logical—when the leading tone is needed, move the submediant, and when the leading tone is not needed, move *it*.

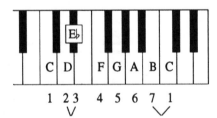

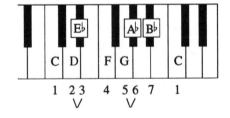

The practical application of this formula, then, is to retain the leading tone when dominant harmony prevails, so the tritone (leading tone and dominant seventh pitch) will be able to do its dominant-function job. When tonic or subdominant harmonies prevail, the leading tone is not needed, and is therefore free to travel, allowing the submediant to do *its* job of providing minor modality. In either situation, contrary to most teaching, melodic direction can be upward or downward (see sidebar "Three Minor Scales?" on p. 131). In both cases, the adjustment enables smooth stepwise movement.

# Three Minor Scales?

The "pothole" problem in the minor scale (the step and a half between the lowered sixth scale step and the leading tone) is treated somewhat logically by music theorists and educators, but, unfortunately, the construct they offer doesn't quite agree with the musical facts. Traditional teaching presents three different minor scales, giving the impression that there are three kinds of minor mode. Textbook authors frequently provide examples of compositions presumably based on each of the three scales.

One of these scales is called **natural minor**, or **pure minor**. Its scale members are those of the aeolian mode. Interestingly, the melodies often selected to illustrate "natural minor" are drawn from Renaissance or folk literature, and are, in fact, examples of the aeolian mode. Confusing the aeolian mode with the revolutionary minor mode that emerged in the seventeenth century requires that the principal ingredient in that revolution, the functional tritone, be ignored. The aeolian mode has no functional tritone.

The name, "natural" minor, is likely a result of the notational practice of borrowing a diatonic key signature from the major scale having the same seven scale pitches. (Further discussion of this point will be presented later under *Notation Of Music*.) The real danger in using this name is that it gives the impression that this is the "natural" configuration of pitches for the minor mode. It is not.

Another traditional minor scale is **harmonic minor**. This one is on the right track in that it correctly shows the "pothole" caused by the lowered submediant. The name "harmonic" indicates that these pitches are used for *chord* building rather than melody building. Nevertheless, textbooks frequently provide melodic examples that leap over the step-and-a-half gap. That such examples are somewhat difficult to find in the literature doesn't seem to affect the decision to use them. The fact that this scale appears to have been invented to explain harmonic principle seems lost on such authors, and indeed, is lost on many music teachers who also seem to miss this point.

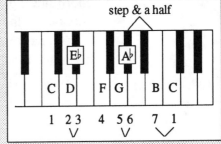

The third traditional minor scale is the **melodic minor**. Again, the name implies the purpose—in this case, to fix the melodic gap in the harmonic minor scale. Unfortunately, the customary description of this scale says nothing about harmonic context or functional roles of the pitches affected. Instead, the "rule" is to raise steps 6 and 7 in ascending passages (matching those in the major scale), and to lower those steps in descending passages (matching those in the natural minor scale). Probably, scale direction is offered as the reason for selecting the appropriate adjustment because this material is normally presented prior to discussing harmony, Unhappily, this misinformation is seldom corrected even *after* harmony is discussed.

It seems that music educators of the past created these scales as "temporary models" for students to follow until such time as they were able to handle the real musical facts. The tragedy is that most former music students, including many who later became theory teachers, have never outgrown that information and continue to look for truth in these misleading constructs.

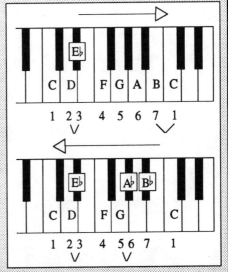

Some composers have preferred to retain the step-and-a-half melodic interval. Sometimes this is done for harmonic reasons—for example, arpeggiating a chord that contains this interval. (On the keyboard it sounds like a minor third.) At other times, it might be retained to express an ethnic melodic style— for example, traditional Slavic or Israeli music. Such styles are exotic from the point of view of traditional Western music; however, European and American composers have occasionally incorporated this element specifically for that effect.

Use the chart "Minor Mode - Diatonic" (p. 78) to practice appropriate melodic adjustments to scale steps 6 and 7 in the context of different primary chords. Remember, the leading tone is needed only when dominant harmony prevails. Therefore, melodic fragments occurring within tonic and subdominant harmonies use the subtonic pitch instead. Notice that the appropriate designations of scale steps 6 and 7 are shown on this chart within each harmonic function. Be sure to drill melodic fragments in both directions in all three harmonic contexts.

Also, note how these melodic adjustments in the minor mode affect the secondary triads. In general, the same scale steps that are modified in a primary chord are the same ones that are modified in its secondary partner. Both versions of the III chord are shown with dotted brackets. The difference, of course, has to do with whether the chord is performing a tonic or dominant harmonic function.

# 14

# Other Melodic Systems

Melodic traditions are as numerous as the cultures of the world. To describe a significant number of them would be to expand this book far beyond its intended purpose. Instead, we will look at those few most likely to appear in the international mainstream of world music.

## Melody in Blues and Jazz

The art of jazz blossomed from the nourishment of two traditions—folk blues and functional harmony. From the former, jazz inherited its blue-note tuning; from the latter came its chordal underpinnings. Much of early jazz was simply a mattter of creating free improvisation around a popular melody set to a "swing" rhythm (described later). However, one chordal pattern became not only the harmonic matrix for much early jazz but has been used throughout the twentieth century in big-band tunes, rhythm and blues favorites, hot jazz, cool jazz and rock-and-roll classics. This chord pattern, called the **twelve-bar blues**, has provided the harmonic structure for melody composed by such diverse artists as Pinetop Smith (the "inventor" of *Boogie Woogie*), Woody Herman (whose big-band hits included W*oodchopper's Ball*) and Bill Haley & His Comets (with the classic *Rock Around The Clock*). Whenever musicians get together to "jam" (improvise), chances are that the twelve-bar-blues chord pattern will appear. Each chord symbol here lasts for one measure (usually four beats).

I I I I, IV IV I I, V V(or IV) I I

14-1

As you can see, the harmonies used in this standard pattern are basically the three principle chords of the major mode. However, minor-mode elements, more correctly "blue" elements, commonly appear in melodic lines performed over these major chords. When more choruses are to follow, appropriate chords are added in the last bar to create a "turnaround," a punctuation-like ending formula that leads back to the tonic chord which marks the beginning of the next chorus.

The twelve-bar-blues chorus normally breaks down into three parts (indicated by commas in the above graphic). When a lyric is set to this chord pattern, it usually consists of two rhyming phrases, the first of which is repeated during the middle four-bar phrase, creating a three-part (a-a-b) poetic form.

> You ain't nothin' but a Hound Dog, cryin' all the time.
> You ain't nothin' but a Hound Dog, cryin' all the time.
> Well, you ain't never caught a rabbit and you ain't no friend of mine.

Earlier, we noted that folk-blues melodies usually are performed over an unchanging tonic chord, employing a blue seventh below the high tonic pitch and usually a blue third in the lower half of the scale. A blue third is often used melodically, even when the accompanying tonic chord contains a major third. The choice of which third to use somewhat depends on melodic direction. The blue third is preferred when the melody descends to tonic, with or without a passing tone on scale step two. The major third is preferred when the melody goes up to the dominant pitch, with or without a passing tone on scale step four.

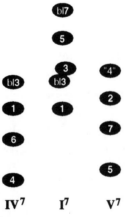

Any or all of the three chords in the twelve-bar-blues style can contain the seventh partial, or seventh interval (coincidentally the same number), and in all three cases any "tritone tendency" is usually ignored. Chord sevenths are commonly left hanging and unresolved. Even the dominant chord, with its leading tone shining for all to hear, often goes directly to the subdominant chord instead of to tonic. It would seem that the seventh in these chords is simply adding its "blue" flavor to the music and makes no promises regarding its melodic direction.

The blue third step described above in tonic harmony also appears in the subdominant chord as a chord seventh. Composers and improvisors delight in repeating melodic figures containing this characteristic while the harmony changes to and from tonic and subdominant. After eight bars of "blue third," both performer and listener are ready for the change demanded by the arrival of the dominant chord.

To the pitches contained in the blue chords described above, jazz, blues and pop musicians commonly add many chromatic inflections. These "bent" pitches cannot be duplicated on a keyboard nor can they be accurately written on paper. It is probably true that no musical tradition can be learned solely by reading a book, but that is especially true of jazz and blues. The vocabulary of this rich heritage can only be learned by listening. The expressive nuances are far too subtle to describe in words, particularly by the few words we have space for here.

**ear-training drill**

"The Blues" chart on the following page contains harmonic structures for two American traditions—simple folk blues and the more sophisticated twelve-bar blues. Actually, the twelve-bar-blues chart can be used for drill on any pattern of primary chords, no matter the number of measures. As before, listen to audible fundamental pitches (played or sung) to help your ear focus on the shifting harmonies, giving particular attention to the tuning of scale step 3 as a blue interval (6:7). Just like the other more conventional thirds, the "blue" third can be perceived as a locked-in consonance. If you have difficulty hearing it, tune scale step 3 as a seventh to the subdominant fundamental, then hold that tuning as you change the sounding root to tonic.

Hearing the blue seventh over the tonic root is essential to learning blues style. The ratio is the same as in the dominant seventh chord, but it has a different "flavor" in this context. Notice how large the distance seems between the well-tuned blue seventh and the tonic above it. It is much larger than a "normal" whole-step second. Experienced blues singers sometimes sing the blue seventh so low it almost sounds like scale step 6.

Speaking of scale step 6, it appears here as a chord tone in the tonic chord. The tonic chord in jazz often includes the "added sixth" pitch, which brings a mild and interesting dissonance to this harmony.

As the chart shows, chromatic appoggiaturas are a vital part of the blues style. In general, chromatic neighbors tune very closely to the pitch to which they resolve. For example, the pitch of ♯5 (leaning upward toward scale step 6) is considerably higher than ♭6 (leaning downward toward scale step 5) even though both pitches would be played with the same black digital on a keyboard. (Incidentally, this tendency of chromatic embellishments to tune toward their destination pitches is not limited to jazz and blues, but is commonly heard in most music having chromatic elements.)

# THE BLUES

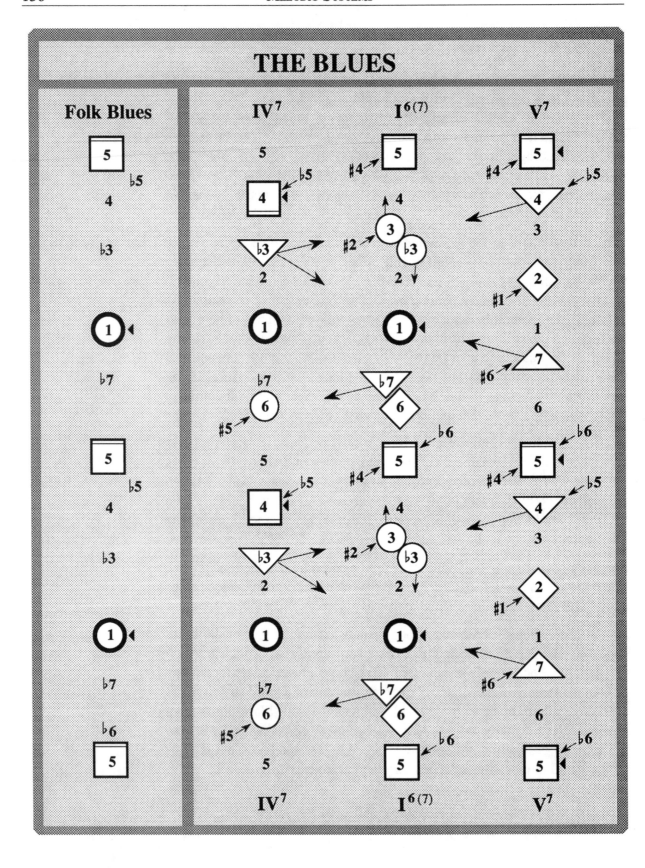

# Modal Melody

During the early Middle Ages, harmonic consideration was far less important in selecting melodic pitches than is melodic construction in major/minor music. Therefore, the earlier discussion regarding harmonic influence on melodic structure does not apply here. Gregorian chant, the principle body of medieval song, floated through virtual time in linear arches of melody with little regard for chordal underpinnings.

**medieval melody**

14-2

Nevertheless, the medieval composer's awareness of the importance of the perfect fifth, or 2:3 ratio, is evident in the descriptive "rules" set out by that era's music theorists. The range of each mode was considered to be one octave. When the tonic pitch was at the bottom (and top) of this one-octave range, the pitch a fifth higher than tonic was designated as "dominant." When the tonic was near the center of this one-octave range, that mode carried the prefix "hypo-" (as in hypodorian). The "dominant" pitch in those modes was usually a major or minor third above tonic, and sometimes a fourth or sixth above. Clearly, this concept of "dominant" was not the same as it is in major/minor music, but rather a kind of secondary "tonal center" pitch.

Popular street music in medieval Europe was a mix of church modes and pentatonic elements. It generally contained more melodic skips than traditional church music.

14-3

During the seventeenth and eighteenth centuries, European music was wholly captured by the dynamic energy of the major/minor system. The classicism of Mozart, Haydn and early Beethoven brought this style to perhaps its highest pinnacle. However, it was the transformed "romantic" Beethoven of the early nineteenth century who was among the first to break tradition in regard to mode. His String Quartet in A minor, opus 132, included music in the lydian mode.

**modes in classical melody**

Others followed, some reflecting earlier times, some expressing nationalistic folk traditions, and others simply reacting against classical tradition. Chopin, Tchaikovsky, and later, Debussy, frequently incorporated modal elements in their compositions.

Since traditional English folk music is quite modal, it is hardly surprising that twentieth century English composers frequently employed modes. This excerpt is from Gustav Holst's *The Planets*.

14-4

Speaking of the English, the influence of the Beatles was enormous in regard to introducing modal elements, as well as other exotic styles, into American popular music. The Liverpool quartet's centuries-old sounds breathed freshness into a pop culture suffocating in a three-chord compositional style.

**modes in popular melody**

14-5

To further facilitate the move toward modal harmonies, pop guitarists found it convenient to move the finger configuration a few frets from tonic to find the subtonic chord. Functional harmonies of early "rock and roll" and "rhythm and blues" gradually gave way to the modal non-functional chord progressions in the "hard rock" and "heavy metal" sounds of the 1980s. The melodies in these styles are a mixture of modal and blues scales.

**modes in jazz**

14-6

As the chord-based bebop styles of the 1950s and '60s began to wear thin, some jazz musicians turned to the modes to inspire fresh-sounding melodic improvisation. Modal scale patterns were used to achieve sounds that were considered "cutting edge."

## "Formula" as a Basis for Melodic Tradition

Some musical cultures, ancient and modern, are based on a "vocabulary" of melodic elements and styles rather than abstract configurations of scales. Instead of fostering melodic creativity, as in most Western cultures, these formula-based systems require performers to employ traditional melodic patterns.

The music of India is an important example of this kind of tradition. Its collection of *ragas* (pitch formulas) and *talea* (rhythmic formulas) form the basis for musical performances. Other Eastern and Middle Eastern systems that are based on melodic formulas include the ancient Greeks *nomos*, the Byzantine and Armenian *echoi*, the Syrian *risqolo*, the Javanese *patet*, the Arabian *maqam*, and the Russian *popievki* .

Melodies in these cultures are seldom written in notation for others to use to recreate them, as in Western musical culture. Each performance is, in that sense, a creation of the moment—similar to American jazz but without free improvisation. Even the formulas are not written, but are handed down aurally from teacher to pupil.

Since harmony, in the usual sense, is not a part of these systems, expressive subtleties often depend on melodic pitch deviations rather than chordal variety. Therefore, many of these melodic traditions employ pitches that appear to be "in the cracks." Musicologists commonly refer to these deviations from acoustic simplicity as "quarter tones," a term clearly based on keyboard concepts. Since the modern keyboard is a recent development which employs an artificial system of tuning, it seems quite inappropriate to describe these pitch deviations in such terms.

It would seem more accurate to consider pitches that sound "bent" to Western ears, and perhaps to Eastern ears as well, as simply expressive distortions of acoustically stable pitches. In such cases, it is the distortion (a relational concept) that is important, not the absolute pitch itself. Distortion is an important element in many art forms, most of which do not require an artificial concept by which to capture deviations as independent "things." Of course, if a recognizable genre of distortion is repeated sufficiently, it certainly could rise to the level of "concept," regardless whether it is named. Such a concept would, of course, be a *relational* rather than an absolute one.

Empirical evidence regarding human perception of pitch relations strongly suggests that *any* accurate melodic conception would be based on acoustical perception. The specific ways in which deviant melodic formulas in various cultures are related to acoustical principles is beyond the scope of this book.

## Melody in Equal-Division Scales

Melody in Schoenberg's twelve-tone style is often constructed of wide leaps between distant pitches, distant in both intervalic and harmonic relationships. This sort of melody is more easily performed instrumentally than vocally, and appears plentifully in chamber music, orchestral pieces and piano music of the 1930s, '40s, and '50s. These compositions tend to be rather short, perhaps thankfully so, in that extended excursions into tonal "nongravity" could, for some listeners, result in a bit of musical vertigo.

14-7

One of Schoenberg's disciples, Alban Berg, employed the twelve-tone compositional system; however, his tone rows contain fairly consonant intervals. As a result, his melodies are palatable to a wide audience of listeners. His violin concerto and his opera *Wozzeck* have become "classics" and are frequently programmed today.

Arnold Schoenberg's attempt to overthrow tonal music was not the first effort in that direction. Indeed, it may have been Schoenberg's observation of the trend toward atonality among certain nineteenth century composers that prompted his thinking. For example, Debussy, whose music predates Schoenberg's by only a few years, frequently included melodic passages based on the **whole-tone scale**, which consists entirely of whole steps, eliminating the characteristic half steps that define a mode and therefore establish tonality. Debussy also continued and expanded upon Wagner's practice of using the **chromatic scale**, consisting entirely of half steps, which also tends to blur tonality.

14-8

Melodic elements in whole-tone and chromatic patterns are not conducive to perceiving small-number ratios, making accurate vocal performance quite difficult. In short passages, one can usually anchor to harmonically stable pitches, but in extended passages in which pitches are related only by half or whole "steps" is doomed to some degree of inaccuracy, even for experi-

## Melody: A Series of Steps and Skips?

Since nature has kindly provided us with an observable means of melodic perception, it makes no sense to ignore it. Yet many do. Music educators seem to view melody as a "chain" of intervals (steps and skips). Propagating this notion encourages students to ignore the harmonic structure on which a melody might be based. It also fosters a music reading technique that will automatically fail upon making a single error in "distance," thereby breaking the "chain."

The emphasis on reading music "by interval" is probably related to the importance placed on atonality in the early-to-middle decades of the twentieth century. Many established and influential music educators were educated during this "atonal period." Perhaps it was believed that focusing on harmony as the basis for melody would prevent music students from developing an ability to read music having no tonal center. Although the influence of atonal music on current practice has diminished, any effect it may have had on music teaching has not.

It is entirely possible for a singer who does not have a sense of absolute pitch to perform atonal music using a sound vocabulary developed from experience with tonal music. By using the "bag of tricks" learned in a tonal context, an experienced singer can quickly move his or her sense of tonal center to interpret and perform a series of seemingly unrelated pitches.

It seems doubtful that we can conceive intervals as abstract "distances." Experience indicates that we tend to imagine a "minor third," for example, in one harmonic context or another—as the third and fifth of a major tonic triad, or as the root and third of a tonic minor triad, or perhaps "down from tonic" with a subdominant flavor, or maybe with a "dominant-seventh" flavor or even as a "blue" third. While the "real truth" awaits research, it seems prudent to base ear training on something we already know—that composers in almost all traditions (other than those using artificial scales) base melody on harmonic principles and/or structures.

enced vocalists. This is understandable, as performing a melodic passage based solely on synthetic equal-divisions of the octave is frequently executed by guessing, sometimes even by singers having some innate pitch recognition.

From a listener's standpoint, music based on equal divisions of the octave can be interesting and often fascinating, if for no other reason than to create mystery and unrest. The Javanese equidistant pentatonic scale (mentioned earlier), and other synthetic scales in various numbers of equally-spaced pitches offer an unlimited source of melodic and harmonic materials. The American composer Harry Partch has employed this kind of scale building in unique ways, creating scales with as many as forty three pitches. Clearly, music employing such scales is better performed through mechanical means, such as a keyboard or other instrument having fixed pitches.

There have been a few professional vocal ensembles that have specialized in atonal vocal music. The extent to which singers in such groups tune their unaccompanied pitches acoustically would be an interesting thing to know. Seldom do they all have "pitch recognition." That being the case, do they concentrate solely on linear relationship of pitches? To what extent do they tune to the harmonic relationship of simultaneous pitches? Perhaps these questions will be researched someday.

## Melody in Electronic and Aleatory music

The application of traditional concepts of melody begins to fade when applied to electronic and aleatory music. Not only is harmony seldom a combination of pitches in small-number relationships, but melody is rarely a series of pitches selected from a scale. Instead, "harmony" is more likely to be perceived as "timbre," and "melody" can be described mostly in terms of its **contour** (general shape), **tessitura** (generally high in pitch or generally low in pitch) and **range** (distance from lowest pitch to highest pitch). The classic example of such melody (although not electronic) is Schoenberg's 1912 song cycle for solo voice and five instruments, *Pierrot lunaire*.

## Melody Wrap-up

Practical experience plus our knowledge of the physical nature of sound indicates that melodic pitch relations, like harmonic pitch relations, are more easily perceived and conceived when elements are related in consonant small-number ratios. This principle applies no matter what the musical style or tradition. That one tradition is melodically more complex than another does not invalidate this fact, rather it verifies it, since complexities themselves would be perceived in contrast to simplicity.

Just as the idea of what constitutes "consonance" changes from age to age, the pitch on which to conclude a melodic journey has changed from era to era. For many centuries, the only acceptable concluding pitch was the tonic. In the nineteenth century, romantic composers often found it effective to leave the listener "up in the air" on the dominant pitch (over tonic harmony) or "mellowed" by a concluding major or minor third step. In the twentieth century, melodies end on just about any scale step, and jazz performers often delight in concluding on the most "far out" chromatic pitches, stretching the melodic imaginations of their listeners.

When using the term *melody*, one should be careful to determine which of two meanings is intended. On one hand, the word is commonly used to mean "the line of pitches most prominent to the ear." On the other, the same word frequently means "pitches in a series," applying to any melodic activity, regardless whether it is compositionally prominent.

# III

# Musical Time

While most visual arts communicate in motionless space, musical artistry requires the flow of time for its expression. A listener is obliged to remember the early events in a composition in order to discover their full meaning as a work unfolds. Long-term memory chronicles the **form** of a piece, storing thematic elements to be recognized later with increased significance. Short-term memory captures the pulsation of repetitive events. It is the latter that we refer to as **rhythm**.

Before we talk about what rhythm is, we might clarify what it is not. In case you thought it might, we should point out that rhythm has nothing to do with clock time. We don't measure rhythmic events in terms of seconds and minutes, largely because humans don't possess an innate or accurate sense of clock time. "I'll be back in ten minutes" is never understood to mean "exactly ten minutes and not a second earlier or later." Returning in seven or eight minutes is considered to be within the concept, but returning in one or two might evoke, "Did you forget something?" Fifteen minutes is deemed "acceptably late," but after eighteen or more one might inquire, "What kept you?" In any case, returning in *exactly* ten minutes is likely impossible without referring to a time piece.

Our concept of a few seconds is not any more accurate than our concept of a few minutes. Students, when asked to clap ten seconds after a given signal, invariably scatter their responses over a window of three or four seconds. Clearly, if we depended on our sense of clock time for organizing the "time" of music, **ensemble** (group) performances would be disastrous. Perception of musical temporal patterns would require incredibly complex mathematical computations. Thank goodness, nature has provided another means of performing and listening to music. In a sense, it is similar to the way we perceive pitch relations. As noted earlier, we can't (and needn't) accurately perceive the *distance* between pitches; instead, we listen for relational perceptions based on simple ratios of regularly-repeated vibrations. Temporal perception in music also has to do with repeated events, and here, too, measuring the distance between repetitions is not of primary importance. It is the perception of *repetition* itself between a series of events that provides the basis for perception of rhythm in music; again, a relational matter.

But let's not get ahead of our practice of describing each concept in its simplest terms and logical relation to other concepts. We need to clarify some of the terms used in the preceding paragraphs.

# 15

# Rhythm

One dictionary defines rhythm as "movement with a regular repetition of a beat, accent, rise and fall, or the like." Another says it is "movement characterized by regular recurrence of beat, accent, etc." These authorities seem to agree that rhythm has to do with "movement" and the regular recurrence of events. The term *regular* seems fairly straightforward, in contrast to *irregular*, and is easily understood in regard to temporal flow. The idea of "movement," on the other hand, has to do with both time and space, as a *relational* concept in which an object changes its location during a period of time. So, rhythm has to do with time. But what does rhythm have to do with space?

A third definition, this from a music dictionary, suggests that rhythm is "the whole feeling of movement in music, with a strong implication of both regularity and differentiation." This article goes on to describe two kinds of rhythm: "isometric," in which "every time value is a multiple (or fraction) of a beat, and the measures are equal and are normally accented on the first beat.," and "multimetric," in which "every time value is a multiple (or fraction) of a beat, but there is no regularly recurrent accent, owing to free alternation of different measures." Is this authority saying that sometimes regularity is *not* an essential characteristic of rhythm?

Now let's consult a few music textbooks for their definitions of *rhythm*. One uses the simple phrase "organization of time in music." This is quite attractive. It possesses a simple elegance. But, what about the regularity question?

Another textbook says that "rhythm is a general term used to refer to the time aspect of music, as contrasted with the pitch aspect." This definition agrees with the previous one in pointing out that rhythm is a temporal matter, but it also says nothing about recurrence. Could the dictionary definitions above be wrong?

Both textbook definitions limit the concept of rhythm to music. Neither includes rhythm in other media. Aren't a dancer's movements rhythmic? What about flashing lights, assembly-line events, jumping rope and hundreds of other repetitive experiences? Does the term *rhythm* have only to do with music, making any other use of the word metaphoric?

The second textbook definition explicitly points out that rhythm has nothing to do with pitch. Can this be true? Perhaps a book devoted to rhythm can provide an answer:

> To study rhythm is to study all of music. Rhythm both organizes, and is itself organized by, all the elements which create and shape musical processes.... To experience rhythm is to group separate sounds into structured patterns. Such grouping is the result of the interaction among the various aspects of the materials of music: pitch, intensity, timbre, texture, and harmony—as well as duration. (*The Rhythmic Structure Of Music*, Cooper and Meyer, 1960, p. 1)

This clearly disagrees with the phrase "as opposed to pitch" used in the second textbook definition. It seems to include just about everything in music, and in fact, sounds very similar to the definition of "music" that we worked out near the beginning of this book. So, what about repetition? Does the concept "grouping" relate to "regular repetition"? How about "structured patterns"? Does that imply "regular repetition"?

Perhaps we should turn to philosophy for some light on the subject. Philosophers specialize in careful thinking and use words with precise meanings. Suzanne Langer, a modern idealist, talks about "regular repetition" in rhythm:

> The essence of rhythm is the preparation of a new event by the ending of a previous one. A person who moves rhythmically need not repeat a single motion exactly. His movements, however, must be complete gestures, so that one can sense a beginning, intent, and consummation, and see in the last stage of one the condition and indeed the rise of another. Rhythm is the setting-up of new tensions by the resolution of former ones. They need not be of equal duration at all; but the situation that begets the new crisis must be inherent in the denouement of its forerunner. (*Feeling And Form*, 1953, p. 127.)

Langer clearly suggests that rhythm has to do with the repetition of "events," implying a temporal mode of perception. And not only are events involved, but their approach and fade-out as well. The idea of "tension" and "resolution" in rhythm is interesting.

The recurrence of events need not be exact, Langer says. Would this freedom apply both to the time intervals between repetitions and also to the perceptual similarity of the events? ("Similarity," of course, is the quality that suggests the events are participating in a series.) In other words, does "need not be exact" refer to spacing, or event matching, or both?

John Dewey, a pragmatic philosopher who lived in the early twentieth century, believed that the concept of rhythm applies to life experience in general:

> Attainment of a period of equilibrium is at the same time the initiation of a new relation to the environment, one that brings with it potency of new adjustments to be made through struggle. The time of consummation is also one of beginning anew. (*Art As Experience*, 1934, p. 17.)

Dewey seems to agree with Langer that one event, "resolution" or "equilibrium," sets up the quest for the next state of equilibrium and that these events are separated by "tensions" or "struggle." Both philosophers view music, indeed all art, as a reflection of life experiences. Langer says that art is a "symbol" of emotional life. Dewey says that art reflects the dynamic struggles of life experience.

These philosophical descriptions clearly support the idea that repetition is an essential part of rhythm. They also suggest that such phrases as "the temporal aspect of music" are both too vague and too specific. "Temporal" does not connote perceptual repetition, and "music" is not the only thing in life that has rhythm. And what about "pitches," "beats," "accents" and other concepts used in the definitions above? What do these have to do with rhythm?

Both Latin and Greek contain the word *rhythmos*, meaning "to flow." Could this concept be helpful in finding a practical and precise meaning for our modern use of the word?

Perhaps we can eliminate some confusion by looking at a few everyday experiences containing repetitive events. The alternation of day and night is certainly repetitive and quite regular, allowing for seasonal variations. Is this rhythmic? It seems to fit Langer's and Dewey's requirement of related repetition, but there really isn't much "struggle" involved, except perhaps in getting out of bed in the morning. Also, which one is the "event" —day or night, either or both? In any case, should a series of rhythmic events be perceptually frequent enough to create some sort of cohesive and dynamic feeling? What do we mean when we say we are "feeling the rhythm"? The night/day experience doesn't provide much sense of flow, particularly not a flow that is "felt."

Let's try again. How about the rhythm of eating meals? The unrest of hunger drives one to find gastronomic satisfaction and then the cycle begins again. This seems to fit the philosophers' parameters fairly well; at least there is some personal urgency involved in this process. The matter of regularity of these events, of course, will vary, depending on one's personal discipline and appetite. But this example, too, lacks perceptual frequency. We may "feel" the hunger, but the intervals between events are too far apart to create any feeling about pattern or organization in the experience. They don't *flow*.

Speaking of flow, what about waves at the seashore? This experience seems to satisfy the philosophers' requirement of anticipation, culmination, and subsidence; and each wave seems to create the expectation of the next. We can usually make some feeling-based judgment of the experience, like "peaceful," "exhilarating" or "terrifying." The events are sufficiently close together to perceive an organizational pattern, for example, anticipation of the next "big" wave. The term *rhythm* seems to fit this experience quite well. Waves *do* seem to flow.

Streams also flow but usually not because of waves. Before we cast our definition, let's consider a hypothetical experience. Imagine standing beside a stream in which there are no visible ripples or floating objects. You might assume the water is moving simply from your knowledge of streams in general, but there is no visual verification of it.

Then you notice a twig coming down the stream, which provides a visual impression of motion in the stream. This may constitute "movement," and perhaps "flow," but is it rhythm? Probably not. Although this single event contains anticipation, consumation, and subsidence, it doesn't provide the repetitive series that seems essential for rhythm to exist.

Suppose, now, that another twig appears, followed a few yards behind by another twig, then another, and another, all having some space in between. Is this rhythm? Probably so. The flow of twigs continues, some larger than others, creating another layer of meaning in the rhythmic perception. Then some twigs appear in closer proximity, and by that contrast they earn your attention. You begin to notice other twigs in pairs, as well as other interesting configurations. The experience continues to draw you into its flow of repetitive patterns. Is this rhythm? It would seem so.

As you watch, the number of twigs begins to increase greatly, until they begin to merge into floating islands of matted twigs. The individual twigs are no longer the center of your attention, so the "events" are now islands. Your "feeling" for the experience focuses on the frequency and size of the islands. Is this still rhythm? As long as "events" continue to flow in some perceptual frequency, there is rhythm.

Eventually, the stream is jammed with twigs. There are no more islands, only one continuous mass of tangled twigs. The whole thing is moving, but there are no longer any "events." Is this rhythm? Probably not.

The word "flow," or even the phrase "sense of flow," in itself doesn't define rhythm, so simply borrowing the ancient definition doesn't complete the job. "Movement" is troublesome, in that it is not a purely temporal concept. The concept "repetition" by itself also falls short when events are so far apart that they don't evoke a single dynamic relational perception. The concept "regular" does not apply if one takes it to mean "occurring in *equal* intervals of time." Terms such as *beat*, *accent*, *pitch*, *intensity*, *timbre*, *texture*, and *harmony* may affect musical rhythm, but it appears that rhythm is present in media other than music. Therefore, it would seem wise to first define the concept in a universal sense, and *then* make application to music, perhaps using some of the terms listed above.

In consideration of the preceding discussion, this definition of **rhythm** may be useful: "the sense of temporal flow, created by repeated events within a field of dynamic perception." This allows application to temporal media other than music—dance, for example. It restricts the concept to immediate sensory experience and excludes abstract constructs, such as "rhythm" of the planets. It favors temporal media, where the term seems most at home, over spacial media. Applying this definition of rhythm to painting and architecture, then, would be using it metaphorically, except when referring to the eye's movements among and across static elements.

**a working definition**

In the preceding discussion, we left the business of *regular* recurrence unfinished. We observed that it wasn't essential to the concept of rhythm, but regularity clearly plays a large part in the temporal organization of music. In fact, music without it is rarer than music with it. So, we need to know how regularity fits into the overall picture.

**regularity?**

Anything this important surely deserves its own terms, and, as a matter of fact, we have some. The word **pulse** is shared by music and medicine, and in both it means roughly the same thing: "a regularly recurrent series of events." Rhythm, as we know, may or may not be regularly recurrent, therefore it is a *different* concept from "pulse." Combining the two concepts gives us two kinds of rhythms: those having pulse and those not having pulse. Logically, then, all pulses are rhythmic, but not all rhythms have pulse. Incidentally, the word **beat** usually means the same thing as *pulse*. The two terms are used interchangeably.

*Pulse* is sometimes confused with another term, *meter* (which we will discuss shortly), and both of these are often confused with *rhythm*. For example, the piano, bass, guitar and drums in a jazz ensemble are traditionally referred to as the "rhythm section" when their true function suggests that they be called the "pulse section," or perhaps the "meter section." You see, most of the interesting *rhythms* in a traditional jazz ensemble are supplied by the wind instruments. We noticed earlier that even authorities who write dictionaries and textbooks seem unsure of the difference. Let's see if we can find some conceptual logic in this regard.

The words "regularly recurrent" are vital to our definition of *pulse*. If temporal events in a series are not perceived as equally spaced, there is no pulse series. For example, reading prose aloud is not likely to create a pulse series because the time intervals between the events (syllables, accents, etc.) are not symmetrical and predictable. Such reading may contain some rhythmic elements (a sense of flow, for example) but usually not a pulse. On the other hand, the reading of poetry, particularly modern "rap," is usually performed with a feeling of pulse.

One might think that **rubato**, the practice of slightly slowing or hurrying the pulse, as one would do in a very expressive passage of Romantic style music, would argue against including "regularity" in our definition. Actually, it proves the point. *Rubato* is a combination of *two* concepts: "regularity of beats" and "regularity in the rate of slowing or hurrying." If rubato is jerky or sudden, the flow is destroyed. Again, if there is no perceptual regularity, there is no pulse, or beat.

The word "series" is important to our definition because a single event doesn't create flow, as we noted in our discussion of rhythm. Also, it takes at least two events to know what the time interval is between pulses. The same students who couldn't clap together after ten seconds of silence had no problem coordinating a "third clap" when two audible claps pre-established a time interval (provided the time interval was not too short or too long). Once established, time intervals are predictable and a series can be maintained with minimal thought or effort. With a little practice, a pulse series can be placed on "automatic," leaving conscious attention free to attend to more interesting aspects of the music.

The word "events" was selected instead of "sounds", "clicks," "taps" or other "musical" terms because pulse, like all rhythm, can also be perceived in media other than sound (light flashes, bouncing balls, back scratching, arm swinging, etc.), or simply imagined. Our clapping students had no trouble coordinating their response after a silent count of ten when only the first two or three audible pulses were provided. Clearly, they were "feeling" the pulse, since there was no audible or visual representation of it during the silent counts. "Events," then, seems the best word to include in our definition because it doesn't specify a perceptual source.

It appears that the essence of pulse is not so much "out there" as it is "in here." As with any perception based on concept, a concept must pre-exist in order to focus perception on the right thing. In this case, one must have already developed a sense of pulse in order to recognize and "feel" it in a musical situation. If this is true, where does the sense of pulse come from in the first place?

In the nineteen twenties and thirties, music psychologists conducted experiments to discover the nature of this sense of pulse. (They called it a sense of *rhythm*, but it was, in fact, *pulse* by our definition.) Their experiments focused on heartbeats, brain waves, and other "regularly recurrent" phenomena. They discovered that blood-flow pulse, contrary to popular belief (both then and now), has nothing to do with musical pulse. Neither do brain waves, they found out. What *does* seem to relate to developing of a sense of musical pulse is kinesthetic movement, or muscle movement. Apparently, when we are learning to walk, we are also learning to "feel the beat."

**kinesthetic pulse**

Just a note on language before we proceed. Notice that just one step is not really walking, just as one "pulse" does not create a series. We use two different words to refer to the distinct concepts "step" and "walk" and only one word—"pulse"—to refer to both a single event and to a series of events. Applying the word *pulse* to a single event is only appropriate when referring to one pulse in a particular location, for example "on the strong beat of a measure." A single "pulse" by itself, without context, is not a pulse at all. Okay, let's continue.

Evidently, the act of moving one foot in front of the other in a regularly spaced time interval is conceptualized so generically that the information can be used for purposes other than walking. The musical terms we use to indicate **tempo**, or speed of beats, offer practical support for this view. The Italian word "moderato" indicates a normal walking speed, and all the other terms, indicating faster and slower tempos, are understood relative to this one.

In perceiving a pulse in music, it is the *regularity* that is perceived, not just the sounds themselves. A series of sound events is deemed to "contain" a pulse by the listener, who determines that the time interval between related events is "regular." Remember, we don't *hear* a pulse series, we *feel* it. In other words, if a series of sounds appears to be regularly recurrent, it can be perceived as "pulse." If a series of sounds fails to evoke such a perception, no pulse is present for that listener.

If that seems unclear, try this experiment. Without moving a muscle, imagine that you are walking. That image *is* the human phenomenon we call a "sense of pulse." When you hear music, you use that imagined feeling of "walking," or other kinesthetic experience, to "measure" the regularity of musical events. If a series of events in the music seems to evoke that feeling, you are perceiving pulse in the music. There is no guarantee, however, that your perceived pulse is the same one the composer had in mind.

This view is supported by the observation that individuals who have never walked seldom have a highly precise sense of rhythmic pulse. Rhythmic sensitivity for such performers is more likely a sense of comparative durations than metric proportions, somewhat like pitch intervals perceived as "distances" instead of as harmonic ratios.

In dance music, the pulse the composer wants the listener to respond to is unmistakably displayed in the music. On the other hand, not all music based on pulse provides a prominent aural suggestion of a pulse series. Nevertheless, sensitive listeners are often able to perceive a sense of pulse from the overall configuration of the various events they hear. See if you can feel a pulse expressed in these musical excerpts. Alternate being persistent with your selected pulse and being sensitive to the events in the music.

15-1

Basically, that is how pulse operates in music. As a performer organizes the elements in a pulse-based piece, his or her own sense of pulse orders the events. An experienced listener instinctively searches for pulse clues in the combination of sounds, using the sense of pulse by which to conduct the search. Any two or more recurrent events can evoke a pulse concept in the listener. It may even be the "wrong" one from the composer's point of view, nevertheless the listener can maintain it as long as he or she likes. It is a personal choice. If that pulse proves unsuccessful in making rhythmic sense of the music, the listener probably will abandon it in favor of another. If the listener "discovers" the one the composer had in mind, the music will be heard as per the composer's "intent." That doesn't necessarily make the listener "right" in any cosmic sense. One is free to interpret music in any way that seems satisfying. Remember, the sense of pulse is in people, not in sounds.

# 16

# Meter

A single pulse series by itself is a simple thing—soon boring, and eventually annoying.

(The graphic illustrations in this section are a spacial representation of temporal relationships. To translate these graphics, move a pointer slowly from left to right and feel the "event" as you pass over each vertical line.)

People tend to "do something with" the stimulus of a regular unchanging pulse, such as the incessant drip of a leaky faucet, the nerve-wracking pounding of a pile driver, the sleep-disturbing ticking of a wind-up clock. It is perfectly human to defend one's sanity by imagining an accentuation of every second pulse to make the sound more interesting and/or tolerable. Have you done this? Try it now, if you haven't.    16-1

Notice that adding your accentuation actually creates a *new* pulse series, one half the speed of the series of sounds. Also, note that the new pulse series is purely subjective, since there is no perception of anything in the actual sound to evoke it.

Observe that you don't have to count beats to experience a back-forth-back-forth duple pattern. Even though you could have focused on the quantitative and counted "one, two, one, two, etc." you find that the qualitative is perfectly adequate to the task.

There are plenty of examples of duple-pattern pulses in everyday life. Windshield wipers, mechanical clocks, and squeaky porch swings all evoke a duple feeling. In all of these, one *feels* the "two-ness" without really counting it. Examples of the qualitative concept of "two-ness" can be found in other modes of experience as well: spacial (up-down, in-out, left-right), moral (right-wrong), practical (good-bad), communication (yes-no), etc.

Scientists tell us that there are biological examples of "duple patterns" in the form of "digital" signals such as neuron firings, chemotaxis, phototaxis and vision (such as in insects' light/dark sensing). We may even be programmed to "sense" on/off signals and have a "natural" tendency to detect things "digitally"—or in terms of duple patterns. In any case, the kinesthetic experience of muscle movement—particularly walking—provides plenty of support for the notion that "two-ness" is a basic metric concept.

16-2  Let's see how all of this works in music. You may have noticed that music based on pulse frequently offers a choice of pulses by which to organize listening. How many different pulse series can you find in "Yankee Doodle"?

Most listeners will easily feel the pulse series that occurs on "Yank," "doo," "went," "town," etc., probably because it is close to walking speed. Did you also feel the one that occurs on every syllable?—"Yank," "kee," "doo," "dle," etc. How about the pulse series on "Yank," "went," "ride," etc.? Were all of these pulse series included in the composer's sense of rhythmic flow? Probably so (although it may not have been consciously recognized). How does a composer do that? Can anyone do that? Yes, anyone can, provided he or she has developed the kinesthetic concept of "walking."

**duple meter**

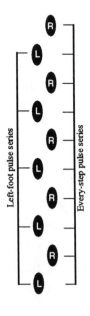

Left-foot pulse series

Every-step pulse series

It is the *feeling* of walking that supplies the raw material for the concept of musical **meter**, "the combination of pulse series in small-number ratios." (Sound familiar?) Walking simulates pulse in that *every* step (both left and right) is a similar event in a series, somewhat like the sound source in the audio illustration above. Walking also simulates meter in that the left foot takes half the number of steps that both feet take, something like the subjective pulse you supplied in that same illustration. This creates a ratio of 1:2. By walking, we teach ourselves to feel the combination of two related pulse series: one series focusing on every step, and one series focusing only on left-foot (or right-foot) steps. This is probably one of the important reasons we tend to supply a subjective accent on every second event when we hear a single "boring" pulse series.

Perhaps a caution here might be helpful to some readers. If you think of meter and accent as more or less the same thing, you should consider re-examining your concept. This popular notion can get in the way of your understanding the discussion that follows.

Again, counting is not required to feel this qualitative flow (although you may *choose* to count). Just as you can learn to recognize the harmonic relationship of "same name" octaves by a *quality* (due to vibrational ratios of 1:2, 1:4, 2:4, etc.), you can learn to recognize the perceivable quality of a duple ratio of pulses. As with vibrational ratios in octaves, pulse ratios of 1:2, 1:4, 2:4, etc., are simply different ways of expressing the same thing. All these reduce to and have the feeling of 1:2. Notice that it doesn't really matter which pulse series you choose in *Yankee Doodle*. The feeling is twice as fast as another pulse, or twice as slow. A duple-pulse-ratio feeling is a duple-pulse-ratio feeling, regardless of speed.

As you probably know, pulse ratios also work in triple patterns. The triple-pattern feeling sometimes is explained as a feeling of alternating an emphasis left and right on every third step. First one foot, then the other, has the privilege of beginning the grouping. Alternating emphasis left and right also creates a duple feeling (shown by the heavy bars).

**triple meter**

It seems improbable that we learn triple pulse patterns directly from walking, since we have *two* legs. This illustration does not represent a basic triple feeling in the same sense as the basic duple feeling described above. It is created by imposing a duple left/right pattern (illustrated by the rectangles) over the little groups of threes. This seems fairly complicated. It certainly is not a basic "natural" function, like walking. It feels more like dancing. Not that dancing isn't a good thing to do in order to feel pulse; it simply isn't as basic as walking.

Another theory of triple-pulse feeling is the short-long pattern. Have you noticed that when one recites "Mary had a little lamb," usually all the syllables are given equal time and a duple pattern results. On the other hand, when one recites "Jack and Jill went up the hill" it usually is in a "singsong" manner, giving more time to "Jack," "Jill," "up" and "hill," and less time to "and," "went" and "the." If you attend closely to the time difference between the longer syllables and the shorter ones, you will notice that the longer ones are twice as long as the shorter ones. (long = 2, short = 1, total each pattern = 3)

 16-3

Reciting poetry certainly is not as physical as walking, so it's not very logical to suggest that poetic flow is the basis for feeling triple kinesthetic patterns.

Any cause and effect in this regard would happen the other way around. However, about the only time we walk in a long-short pattern is when an injury causes us to limp. What do you think?

Let's consider the possibility that the triple-pattern feeling is simply a product of logic, and that the kinesthetic feeling of "two-ness," once established, is simply expanded to include "three-ness," perhaps as a means of contrast. Mathematicians consider *two* and *three* as "prime numbers," being the only ones that cannot be further reduced, except by *one*, which, being a "unit," doesn't count (in both senses). Applying that logic to meter, we might say that a simple pulse series is a flow of "ones," and duple-pulse and triple pulse are two alternate ways to organize or evoke the feeling of meter. A flow of single beats, as we noted above, is *not* meter, just as the number *one* is not a relational math concept. A flow of either a duple or a triple ratio might be thought of as "prime meter." All other pulse ratios are then simply combinations or multiples of these two basic patterns.

Mathematicians also consider 5, 7, 11, 13, etc. to be prime numbers, but we don't seem to *feel* these higher primes as musical metric elements. In any case, we don't have to. We can simply combine sets of twos and threes to handle **asymmetrical** meters in music. The same is true in math, in that fives, sevens, elevens and thirteens *can* be considered as sets of twos and threes. Of course, so can 4, 6, 8, 9 and 12. It seems that *all* numbers higher

## Physical Reality vs. Perceptual Reality

It is interesting to consider that "pitch," "pulse" and perhaps "phrase" are perceived from the same physical raw material—regularly recurrent events. In pitch perception, the events occur too rapidly to count. In pulse perception, the events occur slowly enough to allow for it. When the individual vibrations we perceive as "pitch" become too slow to process that way, the brain seems to shift gears and translate those slower events as "pulse."

When "pulses" become too slow to be felt as a kinesthetic flow, we describe these events in terms of musical form. Our sense of proportion that responds to symmetry (or asymmetry) of phrasing seems more a durational perception than a body-felt rhythmic sensation. Although the concept of "regularity" seems to apply to smaller segments, like phrasing, perception of balance in larger formal sections of a work seems a matter of "temporal space," if we may use these contrasting terms meaningfully.

Likewise, the sense of "harmony" and "meter" are made of the same physical phenomena—relationships in small-number ratios. Again, harmony does not allow for counting, and meter does. The difference between these two perceptual fields is, in the physical sense, simply one of speed. Just as the slowing vibrational rate of "pitch" shifts to become "beats," in this sense harmonic "octaves" (1:2) and "fifths" (1:3) become "duple meter" (1:2) and "triple meter" (1:3).

Contemplating these ideas may not improve your musical perceptions, but it might increase your appreciation of nature's gifts.

than three can be considered combinations of twos and/or threes, prime or not. So why make something difficult when it can be easy?

Musical meter, then, comes down to simply a matter of twos and threes. Isn't it comforting to realize that something you once considered complicated is actually quite simple? In this case, all we need to do is learn to differentiate the *feeling* of "two-ness" and "three-ness." Essentially, those two concepts provide the basic elements of all musical meter.

We noted earlier that the minor triad is a logical alternative to the major triad (p. 65). In meter, then, we seem to have another pair of logical alternatives—duple meter and triple meter. In both cases, one entity is more basic than the other: the major triad corresponds to nature's partial series and duple meter corresponds to having two feet. And in both cases, the "alternative" system—minor triad and triple meter—is an "only possible other" modification: a closed system.

**a closed system?**

So, what do you think? Which of these explanations works for you? Or do you have a better idea? In any case, we are not limited to feeling drips, bangs and ticks only in a duple pattern. With a little concentration, we can impose a subjective *triple* pattern on those unit-based aural data streams as well. Would you like to try it?

16-4

Most people find a duple pattern easier to feel. Perhaps that is why most popular music today is based on a duple-pulse feeling. Examples of the qualitative concept of "three-ness" in life are not so plentiful as "two-ness." After "triangle," "tripod," "Hegelian dialectic," and attempts to include the elusive "present" between "past" and "future," they grow scarce. Nevertheless, it is quite clear that people *can* develop a kinesthetic feel for "three-ness." As might be expected, this "alternative" meter is a little harder to create and maintain than "two-ness," but then, an occasional challenge is not a bad thing.

If you have difficulty identifying triple pulse patterns, think of it this way: if it doesn't feel like a windshield wiper, it must be "the other one." Listen to these excerpts and try to feel triple patterns in the rhythmic flow. Notice that duple patterns can coexist with triple patterns, usually in different ways. (Remember the triple walking pattern?) Also, remember that you can *impose* any pulse patterns on any music; so, the idea here is to attempt to discover what the composer probably had in mind.

16-5

**structuring pulse-ratio patterns** We have observed that most pulse-based music contains more than one pulse series, and that these pulse series usually are related in duple and/or triple ratios. You may be wondering whether these various pulse series have names, like *tonic*, *dominant* and so forth. The answer is both "yes" and "no."

"Yes" refers to the fact that we tend to seek out the pulse series that seems to evoke the most kinesthetic response, usually the one that is closest to walking speed; we call that one the **primary pulse**. "No" refers to the fact that people don't always agree on which pulse is primary in a specific musical experience. Therefore, when the starting point of reference is different, the application of the terminology will be different, and two people talking about the same music may describe it differently.

While the *application* of the terminology is sometimes tricky, the terminology itself is not. Once a primary pulse series is designated, the other pulse series in a metric superstructure automatically receive relational names. The words are borrowed from the spacial realm, but seem to translate reasonably well into temporal concepts. The next-related pulse series *slower* than the main pulse is called the **grouping pulse**, the next one slower than that is the **second grouping pulse**, and so on, until a pulse series is too slow to be felt kinesthetically. (Widely-spaced regular events are organized in the realm of musical architecture, or form, which uses different terminology.)

The next-related pulse series *faster* than the main pulse is called the **division pulse**, the next one faster than that is the **second division pulse**, and so on, until the pulses are too fast to be felt kinesthetically. Seldom is it necessary to feel more than one or two simultaneous division-pulse series in a metric superstructure. Many fine performers simply let the faster ones lie dormant until needed for action. Listeners, of course, can assume a more passive demeanor, but it is helpful to know something about how a blur of fast sounds relates to the rest of the metric scheme.

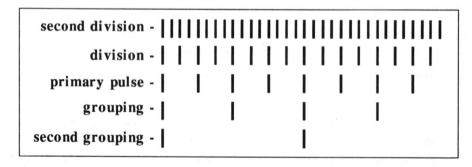

Each pulse series in a superstructure relates to its neighboring series in either a duple or triple ratio. (In the above graphic, all the levels are in duple ratios.) A composer and/or performer makes those decisions (at some level of consciousness) and the musical product reflects them. A listener responds to the performance using his or her sense of metric flow to discover its metric structure (at some level of consciousness). Feeling a metric flow is one thing, of course, but describing it is another. So, let's continue describing.

Students sometimes have difficulty translating the spacial concept **grouping** to a temporal application. Let's see if this illustration helps. Below is a row of equally spaced pies. Hold a pointer above the pie on the left; then, in a steady motion, move your pointer to the right, thinking a "click" as your pointer passes over the left edge of each pie. You probably realize that those imaginary clicks are a pulse series.

**grouping**

Now, impose an imaginary spacial grouping on the line of pies, seeing the pies in groups of two. Now, view it in groups of three. When you group the pies spacially, you have a feeling of "grabbing" each set of pies in a single visual event. To get a *temporal* feeling of grouping these pies, move your pointer over the pies again, this time thinking a click at the left edge of every *second* pie. Then do it with a click on every *third* pie. To group the pies temporally, you used an imaginary "click" or pulse to create the grouping. You didn't move them closer or farther from each other. The grouping was an imaginary one, similar to your adding a subjective pulse earlier to the audible single-pulse series.

In musical meter, *we use pulses to group other pulses*. Remember that a single-pulse series by itself is neither duple nor triple. In order to create the feeling of grouping, an additional pulse series must be supplied that "clicks" simultaneously with every second or every third pulse in the original series. In these graphics, the every-pie click series is a primary pulse and the every-other-pie or every-third-pie click series represents a grouping pulse.

To further realize the *relational* nature of the concepts "duple" and "triple," try this exercise. In the duple-grouping graphic on the next page, cover up the main pulse series and notice that the grouping pulse is, by itself, just a simple pulse series. Then view both series together and focus on their relationship. Do the same exercise in the triple-grouping graphic. Now glance back and forth between the duple and triple graphics. Notice the *qualitative* difference (as opposed to the numerical difference) between duple grouping and triple grouping. If you can *see* the difference here, you likely can *feel* the difference in musical meter.

**DUPLE GROUPING**

primary pulse - | | | | | | | | | | | |

grouping pulse - |  |  |  |  |  |  |

**TRIPLE GROUPING**

primary pulse - | | | | | | | | | | | | |

grouping pulse - |    |    |    |    |

**division**     The relationship of a primary pulse to a division pulse is the same as the relationship of a grouping pulse to a primary pulse. However, from the point of view of the primary pulse, a division is a different concept. Here the added pulse series is *faster* than the primary pulse series, which, in effect, divides the time between each main pulse event into two or three equal parts.

**DUPLE DIVISION**

division pulse - | | | | | | | | | | | |

primary pulse - |  |  |  |  |  |  |

**TRIPLE DIVISION**

division pulse - | | | | | | | | | | | | | |

primary pulse - |    |    |    |    |

If that seems unclear, we can go back to the row of pies. If we divide each pie into two parts the result looks like this:

To get the temporal effect of dividing, move your pointer across the pies clicking on the left edge of each pie and also on the slice line of each pie. The pulse series this creates is *twice* as fast as clicking on only the left edge of each pie. The effect is that you have created a duple division of each beat in the main pulse series. To confirm that *you* are doing the dividing and not just the graphic, go back to the whole pies and add the "division" click at the center of each pie. Be sure your division-click series is evenly spaced, otherwise it is not a true pulse.

It might be interesting to look at pies divided in other ways. We won't move across the pies as we did above to translate their spacial divisions into a temporal mode. That doesn't work beyond the duple division. But pies sliced in equal parts is a good way to translate numerical concepts into perceptual ones. Looking at numbers spacially may help you to understand them better temporally. Let's see what happens.

Notice that in dividing each pie into fourths, we reused the slice lines that divided them in two. This indicates that four is simply two sets of twos. In terms of musical meter, four is simply a matter of adding a second-division duple pulse level to the superstructure (see graphic, p. 158).

A division of three does not generate from a division of two, as four does. "Triple" really is qualitatively different. Beginning music students often have difficulty shifting from a duple to a triple division. When they try to shift, they fall into a division of four, the next faster duple division. Once they realize that the duple feel must completely shut down and get out of the way in order for the triple feel to take over, they usually find success.

Notice that there is no "left-right, left-right" feeling in pies divided into three equal parts. Moving a pointer over these pies doesn't work as it did before. In short, "three-ness" is *different* from "two-ness." Remember, if it doesn't feel like two-legged walking, it must be the other one. These excerpts contain either duple or triple divisions of the main beat. Can you feel the difference?  16-6

Let's look at a few more divisions (see graphic, p. 162). We've already looked at a division in four. Division in five is asymmetrical and more difficult to perceive in time than in space. Six is easier to see and feel symmetrically since it generates from either two or three, and can be perceived as either two sets of three or three sets of two. Seven is asymmetrical and is difficult to perceive in both modes. Eight generates from two, as did four. Nine is simply three sets of three. Ten is difficult and eleven is out of the question.

Twelve is easily perceived by virtue of its breakdown into two doubled sets of three. The bottom line is that the patterns consisting of symmetrical sets of two and/or three are easier to handle than those that don't. This is true in temporal as well as spacial perceptions.

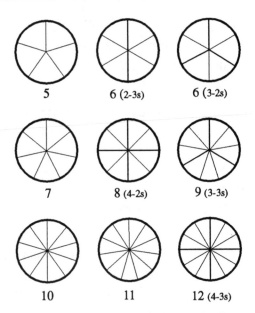

**four basic metric superstructures**

There are only four ways to combine groupings of twos and threes with divisions of twos and threes. In other words, these four metric combinations are a logically closed system. As you can see, the basic nature of meter is rather simple. Unfortunately, our system of rhythm notation is not so simple, and often creates considerable confusion. However, the clearer grasp you have of the concepts described in this chapter, the better prepared you will be to deal with the problems of notating music in these four constructs.

Also, mastery of the four basic meter constructs will prepare you for handling any pulse-based music. Even asymmetrical structures pictured in the graphic at the top of this page can easily be handled by conceiving and feeling them in multiple patterns of twos and threes.

Some musicians insist that quadruple grouping "feels" different from duple grouping, but if our description of basic meter is logical and accurate, then that notion doesn't make sense. A duple grouping is the relationship between a primary pulse series and a grouping pulse series. A quadruple grouping is simply focusing on the relationships between a primary pulse and a *second* grouping (see graphic, top of p. 163). This doesn't make it different from duple grouping because the "feeling" in duple meter also places a subjective event on every second grouping. Since both are derived from the same pulse grid, any differences we feel between metric twos and fours

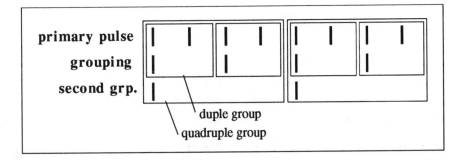

duple group
quadruple group

must have to do with other factors. We'll look at this notion again when we discuss "metric accent."

Asymmetrical combinations are another matter since they produce a pseudo pulse level (meaning one that is not regularly recurrent, therefore not really a pulse at all). **Asymmetrical groupings** are fairly easy to feel and are quite common, particularly in twentieth century art music. They are created by combining duple and triple groupings at the same level. Notice that a pseudo pulse series is created at the grouping level as a result of these asymmetrical groupings.

**asymmetrical meters**

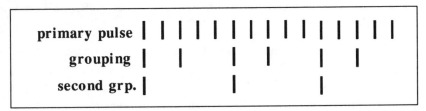

16-7

One can feel the unbalanced flow of this "pulse," but not in the usual sense of regular recurrence. It depends on the regularity of the primary pulse for security. The second-grouping series is a legitimate pulse, although sometimes too slow for kinesthetic feel. Here is a Milcho Leviev song having seven beats per measure, recorded by the L.A. Jazz Choir. If you select the pulse series near walking speed as the primary pulse, you will feel a pattern of two groupings of two beats followed by a grouping of three.

16-8

Twentieth-century composers have been fond of creating **asymmetrical divisions** as well; however, this causes the *primary* pulse to become a pseudo series, relying on the division-level pulse for security. These patterns are more difficult to perform than asymmetrical groupings. Precise regularity

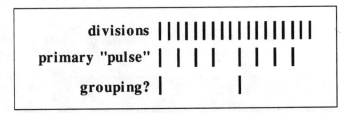

16-9

depends on a pulse level that is often too fast to feel kinesthetically, and control becomes more cerebral than physical.

16-10 👂 In this audio example, the meter has an asymmetrical division of five—alternating sets of threes and twos. The pulse near walking speed is a pseudo pulse since the events are not regularly recurrent, The division and grouping pulses are true pulses since they are regularly recurrent.

It seems unlikely that musicians would *feel* a pure quintuple or septuple division of a beat. It is difficult to avoid breaking an asymmetrical pattern

---

# A Very Old Idea

Although most current music textbooks do not describe this four-construct concept of meter, the idea is not a new one. Music theorists of the eleventh to fourteenth century, the Gothic period, realized meter's logical nature and devised systematic terminology by which to refer to its components.

tempus perfectum
(triple grp.)

tempus imperfectum
(duple grp.)

These theorists, who were very religious and very Christian, called triple elements *perfectum* (as in the Holy Trinity) and duple elements *imperfectum* (as in a two-legged human doing a two-beat dance). While some of us may not relate to their reasons for selecting these terms, we can appreciate their logical and accurate description of meter.

Their system was based on the idea (and probably practical observation) that a main series can be *grouped* in regular sets of twos or threes and can also be *divided* into sets of twos or threes. They realized these two relationships (groupings and divisions) can be combined in four ways, creating the four basic multi-level metric structures.

Meters having a triple grouping were called *tempus perfectum.* They indicated this metric flow with a "perfect" circle. Meters having a duple grouping were called *tempus imperfectum* and were indicated by a half circle. Our modern terms for these patterns are *triple meter* and *duple meter.*

When the Gothics *divided* the beat into two or three parts, they called it *prolatium* (pro-laht-si-um) *imperfectum* and *prolatium perfectum.* Their method of indicating *prolatium perfectum* was to place a dot in the circle (or half circle) and show no dot in the circle (or half circle) indicating *prolatium imperfectum.* They viewed meter as having "layers" of relationships: (1) the ratio between a given pulse and its grouping (*tempus*), and (2) the ratio between a given pulse and its division (*prolatium*). Here's how they combined these factors into their four basic meters.

prolatium perfectum (triple div.)
tempus perfectum (triple grp.)

prolatium imperfectum (duple div.)
tempus perfectum (triple grp.)

prolatium perfectum (triple div.)
tempus imperfectum (duple grp.)

prolatium imperfectum (duple div.)
tempus imperfectum (duple grp.)

into 2+3, 3+2, 3+2+2 or the like. Since duple and triple perceptions are so easy to feel, it makes sense to take advantage of them. Conductors use these "breakdowns" regularly and experienced musicians seem to understand them with little or no difficulty.

In this audio example, the Valley Master Chorale sings both asymmetrical groupings and asymmetrical divisions .

16-11

Another type of asymmetrical metric device is common in music, and its use goes back many centuries. When a composer imposes an occasional triple pattern into a flow which is largely duple, it's called a **triplet**. When a composer imposes an occasional duple pattern into a flow which is largely triple, it's called a **duplet**.

**tuplets**

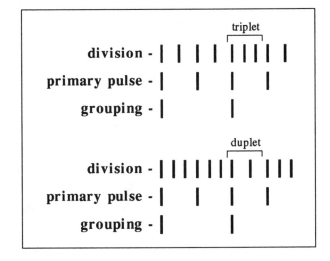

Duplets and triplets can be inserted at any pulse level. Duplets replace triple ratio beats and triplets replace duple ratio beats. Any number of these **tuplets**, as these "replacement" patterns are sometimes called, can occur in succession; however, if they begin to outnumber the resident patterns the overall meter should be redefined to reflect the more frequent grouping or division. Try to pick out the duplets and triplets in these selections.

16-12

Tuplets of five, seven, or other asymmetrical numbers of equal values, are quite rare, probably because they are hard to handle. A practical way to perform them is to think "slightly faster than four" for a division of five, or "a bit slower than eight" for a division of seven. The only practical way to regulate such figures is to maintain the tempo of the primary pulse series. Allowing deviations in tempo while executing tuplets disrupts the flow of the music. If it feels awkward to the performer, it will surely feel awkward to the listener.

# Meter Wrap-Up

**Meter** is created by combining two or more **pulse series** related in duple or triple ratios. The pulse having a tempo closest to walking speed usually is selected as **primary**. Pulses in a metric structure having tempos slower than the primary pulse are called **grouping** pulses. Pulses in a metric structure having tempos are faster than the primary pulse are called **division** pulses.

There are only four ways to combine duple and triple relationships within three levels of related pulses—duple grouping/duple division, duple grouping/triple division, triple grouping/duple division, and triple grouping/triple division. All other meters are variations on these **four basic metric structures**.

It is possible to include random "foreign" metric patterns within a duple or triple flow. This type of event is called a **tuplet**. The most common tuplets are the **triplet** and the **duplet**, each occurring within the other's metric flow. Other tuplets are possible but are far less common.

Like pulse, meter is a **silent** means of organizing musical events and is imagined, or "felt," by the composer and/or the listener according to previous conceptual experience. It appears that pulse and metric concepts are initially generated through **kinesthetic** activity, such as walking. That is why we tend to "feel" the metric flow while listening to music. While duple patterns appear more basic than triple ones, both can be practiced and learned, providing a qualitative and simple "closed system" by which to perceive both simple and rather complex metric patterns.

Just as we are able to learn to perceive pitch-based musical materials without naming them, we are also able to learn to perceive metric-based musical materials without naming them. If this were not true, no one could enjoy music without extensive study. However, in order to clearly communicate musical constructs in notation, it is important to understand the basic principles by which music is perceived and conceived, and that, of course, is what this book is all about.

# 17

# Accent

Some of the definitions of rhythm we considered earlier held that patterns contributing to rhythmic perception have to do with concepts that, in themselves, are not particularly temporal in nature. Cooper and Meyer, you may remember, said that "grouping is the result of the interaction among the various aspects of the materials of music: pitch, intensity, timbre, texture, and harmony—as well as duration." We won't deal exhaustively with all these aspects, but we will look at some of them as the principal means by which composers create rhythmic flow in music.

In all art, indeed in all of life, some things stand out and grab our attention because they contrast with other things within our perceptual field. In interior decorating, it might be an orange pillow in a room otherwise filled with cool blues and greens. In theater, one performer might dominate the rest, not only because the actor appears on stage or camera for long periods, but because his or her character exhibits some outstanding trait—strength of character, physical attractiveness, or predilection toward reckless abandon. In painting, the composition frequently leads the eye to focus on some strong element within the frame.

Any element that stands out from its surroundings is an **accent**. In music, the word often is misunderstood to mean "a stress in loudness," but loudness is only *one* kind of musical accent. In fact, it probably is not the most important kind.

## Metric Accent

We already have discussed the element in music that is perhaps the most influential in creating rhythmic flow in music—the sense of pulse. Ironically, it is the element that doesn't make any sound at all. How, then, does a silent pulse create an accent in a field of metric pulses which are also silent?

The answer is that musicians (and listenters) do, in fact, feel multiple pulse series, provided the series is flowing in small-number relationships. Observation indicates that maintaining three or four series, or metric superstructure levels, is not unusual, and can be accomplished by performers and listeners with even modest experience.

The feeling of metric accent is produced by the regular simultaneous recurrence of pulses at different levels. The graphic below demonstrates how this works. Scan the graphic from left to right, as you did with the pies earlier, and notice that as you pass certain events there are simultaneous pulses occurring in many related pulse series. The more levels  that contribute strength at a given point, the stronger that event is within the overall flow. This point of strength, or accent, is not caused by loudness. Being silent, how could it? It is imagined, or felt, in terms of learned kinesthetic concepts.

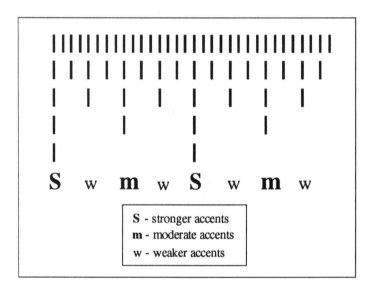

**Metric accents**, then, are created by the contrasting strengths of coinciding pulses in a metric structure. The relative strength of any specific accent is proportional to the number of pulses that coincide with it at other levels. It is important to realize, thus we repeat, that none of this has anything to do with loudness, or any other sound-related perception. Metric accent is a matter of imagined kinesthetic feeling. Just as the hierarchical marks on a ruler are not the thing being measured, musical meter is not the sounds being "measured," or organized, whether by composer or listener.

There is an important difference in using a ruler and using musical meter. The designations on a ruler, or yard stick, represent *fixed* units of space. That is why no one makes elastic rulers. The "designations" in musical meter are quite elastic, however, and all the "distances," or durations, are relative, not

# Meter? Accent? Help!!!

Music textbooks are often vague about the nature of metric accent. One, for instance, states:

> The gathering of beats into regular groups is called *meter*. Instead of having a steady stream of undifferentiated beats, we instinctively stress some more than others in a regular and repeating fashion.

The word "gathering" is particularly disturbing, implying that beats are like wandering sheep needing to be brought into meaningful formations by "stressing" them. The method of applying stress to "undifferentiated beats," or a definition of stress, is not mentioned. The reader is left to assume that loudness is somehow involved.

Another textbook's description says that "sounds that are stressed (your louder claps, for example) are said to be accented." A few lines later this same author says that "*meter* is a regular pattern of accented and unaccented beats." Here the student is clearly misled to the idea that meter is a matter of loudness.

An English dictionary defines accent as "emphasis on certain chords or tones," but leaves us without information regarding the means of emphasis. A general dictionary has no particular obligation to explain methods of achieving a described condition, of course. The point here is simply that it was no help in that regard.

Another dictionary defines accent as "rhythmic stress," which sheds no further light on the subject. While authorities agree that a metric accent "feels" stronger, and some specify that the matter is wholly silent, logical explanations of how metric pulse is perceived are virtually absent in the literature.

Music textbooks are nearly universal in describing "basic" meters as *duple, triple* and *quadruple*. Authors are understandably hard pressed to explain a difference between duple and quadruple meter. Here is an example:

> This pattern of two beats to a measure is known as *duple meter* and occurs in many nursery rhymes and marching songs, as well as in other kinds of music.... *Quadruple meter*, also known as *common time*, contains four beats to the measure, with a primary accent on the first beat and a secondary accent on the third. Although it is sometimes not easy to tell duple and quadruple meter apart, quadruple meter usually has a broader feeling.

The idea of "primary" and "secondary" accents is a clue to meter's hierarchical nature, but few seem to realize that a grouping of four main beats is *identical* to two sets of two main beats, since duple meter also provides a "primary" accent on the first beat of every other group as a second grouping level (see p. 163). The "difference" is purely notational, not perceptual.

The author quoted above implies, as do many others, that meter influences (or is influenced by) performance style when he refers to "a broader feeling." That statement says more about the confusion surrounding the conceptual nature of meter than about any differences between duple and quadruple meter. Meter, by virtue of its conception from kinesthetic experience, is concerned only with ratios between pulse series and has nothing to do with "broader feeling" or any other expressive element in music. Tempo and style are irrelevant to meter.

absolute. It is the user's responsibility to preserve the equality of the relative durations by maintaining a steady flow.

All too frequently, music students focus more on *counting* beats than on feeling metric flow, resulting in erratic performances. It is far more important to feel meter than to assign names to relative pulses. What is worse, of course, is a teacher who assigns names and leaves it at that, rewarding the student performer who counts the beats properly but who doesn't realize those beats must be performed in equal spacing to have musical worth.

Now let's discuss a number of musical accents that are qualitatively different from metric accent in that they have to do with contrasts in *sound*. A composer can use any perceiveable sound concept to create accent simply by modifying that element to provide temporal "contrast" in the music.

## Dynamic Accent

Considerable confusion comes from not realizing that there are *different* kinds of accents in music. Accents created by *loudness* are the type most people think of when the word is used. It's the only type of accent that has a notational sign (>), so it's easy to get the idea that it is the only one there is. When this sign is encountered, the performer is being instructed to make that event louder than the surrounding ones so it will stand out. The amount of contrast is up to the performer's musical taste as he or she senses the character of the music.

A loudness accent, commonly called a **dynamic accent**, can be placed in any metric position. It needn't be limited to strong metric beats. Notice that this familiar dynamic accent falls on a relatively weak metric beat.

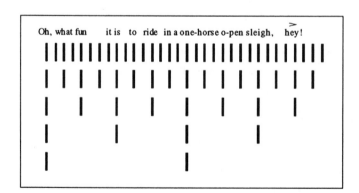

On the other hand, it is common to compose music with dynamic accents on strong metric beats. In dance music, a composer wants the meter to be easily discovered. Therefore, heavy sounds such as bass drum, string bass, guitar strums, etc. are placed at regular recurrences of strong metric beats (and not other beats). The conductor may also invite those playing melodic lines to place a dynamic emphasis on those events occurring on these stronger metric locations. Indeed, those players may provide this dynamic emphasis without invitation simply on the basis of their own sense of rhythmic flow.

But remember, even though musicians frequently play dynamic accents on strong metric beats, a perceptual variation in loudness is a *dynamic* accent and not a metric one. Dynamic accents exist in sound, metric accents exist in silent kinesthetic multilevel metric structures.

## Agogic Accent

Given a series of musical events of unequal durations, a listener tends to feel the longer durations as accents. These are called **agogic** accents. They are not necessarily louder than surrounding events, although they can be. Just as dynamic accents can, and frequently do, coincide with metric accents, so agogic accents can, and frequently do, coincide with accents in other modes of contrast. Translate this graphic to the temporal mode by scanning from left to right and notice how the longer durations feel "stronger."

Also, notice longer durations are still felt as accents even when the short durations are at the beginning of the series.

There are some tricky aspects of durational, or agogic, accents that must be clearly understood to prevent erroneous conclusions regarding the relationship of mixed durational patterns to meter. Notice the placement of agogic accents on every third duration does not create a triple metric pattern, but rather a duple one. The reason is that metric durations are equal, while agogic accents are, by definition, longer than surrounding durations.

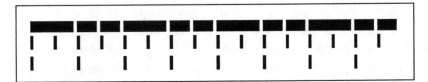

While that may seem obvious, it is amazing how much trouble it causes for many beginning music students. Hopefully, realizing the difference and the relationship between metric and agogic accents will clarify the concepts and alleviate the perceptual/conceptual problem. Since agogic accents can relate to surrounding durations in a wide variety of proportions, there is no rule for determining how many durations will fit a given metric pattern. They are simply two different things, and it is up to the composer and then the listener to perceive them separately and coordinate them.

To illustrate, consider a picket fence in which every fourth picket is "missing." The visual impression is that the remaining pickets are grouped in threes, the space left by the missing picket is perceived as a vacancy, a negative value.

Now, move a pointer from left to right over the fence, imagining a "click" on each picket. Influenced by the visual experience, you may feel that the first picket in each group is accented, reinforcing the visual grouping of three pickets. But feel the metric pattern carefully. Notice that the meter is not triple, but duple, having two short durations followed by a long one.

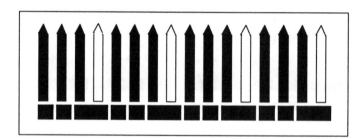

As you continue the flow, you may feel the accent switch to the last picket in the visual grouping. If so, you have just been influenced by the agogic accent principle. In other words, because the time duration is greater between the last picket of each visual group to the first picket of the next group, that longer duration wants to be felt as the accent, a positive value.

**space vs. time** There appears to be a difference in the way this pattern is perceived in the spacial and temporal modes. On one hand, the larger *distance* in the spacial mode arranged the pickets into a static visual grouping of threes, while the larger *duration* in the temporal mode grouped the "events" into a metric duple pattern. Influenced by agogic accent, the spacial "negative" was transformed into a temporal "positive."

But we're not quite out of the woods yet. The feeling of a three-click grouping is still present. The grouping-by-proximity concept is a strong one and works in the temporal mode as well as the spacial one. Listen to this audio example. As you can hear, the agogic accent shifts the accent to the *last* of the three events in the proximity grouping. This shows that the "spacial" grouping does not occur *within* the metric beat, but *overlaps* it.

17-1

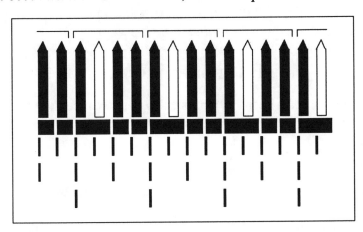

This is one of the most troublesome perceptual translations a music student is asked to conquer, and causes considerable problems in learning to perceive and notate rhythms correctly. The solution is to understand the principle of agogic accent and not be fooled by confusing it with the wrong perception.

## Melodic Accent

Another type of accent is created by pitch patterns. Notice in the following example that accent patterns are created even though the durations are even and regular. These are **melodic accents**. Because the pitches that are different from the repeated pitch happen on every third event, a triple metric pattern is felt.

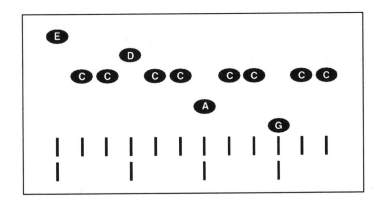

17-2

The melodic accents here suggest a triple metric pattern because the durations are regular and because every *third* pitch is heard as "different" from the repeated pitch. When pitch patterns are not symmetrical, the influence of pitch on the feeling of metric flow is more subtle. Nevertheless, pitch patterns can, and often do, create their own accent series, and when they persist in a regular pattern, they can either confirm or contrast an established metric flow. That is possible, of course, only because the audible accents occurring in the music are something *other than* metric accent.

## Harmonic Accent

17-3

A chord change can be heard as a musical accent. Notice how these chords tend to group in a triple pattern, even though they are all played in equal durations.

17-4

This audio illustration isolates harmonic accent from dynamic and agogic accents, but you may have noticed that some of the pitches changed (inevitably) at the same time the chords changed. Isolating harmonic accent from melodic accent is a bit difficult, but we'll try. This time we'll minimize regular melodic accent patterns by changing the melodic direction asymmetrically. Harmonic accent will be created by using pitches belonging to different chords after each three tones. You may have to play this illustration a few times in order to perceive the harmonic relationships between the pitches. If you hear these pitches in a triple grouping you are probably hearing the **harmonic accent,** or pattern of chord changes.

17-5

Harmonic accent also occurs when dissonance resolves to consonance. The release of tension, particularly when a dominant-function tritone is followed by its tonic-chord destination, creates a feeling of accent. Beethoven uses this principle in the introduction to his first symphony. Even though the tempo is slow, one can feel the rhythmic accentuation on the second of each group of two chords in spite of some conflicting dynamic stresses.

When the release of harmonic tension at a phrase ending coincides with a strong metric beat, the result is called a "strong" **cadence.** When the release occurs in a weak metric position, it is referred to as a "weak" cadence. In

17-6

| strong - | I | ii | I | V₇ | I | | |
| weak - | I | ii | I | vi | V₇ | I |

order to perceive the difference illustrated in this audio example, you need to feel the underlying duple (quadruple) pulse pattern.

In the strong cadence, the harmonic accent (release of tension) coincides with the strong metric pulse. In the weak cadence, the harmonic accent works against the metric accent pattern. This doesn't make it better or worse; it just makes it different.

## Timbral Accent

Speaking of Beethoven, in the first movement of his Fifth Symphony, he creates a metric pattern by alternating strings and woodwinds on the same chord in equal durations. This, of course, sets up a duple pattern; the timbre of one section contrasts the timbre of the other, a **timbral accent**. Needless to say, Beethoven was not the only composer to use this technique.  17-7

## Syncopation

As you can see, a composer has many more ways than loudness to create accent. As you listen to music in the future, notice when various kinds of accent *verify* an established metric flow and when they *negate* an established metric flow. The latter is used frequently enough to have its own name—**syncopation**.

Depending on the musical style, accents—dynamic, agogic, melodic, and/or others—usually occur simultaneously near the beginning of a composition, communicating clearly an appropriate metric pattern to help the listener feel the ongoing rhythmic flow. The listener responds by generating an appropriate metric superstructure (whether analyzed consciously or not) by which to predict future rhythmic accents in the music. Once established, this sense of pulse and meter becomes the "ruler" the listener uses to "measure," or interpret, musical events that follow.

In contrast, the performer generates the metric structure in advance, feeling the silent flow of the pattern for a few seconds before creating any sounds. This silent metric flow provides the temporal "measurements" he or she needs in order to place the musical events in their proper relationships.

In very simple music, the flow of simultaneous accents might continue unchanged throughout a whole piece. Nursery songs tend to be this way, encouraging young listeners and performers to develop a secure sense of metric and rhythmic flow. 17-8

But experienced listeners are soon bored with music that offers no rhythmic challenges. The most common method of creating rhythmic interest is to employ sound accents that do not synchronize with the ongoing pattern of metric accents. For example, placing longer durations on weaker metric beats creates a conflict of accents. Not only is the listener asked to feel the basic metric flow, he or she is invited to feel an additional rhythmic event— an agogic accent that is out of sync. Beethoven presents an agogic accent out of meter near the end of the famous "Ode To Joy" theme in his Ninth Symphony.

17-9

When a sound-accent pattern in any perceptual aspect does not agree with the basic metric flow, the resulting conflict is called **syncopation**. In case there is any doubt that pulse and meter are silent phenomena, the fact that one *can* feel syncopation shows that an ongoing sense of regular meter is being maintained, enabling the conflicting accent to be noticed.

17-10

Unaccompanied pitch patterns, even when durations are even, can create a sense of syncopation. In this example, the four ascending pitches are answered by four descending pitches, confirming a duple meter. The following pitches, however, seem to group in two sets of three, due to changes in melodic direction. Assuming the middle pulse (shown below) is primary, syncopated melodic accents occur near the end of the third grouping and in the middle of the fourth grouping.

17-11

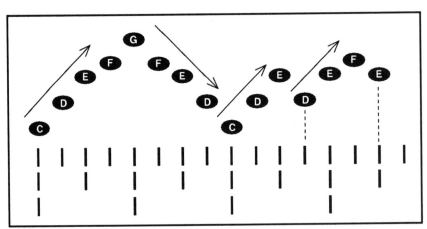

Dynamic accents, the ones usually associated with the word "accent," can also be used to create syncopation simply by placing them in locations that are not otherwise accented. In the example at the top of the next page, the sounds are evenly placed, which, with no other modifications, would simply represent a pulse pattern. Meter is suggested at the beginning by placing louder sounds on the first and fourth events, creating a triple pattern. This then is negated by placing louder events in a duple pattern, dynamically accenting sounds that do not occur on established metric accents. The phrase is concluded with a set of three accents, placing an agogic "picket fence" accent (the last sound) on a moderate accent (a mild syncopation).

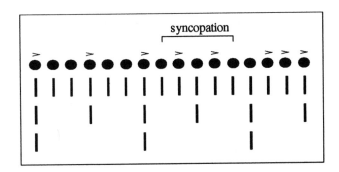

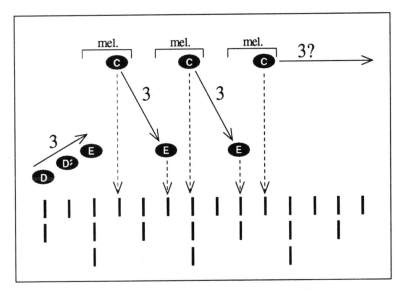

17-12

The type of sound accents discussed here, or any other types for that matter, can be used together or separately to create syncopated events in relation to an ongoing basic metric flow. If an out-of-sync pattern continues, the music is said to contain a **cross rhythm** (perhaps more correctly, **cross meter**). An excellent example of this is Scott Joplin's ragtime composition "The Entertainer." While the left hand plays an unmistakeable duple pattern (represented below by the meter grid), the right hand plays a triple-meter pattern, largely created by agogic accents. If heard without the left-hand accompaniment, this melody would evoke a triple metric flow (assuming that its famous ragtime setting can be temporarily ignored).

17-13

Of the three agogic C's, only the second occurs on a strong metric pulse. Also, notice that the repeated melodic pitch-pairs E-C contribute their own syncopated pattern to the mix of rhythmic information. Only the first of three sets begins on the strongest metric beat. It is clearly the relationship of this "triple meter" melody to its duple meter accompaniment that evokes the fascination surrounding this "catchy" tune.

# Rhythm Wrap-Up

Not only do we see that rhythm involves "flow," as was understood by the ancient Greeks and Romans, but we know something about what causes that sense of flow. We also realize now why one of the definitions of rhythm quoted earlier included "pitch, intensity, timbre, texture, and harmony" even though these are not, strictly speaking, durational concepts.

We know that *pulse*, the concept that many people confuse with *rhythm*, is not even an essential part of rhythm. In fact, some music that has no pulse has rhythm. We realize that pulse and meter are silent kinesthetic "rulers" by which audible rhythmic elements within a composition can be coordinated, first by the composer, and then by the listener. Therefore, we don't hear meter—we feel it. What we actually hear are sound accents in the music created by various means, and then we perceive meter when accents are heard in symmetrical patterns.

Although the concept of rhythm is not limited to music, we can appreciate composer Roger Sessions's remark that "an adequate definition of rhythm comes close to defining music itself." This view certainly reinforces our own definition of music—"organized sound"—and provides additional insight into the means by which musical organization is acheived.

# IV

# Musical Meaning

In any aspect of human experience, meaning is shaped by the interplay of two opposing concepts—continuity and contrast. Continuity, an unchanging condition or continuous series of predictable events, is, by itself, essentially meaningless. The things in life that usually continue unnoticed—light, breathing, furnace fans—don't require our attention. But don't confuse "meaning" with "importance." Light, breathing, and perhaps furnace fans are certainly important, but as long as they are working well we tend to be unaware of them and, for a time at least, they are perceptually meaningless.

continuity and
contrast

However, when any of these things loses continuity—meaning immediately springs into existence. If the lights go out, or even flicker threateningly, we take notice. If suddenly we can't breathe, our condition rivets our attention. If the furnace fan starts rattling, we begin to wonder how much the repair is going to cost. It is *discontinuity*, or contrast, that captures our attention and brings meaning to perception. However, before we totally depreciate continuity's role in the scheme of things, we should point out that without continuity, contrast is not possible.

To illustrate, imagine driving through a thickly-wooded area. At first you may notice that some trees are larger than others, but not in any meaningful pattern, so this soon fades from your awareness and the experience reduces to a semi-conscious blur of trees flowing along the periphery of your vision. Suddenly you see a fallen tree. You wonder how it happened. Lightning? Disease? Vandalism? The contrast of the fallen tree to the standing trees creates meaning for you.

A little later, you drive past an area where *all* the trees are fallen. After remarking to yourself that the area looks bleak and devastated, you eventually lose interest and continue driving. When you observe a lone tree standing erect among the horizontal trunks, you wonder why this particular tree was spared. Had this tree been surrounded by a forest of other erect trees you wouldn't even have noticed it. It was *contrast* that gave meaning to the experience.

As you continue your drive, you pass through an area where about half the trees are fallen, with no particular pattern to the fallen and erect trees. Now, neither the fallen nor the standing trees attracts your attention. Once you become aware of the continuity of the perceptual field, it begins to fade from your conscious awareness. So, looking back on all three perceptual situations, it wasn't just "fallen tree" or "standing tree" that caught your attention and contributed perceptual meaning—it was "different tree."

Visual artists understand this principle. That's why painters normally don't portray a red wall behind red roses in a red vase. The viewer wouldn't see anything. However, by adding a bit of light and shadow (visual contrast), red roses in a red vase against a red wall might make a bold statement (stylistic contrast), compared to just another traditional painting of a vase of flowers.

In music, the composer (as well as his or her representative, the performer) provides both continuity and contrast. Music without continuity is, of course, not music; there is no opportunity for contrast until continuity is established. A simple illustration is the sounding of a single tone. If it continues unchanged for more than a few seconds, a listener may become disinterested. If a meaningful musical experience was expected, the listener may become annoyed. The composer/performer, then, must judge when contrast should be provided to make the experience meaningful to the listener. If the long tone is contrasted with a flurry of fast pitch changes, this too will hold interest only for a short time and must again be contrasted, either by going on to something new, or by returning to the long-tone idea. The process then continues throughout the composition, creating continuities that set up meaningful contrasts.

In the following chapters, we will look at some of the ways composers create meaning through continuity and contrast. We've already seen how the use of accents in various perceptual modes helps shape music in its smaller segments. Now we will look at some ways musical components discussed earlier are used to configure music in its larger formal proportions.

# 18

# Melody As Meaning

Of all the musical components that convey artistic meaning, melody plays the prominent role. The principle of continuity and contrast applies to melody in two different ways—internally and externally. By **internal meaning**, we are referring to the way a melody is put together, specifically in terms of the continuity/contrast principle. By **external meaning**, we are referring to the relationship of a melody, taken as a whole, to a composition's overall structure.

## Internal Melodic Meaning

A large part of meaning in melody is related to the use of standard scales, or modes. A listener's recognition of a melodic style serves as a point of reference (continuity of familiarity), as opposed to an exotic, or "strange sounding" style (contrast), enabling the listener to evaluate events in a given melody. Tonality provides continuity in much of the world's melody, past and present. Pitches closely related harmonically to tonic (consonance) provide continuity while more distantly related pitches (dissonance) create contrast.

**Contour**, the shape of melodic movement up and down in pitch, can be used to create meaning. Plentiful use of consecutive scale steps provides **conjunct** motion, which can then be contrasted by **disjunct** motion, the use of melodic skips, or leaps. Any or all of the other perceptual attributes of tone—loudness, timbre and duration—can add meaning to a series of melodic pitches. We will discuss those attributes in upcoming chapters.

The expression of melodic meaning has changed over the past two millennia. Each major period has made significant advances in the art of melody writing. Early "melodies" were not much more than pitches, sometimes with meter and sometimes not, on which lyrics were recited. Gradually, melody came to stand on its own, conveying its own meanings without the need for language.

**the early periods**

18-1

It would be inaccurate to suggest that the monophonic chants of the **Middle Ages** (300-1100) were *without* internal meaning, but compared to melodies of later centuries, it seems clear that these chants were not designed with continuity and contrast in mind. The purpose of much early chant was to convey sacred texts in a manner more compelling than simple recitation. What's more, *singing* the words added mystique and enhanced the ritual of the Mass.

18-2

With the advent of **polyphonic** church music toward the end of the first millennium and into the **Gothic** period (1100-1450), it became essential to anchor multiple voices (melodic lines) to an ongoing pulse and meter in order to keep them in their proper temporal relationships. Although much effort was spent harmonically securing added voices to elongated chant melodies, little thought was given to arranging pitches in melodic patterns using continuity and contrast.

Remember that the Gothic period was not noted for its sensitivity to human aesthetic needs. Life's values were a matter of obeying those in authority and following the rules. Church music was an expression of religious devotion and most certainly was not intended to entertain. Its purpose was to provide mystery, not stimulate the intellect.

18-3

Secular music was another matter entirely. Minstrels composed and performed music purely for entertainment. Fortunately, Medieval monks skilled at notation were often kind enough to preserve this music for posterity. As a result, we know these "street" songs often contained repeated and contrasting phrases. They were simple one-voiced **monophonic** compositions—no polyphonic complexities and no chordal accompaniments—just a single series of pitches, but in this case the pitches were arranged with some sense of artistic meaning.

In the late fifteenth century and into the sixteenth, life changed radically. Columbus's ships were by no means the only ones at sea in 1492. World exploration brought wealth, education, culture and technology to the emerging cities of Europe. This period is known as the **Renaissance** (1450-1600), or the age of Humanism. This new climate gave rise to the Protestant Reformation, Gutenberg's printing press and Michelangelo's graceful art.

**melodic imitation**

As Western society was relaxing its "heavenly" values to allow for more "human" ones, music began to incorporate increased internal meaning. Even church music changed, embodying artistic expression while continuing to convey religious meaning. All polyphonic melodic lines were considered equally important, and melodic shapes were passed from one voice to another, creating artistic continuity. This compositional technique, called **imitation**, became the principle means of achieving musical cohesiveness throughout the Renaissance. The Los Angeles Chamber Singers illustrate this device as employed by the English composer Orlando Gibbons.

18-4

One of the most dramatic stylistic changes in music history occurred between the sixteenth and seventeenth centuries. Polyphony was becoming overly complex and reform was in the air. The piano's predecessor, the harpsichord, was invented and became very popular. This keyboard instrument made it possible for one performer to supply a harmonic accompaniment to a melodic line, thus **homophonic** texture was born. It was a short step to incorporate this new musical structure into the theater—giving rise to opera. By the middle of the seventeenth century, the sweet-sounding violin replaced the strident viol and the orchestra emerged.

**melodic sequence**

But the new musical texture, consisting of a melody with chords, couldn't use imitation to create internal meaning—there was no other melodic voice to which a melodic shape might be tossed (except perhaps the bass line, which usually was played by another instrument along with the keyboard). So, a new way to create continuity and contrast was developed. Melody tossed melodic shapes to *itself*. More specifically, a melodic idea would be stated and then immediately repeated within that same melodic voice, as many as four or five times. Each repetition of the pattern occurred one scale-step higher or one scale-step lower. This new compositional technique was called **melodic sequence**. The idea quickly caught on and sequences abounded in the music of the **Baroque** period (1600-1750).

18-5

In the late Baroque, a new kind of polyphony emerged in which multi-voiced music was threaded through chordal structures. This made it possible for J. S. Bach, as well as others, to combine *both* imitation and sequence in order to create considerable internal meaning within a musical composition. Bach's fugues abound with combinations of imitation and sequence.

18-6

At no time in history was the internal shape of a melody more important than in the late eighteenth century. During that period, called the **Classical** era (1750-1820), formal design dominated not only music, but all genres of art. The traditional American melody "Yankee Doodle," associated with the Revolutionary War, was very popular then. This Classical melody is an excellent example of how the two principles—continuity and contrast—can be used to create internal meaning.

**classical melody**

18-7

One of the most prominent features contributing to continuity in this melody is the pattern of two tonic pitches that recur at the beginning of each of the first three phrases. Notice that the repeated pitches do not occur at the beginning of the fourth phrase.

Had the repeated-pitch figure occurred in the fourth phrase just as it had in the first three, no artistic meaning (contrast) would have resulted. The pattern's continuity then would only have meaning by its contrast to all the non-repeated pitches in the melody. Incidentally, it still has that meaning on the basis of only the three repetitions. That's why it generates such a strong expectation, or sense of continuity, in the first place. If there were sets of repeated tonic pitches throughout the melody, this characteristic would have far less internal meaning, even while opening each phrase.

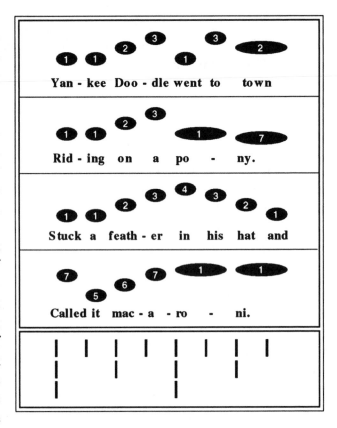

Another repeated element in this melody is the set of three pitches on consecutive scale steps 1-2-3, placed just after the first strong metric beat. The first three times this element appears, the direction is upward. The next time it appears ("his hat and"), those same steps (continuity) are going downward (contrast). The downward appearance occurs later in the phrase instead of at the beginning (contrast), but still follows a strong metric beat (continuity). The last appearance of this element occurs on a new set of pitches, 5-6-7, a strongly significant point of contrast, made even more vivid by the fact that it occurs in the expected metric placement (continuity).

**motive**     These two elements—the opening repeated pitch and the 3-pitch scalewise series—are **motives**, since they are small melodic/rhythmic figures that recur. (The meaning of *motive* in music is essentially the same as *motif* in the graphic arts.) Or, if preferred, the combination of these two smaller motives can be taken as a whole, since they appear together consistently, and can be designated as the motive here. Since this motive appears at the beginning of the melody, it is called a **head motive**.

The head motive occurs at the beginning of each of the first three phrases, creating the continuity that provides for contrast. The contrast here is achieved by answering the head motive in three different ways. The three answers also contain points of continuity and contrast.

The first answer ("went to town") begins on the tonic pitch, leaps up to scale step 3, then fills in the interval by turning downward to scale step 2. It contributes continuity by using the same pitches as the motive, and contributes contrast by changing their order and contour. It states its answer inside the high and low "boundaries" suggested by the motive.

The second answer ("pony") provides continuity with the first answer by also beginning on the tonic pitch. It provides significant contrast by moving downward, but perhaps more importantly, by introducing a new pitch, scale step 7, which is one step outside the boundaries set by the motive. The longer duration on the tonic pitch also adds significant contrast.

The third answer ("in his hat and") does not start on tonic, a very important point of contrast. Instead, it begins on scale step 4, one step outside the motive's boundaries, as in the second answer (continuity), but this time on its high side (contrast).

Rhythmically, continuity is established by the steady flow of division-pulse syllables. Contrast and continuity are both supplied by the manner in which each of the four phrases is finished. The first phrase concludes with a longer duration on a relatively weak beat ("town"). The second phrase concludes with *two* (contrast) longer durations (continuity) on consecutive strong and weak beats ("pony"). The third phrase has no long durations (contrast), and simply continues the flow of division-pulse syllables into the beginning of the fourth phrase, which concludes with two longer durations ("-roni") in the same metric position as the second phrase (continuity).

The repeated tonic tones at the end relate to the repeated tonic tones that open each of the first three phrases. The repeated-pitch idea contributes continuity, as does the fact that it is on tonic. The final occurrence falls on a relatively strong metric position, as do the first three, but it is not quite as strong, thus contributing contrast. Of utmost importance is the fact that the final tones, being twice as long as the earlier ones (contrast), answer the long tones of the second phrase ending (continuity).

**phrases and periods**

Phrases in classically designed melodies are usually shaped into a balanced pattern. When a group of two or more phrases depend on each other for their internal meaning, and the last phrase leads to the feeling of closure, the result is called a **period**. In the portion of "Yankee Doodle" examined above, the first and second halves begin with the same melodic idea, which is called a **parallel period**.

"Wait a minute," you say. "The second half of 'Yankee Doodle' is very different from the first half." If that is your judgment, you will call this structure a **contrasting period**, but you are going to get a lot of arguments from a lot of musicians. "Over those four little syllables?" Yes, because, remember, it's a *head motive*. That makes a big difference.

**recent trends**   In the more romantic nineteenth century, melodic construction became freer and less formal; nevertheless, the principles of continuity and contrast continued to be the criteria by which an expression was deemed meaningful. Richard Wagner's composing of what has been called "endless melody" opened new ways to bend melodic shapes into significant flights of musical fancy.

18-8

Twentieth-century composers seemed anxious to continue the struggle to free melody from traditional boundaries. Nevertheless, they realized that total freedom would risk meaninglessness. Even Schoenberg and his disciples confined "freedom" to a tone row. Some chose to reinstate the formal values of classicism, employing well-proven devices such as imitation, sequences and formal phrasing. Although Prokofiev's melodies often slide easily from one tonality to another, even within a single phrase, they are never allowed to wander freely and meaninglessly.

18-9

Recent trends in internal meaning seem to focus less on melody, in the traditional sense, and more on other perceptual components. The essence of **minimalism**, for example, is the creation of almost imperceptible changes in some aspect of a repeated melodic figure which become consciously noticeable only after the passage of time. As a listener might begin to question the meaning of so many unchanging repetitions, he or she begins to realize that change is in fact taking place. Listening to minimalistic music can be compared to seeing your image in the mirror each day and remembering what you looked like some years earlier, except that the changes do take place considerably faster in this music. Although memory is required to perceive *any* musical meaning, it is particularly important to perceiving meaning in this genre.

18-10

No matter what the style, internal melodic meaning is conveyed by the universal perceptual principles of continuity and contrast. The means of infusing these principles into the organization of pitch patterns is limited only by the composer's imagination and assessment of the audience he or she hopes to reach.

# External Melodic Meaning

Once a melodic pattern achieves closure (form) in terms of its internal meaning, the composer must decide whether to repeat the pattern or contrast it. If repetition is selected, another decision must be made to modify it or repeat it exactly. In the nursery song "Mary Had A Little Lamb," the option favored repetition (continuity). The pattern of two related phrases, which constitute a parallel period, is repeated exactly. Only the lyric is changed.

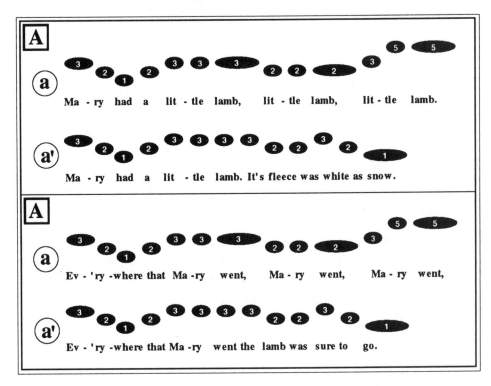

18-11

The standard method of representing melodic structures is to use letters to indicate repetition and contrast. When structural elements are smaller—phrases for example—lower case letters are used. When structural elements are larger, upper-case letters are used. If a section is clearly based on an earlier one but is significantly modified in some way, the same letter is used with a prime mark added (a') to indicate the change. If other modifications occur in later phrases, they are indicated with a double prime (a"), and so on. Sometimes superscript numbers (a$^2$) are used instead of prime marks.

In the case of "Yankee Doodle" (see graphic, p. 188), the contrast option was taken. Here, the first parallel period is followed by a contrasting parallel period. Some authorities call this form a **contrasting double period**. Others reserve the term for four-phrase structures that do not close until the end of the last phrase. We will not argue the point; the focus of this discussion is on meaning in sound patterns, so this need not be settled here.

18-12

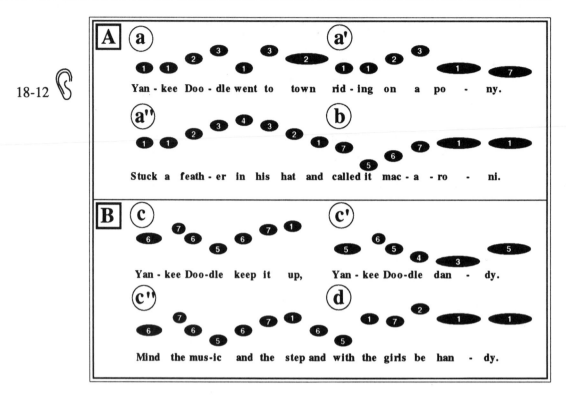

The song form of "Yankee Doodle" is **binary**, in that the first melodic entity is followed by a contrasting melodic entity of comparable size. When a melodic entity is followed by a contrasting entity and then by a return of the original entity, the form is said to be **ternary**. "Twinkle, Twinkle Little Star" is an example.

18-13

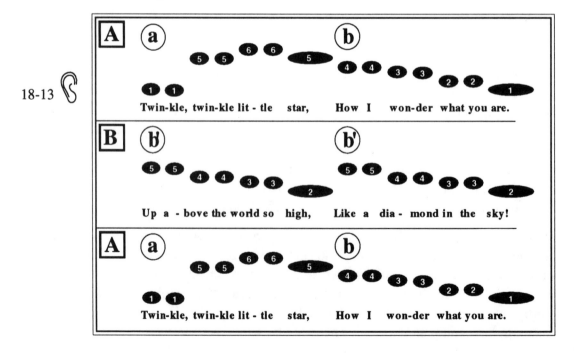

A common formal phrase pattern employs both options—to contrast *and* repeat. An example of this pattern is "Home On The Range" (see graphic below). The first period is in parallel construction, the first phrase (a) ending on an inconclusive dominant chord, called a **half cadence**, and the second phrase (a') ending on a conclusive tonic chord, called a **full cadence**. These phrases together constitute a parallel period. This is followed by a contrasting phrase (b) which is answered by a return of the second phrase of the first period (a'), constituting a contrasting period, but one which relates back to the first period.

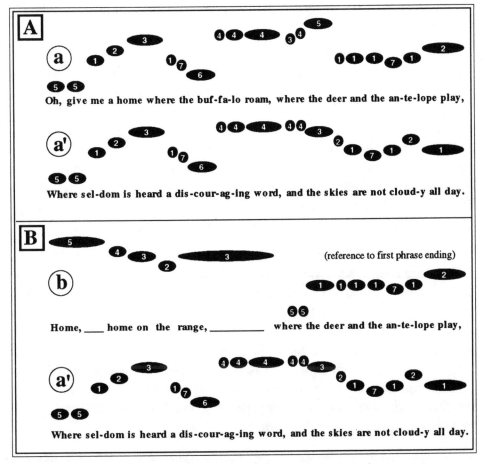

18-14

This is sometimes called a **rounded binary**, rather than ternary, largely because of the proportions of the phrases and periods. Some other traditional songs having this form are "Beautiful Dreamer," "Carry Me Back To Old Virginny," and "Drink To Me Only With Thine Eyes."

Many popular songs, such as "Blue Moon," "I've Got The World On A String," "We've Only Just Begun" and "A Hard Day's Night" employ an AABA song form in which each letter represents at least one complete period.

**the big picture**    In a larger context, external melodic meaning is created when a recognizable melodic entity returns within the course of an extended composition. A melody that recurs in this way is called a **theme**. Depending on its overall structural concept, a composition might have one, two, three or more themes arranged in such a way as to complement, enhance, and (most importantly) to contrast each other.

The precision of this definition is doubtful because the term is also used to refer to a melody that appears only once within a multi-theme composition, as in an ABA form. In a sense, it might be said that these "one-time" melodies earn the status of *theme* by providing contrast to melodies that actually do recur.

We might be tempted to modify our definition to read "melodies used to create formal meaning," except that if no melody recurs we have only contrast—no continuity—therefore, no thematic meaning. A continuous parade of different entities does not particularly create artistic meaning. There is no expectation and fulfillment, no balance, no sense of closure. For example, a **medley** of songs is not required to include or exclude any particular selection, except that they are all by the same composer, or all have to do with a single topic, or are all simply "my favorites." Musically, they are unrelated. They may be tastefully ordered in terms of tempo, key, or topic, but any song could be replaced by other selections that fit the criteria.

To further illustrate this point, let us suppose the arranger decides to repeat the opening song at some point later in the medley. Does that song become a theme by virtue of the repetition? The answer is "yes." The first time it recurs, the listener wonders whether the medley is now complete, having been "rounded off" by this repetition. If the medley continues beyond that point, the listener knows the song will be heard again, since it doesn't make artistic sense to include it twice for no reason. It can be repeated any number of times thereafter since it has been established as a theme. It is logical to expect this theme will conclude the medley, perhaps with flourishes and embellishments added to emphasize the ending.

Unfortunately, the word "theme" is commonly used to refer to a melodic entity that appears only once within a compostion. Since it is beyond our scope to try to solve every problem of this nature, we can hope that a new and better term for this concept will someday emerge, thereby improving the vocabulary we commonly use to describe musical form.

**rondo**    Perhaps the most common musical form is the **rondo**. The organizational principle of a rondo is the reappearance of an initial theme after the inclusion of one or more contrasting "themes" (reluctantly used here). The simplest rondo form is ABA. Other common rondo forms include ABACA, or ABACABA, or ABACADAEA, etc.

The rondo is not entirely an eighteenth-century Classical invention. While Baroque composers created continuity and contrast by other means, usually by employing key changes and various manipulations of a single melodic idea, they did use a **ritornello**, a kind of recurring instrumental "chorus." Also, the *da capo* aria, a Baroque operatic form in which the opening melody returns (exactly) after a contrasting one, was fairly standard.

Another favorite technique Classical composers used for achieving musical meaning was to introduce a theme and then repeat it a number of times (continuity), each time varying some aspect of the melody (contrast). This formal design, known as **theme and variations**, employs one basic melody which the composer dresses up in new clothes each time it is heard. Variations might appear as changes in mode, tempo, meter, melodic embellishments, instrumentation or other perceptible characteristics.

**theme and variations**

Usually, the formal proportions of the theme are preserved, enabling the listener to compare each variation to the original. With this in mind, the composer usually retains more of the theme's recognizability during early variations, and later challenges the listener by venturing farther afield.

Twentieth-century jazz is replete with examples of theme and variations. Since improvisation is an important aspect of this American art form, variation is particularly appropriate to the genre. Typically, a song is initially played more or less as originally composed (called "the head"). As the song is repeated a number of times, one or more performers create "variations" on the melody. As in the Classical theme-and-variations form, the improviser tends to stay closer to the tune during early repetitions and then moves "far out" during the later ones. Usually, the performance ends with a return to "the head."

These two schemes—rondo and thematic variation—represent the two basic ways formal contrast is created in music, (1) by introducing new material and (2) by modifying material already present. The relationship of these two ideas is, in a sense, similar in principle to major/minor, twoness/threeness, or any other logically related contrasting pairs. Innovator Ludwig Beethoven combined these two options in the second movement of his famous Fifth Symphony, in which he employs two contrasting themes, each of which he modifies during the course of the movement.

Perhaps the most sophisticated use of these combined principles is the **sonata-allegro** form, also a product of eighteenth century Classicism. This form was used to shape the opening movement of symphonies, concertos, sonatas,

**sonata-allegro**

string quartets, and any other multi-movement genre. The details of sonata-allegro form (also known as sonata form or first-movement form) are interesting and worth knowing but are largely outside the purpose of this book. We will look only at its overall shape.

Sonata-allegro form has three major sections: exposition, development, and recapitulation (or recap). Continuity is served in that the recapitulation is a restatement of the themes introduced in the exposition. Contrast is served in that themes heard in the exposition are significantly modified during the development section.

Contrast within the exposition (and therefore within the recap) is created by incorporating at least two different themes, the first one usually rugged in character and the second usually **lyrical** (smooth, conjunct). While the recap largely provides for continuity, it is common to modify the themes when they reappear there. Usually, a composer sprinkles small fragments of themes (motives) throughout the composition, particularly in a closing section added at the end, called the **coda**.

One of the most succinct examples of sonata-allegro form is the well-known first movement of Mozart's "Eine Kleine Nachtmusik." It is customary to repeat the exposition, giving listeners opportunity to memorize its themes. If you have a recording of this work (or other classical example), focus on how various thematic elements create continuity, contrast, or both.

Late Baroque and Classical periods provide the clearest examples of pure musical meaning. Such meaning involves the relational interplay of all its elements—specifically, the cumulative use of continuity and contrast. Music of this type is said to be **absolute music** in that it expresses no extra-musical meanings. In short, such music means *itself* and nothing more.

**extra-musical meaning**  Melodies can have yet another kind of "meaning." Some melodies can be said to express such feelings as "mournful," "jubilant," "angry," "tender," and so on. They seems to embody the essence of various human experiences. There is no doubt that this is true. Film composers, for example, are particularly aware of music's ability to create emotional environments appropriate to the dramatic moments in a film.

Throughout music history, compositions have been created around extra-musical ideas. Vivaldi's four concerti entitled "The Four Seasons," Tchaikovsky's "Romeo and Juliet" concert overture, and Debussy's symphonic poem "La Mer" ("The Sea") are examples. Listening to Ferdi Grofe's "Grand Canyon Suite" one can hear the clopping and braying of the donkeys "On The Trail" and almost feel the stagnant heat of the "Painted Desert." Such compositions are described as **program music**.

When these compositions are performed, it is customary to provide the listener with a description of the extra-musical ideas the composer had in mind. But the music must still stand on its own. If the music doesn't "work" without the program, it probably isn't good music. The program may enhance the listening experience, but it can't enhance the musical integrity of the work.

Along this same line, if one cannot appreciate in some way an operatic aria sung in a foreign language unless it is translated, it probably is not a good musical composition, or not a good performance, or both. Again, knowing the meaning of the lyric can certainly enhance one's listening. We are simply distinguishing between *musical* meaning and *extra-musical* meanings.

Renaissance composers of masses, motets and madrigals were particularly fond of using musical elements to express the essence of a lyric. When the words were "ascending to heaven," the melodic setting ascended in pitch. When expressing the pain of unrequited love, appropriate dissonances and chromatic pitches would be included. Handel and other Baroque composers often expressed qualitative ideas in their music. In Handel's aria "Every valley shall be exalted," a long extended rising **melisma** (many pitches on one syllable) dramatizes the elevating process.

However, it is important to separate this kind of meaning from musical meaning described in these chapters. Remember that while art might be said to reflect human experience, it is not a photograph of it. The bottom line is that purely musical meaning, melodic or otherwise, does not include extra-musical descriptive meanings. True meaning rests in the clear and logical use of the principles of continuity and contrast in organizing the sounds of music.

"It is the melody which is the charm of music, and it is that which is most difficult to produce. The invention of a fine melody is a work of genius."
—Joseph Haydn

# 19
# Other Sound-Based Elements As Meaning

After suggesting that it might be best to ignore connotative meanings in order to focus on "musical" ones, what follows may seem to contradict that idea. The harmonic property called consonance/dissonance, a somewhat subjective and connotative perception, appears to have a great deal to do with musical meaning. Aren't dissonance and consonance the musical equivalent of "restlessness" and "repose"? For someone living in the sixteenth to nineteenth centuries, the answer was easy: a resounding, "Yes." A twentieth-century musician might say, "No, consonance/dissonance is simply an extension of timbre, or tonal color, and has little to do with subjective notions.

Is it possible to experience loudness contrasts in music without feeling "tenderness," "elation," "terror," or the like? Are the dynamic changes in a Classical symphony less emotional that those in a Romantic one? Do the controlled tonal schemes in a Classical piece evoke more or less musical meaning than the seemingly unbridled tonal diversions of an early twentieth-century composition? Is timbre simply a means of identifying the various instruments used in a composition, or is timbre an integral part of musical meaning? We won't be able to settle all these questions here, but hopefully we can find a practical perspective on most of them.

## Harmony As Meaning

Does dissonance automatically create a feeling of "disturbance"? If so, does "disturbance" demand resolution, or is it simply a contrast to "pacificity"?

Perhaps revisiting our discussion of consonance/dissonance will yield some insight. We noted that to the extent two or more simultaneously sounded pitches acoustically agree, their combined sound is consonant; and to the extent two or more simultaneously sounded pitches acoustically disagree, their combined sound is dissonant.

It is important to remember that this is not an either/or issue. There is a gradual progression from pure consonance (two voices in a 1:1 ratio) to an infinity of dissonance. At what point does consonance become dissonance? The answer to that question has changed throughout music history. The only factor that is certain is that pitch intervals which have smaller-number vibration ratios (1:2, 2:3, 3:4, for example) are more consonant than those which have higher-number vibrations ratios (7:8, 8:9, 9:10, for example). Does that mean the twentieth-century values expressed above are correct? Is the dissonance/consonance continuum simply a matter of "color"?

Let's look at the other point of view, that of "functional harmony." Music theorists from the sixteenth through the nineteenth centuries have agreed on the need to "resolve" dissonances. Notice that their "dissonances," compared to the infinite possibility of dissonance, constitutes a very short list: seconds/sevenths, certain fourths, and tritones. Might functional dissonances be different from acoustic ones? What role does style play?

Consider another point. While a dominant triad is neither more nor less dissonant than a tonic triad, ending on dominant harmony leaves a phrase in a state of unrest while ending on a tonic triad produces a feeling of resolve. Clearly, there is more to harmonic restlessness than simple dissonance. Furthermore, in functional contemporary music, such as jazz, the final arrival at tonic harmony seems to produce a feeling of closure even when its collection of pitches include some with quite dissonant relationships to the tonic root (including scale steps 6, 7, 9, and ♯4). Here, *tonal* arrival seems more important than resolving dissonance when creating final cadences.

19-1

So what is the relationship of dissonance and tonality in creating unrest and closure? Even ♭7, the pitch that creates a tritone relationship with scale step 3 can, in a blues style, participate in a conclusive tonic-chord. Does this information then negate everything we discussed earlier about the tritone's ability to turn tonality alternately away from and back toward an established tonal center? Not at all. Three hundred years of success shouldn't be taken lightly. The question is not *whether* the tritone affects tonal direction, but rather *how* it affects it.

Disregarding style for the moment, let's consider the basic nature of dissonance/consonance. During a discussion on this topic, a musician pointed out that while he is tuning his electric bass, he actually can feel dissonant vibrations in the neck of the instrument. His method is to stop (place a finger on) an already-tuned string at a point where it will produce the pitch to which he wishes to tune the next string. By plucking both strings simultaneously he not only can hear the pitch relationship between the two strings but he can feel it as well. When the strings are only slightly out of tune, a rough vibration is felt in the neck of the instrument. As he turns the tuning peg toward consonance, the roughness disappears. He demonstrated this phenomenon for all in the room to feel. The inevitable conclusion is that dissonance, in itself, *is* a matter of unrest while consonance *is* the reciprocal absence of that unrest.

Is there a logical answer to the question of harmony as "resolution" or harmony as "color"? Earlier, we defined *harmony* as "combinations of pitches." This definition, while concise and reasonably clear, does not deal with the various *results* of combining pitches. Clearly, "resolution" and "color" are separate concepts from "harmony."

Harmony, then, in its larger generic sense, probably does not directly contribute to artistic meaning. Likely it is the perceptual *components* of harmony that do the job. Therein lies a solution to the apparent problems noted above—harmony's role in creating musical meaning must be viewed in terms of its individual perceptual elements.

It seems clear that dissonance, *assuming all other things are equal*, symbolizes unrest while consonance symbolizes calm. To be sure, there is a "color" aspect to dissonance. Isn't it true that certain visual colors are said to be "hot" and others "cool"? It is not surprising, then, that dissonance inhabits a similar continuum from "restless" to "restful." The subjective, connotative "meaning" of dissonance seems to be inevitable. It carries this meaning *in addition* to any continuity/contrast meaning a composer might create by its use. The artist who uses dissonance for aesthetic purpose needs to be aware of that reality.

What about the tritone effect in music? The fact is that chords—even ones containing "everything but the kitchen sink"—sound different when they do or do not contain a tritone. Twentieth-century theorist/composer Paul Hindemith, in his book *The Craft Of Musical Composition*, emphasizes the special role of the tritone. A tritone's presence, then, is *one factor* in determining restlessness in music. In this audio example, the first three chords do  19-2 not contain a tritone and the last three chords do.

## Tonality As Meaning

19-3

The shifting of harmonic roots away from and toward an established tonal center is also a separate perceptual matter. In this audio example, even though all the chords are major triads (equally consonant), a feeling of restlessness is created at the end of the phrase. Is that because it relates to our real-life experience of leaving home? Perhaps. Or is this simply setting up a contrast to the next phrase which will return us back home? What do you think? In any case, the trip was accomplished without dissonance or tritones.

Either or both aspects of harmony—tonality and dissonance, including the unique function of the tritone—can be used separately or combined to create patterns of continuity and contrast. In addition, immediate connotative meanings of "restlessness" and "repose" seem inevitable in both aspects

19-4

The notion of tonality is probably as old as music itself. The most ancient cultures seem to have been aware that one pitch in a system somehow provides relative meaning to the others. However, it wasn't until recently that changes in tonality became part of music's meaning. Renaissance composers hinted at tonal shifting when they caused various voices within a polyphonic texture to imitate musical motives at different pitch levels, but these seldom produced the impression of true key changes.

19-5

Chromaticism was used in the Renaissance; however, much of it was a matter of inserting F-sharps and B-flats in order to *avoid* tritones, not create them. In the period's later years, out-of-key pitches and startling chord progressions abound. The Los Angeles Chamber Singers demonstrate.

19-6

When Baroque composers discovered the tritone's power to turn tonality in whatever direction they fancied, they frequently used that information to create adventurous introductions that were kaleidoscopic in their tonal varieties. However, once the steady tempo began, signaling the commencement of the formal part of the piece, freedom gave way to discipline and logically structured key relationships guided the music through its tonal journey. Tonality became part of the artistic import of the music. This J. S. Bach excerpt travels through a number of keys—some near and some distant.

Relationships between two keys are said to be close or distant in somewhat the same sense that intervals are said to be consonant or dissonant. The key of G major is closely related to C major since the two scales share six out of seven pitches. On the other hand, the key of E major is distantly related to C major in that the two scales share only three out of seven pitches. Incidentally, a change of mode, for example going from C major to C minor, isn't really a modulation, even though it involves some changes in scale members, because the tonic remains unchanged.

Although Classical compositions are frequently named by key, for example, "Symphony No. 5 In C Minor" or "Mass In G Major," they are not limited to a single tonality. Such titles only indicate that the piece begins and ends in that key. Tonal variety is achieved in two ways within a multi-movement work: (1) individual movements are composed in different keys, usually closely related, and (2) modulations occur within each movement, usually to closely related keys during thematic sections and to more distantly related keys during transitional and developmental sections.

While Classical composers usually kept their modulations fairly close to the tonic key, fanciful Romantic composers embarked on more daring tonal adventures. The difference is like comparing a trip from New York to Chicago and a trip from New York to Borneo. Just as traveling to more distant cultures provides sharper contrasts to one's point of origin, traveling to more distant tonalities provides sharper contrasts to the home key.

On the other hand, if one constantly traveled to exotic lands until the experience became commonplace, the contrast would be diminished. Likewise, in a musical environment in which free passage in tonality is the norm, artistic meaning in this regard would be minimal. This, as we noted earlier, was the main issue separating Schoenberg's supporters from his antagonists. Of course, where no tonality is established no deviation is possible. Therefore, certain kinds of aleatory, electronic or minimalist music would contain little or no meaning in this regard.

There is another way in which change in tonality creates musical meaning. This has nothing to do with close or distant relationships, rather it involves highness/lowness of pitch. When an establish key is contrasted by a sudden shift to a key a half step higher, it creates a certain sense of exhilaration. Although probably a cheap thrill, arrangers of show music often use this device to create an emotional lift at strategic moments. Many a Las Vegas star has ensured a second encore, and therefore a renewed contract, using this technique. Needless to say, sudden modulation to a lower key is not as popular.

One of the innovations of twentieth century musicians was to compose in two or more keys simlutaneously, called **polytonality**. In this audio example, Milcho Leviev pits one tonality against another to create a very interesting effect. 19-7

As with any element of music, tonality is meaningful only to the extent that a listener is able to perceive it. Perhaps listeners with pitch recognition have a slight advantage here, being able to identify and "catalogue" tonal events that occur during an extended composition. Nevertheless, any of us can increase our perception of *relative* tonality through awareness and practice.

# Loudness and Timbre as Meaning

Like harmony, loudness/softness and timbre offer their own possibilities toward meaning in terms of continuity and contrast, and can also carry connotative meanings. Loud sounds can mean "strength" but not "tenderness," "immensity" but not "intimacy," "forcefulness" but not "submissiveness." Trumpets can make musical statements that flutes can only dream about.

Apparently, loudness was not considered a meaningful component of music until the seventeenth century. Although Gothic and Renaissance instruments were designated as "indoor" or "outdoor" depending on their ability to play loudly, it appears that the Baroque idea of *contrasting* loudness and softness within the same composition was quite original. The idea might have been, to some extent, a by-product of technology (see sidebar "Technology Versus Imagination," p. 201).

The realization that loudness and timbre could be used as artistic ingredients to communicate musical meaning first appeared in Venice in the early seventeenth century when Gabrielli specified dynamics in his compositions. He also composed music in which choirs of various sizes and voice types were used to contrast each other. The resulting music was called **polychoral**.

19-8

The practice of pitting one timbre against another became a major element in Baroque music. For the first time, music was composed specifically for instruments, making possible a contrast between an orchestra and chorus in the same composition. Previously, instruments merely played one or more of the vocal lines. Instrumental music also flourished on its own, giving rise to the **concerto grosso**, in which a small group of solo instrumentalists (usually from three to five) contrasted with the orchestra as a whole.

19-9

Contrast of timbre and loudness continued during the Classical period; however, the notion of *gradual* changes in loudness, called **crescendo** (gradually louder) and **diminuendo** (gradually quieter), also appeared. The piano-forte was invented, replacing the Baroque harpsichord. The earlier instrument suffered from an inability to change dynamics gradually. No matter how hard one struck its digitals, the loudness was unaffected. The new piano made it possible for a keyboardist to take full advantage of gradual dynamic changes.

However, it was the nineteenth century Romantic composers who took full advantage of the artistic possibilities of dynamics (changes in loudness). Beethoven used this device as no one had before, creating enormous emotional contrasts in his symphonies and other compositions. The piano moved into its golden era in the hands of Chopin, Liszt, Schumann, Brahms and many others.

## Technology Versus Imagination

An interesting observation can be made regarding the conceptual limitations placed on vocal sounds through the ages. It seems that we have historically depended upon musical technology to take the lead in differentiating between the kinds of vocal sounds that are "musical" and those that are not. For example, voices singing different pitches simultaneously became common late in the first millennium, at about the same time early versions of the keyboard were developed.

In the seventeenth century, organs and harpsichords were built that could change timbres and loudness by mechanical means, which seemed to lead the way for polychoric vocal compositions, combining choirs of varying sizes and vocal combinations. During that period, changes in loudness within a composition, both instrumentally and vocally, were executed suddenly. It wasn't until the development of the dynamically flexible piano that **crescendos** and **diminuendos** (gradual changes in loudness) commonly appeared in music, again, both instrumentally and vocally.

In our own time, the voice is frequently invited by composers to slide up and down without regard for traditional pitch systems. It's as if the voice had been waiting all these centuries for the advent of electronic music to validate its freedom from scales.

Clearly, the voice was always physically able to do *all* of these things, even before technology made them possible instrumentally. Somehow it didn't seem"musical" to do them until technological developments in instrumental music led the way. What caused this vocal inhibition toward "progress"? Has this happened in other areas of creative expression? What are your thoughts?

While Classical composers commonly used contrasting timbres to add abstract (non-specific) meaning, nineteenth-century masters of orchestration, notably the Russian composers Rimsky-Korsakov, Mussorgsky and Tchaikovsky, painted exotic musical tapestries using orchestral colors and emotion-packed crescendos. Their descriptive compositions convey both absolute musical meanings and extra-musical ones.

19-10

While Bach's abstract music can be performed in almost any medium, it is difficult to imagine Debussy's tone poems "Prelude To The Afternoon Of A Fawn" played by any medium other than a symphony orchestra. The timbres and expressive degrees of loudness are an essential part of the musical meaning of this work. The dynamics and instrumental colors chosen to represent its program are essential to its musical import, as well.

Remember, a descriptive musical composition cannot rely on its program to elevate it to an artistic level. Its value as art always depends on its musical integrity alone. While some of our candid photos contain a realistic representation of the subject, we tend to reject them when the photo's composition is not pleasing. On the other hand, we tend to keep a photo that contains a "life of its own," a dynamic balance, even when the likenesses may not be perfect. Just as a well-composed photograph can be enjoyed over and over for many years, so can a well-formed musical composition, regardless of how accurately it describes or imitates its programmatic subject.

19-11

In the past, timbre has been used as a meaningful element in music largely by contrasting one continuous sound against another continuous sound. In this audio example, recorded in India, the jew's harp player demonstrates a constantly changing timbre created by modifying the shape of the mouth while striking a plectrum on the instrument. Electronic music has used similar changes in timbre to convey musical meaning. Very likely, changes in timbre will play an even more significant role in music of the future.

20

# Temporal Elements As Meaning

We observed earlier that the temporal aspects of music are not the sounds themselves, but the organization of the sounds. It is important to keep this in mind as we discuss musical meanings that arise from the perception of temporal relationships between significant sound events. While events in music are necessarily communicated in sound, we want to avoid confusing meanings in sound with meanings in time. Again, as with all meaning, perception of temporal meaning depends on continuity and contrast.

## Meter as Meaning

Almost every composition (or section of a multi-movement work) in the seventeenth, eighteenth and early nineteenth centuries contains a single metric pattern which continues unchanged throughout. That metric pattern is communicated in various ways—a left-hand pattern played by a pianist, or the bass playing on regular metric pulses with other instruments answering on intervening pulses, or perhaps repeated patterns of pitches. In such pieces, the meter, once established, carries no further musical import in itself. All significant musical events occur in *other* elements of the music—melody, harmony, rhythm, dynamics, etc.

In these audio examples, the meter is continuous, therefore it doesn't contribute any musical meaning to the overall import of the piece. Once a listener perceives the meter, it can be put on "automatic" and more or less forgotten about. 20-1

In twentieth-century music, meter frequently participates in the expression of musical meaning. Audiences at the turn of the twentieth century were both annoyed and intrigued by Igor Stravinsky's proclivity for frequently changing meters during a work, sometimes using a pattern only once, merely to disrupt meaningless repetition. Other modern composers followed suit and began to use meter change to add meaning to their creations.

20-2

It should be noted that using meter change meaningfully can be tricky. Since meter exists only in the minds of the participants—including composer, performer and listener—there is no guarantee that they will all sense or interpret the meter in the same way at any given point in the music. The performer has the best chance of perceiving the metric scheme the composer had in mind, assuming he or she is working from the written score. The listener, on the other hand, has only the aural clues received from the performance itself from which to create a metric feeling that seems to fit the sound patterns being heard.

An illustration of this potential confusion can be found in Stravinsky's "L'Histoire du soldat." At first, there are few aural clues to suggest a meter. Then a steady flow of bass sounds appears on two alternating pitches, related as "tonic and dominant," evoking an obvious duple meter. Stravinsky doesn't seem to regard this duple pattern as the principal organizing meter. According to the notation, the meter is constantly changing while the bass line continues its regular duple pattern. One might speculate that it would have been easier (especially for the performers) had he used a continuous duple meter and notated his cross-meter melodic ideas as syncopations. However, it is perhaps foolish to try to second-guess a genius. So we will just leave it at that.

20-3

It does seem, however, that if a composer intends to make the metric flow of import to the music, it is critical to offer sufficient aural clues that allow the listener to enter the game.

## Tempo as Meaning

In one sense, a selected tempo is usually little more than a place to hang one's musical hat. In other words, an established tempo continuing throughout a piece contributes no artistic meaning. Unless it changes during the course of the piece in some significant way, it is simply a meaningless utility.

In another sense, tempo contributes a continuity/contrast meaning to a piece even if the tempo doesn't vary. Any tempo has meaning in terms of all other possible tempos. In other words, a moderately fast tempo has a distinct quality while a very slow one also has a distinct quality. It doesn't matter that a given tempo is exactly one speed or another in terms of clock time, only that it seems appropriate to the mood of the music. In this sense, even absolute music contains a kind of subjective "program" which is determined by its tempo, even though a specific story line is not intended. A slow tempo might be thought of as "meditative," but never as "frantic." A fast tempo might be thought of as "urgent," but never as "sad."

In the seventeenth and eighteenth centuries, tempo became a meaningful element in continuity/contrast when composers organized separate "movements" into suites, symphonies, song cycles and the like. The favorite pattern historically is fast-slow-fast. Multi-movement works from this period which do not follow this pattern are conspicuous by their deviation. Generally, a tempo established at the beginning of a movement was maintained throughout—the principal exception being a slow introduction to an otherwise fast-tempo movement.

**rubato**

As Beethoven was negotiating his steady turn from Classicism toward Romanticism, his established tempos became less resistant to modification for expressive purposes. By the mid nineteenth century, flexible tempo had become the norm, not the exception, and tempo markings were interpreted with considerable latitude. A new kind of flexible-pulse tempo was developed, called **rubato**, in which the tempo alternately rushes ahead and holds back. This new technique provided the means for immediate emotional tension and release, even within a single phrase, which was particularly suited to emotion-based music.

20-4

**accelerando and ritardando**

Another device which was particularly useful in nineteenth century music is the gradual change of tempo. When an established speed of beat gradually increases, the event is called an **accelerando**. A common place to find an accelerando is at the beginning of a **coda**, or ending section. Composers sometimes use it to affect urgency, signalling the listener that the piece is approaching the end.

Another use of accelerando is to connect a slower tempo to a faster one—for example, in a medley of songs or in a Broadway show. The gradual speeding up of the tempo tells the listener that the previous section is coming to a close and to expect something new.

**Ritardando**, or simply **ritard**, is a more universal device, commonly used to signal an ending. The amount of slowing can vary from a slight delay of the last few beats of the last phrase to a grandiose broadening of the final ten or fifteen seconds.

Hurrying and slowing in music are clearly symbolic of hurrying and slowing in life itself. The subjective and emotional meaning these devices bring to music appears fairly obvious.

**tempo vs. pace**

20-5

A potentially confusing aspect of tempo occurs when a melody's rhythmic events move from slower pulse levels to faster ones. Because the events appear to happen faster, a listener is sometimes fooled into thinking that the tempo has changed. Consider this **subject** (theme) from Bach's "Organ Fugue In G Minor." Notice that the first few melodic events occur at the speed of the primary organizing pulse. As the melody proceeds, the events become faster—two events per beat, then four events per beat. Listen again and tap the tempo set by the first three events and maintain that steady pulse series. Don't speed up. You will see that the tempo has not changed even though the impression of increased "speed" is conveyed in the music.

Some musicologists have adopted the term **pace** to identify this characteristic. It is a very handy concept and can clarify changes in the frequency of sound events while pulse and meter maintain the original tempo.

20-6

Another example of a change of pace without change of tempo occurs when a section of a composition is followed by another section containing faster-paced or slower-paced melodic events. In such cases, it is the *pace* of the music that creates the contrast, not the tempo. This audio example contains a steady tempo with contrasts in melodic pace.

**"free" tempo**

20-7

Some music that flows rhythmically seems not to be anchored to a pulse, not even a rubato pulse. One example is **chant**, in which a singer intones text in the rhythm of speech. Syllable stresses are allowed to fall where they will, without regard for an imposed feeling of duple or triple patterns. If any sense of "two-ness" or "three-ness" is felt, it is usually a result of the flow of language rather than kinesthetic regularity.

Strictly speaking, since chant is not based on regularly recurrent pulse, it seems somewhat inappropriate to refer to the speed of chant as *tempo*. Perhaps this would be a good use of the term *pace*. What do you think? In any case, there is seldom any formal artistic meaning carried in the pace of a chant, other than perhaps choosing a rate of speed that is in keeping with the mood of the lyric.

In most structured songs, it takes time to deliver a lyric in an artistic and expressive way. Sometimes syllables are sustained over many beats. Often whole phrases, even sections, are repeated for the sake of musical form and artistic meaning. In opera, such a song is called an **aria**. If all the lyrics in an opera were set as arias, it would take an extraordinary amount of time to tell the story. In order to advance the plot efficiently, a singing style was adopted called **recitative** (pronounced re-si-tah-teev). The orchestral (or keyboard) accompaniment simply sounds a chord or two establishing tonality and the singer delivers large amounts of lyric in a few seconds, without regard for beat, tempo or meter. Phrase endings are sometimes punctuated with additional chords, selected to enhance the mood. This style might continue for a few seconds or a few minutes. Eventually, an emphatic V-I chord progression signals the end of the recitative.

 20-8

A similar style occurs in instrumental music wherein an accompanying orchestra or keyboardist waits in silence for a few moments while an instrumental soloist engages in flights of fancy (the soloist's or the composer's) without the constraints of tempo or meter. During this brief section, called a **cadenza**, the soloist stretches his or her musical wings, taking the opportunity to charm and amaze the listener with technical skills and imaginative manipulations of thematic material heard earlier in the piece. Since the cadenza is totally within the control of the soloist, he or she may choose to play phrases in or out of tempo, in or out of key, or use any other means by which to create artistic meaning.

 20-9

In a sense, the freedom of a recitative or a cadenza can be considered a part of overall meaning in that it contrasts with the normally strict tempo of the surrounding music. However, since the use of these devices seem to have arisen for more or less utilitarian purposes, it seems possible that composers seldom think about the "meaning" created by these "gaps" in the overall continuity of their works.

## Rhythm as Meaning

Rhythm is not so much a *creator* of meaning as it is a *creation* of the combined meanings of other elements. As many of the authors quoted earlier apparently believe, rhythm is created by the interplay of the various aural perceptual events that combine to create the sense of "movement" in music. This impression of flow is created by the anticipation, arrival, and fading of events in a related series.

Experiencing rhythm is largely subjective. A listener with a substantial musical background is more likely to extract multiple layers of rhythmic subtleties from a performance than a listener having limited listening experience. Are those rhythmic subtleties *in* the performance? Or are they in the listener? The answer is "both."

To illustrate, consider the scene from the movie version of "The Music Man" in which the new school band is alternately heard "as it really sounds" and "as heard by the audience of proud parents." Then there is the self-deluding choral conductor who seems incapable of hearing his singers flaws because he is enjoying that "perfect choir of angels" in his imagination. While these two situations might seem extreme, they indicate that beauty—including rhythm—is largely in the eye, or in this case, the ear, of the beholder.

In both illustrations, the listeners took the lead in creating a rhythmic experience, mostly by and for themselves. In contrast, when a great performer shapes and molds sound elements in such a way that a listener is transported to *new* heights and depths of aesthetic meaning, the *performer* has taken the lead. Still, the experienced listener will come away from the performance with much more than the novice. Perception, even of rhythmic meanings, depends on previously formed concepts by which to bring significance to the sounds being heard.

Hopefully, this discussion has shown that rhythm is much more than just "a good beat." Even *meter* and *tempo*, important elements in generating the flow of rhythm, do not constitute the whole of it. And don't forget that rhythms in life itself help us form the concepts by which musical and other artistic rhythmic experiences become aesthetically significant.

## Musical Meaning Wrap-Up

To bring this discussion back where we started, the basis of all meaning—whether verbal, conceptual, perceptual, or aesthetic—arises from the interplay of continuity and contrast. Words have meaning only in terms of how they consistently connote "something" as opposed to "everything." Ideas have meaning within a stream of logic—real or imagined—and are perhaps more wisely used when not confused with reality. Perceiving musical meaning occurs when an event is recognized in terms of previous perceptions and how it stands out from the whirl of other sensory data.

In order for music to communicate meaning, all the participants—composer, performer, and listener—must share a similar vocabulary of musical concepts. The perceptual/conceptual components must operate reasonably well, each contributing its own special significance to the whole. On one hand, they must operate in reasonable agreement to create continuity, and on the other, they must operate in organized conflict in order to produce the essential artistic contrast needed for aesthetic meaning to occur.

**world-wide view revisited**    In the remaining chapters we will turn our attention to music notation, so this would be an excellent time to replay the audio examples in chapter one and reevaluate the musical meaning expressed in those items. It will be interesting to see if you now find more musical significance in those excerpts than when you heard them the first time. Listen in particular for the sense of tonality, specific scale steps, harmonic relationships, meter, formal melodic patterns, and so forth. Very likely, this exercise will bring you a great deal of personal satisfaction that your efforts here are paying off richly.

# V
# Music
# Notation

An important thing to keep in mind as we discuss music notation is that notational symbols, in any field of knowledge, are *not* the things they represent. We understand this in regard to language. As adults, we don't expect the word *elephant* to come rushing off the page and threaten our safety. We know the word is used as a communication tool to cause us to activate our *concept* of that particular animal. Yet many novice music readers seem to have the idea that the music is somehow embedded in the page and that counting beats and pushing the right buttons on an instrument will produce "that" music.

Continuing the analogy, knowing *why* the elephant is mentioned is likely more important than simply knowing what an elephant is. The writer is probably concerned with more than just getting the reader to think "elephant." How does the elephant relate to the discussion, situation or action? Similarly, a composer does not write an "eighth note" or an "F-sharp" just to evoke an isolated response.

The eighth note and the F-sharp are meaningful only as part of a larger notational construct, which in turn represents a larger musical idea. In literary communication, it is the *relationships* between concepts represented by words that are the "meaning," not just the individual words themselves. That is even more true with music symbols, of which most have absolutely no connotative meanings. Furthermore, it is only by realizing the *relationships* between sounds represented by *collective* symbols that meaning is discovered through reading music.

Just as a real elephant is not present on the page but is conceived in the writer's mind, music is not contained on the page but is conceived in the composer's mind. In both cases, the reader's challenge is to discover the idea that was in the writer/composer's thinking and *reconstruct* it for him or herself.

In order to do that, the reader must have assimilated sufficient practical experience by which to understand the creator's intent. When we learned to read language, the subject matter usually dealt with things with which we were already familiar. To learn to read music, it is important first to have some idea about how music works. Otherwise, "music reading" will consist only of robot like responses to individual symbols with little or no apprehension of real musical meaning.

A singer who learns German phonetically for the purpose of singing lieder is not automatically literate in the German language. A literate person is one who has developed the ability to understand *meanings* represented by printed symbols. That does not mean merely creating sounds from printed symbols, but understanding the collective significance of those symbols. Hundreds of hours spent singing the sounds of German lieder will not produce literacy. Likewise, many hundreds of hours counting eighth notes and playing F-sharps will not produce musical literacy.

It is certainly possible for diligent people to spend hours learning to respond mechanically to music symbols and thereby learn to "play" an instrument reasonably well. It is also possible that such people do not have a clue regarding the musical meaning of the pieces they are "playing."

Surely, many intelligent and sensitive "players" will discover musical meaning by listening to the results of their own mechanical accomplishments, as well as by analyzing the musical performances of others. Leaving this discovery to chance can be hazardous, however. When we are left to discover meaning on our own, the result is often intuitive and shrouded in mystery. That is why some music teachers who learned music intuitively are able to share the mechanics of music reading very well but are less successful in communicating the logic of musical meaning to their students.

As mysterious as basic musical meanings might appear to one who learned to perform music in a mechanical way, music notation is far more mysterious to someone who has little or no experience *making* music. It is for this reason that the topics in this book are ordered as they are. If you feel your grasp of the systematic structure of the major/minor system and/or the kinesthetic logic of musical meter is uncertain, please take the time to review these discussions until you feel you understand them. Otherwise, there is little practical reason for studying music notation. It will only add to your confusion or put you at risk of becoming a mechanical performer. On the other hand, if you feel you have a reasonably clear understanding of the ideas and principles described thus far, you are ready to proceed.

# 21

# Meter

# Notation

The written symbols used to represent the temporal aspect of music are often referred to as "rhythm notation," however, a systematic method of notation has not been, nor likely will be, developed to represent rhythm as we have defined it. Rhythm is far too complex to be effectively captured in clear cognitive terms and translated into symbols. The subject normally discussed under that heading is more correctly called "meter notation."

In general, meter notation records relative durations of sounds events (and sometimes silences) heard or imagined within the flow of a musical performance. Some historical attempts to record musical durations were satisfied with symbols that only approximated the rhythmic effect while others developed systems with considerable precision.

Of those concerned only with a general flow of accent, the notion of **poetic meter** is most well-known. Based on the syllabic accent of language, poetic meter differentiates between two rhythmic values—accent and unaccent. Various accent patterns have been identified and named based on the number of syllables per "foot" (grouping) and number of feet per line.

poetic meter

Here are the standard patterns. Notice that, when repeated, the iamb and the trochee result in the same pattern—alternating one accent with one unaccent. Also notice that the dactyl and the anapest have a similar relationship and that both generate a continuous pattern of two unaccents between each accent. Clearly, the difference in both cases has to do with whether the pattern begins with an accent or with an unaccent.

| | |
|---|---|
| Iamb | ˘ — |
| Trochee | — ˘ |
| Dactyl | — ˘ ˘ |
| Anapest | ˘ ˘ — |
| Spondee | — — |
| Tribrach | ˘ ˘ ˘ |
| — accent | ˘ unaccent |

Apparently, the difference between a spondee and a trochee (or iamb) has to do with a subjective evaluation of the amount of stress placed on consecutive syllables. The same seems to be true of the tribrach and the dactyl (or anapest). However, both the spondee and the tribrach create a dilemma in that, having no "unaccents" in one case and no "accents" in the other, it would be impossible to perceive a sense of "feet" when either of these patterns is repeated in a series. Perhaps context provides the clue.

The ancient Greeks' concepts of *thesis* and *arsis* reflect this either-or idea of rhythm. In fact, the traditional system of poetic metric analysis described above is based on the Greek model. A more modern system of analysis, rather than describing poetic flow as repeated patterns of "feet," indicates syllabic accents more in the style of prose, marking stresses with an "x." This system also allows for multiple levels of rhythmic activity by treating smaller patterns separately from larger ones, somewhat like the melodic phrases and periods we described earlier.

Musicologists have used a similar system to describe levels of rhythmic flow. Cooper and Meyer in their book "The Rhythmic Structure Of Music," which was quoted during the discussion of definitions, use such a method. While some of their conclusions are subjective and thus are debatable, the principles of analysis they outline are sound.

**notation and communication**  Of course, these descriptive systems cannot (nor are intended to) represent specific rhythms in a way that would enable a reader to re-create a composer's music. A system of notation must clearly and specifically communicate a writer's ideas so that others can reconstruct those ideas in terms of their own experience—both experience with the symbols and experience with the conventional ideas they represent. As noted above, meter is elemental and systematic, consisting of kinesthetic combinations of pulse series in duple and/or triple groupings and divisions. Meter, in contrast to rhythm, is easy to notate due to its simple logical structure.

Nevertheless, considerable confusion and misconceptions have plagued the study of meter, particularly when the notational system is taught before the nature of meter is clearly understood. If you have previously studied meter and memorized such phrases as "the top number tells how many beats in a measure and the bottom number tells what note value gets one beat," you might find it profitable to suspend those "rules" and re-evaluate them in relation to the facts of practical music making. In fact, there is a good chance that any misleading or unclear ideas you may have will hinder your ability to translate real kinesthetic metric concepts to notational ones, and vice versa.

So, as you proceed through the following pages, be on guard for ideas you find hard to assimilate. If something you read seems at odds with an assumption you have, take the time to think through the apparent conflict. Does your assumption line up with basic experience? Is it a logical conclusion that you worked out on your own? Is it something someone else told you? Did you really understand what they said? Don't be satisfied until an idea *makes sense to you.*

With that in mind, see if the following statements are clear to you. Do they fit logically into your understanding of meter?      **self check**

- Although human beings do not have an accurate sense of "clock" time, we do have the capacity for sensing regular recurrence, evidently learned from kinesthetic experience, particularly walking.

- That sense, called *pulse*, or *beat*, manifests itself as the ability to predict when the next event in an established series should occur in order to maintain an apparent temporal regularity between the individual events. Like all concepts, it can exist in imagination, with or without the presence of actual sounds.

- The sense of musical pulse does not reside in the sounds themselves, but in the performer and/or listener. The critical factor is not whether sounds *are* measurably regular, but whether they *feel* regular. A listener can invoke his or her own sense of pulse by which to interpret a musical phrase, even when the music's "apparent pulse" might be ambiguous .

- *Tempo* is the term we use for designating the speed of a pulse series. The descriptive terminology we use to indicate various speeds assumes moderate walking speed as the basic standard from which "fast" and "slow" are determined.

- Human beings appear to create subjective combinations of pulse series related in ratios of two to one and/or three to one. Slower pulse series (in ratio) can be said to be *groupings* of a primary series and faster pulse series (in ratio) can be said to be *divisions* of a primary series.

- A primary pulse series (usually the one closest to walking speed) combined with one or more grouping series and one or more division series constitutes a metric pattern, or structure. The number of series activated depends largely upon the variety of durational elements in the music under consideration.

- Logically, there are only *four basic metric structures* possible when the primary pulse series is combined with one *grouping* pulse series, in either a duple or triple ratio, and one *division* pulse, in either a duple or triple ratio. These four metric structures can accommodate most of the metered music composed in the last four centuries.

- An occasional triple element imposed on a duple series is called a *triplet*. An occasional duple element imposed on a triple series is called a *duplet*. Other numbers of evenly spaced durations can be similarly imposed as well. All these impositions of "foreign" metric elements are sometimes collectively referred to as *tuplets*.

So, how did you do? Does everything check out? If not, you know what to do. If so, here we go.

# 22

# Durational Symbols

It was the musicians of the Gothic period who first systematized metric notation. The Gothics did not invent pulse-based music. It most certainly had
existed for thousands of years in folk traditions. Although we don't know
much about folk music before the second millennium, it seems reasonable to
assume that some early European melodies were associated with dance, and
therefore metric-based. In any case, such music was most likely secular,
since we know Western church music, specifically Gregorian chant, was
based more on the flow of language than on pulse.

The development of metric notation in the Gothic period probably occurred
out of necessity, since compositions having simultaneous melodies appeared
during this period. The obvious way to coordinate multiple lines of music is
to align them by means of pulse. It was then a short logical step to realize
that pulse-based music organizes into the four basic structures we described
earlier—by grouping and dividing pulse series in patterns of twos and threes
(see sidebar, "A Very Old Idea," p. 164).

What remained was to develop a notational system to represent related sound
durations. Perhaps some attempts were made to represent durations by graphic
means, similar to what appears on pp.187-9. Since our  sense of spacial
distance is no more accurate than our sense of temporal duration, such a
method would soon have been judged
impractical. Evidently, it became clear that
relating symbols to the sense of pulse was
the only way to go. Relational symbols
were invented to notate longer, medium,
and shorter durations.

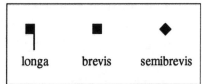

The main problem the Gothics faced in developing these symbols was that sometimes values divided and/or grouped in twos and other times in threes. A reader needed to know how different values related to each other in order to recreate the metric relationships the composer intended.

A fairly satisfactory method was developed in which metric structures were specified by a "mensuration sign" consisting of circles, half circles, and dots. These signs instructed the reader to group and divide values in duple and/or triple patterns. In this system, the same notational symbol could be used for durations that divide or group either way.

| Mensuration | Grouping | Division | Proportions | |
|---|---|---|---|---|
| ( | 2 | 2 | ¶ = ■ ■ | ■ = ◆ ◆ |
| ○ | 3 | 2 | ¶ = ■ ■ ■ | ■ = ◆ ◆ |
| (· | 2 | 3 | ¶ = ■ ■ | ■ = ◆ ◆ ◆ |
| ⊙ | 3 | 3 | ¶ = ■ ■ ■ | ■ = ◆ ◆ ◆ |

This method worked quite well, provided the designated metric flow remained unchanged. A clever device was developed to accommodate occasional triplets and duplets. A different color ink signified the imposition of the contrasting element. This also worked well until the invention of the printing press, when changing ink color became inconvenient.

Renaissance composers used and expanded this system, adding symbols to represent additional longer and shorter values. They also changed from "black" notation to "white" notation, showing only the outline of the note heads, perhaps for greater clarity or economy of ink use in press printing.

During the sixteenth century, a small and seemingly insignificant invention completely revolutionized music notation. It was somewhat akin to the invention of the modest paper clip which has contributed so immeasurably to the organization of our endless sea of paper. What was this amazing new element that provided the basis for modern music notation? It was the *dot*.

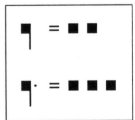

A dot increased a symbol's value by half. Therefore, a plain longa would always equal two brevi and a dotted longa would always equal three brevi. This allowed for triple divisions within a duple metric system, therefore rendering mensuration unnecessary and providing the basis for our current system of metric notation. We'll get back to dotted values shortly. First, let's look at modern notational symbols.

Today, many countries use the same symbols to represent metric values; however, they refer to them by different names.

|   | United States | England | France | Germany | Spain | Italy |
|---|---|---|---|---|---|---|
| o | whole note | semibreve | ronde | Ganze | redonda | semibreve |
| ♩ | half note | minim | blanche | Halbe | blanca | bianca |
| ♩ | quarter note | crotchet | noire | Viertel | negra | nera |
| ♪ | eighth note | quaver | croche | Achtel | corchea | croma |
| ♪ | sixteenth note | semiquaver | double-croche | Sechzehntel | semicorchea | semichroma |

A "flag" added to the stem of a note decreases its value by half. A sixteenth note has two flags, a thirty-second note has three, and so on. Among the countries listed above, only the United States uses a thoroughly systematic method of naming these symbols. All others use more or less arbitrary names for values that are clearly related in a systematic way. (How interesting! While most of the rest of the world uses the systematic metric system of measurement, Americans still fumble with feet, pounds and quarts? It would be interesting to know why this circumstance is reversed in regard to music.)

Here is a convenient way of looking at the system. The language of fractions works well in that any durational symbol has no meaning in itself except as it relates to other symbols within a relational concept. If you were asked, "How big is a half?," you would probably respond by asking, "Half of what?" Likewise, if asked "How long is a quarter note?," you might respond, "Compared to what?" Such questions, of course, have

| 1 whole note | o |
|---|---|
| equals 2 half notes | ♩ ♩ |
| equals 4 quarter notes | ♩ ♩ ♩ ♩ |
| equals 8 eighth notes | ♪♪ ♪♪ ♪♪ ♪♪ |
| equals 16 sixteenth notes | ♬♬ ♬♬ ♬♬ ♬♬ |

no logical answer because both fractions and metric durational symbols have meaning only in relation to other values.

On the other hand, a question such as "How many eighths are in a half?" does have a logical answer. The correct response, of course, is "four." However, that answer assumes that "eighth" and "half" are related to the same "whole." Here's a riddle. "When is a quarter note shorter than an eighth note?" You have the information you need to figure it out. Do you have the answer? Give up? The answer is "When they belong to different pieces of music."

Remember, there is no specific answer to the question "How long is a quarter note?" A quarter note, or any value for that matter, can have any duration specified by the user. However, once the assignment of any note value in a metric flow is established, all other values in that context are automatically determined by their relation to that value.

Before going further, we might clarify and define the term **note**. As the word implies, a note has to do with notation. In other words, it is what one puts on paper to represent a musical sound. Being a symbol, it is not the sound itself. That being the case, it is not logical to "sing a note" or "hear a note." Strictly speaking, both are impossible, since a "note" is a silent symbol. Also, one would more correctly sing a "high *pitch*" than sing a "high note." Nevertheless, these expressions are well entrenched in the common language of music, so it is not likely that this paragraph is going to influence much change in that regard. Perhaps the best that might be hoped for is that when we hear (or use) these expressions we can smile knowingly and then go on with our musical lives.

**triple elements**   Let's get back now to more practical matters. As you may have noticed, there are no "third notes" or "ninth notes" in our list.

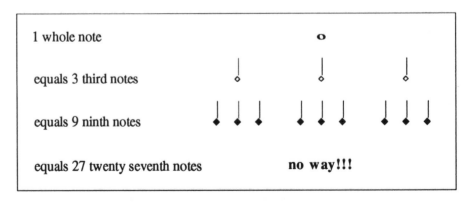

We probably should be thankful for that. Metric notation is tricky enough without having to learn *two* systems using *two* sets of symbols. It boggles the mind to imagine *mixing* quarter notes and eighth notes with "third notes" and the like within a piece of music.

| | |
|---|---|
| 1 whole note | 𝅝 |
| equals 2 half notes | 𝅗𝅥 𝅗𝅥 |
| equals 6 sixth notes | ? ? ?  ? ? ? |
| equals 12 twelfth notes | *forget it!!!* |

Perhaps now you will realize the importance of the dot which makes it possible to represent triple elements within a duple system of notation. Using the dot is not without its problems, however, as you will soon see, but it is better than the Gothics' mensuration and certainly better than the "third note" idea.

Here is how the dot works in notation. Whenever a triple relationship is present in a metric structure, the slower (larger) of the two pulse series is represented by a dotted note. Here six quarter notes fit into two dotted half notes, three quarter notes per each dotted half note.

| | |
|---|---|
| 1 dotted whole note | 𝅝· |
| equals 2 dotted half notes | 𝅗𝅥· 𝅗𝅥· |
| equals 6 quarter notes | ♩ ♩ ♩ ♩ ♩ ♩ |
| equals 12 eighth notes | ♪♪♪♪♪♪♪♪♪♪♪♪ |

Oh, much better! Love that dot! Notice also that two dotted half notes equal a dotted whole note. That is also very convenient. We can generalize on this. Two dotted notes of any denomination will always equal one dotted note of the next larger denomination.

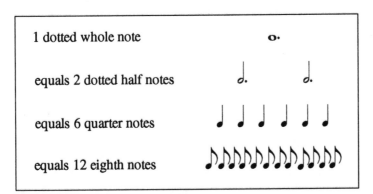

So, by using regular and dotted notes we can notate metric structures having both duple patterns and triple patterns within the same system. Duple divided beats are represented by notes "right off the shelf," and triple divided beats are represented by notes modified by a dot. Very nice!

**swing**     However, as clear and convenient as this system is, it generally is not used in "swing" notation. In this jazz style, pairs of eighth notes are interpreted as "long-short" patterns, creating a triple feel (2+1=3). When all three articulations are present, the pattern is usually written with three eight notes beamed as a triplet. Thus, a simple meter in notation sounds like a compound meter in performance. This may sound like a strange practice, but it is quite standard. Likely, it was developed to avoid having to write lots of dotted notes to represent the primary beat. Usually, the instruction to "swing" the music is provided at the beginning of printed music intended to be performed in this style.

22-1          In this L.A. Jazz Choir excerpt, the feel changes from regular even-eighths to a swing feel. Can you hear and feel the change?

# 23

# Notating Metric Structures

Now let's look at how notes and dotted notes relate to kinesthetic metric structures. We know that a pulse series consists of regularly recurring events. We also know that multiple pulse series can be combined in ratios of twos and/or threes. Since note values relate to each other in ratios of twos (simple notes) and threes (dotted notes), these symbols offer a convenient way to represent durational relationships of sounds organized within metric pulse structures. Here's how it works.

When a composer conceives a metric-based musical idea, some decisions must be made before it can be written in meter notation. First it must be determined which of the four basic metric structures will best fit the music. While performing it in imagination (or in sound), the composer determines a primary pulse series. Normally, the pulse series selected is the one closest to walking speed.

Earlier, you were asked to listen to the song "Yankee Doodle" and to focus on as many pulse series as you could. If you think it might be helpful, go back to p. 154 and do that exercise again to refresh your memory. If you were asked to notate "Yankee Doodle," which pulse would you select as the one closest to walking speed, and therefore the most practical for the primary pulse series?

Once a primary pulse has been established, the next step is to determine whether the grouping and division ratios seem to be duple or triple. In the case of "Yankee Doodle," both are duple. The basic metric structure appropriate for this song, then, is the one having a duple grouping and a duple division. For this discussion, we will assume that you selected the pulse series that falls on the syllables "Yank-," "Doo," "went," and "town" as the primary one. You must now assign a note value to that pulse series.

Here is a piece of information often missed by beginning music students, so you might want to catch a fresh breath and get ready for what might be a surprising fact: A COMPOSER CAN SELECT ANY NOTE VALUE TO REPRESENT THE PRIMARY PULSE SERIES. Since the division level is duple in this song, the note selected does not require a dot.

Once a primary-pulse note value has been selected, all other related pulse series are determined in relation to it. For example, if the half note value is selected to represent the primary pulse, the division pulse is automatically represented by quarter notes and the grouping pulse is represented by whole notes. If eighth notes are selected for the primary pulse, the division uses sixteenth notes and the grouping uses quarter notes.

This principle extends to any additional groupings and divisions that may be needed to express a metric idea. If a second-division series is needed, it will be represented by the next smaller (faster) note value to the division pulse note value. If a second-grouping series is needed, it will be represented by the next larger (slower)

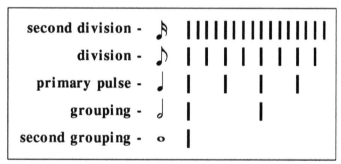

note value to the grouping pulse note value. In this graphic, the quarter note is selected to represent the primary pulse series. All the other pulse series are automatically assigned to values in relation to it. Division values are eighth notes, grouping values are half notes, and so forth.

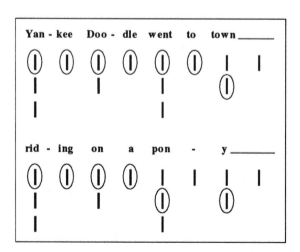

Finding appropriate note values to represent the first two phrases of "Yankee Doodle" is fairly simple, since most of the durations are equal. Most of the syllables (durations) in this phrase occur at the division level, a few at the primary level, and none at the grouping level (or any other level).

To feel the relationship of the musical idea to the pulse structure, tap on the marks of the primary pulse in the graphic (the one falling under "Yank," "doo," "went," etc.) while you say the lyric. Keep your tapping evenly spaced (like walking). DON'T TAP SYLLABLES. Notice that while you are tapping the primary pulse, the durations of the syllables only occasionally correspond to the durations of the primary pulse level.

Also notice while the durations of the melody are "shifting" from one level to another, all levels of the pulse structure continue unchanged. This is important, since the regular steady flow of the meter is the only means of "measuring" the durational values in the melody. If the flow of the meter is not regular, there is no assurance that any notation based on it will be accurate. Remember, an elastic ruler is of little value.

**duple-division notation**

Now that we know how this melody relates to an appropriate metric structure, we are ready to express those durational values as notes. Here are three possibilities.

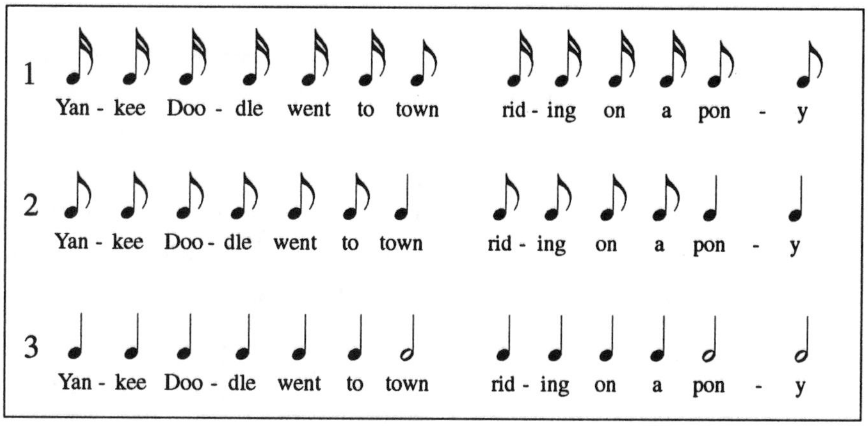

No, the first one is not faster than the other two. Remember, sixteenth notes are only faster than eighth notes when they are related to each other within the same metric flow. Performance of any of these three notations can sound identical. Establishing a tempo is a decision made by the performer. The difference among these three versions is purely notational and is a result of selecting a different note value in each case to represent the primary pulse series. Again, the notation is not the music—it only represents the music.

**decisions**

Listen to a phrase of this Stephen Foster melody and select the pulse series that is closest to walking speed. Most musicians would select the one that corresponds to the two syllables of "dream-er." Assuming that you agree, now identify the division pulse. Clues can be found where the syllables are shorter (faster) than the primary pulse. This occurs in two places—on "beauti-ful" and on "wake un-to." Is it a duple division or a triple division? Does it have the windshield wiper feeling of back and forth? If not, it must be the "other one."

Did you decide that the division is triple? If so, you are correct. We should mention, however, that the division is not judged to be triple merely because there are three syllables within the space of one beat. If "number of syllables" was the basis for your correct response, you may need to be reminded that it is important to make sure that the beats you are imagining are all the same size. If you felt the three syllables in a short-short-long pattern, the divisions would have been duple. In order to be triple division, the beats must be continuously even, and that is the case in this song.

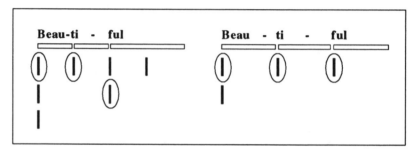

The aural clues that lead to the best grouping for this melody are a bit more subtle. One might feel that either a duple or triple grouping would work; however the decision should favor triple because of the regularly recurrent pattern of the beat having faster syllables. Recite the words in tempo and notice that the three-syllable fragments ("beau-ti-ful" and "wake un-to") create a "faster syllables" accent on every third beat.

Therefore, the metric structure that best fits this melody is a triple grouping with a triple division. On the graphic below, tap the primary pulse series while singing the phrase.

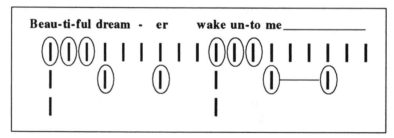

Do you feel the triple division pulse generated by the three-syllable patterns? Notice that you can continue that triple feeling silently in your imagination while you are singing "dream-er" and "me" on the primary pulse series. The reason you can do that, of course, is because meter is a silent feeling of related pulses used to maintain regularity and thereby "measure" the actual sounds. The more securely you are able to maintain that underlying feeling, the more confidence you will have that the "measurements" are correct.

To express this phrase in metric notation we need to assign a note value to the primary pulse series. Because the division is triple, we will use a dotted note for the primary pulse. (As you remember, because our notational symbols are based on a duple system, a simple note will not divide evenly into three of the next smaller denomination.) Here are three possibilities. **triple-division notation**

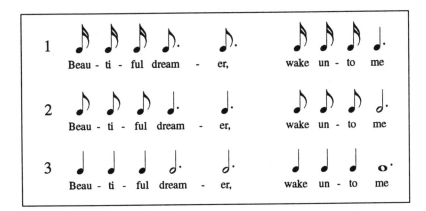

Because the value assigned to the primary pulse is dotted, the values at the division level are simple notes. Don't let that confuse you into thinking the division level is duple. Remember, the designation "triple" describes the *relationship* of the division level to the primary one. Also, the long note on the word "me" sustains for two pulses, twice the duration of a single primary pulse, and is appropriately represented by a dotted note (see p. 219).

Again, all three notational versions represent the same pattern. The selection of the primary note value is arbitrary (provided it is dotted) and all other related pulse series are named in relation to the primary one.

You may have noticed in the above illustrations that a long string of note values is not very user-friendly. One would have to be very quick with mathematical calculations in order to figure out the placement of primary beats, groupings and divisions in even a mildly syncopated phrase. You may be impressed to know that Gothic and early Renaissance music readers had to do exactly that, sometimes with metrically complex music. In addition, they frequently viewed only the notation of their own musical line, needing to coordinate that line with up to five or six other parts. Since the music was usually polyphonic, the lines often interplayed with each other in interesting and tricky cross meters and staggered accents. Misinterpreting even one value would result in disaster. **measures**

Again, a simple device provided a practical solution. A seventeenth-century invention called a **barline** organized notational symbols into segments that roughly correspond to what we have called "groupings." The "space" between one barline and the next is called a **measure**. Although "measure" and "bar-line" are not exactly the same thing, practical use of the phrase "last four bars" means essentially the same as "last four measures." In other words, either expression will lead users to the same location in the printed music.

Inserting barlines into the notation representing the two phrases we just looked at helps considerably to show the kinesthetic organization of metric flow.

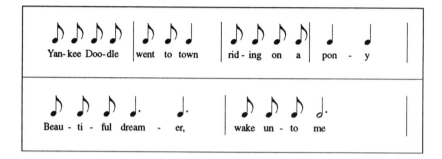

The introduction of barlines was a major step in making music notation look more like the metric flow it is intended to represent. Sing the phrases above and notice the feeling of the grouping metric accent as you pass a barline.

**beaming**     While measures help a reader feel the grouping of metric flow, they do little to shed light on the organization of durations *within* the measure. Long series of notes with various numbers of flags contribute more to confusion than to clarity. A partial solution was found by connecting notes belonging to a single primary beat with **beams** instead of using flags. When notated with beams, the above phrases appear this way:

Of course, notes having no flags can have no beams. Therefore, quarter notes and half notes cannot be grouped into beats using this method. In this case, the reader is obliged to perceive the pulse organization through experience and quick thinking.

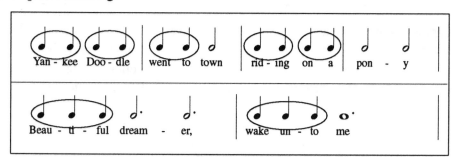

This is probably the reason the quarter note and dotted quarter note are the modern favorites for representing the primary pulse series. They provide for clean uncomplicated single-symbol primary beats that allow for beaming of everything smaller. Because the quarter note is so frequently selected for the job, many people have the idea that it always "gets one beat." If you have been under that impression, you may now retire that misinformation and improve your understanding of quarter notes as simply one of a number of relative values in a duple system of metric notation.

The number of beams used to connect a group of notes corresponds to the number of flags each note would have when presented individually. While the above examples are relatively simple, music often contains some fairly complicated combinations of durations. Beaming may not guarantee error-free perception, but it certainly improves on beamless notation. Here are some examples of unbeamed and beamed patterns based on a quarter note of value.

The unbeamed series of notes appears formidable and chaotic. When beamed, the same series of notes no longer appears "impossible," but merely "difficult."

In some vocal music, beams do not indicate the internal structure of the measure. Many editors use beams in vocal scores only to show where a single syllable is performed on more than one pitch. Syllables to be sung on one pitch having an eighth value (or less) are shown as single flagged notes.

**beams in
vocal music**

Most vocal music is not complex, so this works fairly well. It does not show the metric structure of the measure, however, so the trend seems to be toward using full-beat beaming in vocal music, as in instrumental music. Multiple-pitch syllables are shown by a **slur** connecting the affected notes.

This method shows quite clearly, particularly in the third measure ("glorious song of"), that the metric organization here is a duple grouping with a triple division. The beamed sets of three eighth notes are easily perceived as belonging to a single beat. Because quarter notes have no flag they cannot be beamed, so the quarter-eighth sets (on "came up-," "mid-night" and "clear, That") must be collected into beats by eye.

the tie    While a curved line connecting two or more notes on different pitches is called a slur, a curved line connecting two notes on the same pitch is called a **tie**. Tied notes represent a single uninterrupted sound, just as any single note value would do. You might think that using single notes to represent uninterrupted single-pitch sounds would always be the best way to go, but there are at least two good reasons for not always doing it this way.

Sometimes a durational value is needed that cannot be notated by a single note, not even a dotted one. For example, a sound equal to five eighth notes can be notated only by combining values, for example:

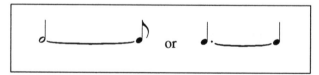

Another reason for notating some single-pitch durations with two tied notes is to show the metric organization within the measure. Students sometimes find this a bit confusing (perhaps because they don't understand meter in the first place).To avoid confusion, keep metric structures in mind during this discussion.

Suppose we want a single pitch to be sustained into the second half of a duple-grouping triple-division measure. The triple division requires that a dotted note be used to represent the primary pulse, so we will assign a dotted quarter note to do this job. The basic metric feeling of this measure is shown here in notation—the barlines represent the grouping pulse, the dotted quarter notes represent the primary pulses (two per measure), and 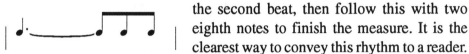 the eighth notes represent the division pulse (three per primary pulse). Perform this metric pattern repeatedly to feel its flow.

With this meter in mind, we will compose a rhythm consisting of one long duration from the beginning of the first beat through the first eighth note of 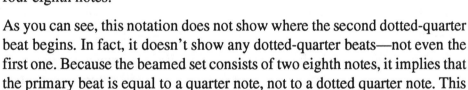 the second beat, then follow this with two eighth notes to finish the measure. It is the clearest way to convey this rhythm to a reader.

The set of beamed eighth notes clearly shows where the second primary beat begins, even though no articulation occurs there in this rhythm. The reader can use that information to create and feel the metric flow needed to accurately re-create and perform these durations.

The mistake that students commonly make in notating this rhythm is to show the long duration as a half note, reasoning that it is equal to four eighth notes.

As you can see, this notation does not show where the second dotted-quarter beat begins. In fact, it doesn't show any dotted-quarter beats—not even the first one. Because the beamed set consists of two eighth notes, it implies that the primary beat is equal to a quarter note, not to a dotted quarter note. This certainly is more confusing than clear.

On the other hand, that notation would work very well in a meter having a triple grouping with duple division.

Perform this pattern repeatedly to experience its feel, then use it to interpret the rhythm above containing the half note. The half note is easily seen as equal to two quarter-note beats and the two beamed eighth notes fill out the third beat and complete the measure.

 Ties can be useful in this meter as well. For example, a tie can be used to show a duration that begins on the first beat and extends into the first part of the second beat. The set of two eighth notes shows clearly where the second beat begins. A secure feeling of the second beat will help to correctly place the eighth-note duration on the second half of the beat.

**dotted notes in**    Earlier, it was shown that a note is increased by half when followed by a dot.
**duple values**    In that discussion, we needed a note to represent a duration that would divide into three equal parts. The dot also works to good advantage in duple values. The rhythm notated with a tie in the preceding paragraph can also be notated using a dot.

The dotted notation is not as clear as the tied notation in regard to locating the second beat. In the dotted verson, the second beat begins on the dot. However, the dotted version looks much cleaner. Experienced musicians generally prefer it.

Using a dot is also preferred to show values smaller than one beat. Here is the same rhythm expressed with ties and dots. Notice how much cleaner the dotted version is.

Although some composers, notably Johannes Brahms, have used the dot to indicate durations extending through barlines, others have used the tie for this purpose. If you believe the tie is clearer, you are in the majority. Using the tie to represent a duration sounding in different measures is the technique of choice in most modern music notation.

**choices**    Remember that meter is the "ruler" by which we "measure" the sounds of music—it is not the sounds themselves. Each user will select a meter that seems to organize in a meaningful way the events being heard or imagined. Therefore, to represent musical ideas in notation, one must develop the ability to choose meters that will best serve that purpose.

Just as there are different ways to express the same ideas in language, there are different ways to express the same music in notation. What is important in both cases is to *understand the system.* Just as understanding syntax provides a basis for clear writing, understanding meter provides a basis for clear music notation.

To be sure, there is some value in learning language skills and music skills by rote. However, the deepest levels of expression are reserved for those who have earned the freedom to choose the most effective template upon which to convey meanings to others.

# 24

# Reading Meter Notation

In some ways, writing and reading are two sides of the same coin. Vocabulary assimilated by reading often becomes vocabulary used in writing. However, assimilating other people's written ideas always depends on at least two factors: (1) the reader's practical experience and accumulation of related concepts, and (2) the reader's knowledge of the symbols commonly used to represent those concepts.

In this chapter, we will look at some practical ways of dealing with meter notation from the reader's standpoint. We will also evaluate some traditional methods of teaching music reading to see how well they line up with what we know about meter and how it works.

A popular method of teaching "rhythm" reading is to *count* beats and sub-beats, or use various systems of syllables to keep track of what articula- **counting beats** tions happen where. Many music teachers and their students seem to thrive on such systems, with some achieving an impressive ability to rattle off difficult rhythms without missing a single syllable. On the other hand, many students are able to rattle off complex lines of rhythms *without* using any syllables or numbers. Still others can rattle off difficult rhythms while getting the syllables *wrong*. It seems that naming metric events does not correlate closely with accurate performance of metric rhythms.

In a strange way, counting rhythms is similar to using phonics to "sound out" words. Breaking down a word into its separate sounds may be helpful in the early stages of learning to read, but at some point, voicing each separate sound becomes cumbersome and actually impedes the reading process. While phonics helps youngsters relate letters to the sounds of language, experienced readers are not concerned with sounds—only with meanings.

The experienced music reader also is not concerned with sounds where meter is concerned. As we know, meter has little to do with sounds. Unlike language, metric symbols have no connotative, or assigned, meanings. Metric meanings are strictly relational and only make sense when conceived and perceived with temporal regularity.

Therefore, one cannot learn anything practical by "sounding out" (counting) individual elements unless it is done with temporal regularity. Perhaps you have seen (or maybe even been) a music student dutifully counting beats while slowing down for, or even pausing at, the "hard" parts during a practice session. Clearly, it isn't counting beats, but feeling a steady flow of metric structure that brings metric notation to life.

The basic question here is whether active counting has any advantage over simply feeling an underlying metric flow and being aware of its groupings and divisions. The evidence of students who accurately perform metric patterns using the wrong names argues that it probably does not. At some point, the experienced music reader, like the experienced language reader, will have no use for sounding out separate elements. If students can learn to read meter notation easily *without* this detour, it probably should be taught that way from the beginning. We need to be wary of teaching techniques that are more helpful to teachers than to their students.

**metric "words"**   Perhaps a more practical method of learning to read metric rhythms is related to another aspect of reading language. Most youngsters soon outgrow the need to "sound out" individual syllables, and learn to read words as units. It becomes inefficient to sound out each syllable, especially of common words. Eventually, whole phrases are scooped up at a glance.

The same occurs in music reading. Very quickly, young readers learn to apprehend *groups* of notes instead of "seeing" each note individually. This sort of perception makes even more sense in music since individual notes have no meaning in themselves. Music readers develop a visual "vocabulary" of metric shapes, just as language readers develop a visual vocabulary of word shapes.

Learning the basic "vocabulary" of metric notation is easier than learning the vocabulary of a language because THERE ARE ONLY EIGHT WORDS TO LEARN. That's right. There are only eight possible durational combinations within a single primary beat having a duple division and duple subdivision. Instead of mastering a counting system, you can go right to the vocabulary and practice "words." Here are the eight "words" notated with the quarter note as the beat unit. In the audio example, each "word" is repeated four times.

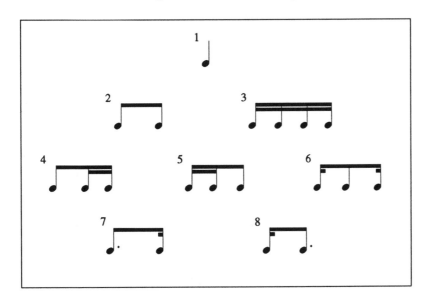

24-1

These metric "words" are not words in the usual sense of "standing for" concepts. These eight words *are* the concepts. We are calling these configurations "words" only in the sense that they can be recognized individually by their shapes and used in combinations to express larger rhythmic ideas. By learning this "vocabulary," you will prepare yourself to easily and correctly notate and/or read rhythms that may otherwise appear "difficult."

Here is an exercise for learning these eight basic patterns. Feel a pulse series at about the tempo of a slow walk. On each beat, tap *once* on a word (not on each note) and articulate its pattern using some syllable ("ta" is a time-honored choice). If reading metric rhythm is new to you, you may want to limit this drill to the first three words until you get the feel of it. Repeat a word if you like, repeat patterns of words, make up interesting metric phrases, pretend you're in a drum section of a marching band. Have fun. Make music!

24-2

In order to benefit from this drill, you must perform it with a strict pulse and evenly placed divisions. When performing "words" 4 through 8, you may find it helpful to include the four-sixteenth-note "word" (number 3) in your drill to help keep the second-division pulse level activated in your silent kinesthetic metric flow. This will provide security for "words" 4 through 8 to make sure they are based on a steady metric flow.

That drill will prepare you to read rhythms based on a quarter-note primary pulse. Try this rhythm. To ensure a steady pulse, point to each "word" (not each note) as you perform it. Maintain a two-beat walking feeling, taking left and right "steps" in each measure.

Notice that the measures here are not spacially (visually) equal. Those containing many notes are larger than those with few. Yet all are equal in metric time. The spacial size of each measure does not affect the time given to the sounds. The experienced reader ignores the amount of space used to draw the notes and uses the sense of steady pulse to regulate placement of the individual sounds represented by the notes (or better yet, by the metric "words").

Once the eight metric "words" are secure, they can be used to read and write music with fairly difficult-sounding syncopations. Most students are surprised at how simple the notation is for what sounds like complex rhythms. In this example, syncopations are created by using **ties** to connect the last note of one beat, or "word," to the first note of the next. Accurate performance is a matter of reading the basic "words" and not articulating between tied notes.

This is not to suggest that one should be able to perform this and similar rhythms after simply reading these descriptions. Like any performance skill, one must pay some dues by regularly practicing the basics and gradually increasing the difficulty of the material. The main reason for mentioning now the use of the tie to create syncopations is to show its relationship to the vocabulary of the eight basic "words."

It would be nice to be able to tell you that there are only a few basic "words" in meters that divide the beat into *three* parts, but adding just one more part brings a flood of additional possibilities. That's the bad news. The good news is that once you have a feel for duple-division words it isn't difficult to get the feel of triple-division words. The same kinds of subdivision patterns you encountered there are present here. Here are some of the more common triple-division "words." The basic "word" is a dotted quarter note.

Each "word" is repeated twice in this audio example. Since the value of the basic "word" here is larger than a quarter note, and because the quarter note has no flag and therefore can't be beamed, four of these "words" must be drawn without beams. Other than this inconvenience, these words are formed just like the duple-based words—with durational combinations from the division and second-division pulse series. Just remember that the basis for the *feel* of this "vocabulary" is the three-eighth pattern. Maintain that feeling in the metric flow as you recite these and other triple-based words.

24-3

Composers frequently want to indicate the passing of metric time in silence rather than sound. Although the symbols used to do this are called **rests**, the music reader should not stop or relax the metric flow during these moments. To do so would result in a collapse of the measuring system that holds everything together. A better name for rests would be "silent notes."

**rests**

For the most part, rests are as much a musical event in the mind of the careful music reader as are notes. Precise metric placement of rests will assure that sound durations end on time. This results in cleaner and more rhythmic performances, particularly by ensembles.

| whole rest | ▬ |
| half rest | ▬ |
| quarter rest | 𝄽 |
| eighth rest | 𝄾 |
| sixteenth rest | 𝄿 |
| thirty-second rest | 𝅀 |

The names of rests, at least in the United States, are the same as notes. The number of flags on rests correspond to the numbers of flags (or beams) on similarly named notes. Learning rests, then, is merely a matter of memorizing the symbols. The only visual difference between the whole and half rests is that the whole rest hangs below a line and the half rest sits above a line. A convenient way to remember which is which is to think of the whole rest as "larger," therefore "heavier," and as a result falls below the line.

While up and down are easy for most people to perceive quickly, left and right are sometimes a problem, particularly for the ambidextrous. Some early European music publishers used a quarter rest that looked like an eighth rest facing the other way. Thankfully, this early quarter rest dropped out of use and now the more distinctive "squiggle" is used exclusively.

Here are some rests at work, making their own positive contribution to the metric flow of this music.

You may have noticed that when rests are present it sometimes becomes more difficult to tell at a glance where the beats fall. This is because notes and rests that belong to the same beat sometimes cannot be beamed together. In the example above, only the rest in the third measure is helped by a beam. Therefore, the reader either has to do some fast math or imagine the rests as "notes not to be sounded." Here is the same rhythm shown with parenthsized notes in place of rests.

The quarter rest at the beginning of the first measure is fairly easy to perceive since it represents a single beat. The eighth rest in that measure can be visualized with the eighth note, reading both the silence and the sound as elements in a single two-eighth word. This is where the concept of "silent note" is valuable. Both the rest and the note are felt metrically as a single "word," but only the note is given sound.

The same procedure can be used to perform the sixteenth rest in the second measure. The music reader can conceive the whole metric "word" (two sixteenths and an eighth), but perform sound only on those values expressed as notes. This sixteenth rest falls on the strong metric accent beginning the measure, so its energetic placement there is critical for knowing where the sounding values are to be placed within that beat.

The silent sixteenth value in the third measure is easy to perceive since the beamed notes surrounding it carry it along visually within a full set of four sixteenths. The performance procedure here is the same as above—think and feel the complete pattern while only sounding the values expressed as notes.

In the last measure, the sixteenth note can be felt as the last part of the complete four-sixteenth "word" leading to the two-eighths "word" in which the second note is silent. To perform this measure accurately, one must feel the flow of the second-division pulse level and sound that value just before the eighth note and feel the "ta-tum" that results. This idea is described more fully below.

Under some circumstances, it is more efficient to ignore rests when the metric placement of a note (or notes) is immediately clear. This may sound strange after discussing the positive value of rests. Nevertheless, some rests can be safely ignored when the metric information is perceived immediately upon seeing only the notes.

**rests as "leftover" values**

When all the notes in a measure have been sounded and only rests remain, there is no practical reason to consciously read those rests, provided a strong sense of metric flow is maintained. In this example, each measure has four quarters of value. By maintaining a strong sense of this repeated pattern, the location of each barline can be felt, whether or not all of the rest values are carefully considered.

"Feeling" the next barline is all the reader needs to perform "leftover" rests correctly. Reading all the individual rest values following the notes and preceding the next barline is not essential. In fact, it might interfere with the flow of metric feel if a reading error occurs, perhaps by counting an extra beat. Sometimes feeling is more important than thinking, and this is probably one of these times.

This "efficiency" method of reading rhythms also applies in circumstances where notes occur on the early side of a barline. In this example, each measure contains four quarters of value. Since the quarter value is assigned to the primary beat, it is clear that the first note occurs on the last beat before the strongly-felt first beat of the next measure. Provided a strong sense of the measure is felt, this single "last beat" quarter note can simply be sounded immediately before the next measure. It isn't really necessary to give dutiful attention to whether the boxlike rest preceding it is a whole or half rest.

Placing the eighth note at the end of the second measure can be easily accomplished by feeling the division pulse and sounding it at the last occurrence of that pulse series before the next "first beat" accent. The same method can be used to place the sixteenth note at the end of the third measure, provided the metric feel includes the second-division pulse series.

With a strong sense of metric flow, all the "pickup" notes above (those immediately preceding the barlines) can be performed by examining the note value, and more or less ignoring the "leftover" rests. Much easier, don't you think?

Incidentally, the formal word for *pickup note* is **anacrusis**. Don't be surprised if you find experienced musicians who have never heard that term. Almost every musician knows what pickup notes are, however.

**practice tip**  Because meter has nothing to do with sound, it is sometimes a good idea to separate rhythm practice from other aspects of music drill to avoid developing habits that can lead to erratic and stilted performances. For example, if fingering a technical passage is a problem, practice it "out of rhythm" until it is comfortable. Then play the passage *in meter* in a slow and steady tempo. Finally, increase tempo until the passage flows musically at performance speed.

If an unfamiliar rhythm pattern is the problem, work it out without performing its pitches. Analyze the metric structure of the passage, noting the metric levels needed to interpret the notation. Establish the feeling of the meter in a slow and deliberate tempo and imagine the rhythm pattern. When it makes sense as a clean rhythmic idea, reintroduce its pitches and perform the excerpt out of context at the slow tempo. Gradually increase the speed, maintaining the metric feel, until the passage is comfortable. Finally, reinsert the passage into the flow of the performance.

25

# Meter Signatures

We observed earlier that the Gothics placed a symbol at the beginning of their music notation to tell readers what metric pattern to use to interpret the notes. We still do this today, but the symbols have changed. While their mensuration sign consisted of circles and dots, the modern meter signature consists of two numbers, one placed over the other.

In general, the top number tells the reader "how many..." and the bottom number tells the reader "...of what." For example, in this music, each measure has the equivalent of two quarter values. The meter signature therefore shows a 2 on top (representing "how many...") and a 4 on the bottom (representing a quarter value).

This meter signature informs the reader that each measure in this composition, until notified otherwise, will contain two quarters of value. As you probably realize by now, that value might be expressed in different measures by different combinations of notes and rests, but always with that exact amount of metric "space."

Because the meter signature assures the reader that each measure will be consistent in value, the reader can confidently set up the appropriate metric flow that will measure the rhythmic events in the music. In the example above, the top number is 2, signifying a grouping of two simple (not dotted) note values. That number 2, *by itself*, specifies that the appropriate basic metric structure to be employed is the one having a grouping in two and a division in two.

**simple meter**    A meter based on this structure is commonly described as **simple duple**. It is called "simple" because the primary-pulse value is a simple note (not dotted) that can

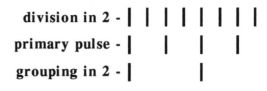

be divided into two equal parts, reflecting the duple division in this metric structure. It is called "duple" because each measure contains two primary pulses, reflecting the duple grouping in this metric structure.

The top number of a simple duple meter will always be 2, but the bottom one can be any number that represents a simple note value—for example, 1 (whole note), 2 (half note), 4 (quarter note), 8 (eighth note), 16 (sixteenth note), etc. As noted earlier, the quarter note is by far the most popular, but the half note and eighth note are also frequently used in modern notation. The music shown on the preceding page in 2/4 meter can be notated as shown here with no change in sound or feel.

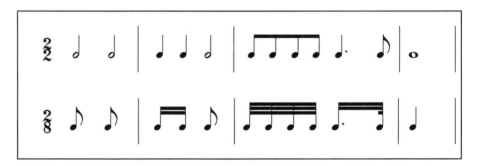

The top number of a **simple triple** meter will always be 3 and the bottom one, as above, can be any number that represents a simple note value. In this case, the meter signature informs the reader that every measure in the piece, until further notice, will contain the equivalent of three of the note value specified by the bottom number.

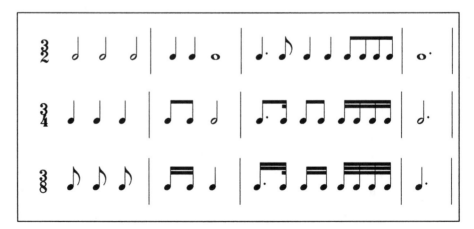

Upon encountering a simple triple meter signature, the reader generates the metric flow of a triple-grouping duple-division structure. As above, the term "simple" refers to the use of a simple (undotted) note value to represent the primary beat. The term "triple" refers to the grouping of primary beats in threes.

**compound meter**

Using the dot to create a primary note value that divides into three equal parts is the clever device that transformed metric notation from the Gothic system to the modern system. However, that transition was not without problems. When a dotted note value is used as a primary pulse series, that value cannot be represented by a whole number. For example, in this metric flow

 there are two dotted-quarter notes per measure, but 2 can't be used as the top number of the meter signature because there is no whole number that will represent a dotted quarter note. Although 2 answers the question "how many...?," there is then no way, using the system, to answer the question "...of what?"

The same is true for *any* meter having a division of three since the primary beat will be represented by a dotted note, which can't be expressed as the bottom number of a meter signature. Having three dotted notes per measure presents the same problem.

Carl Orff, a twentieth-century composer and music educator, offered a brilliant solution to the problem. His meter signatures simply used the note symbol itself instead of representing it by a number. He used this method for both  duple-division meters and triple-division meters. This made it possible to represent all four basic meters with top numbers of either 2 or 3.

| | |
|---|---|
| triple grouping, triple division $=$ | $\frac{3}{d.}$ or $\frac{3}{d.}$ or $\frac{3}{\wedge.}$ etc. |
| triple grouping, duple division $=$ | $\frac{3}{d}$ or $\frac{3}{d}$ or $\frac{3}{\wedge}$ etc. |
| duple grouping, triple division $=$ | $\frac{2}{d.}$ or $\frac{2}{d.}$ or $\frac{2}{\wedge.}$ etc. |
| duple grouping, duple division $=$ | $\frac{2}{d}$ or $\frac{2}{d}$ or $\frac{2}{\wedge}$ etc. |

It would have been helpful had Orff's great idea caught on. Alas, tradition has prevailed, and consequently, we use a method of indicating triple division meters that causes considerable confusion. The method itself is logical enough once basic meter is understood, but attempts to explain meter *in terms of* notation too often result in ill-defined concepts. Since you already understand basic meter, you will be able to avoid this confusion. Here is how triple-division signatures work.

Although a primary pulse having a triple-division cannot be represented by a whole number, its division pulse (since it is expressed in notation as a simple note) *can* be represented by a whole number. So, instead of counting the number of primary-beat values in a measure, the division-beat values are counted. Two dotted-quarter values contains six eighth values, therefore this meter can be expressed with a top number of 6 (the number of division-level beats) and a bottom number of 8 (the value of one division-level beat).

The important thing to remember here is that the signature of a triple-division meter describes the pulse pattern of the division level, NOT of the primary level. Once you have this idea firmly in place, it is a simple matter of remembering that when 6 appears as a top number it always indicates a metric structure having a duple grouping and a triple division—in other words, two sets of three.

If you have been told elsewhere that "the top number of a meter signature tells how many beats there are in each measure," you can see the fallacy in this case (provided the term *beat* is meant to refer to the primary level). There are not six primary beats per measure here, there are two. Likewise, if you have been told that "the bottom number of a meter signature tells what kind of note value gets one beat," you can see that this also is not true in this case. The primary beat value here is the dotted quarter, not the eighth.

Those statements are also true of triple-division metric structures having a triple grouping. In this example, each measure contains the equivalent of three dotted-quarter values (which cannot be expressed by a whole number)  and nine eighth values (which can). Therefore, the top number is 9 and the bottom number is 8. Thus, we have three sets of three.

The term used to describe meters having triple division is **compound meter**. Those having two primary beats per measure (grouping in two) are called **compound duple** meter and those having three primary beats per measure (grouping in three) are called **compound triple** meter.

As in simple meter, compound meter can be written using a variety of values. The top number will be either 6 or 9, indicating the number of division values that fit either two or three primary beats per measure, and the bottom number will be a whole number indicating the note value at the division level.

The logic of the term *compound* is a bit elusive. Presumably, it refers to the combining of simple-triple measures into groups of two or three. Here are the 6/8 and 9/8 examples above notated in 3/8 measures in which each measure represents one primary beat. The numbers above the measures are added here to remind you of the metric grouping in the originals.

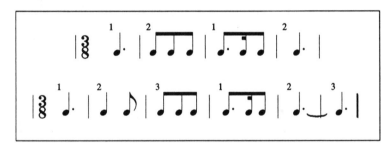

As you can see, if these examples appeared without the numbers added here, it would be impossible to know which grouping pattern the composer intended. Sometimes the rhythmic phrasing provides clues, but the use of compound meter signatures is clearly the better way to go. That way, the reader knows the metric grouping even before looking at the rhythm patterns—two primary beats in a measure when 6 is the top number and three primary beats in a measure when 9 is the top number.

Sometimes tradition gets in the way of clarity. Here are two examples. To the question of what meter—duple or triple—is used for the waltz, the standard answer is "triple meter" (specifically, 3/4). What is seldom realized is that each measure of a waltz constitutes one primary pulse and that these primary pulses always group in sets of two. Therefore, one might answer "duple meter" and be just as correct (although the quiz show host probably would not reward that answer). The best answer is "both," but before you use it, make sure you have time to explain and demonstrate your reasoning.

If you decide to assume the challenge, you might use "Skater's Waltz" as your illustration. It clearly contains a "left-right, left-right" metric feeling that reflects the pattern of a skater's alternating glide.

25-1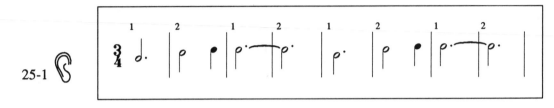

Beethoven had a similar problem with tradition when he notated the *Scherzo* movement of his Ninth Symphony. The scherzo was a fast-tempo nineteenth-century modification of the traditional eighteenth-century minuet, a dance in simple triple meter in which the three beats could be felt as the primary pulse series. Because the minuet was always notated in 3/4 meter, the scherzo was notated the same way, even though the quarter notes were far too fast to be felt as the primary pulse. Earlier Beethoven scherzos were already quite fast, but the one in the Ninth was blazing. After notating the music in the traditional 3/4 meter, Beethoven realized that musicians might easily get lost in the blur of small measures racing past their eyes, so he actually did what we have done above—he numbered the measures in the notation.

**quadruple meter**  Tradition aside, Beethoven might have opted for a compound meter to make the grouping clear. Since his intent was to show four beats to the measure, he might have selected 12/8, a **compound quadruple** meter. Remember, 4 is simply two 2s in meter structure.

The top number 12 is 6 doubled. Compound quadruple meter is based on the same metric structure as compound duple meter. The difference is simply a notational one in which two duple measures are combined into one quadruple measure. The metric feel is identical in both (see sidebar, "Meter? Accent? Help!!!" p. 169).

Simple meters, as well as compound meters, can be notated with four beats per measure, and these are very common. In fact, they are so common that the **simple quadruple** meter using the quarter note as the primary beat value is frequently called "common meter" and its meter signature is the letter "C," which often appears on the staff instead of 4/4.

Quadruple meters are the notational equivalent of the second-grouping pulse feeling in a duple-group metric structure. (If this is not clear, refer to the discussion on pp. 162-163.) Metrically, beat one in each measure is the strongest and beat three is the next strongest. One might imagine a sort of secondary barline between beats two and three.

Another "common" practice is the use of the "alla breve" signature. Its signature is the letter "C" with a vertical line through it. It means the breve, or half note, is to be felt as the primary pulse series. Its metric flow is the same as 2/2 (note the beaming). While the notes are identical to the example above, the primary pulse has shifted to the next slower one—the grouping pulse in the example above.

This is not the only alla breve meter in use. Although not widely known, alla breve signatures have been used with any number of beats per measure. In this illustration, the meter is the same as 4/2 and sounds and feels exactly like all of those above.

**sextuple meter**

Just as two simple duple measures can be combined to create a simple quadruple measure, two simple triple measures can be combined to create a simple sextuple measure. In other words, just as duple and quadruple meters are based on the same metric structure, triple and sextuple meters are based on the same metric structure. In a sextuple meter, the top number 6 counts the number of primary pulses, not the number of division pulses (as in compound duple meter). The difference, then, between simple sextuple meter and compound duple meter is tempo. It is a matter of identifying the primary pulse level.

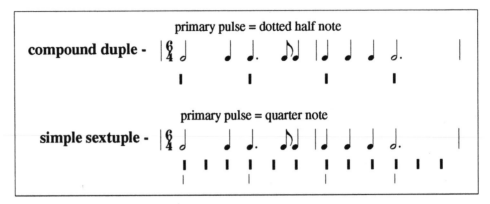

When the rhythm notated above is played in a tempo appropriate to compound duple meter and then repeated at gradually slower tempos, the primary pulse will tend to shift at some point to secure the regularity of flow. Listen to this audio illustration and notice where the shift happens for you.

25-2

Confusion sometimes occurs when comparing the meters above with simple triple meter. For example, 6/4 meter is sometimes confused with 3/2 meter, obviously because these combined numbers mean the same thing in the language of fractions. Remember that the top number in a meter signature tells you much more than the top number in a fraction. As we have demonstrated, the top number of a signature *by itself* indicates the configuration of related pulse ratios. The top number 3 indicates three sets of two (simple triple meter) while the top number 6 indicates two sets of three (compound duple or simple sextuple meter).

## Asymmetrical meters

Mixing duple and triple metric elements at the same metric level is sometimes thought of as an invention of the twentieth century. Actually, the practice goes back to the Middle Ages when Gregorian chant mixed syllabic sets of accents which were dictated by the flow of the language being set to music.

When music became polyphonic, around the beginning of the second millennium, meter was vital to coordinate the simultaneous lines of melody. Nevertheless, Gothic and Renaissance composers found ways to allow the individual voices to interplay in mixed duple and triple patterns. Notating a continuous flow of a single regular metric pattern throughout a composition was a seventeenth century innovation. Even then, composers frequently included melodic and rhythmic elements that conflicted with the prevailing meter established at the outset of the music.

Regular meter was standard musical practice from the seventeenth century through most of the nineteenth century. In the early twentieth century, a host of composers—notably Stravinsky, Bartok and Copland—liberated music from the bonds of regular meter. In the world of jazz, Stan Kenton, Dave Brubeck, "Peanuts" composer Vince Guaraldi and others fascinated audiences with unusual patterns. Brubeck's "Take Five" has become a classic.

There are two ways to create asymmetrical meters—at the grouping "pulse" and at the primary "pulse." When groupings are mixed patterns of twos and threes, the grouping level contains a "pseudo pulse" named thus because it is not regularly recurrent. The primary pulse, then, must take full responsibility for holding things together. In this example, the quarter note value is the primary beat. The grouping is a "pseudo pulse," which, nevertheless, is still felt in the flow of the music. The second grouping (the barline) will be felt as regular.

The difference between this asymmetrical meter and a *triplet* (see p. 165) is that here the primary beat (quarter note in the example above) is held constant, therefore the triple value forces the grouping "pulse" to accommodate the pattern. Performing triplets at the primary-pulse level requires that the grouping beat (half notes in this example) remain constant, therefore forcing the primary pulse to accommodate the modification.

When the primary level alternates between patterns of twos and threes in which the division pulse is steady and constant, the primary level becomes a "pseudo pulse." The division pulse then regulates the feeling of metric flow. In this example, eighth values represent the division pulse (as in a compound meter) and quarter and dotted-quarter values occur at the primary "pulse" level.

The difference between the triple pattern in this asymmetrical meter and a triplet is that in the asymmetrical meter the division pulse (eighth values) is held constant, therefore the triple pattern forces the "primary pulse" to accommodate the modification. Conversely, triplets at the division-pulse level require that the primary pulse be constant, providing the basis for accurately "measuring" the triplet.

In dealing with all asymmetrical meters, a conductor indicates the primary pulse series through gestures. When a grouping is asymmetrical, the gestures will be regular, therefore representing a true pulse. With an asymmetrical primary "pulse," the gestures will not be regular. Therefore, the feeling of regularity is maintained by giving attention to the division-level pulse.

Sometimes asymmetrical meters call for top numbers that might be confused with "normal" meters—for example 8, 9 or 12. When this occurs, composers alert the reader by breaking down the pattern. The possibilities are limited only by imagination and practicality.

## Durational Pattern on Metric Pattern

We have seen how the same metric structure can be expressed notationally in different ways. Now we will see how the same durational pattern (the ratios of longer and/or shorter sounds) takes on quite different rhythmic meanings when combined with different metric placements.

All the examples in this section contain an identical durational pattern. Some values expressed as single notes in one example may appear as tied notes in another example, and vice versa, but all relative values are the same. The order of the durations is also the same in all of the examples.

Earlier, we demonstrated concepts by holding certain characteristics constant while modifying others. We will use that method again here. In the three examples below, the meter and the durational pattern are constant. The point where the durational pattern begins is changed in each example. In the audio illustration of these examples, each is preceded by one measure of pulse patterns to help you establish the metric feeling.

25-3

This demonstration shows the effect of **metric placement** in creating rhythmic meaning. In the first example, sounds begin on the first beat. In the second example, sounds begin on the second beat. In the third, sounds begin halfway through the first beat. Each version feels distinctly different since durations of various lengths begin on beats of varying metric strengths. Where agogic (durational) accents correspond to metric accents, the rhythm seems secure and calm. Where agogic accents do not correspond to metric accents, the rhythm seems active and somewhat "jazzy."

In the following examples, the same durational pattern used above is held constant while the meter signature (metric structure) is varied. The initial simple quadruple version heard above is contrasted here to one using a simple triple meter and one using a compound duple meter. The differences in rhythmic feeling are certainly interesting and hopefully enlightening.

25-4

## Meter Notation Wrap-Up

At this point, you may very well feel that this whole subject is a rather unruly affair. Perhaps you are also unsettled by the realization that the same metric flow can be notated in a variety of ways. The myriad collection of available meter signatures can seem rather formidable, but if you remember that all of them are based on very simple and systematic perceptual principles of duple and triple groupings and divisions, potential confusion can be greatly minimized.

In general, these guidelines should serve well:

- When the top number of a meter signature is 2, the metric structure underlying the music has a grouping of 2 and a division of 2. This pattern is called *simple duple meter*.

- When the top number of a meter signature is 3, the metric structure underlying the music has a grouping of 3 and a division of 2. This pattern is called *simple triple meter*.

- When the top number of a meter signature is 6, the metric structure underlying the music usually has a grouping of 2 and a division of 3. This pattern is called *compound duple meter*.

- When the top number of a meter signature is 9, the metric structure underlying the music has a grouping of 3 and a division of 3. This pattern is called *compound triple meter*.

- The bottom number of a meter signature represents a note value. Under a top number of 2 or 3, the bottom number represents the value assigned to the primary pulse series. Under a 6 or 9, this number represents the division pulse series.

- When the top number of a meter signature is 4, the metric structure underlying the music is the same as a signature having a top number of 2. The difference is purely notational in that the barlines correspond to the *second* grouping pulse instead of the grouping pulse. This pattern is called *simple quadruple meter*.

- When the top number of a meter signature is 12, the metric structure underlying the music is the same as a signature having a top number of 6. Again, the difference is purely notational in that the barlines correspond to the *second* grouping pulse instead of the grouping pulse. This pattern is called *compound quadruple meter*.

- A top number of 6 can indicate *simple sextuple* meter rather than compound duple when the tempo is slow enough to feel the bottom-number value as the primary pulse. This is merely two simple-triple measures combined. Compound sextuple meter (which would have a top number of 18) is impractical and is not used.

- When the top number of a meter signature is 5 or 7, the metric structure underlying the music has an asymmetrical element, meaning that one of the "pulse" series will not be regular. In this case, coordinating the music will depend on maintaining regularity at the series next faster than the asymmetrical one.

- Occasional insertions of triple elements in a predominantly duple pulse series are identified by the number 3 placed over the affected notes, usually enclosed in a bracket. Such events are called *triplets*. Insertions of duple elements in a predominantly triple pulse series are identified by the number 2 placed over the affected notes, usually enclosed in a bracket. Such events are called *duplets*.

- Meters with higher top numbers are not practical because we are not likely to *feel* regularity when many beats are grouped.

Musical meter is a matter of feeling patterns of twos and threes in about three or four levels of related metric series. One should keep in mind that overemphasis on the intellectual side of meter can sometimes get in the way of smooth and graceful performance. Without feeling, not much happens.

# 26

# Pitch
# Notation

Developed over the past five centuries or so, standard pitch notation has made it possible for musicans—most of whom have never met in person—to communicate melodies and harmonies to one another. We can stop by the music store, pick up some sheet music, take it home and recreate, with reasonable correspondence, the sounds originally conceived by the composer. The correspondence increases if we are familiar with the general style of music.

Like meter notation, pitch notation represents the sounds of music in an abstract and generalized way. For example, just as meter is not able to represent the subtle differences between country shuffle, big-band swing and rap hip-hop, pitch notation is not able to represent the difference between a minor third and a "blue" third, nor the difference between scale step 4 tuned as a subdominant root and scale step 4 tuned as a dominant seventh pitch. Standard notation is not designed to provide that information. Such discriminations are the result of one's practical experience with the sound and style of the music itself.

In spite of these shortcomings, standard notation has served well in communicating musical ideas from composer to performer. By combining the information from very old notational manuscripts with general descriptions of early musical styles, we are able to compress centuries of time and perform that music today as if it were composed this morning. Sometimes, even music not intended for notation—aboriginal folk music, for example—can be witnessed by musical anthropologists, notated and included in research documents, making it possible for the reader to gain some understanding of a musical culture he or she has never experienced.

As music became more complex, particularly in the twentieth century, the inadequacies of the standard notation system became more evident. Modern composers have been forced to find new ways to represent their creations on paper. While many of the innovations in this direction are interesting and imaginative, our attention will be focused on traditional ways of conceiving melodic and harmonic structures and casting them in standard modes of written representation.

We will look first at the development of the staff, a system of lines and spaces that provides a matrix on which to represent the ups and downs of pitch. Then we will see how key signatures make the staff more efficient in specifying "raised" or "lowered" pitches throughout a composition. Next, we will continue the discussion of intervals and complete the overall view of that system in terms of notational representation. Finally, we will take a look at how chords appear when written on the staff.

# 27

# The Staff

In one sense, the principles involved in using the staff are fairly simple. Symbols are placed on the five lines and four spaces to represent pitches. The higher the symbol on the staff, the higher the pitch in sound.

However, there are a number of potentially confusing aspects of translating pitch information from the realities of sound to the symbolic abstraction of a staff. For example, while the keyboard clearly shows where half steps occur in diatonic scales, half-step locations are not evident on the staff. Additionally, the lines and spaces of the staff do not always represent the same pitches. Perhaps you have wondered how five-line staves can represent the wide range of pitches used in music. These and other questions will be addressed in the following pages.

## Representing Pitch in Terms of Letters

The idea of referring to pitches by letter names is not new. Ancient Greeks used letters to represent pitch as it related to the kithara (a harp like instrument). Certain Far Eastern systems have employed pitch symbols derived from literary script. In the Middle Ages, several European systems were developed in which letters of the Roman alphabet were used to represent about two octaves of pitches arranged in modal scales. The practice of limiting the system to seven letters repeated in lower and higher octaves began during that period.

Several methods of designating pitches in specific octaves are currently in use. The earliest, and perhaps most widely known, uses upper and lower case letters with the following designations.

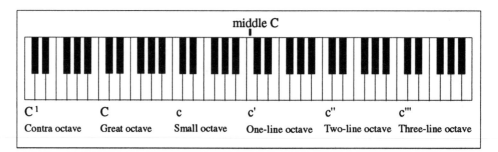

In this system, the octave below middle C (the C nearest the middle of the piano keyboard) is called the "small" octave. The ones below that (in order) are the "great" octave and the "contra" octave. The octave from middle C to the B above it is called the "one-line" octave (or "C one"), the next higher is called "two-line" (or "C two"), and so on.

Another system uses "c" and "C" to represent middle C and the octave below it. Higher and lower octaves are represented with superscripts indicating their position relative to those two pitches.

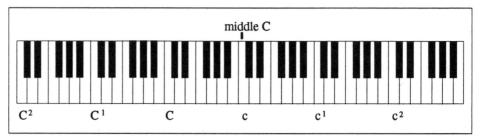

Thus, we have one system using "c'" to represent middle C and another system using "c" to represent middle C. A third system designates middle C as "$C^4$." The higher octaves are designated with higher superscript numbers and lower octaves with lower superscript numbers.

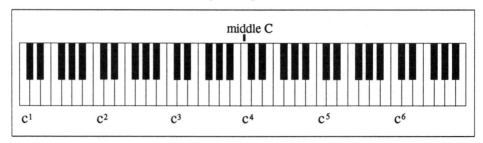

In all three systems, the octave locations of the other pitches (D-E-F-G-A-B) are designated in relation to the nearest C *below* that pitch. For example, in the third system the D above $C^4$ is $D^4$; the B below $C^4$ is $B^3$.

Because none of these systems is universally used, musicians tend to use other terminology to designate pitches in specific octaves. Some of these expressions are a bit ambiguous. For example, the term "high C," when applied to a soprano, refers to the C two octaves above middle C, but when applied to a tenor, it refers to the C one octave above middle C. (The difference, of course, has to do with the difference between the male and female voices.) The ambiguity gets even worse when referring to a soprano's "high F," since most sopranos can sing the F one-and-a-half octaves (roughly) above middle C while some can sing the F two-and-a-half octaves above.

Using the distance from middle C to specify octaves is a bit inconvenient and wordy; however, it is accurate and likely to be understood. A far more convenient and accurate method is to describe octave locations in terms of standard notation. We will revisit this topic when we discuss the *grand staff* below.

## Representing Pitches in Terms of Lines and Spaces

As legend has it, Pope Gregory (reigned 590-604) challenged the monks and priests of the Roman Catholic Church to develop musical notation in order to standardize the performance of liturgical chant throughout the church world. Early efforts consisted of **neumes** (squiggles placed higher and lower on the page to indicate higher and lower pitches). Needless to say, this method left a lot to be desired in terms of specificity of pitch. Unless one already knew the melody, the neumes were not helpful in determining the specific pitches to be sung. The best neumes could do was to remind the reader when the melody went up or down and approximately how far.

A significant breakthrough was achieved when the tonic pitch was indicated by a horizontal line. Neumes that appeared above the line were sung on pitches above tonic and neumes below the line were sung below tonic. While that helped, it did not indicate how far above or below tonic these pitches were to be sung.

Eventually, a second line was added representing the dominant pitch. From there, it was only logical to add more lines to identify more pitches. The standard number of lines used to notate Catholic liturgical chant was four. Because the melodic **range** (distance from the highest to lowest pitches) of most chants was about an octave, the four lines and the three spaces between them served the purpose well.

Ky - ri - e

This system of lines and spaces is called a **staff** (plural, **staves**). Colors were    **the staff** sometimes used to designate pitches. For example, red was often used to signify F and yellow to signify C. This was discontinued, however, after the invention of the printing press, since multicolored printing was quite impractical. Instead, the line designated as middle C was marked by a symbol resembling the letter "C," as seen in the illustration above. Since the tonic was sometimes higher in various chant melodies and sometimes lower, the line selected to represent middle C would change from one chant (and mode) to another.

**multiple staves**  With the development of polyphonic musical textures, more notational space was needed. The Gothic motet included at least three musical lines. A *tenor* (meaning "to hold") voice sang the pitches of the traditional chant in fairly long ("held") durations. Voices added above—the *altus* (meaning "high") and the *superius* (meaning "highest")—sang newly created melodies. By providing separate staves (sometimes containing five or six lines each) and designating various lines within a staff to represent middle C, flexibility was achieved that could accommodate the sustained tenor chant melody as well as the more rhythmic melodic lines sung by the two higher voices.

Coordinating multiple voices required that they be metrically related. The rhythms in this illustration are written in modern notation so you can read them.

In the early Renaissance, a voice was added below the tenor called the *bassus*. As you may have already realized, "superius," "altus," tenor" and "bassus" became our modern "soprano," "alto," "tenor" and "bass." Although all the voices originally were sung by men when the music was sacred, the soprano and alto voices were commonly sung by women when it was secular. Thus the "low female part" is called "alto," a word which means "high." As you can see, knowing the etymology of the term is helpful in resolving the apparent conflict of meaning.

Renaissance choral music was frequently composed in as many as five or six voices (musical lines), and since the music was still mostly polyphonic each voice required its own staff. When musical texture became more homophonic in the Baroque period, it was sometimes practical to place two voices on the same staff. To the extent that voices shared the same rhythmic pattern, the pitches sung by those voices could share the same stems, beams, flags, etc. Therefore, as many as eight voices might be notated on a system of four staves. In some cases, editors indicated separate voices on one staff by showing stems up for the higher voice and stems down for the lower one.

Notating the music played by a modern symphony orchestra sometimes requires as many as thirty or forty staves. As you can imagine, a conductor must have considerable experience to be able to read such complex notation (called a **score**). Incidentally, the players do not have this problem since the notation of their individual music, with few exceptions, is placed on a single staff.

Since various instruments and voices perform in different pitch "neighborhoods," it was important to name staff lines and spaces in a way that was practical for each one. In the seventeenth century, the traditional "C" used to indicate middle C was stylized into a more elaborate symbol named a **clef sign**. This particular sign has been variously called the **C clef** and the **moveable clef**, because it, like its predecessor, can be moved from one line to another to accommodate the ranges of each voice type or instrument. The note shown here in each example is middle C. Of these C clefs, only the alto and tenor clef are commonly used in modern notation.

**clef signs**

Soprano clef

Mezzo-soprano clef

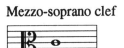

Alto clef

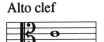

Tenor clef

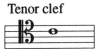

With the development of the violin in the seventeenth century, the need for a clef higher than the soprano clef became evident. Since the soprano clef already used the bottom line for middle C, a "higher" clef would drop middle C off the five lines altogether. A clef symbol was needed that would designate a pitch other than middle C.

Baritone clef

By naming the second line from the bottom "G above middle C," middle C itself could conveniently move to a short added line (called a **ledger** line) below the set of five. This **G clef** provided plenty of

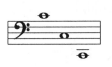

room to notate the pitches played by the violin when it soared into the higher pitches of its range. Pitches above the staff could also be shown on added ledger lines as needed. This example includes the Cs one octave and two octaves above middle C.

A similar problem existed on the lower side of middle C. The violoncello, the bass member of the newly developed violin family, required a clef that would reach down to the C two octaves below middle C. By designating the

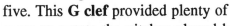

second line from the top as "F below middle C," middle C then appeared on an added line above the set of five. This illustration of the **F clef** shows middle C on the ledger line above the staff and the Cs one octave and two octaves lower.

When the Baroque orchestra grew to a size that required increased bass support, the double bass joined the ranks and played from the same music as the violoncello. Because of the size of the new instrument, it sounded one octave lower than the 'cello, thus automatically providing its lower sounds without using a new clef.

Using the G clef and the F clef in combination has turned out to be very practical in that they interface in a convenient way. Since the G clef designates the pitch a fifth higher than middle C and the F clef designates the pitch a fifth lower than middle C, the ledger lines added below the G clef staff and above the F clef staff represent the same pitch—middle C.

By viewing the two staves one above the other with the lines and spaces consistently spaced vertically through the middle C area, you can see that these two staves, plus two ledger lines above and two ledger lines below, provide sufficient room 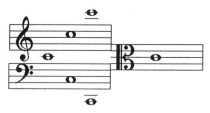 to write four octaves of pitches. This is enough space to notate nearly all vocal music and a large portion of all instrumental music. The moveable C clef (the alto version) is included here to show its relationship to the two "new" clefs.

As it turns out, the invention of these clefs resulted in the near demise of the moveable C clef. The only practical reason today for using a C clef is to avoid having to change from one clef to another when music centers around the middle C area. Therefore, the only instruments that commonly use the C clef today are those that normally play in that space—primarily the viola and occasionally the cello and trombone. Most all other instruments use the G clef, also called the **treble** clef, and/or the F clef, also called the **bass** clef.

**the grand staff**    The treble and bass clefs considered together is referred to as the **grand staff** (occasionally called **great staff**). Publishers commonly show the treble and bass staves spacially separated, which beginning music readers sometimes find confusing. The solution to this visual problem is to remember that the vertical distance between the two staves has no meaning, and that the first ledger line below the treble staff and the first ledger line above the bass staff both represent middle C. Also, notice that a second ledger line added below the treble staff is equivalent to the top line of the bass staff, and a second ledger line added above the bass staff is equivalent to the bottom line of the treble staff. This is true no matter how much space the publisher might allow between the printed staves.

To further illustrate this point, here is the same G major chord (G-B-D-G) written in both the treble clef and the bass clef. The pitches in each notated chord are exactly the same and are played in the same location on the keyboard. If this is not clear to you, find middle C in both clefs and notice how the G chord relates to it. You can see that the notation in either clef leads you to the exact same pitches.

Having considered the "space" between the treble and bass staves, let's look at the "space" outside them. A handy device for notating extremely high or low pitches is the symbol *8va.* (meaning *octava*, Italian for "octave"). Instead of using tall stacks of ledger lines for pitches that are far above or below a staff, this symbol over or under a note (or series of notes) indicates that such pitches are to be sounded one octave further from the staff. The symbol *16va* indicates that such notes are to be sounded two octaves further

**more octaves**

than shown. In this illustration, the second four-note fragment is played on the exact same pitches as the first four-note fragment.

Pitches considerably below the bass clef are similarly designated. The *8va* or *16va* symbols, or the more specific symbols *8bassa* or *16bassa,* can be placed below notated pitches to affect their octave placement.

Regarding specifying octaves in conversation, the staff position of pitches is a handy reference. For example, "top-line F" specifies the F an octave and a half above middle C. "F below the bass staff" is quite clear. "Treble G" is the one above middle C. Some positions require more imagination than others, but musicians operate fairly well using this "system."

## Memorizing Lines and Spaces

Musicians need to respond immediately when translating music notation into performance. There is not enough time to count lines and spaces, or to recite cute little phrases like "**e**very **g**ood **b**oy **d**oes **f**ine" in order to "figure out" the letter names of a clef, while performing a musical phrase in rhythm and in tempo.

When immediate response to visual stimuli is needed, there is no substitute for "drill." By that, we mean learning to respond to a symbol without conscious thought. The classic technique for developing this kind of skill is "flash cards." If you enjoy shuffling through a deck, it is a great way to go. If not, you might consider the "neighborhood" drill that we will describe on the next page.

Fortunately, the five-line staff is well suited for fast perception. Notice how quickly you can focus on "middle line," "top space," "space below the middle," "line next to the top," and so forth. It takes more time to say the words than to locate the line or space being described. This being the case, it is easy to see why "counting" is a diversionary waste of time and effort. If the "locations" are so easily perceived, pitches are also easily named and/or performed.

Naming and performing are the two "automatic" responses a musician makes to pitch notation. Theoretically, it is possible to learn one without knowing the other. Learning pitch names does not necessarily relate to any particular instrument. On the other hand, translating note positions and configurations to fingerings or vocal responses can be done without knowing the names of the pitches performed.

Of course, most musicians prefer to learn both skills and, to some extent, relate "naming" and "performing" to each other as well. While both could be drilled at the same time by performing and naming simultaneously (unless the instrument being used requires blowing), it is more logical to practice them separately. Whatever method is used, the goal is to learn to respond immediately to a line or space location without counting, or any other deliberate process.

Although the actual drill should be done "thoughtlessly," planning the pitch-name drill should involve some awareness about certain helpful visual characteristics of the grand-staff system as well as some information about how the brain works in regard to drill.

**the big picture**    First, let's look at the "playing field." We have already noted the location of five Cs in relation to the treble and bass clefs. Notice in this graphic that the Cs in the two clefs create a mirror effect. The C above middle C is in the space above the middle line of the treble staff and the C below middle C is in

the space below the middle line of the bass staff. A similar relationship occurs between the two Cs next farthest from middle C, in that they both require two ledger lines.

The lines and spaces near each "landmark" can be thought of as "neighborhoods" of pitches. To fill in the gaps between the Cs, additional neighborhoods can be visualized around the Gs in the treble clef and the Fs in the bass clef. These additions also contribute to the mirror relationship of the two clefs. Memorizing these landmarks is a good start toward constructing a framework for learning the remaining pitches.

The mirror-image difference between the two clefs makes it easy to separate them conceptually. The reason for mentioning this point is that sometimes a student who is already familiar with one clef is tempted to learn the other in terms of the one already mastered. For example, a flute player who knows the treble clef can figure out the name of any pitch on the bass clef by counting up two lines and/or spaces. Needless to say, this is not very efficient, nor does it represent the pitch in the appropriate octave. It is much better to learn the "other" clef *as itself* and not as a translation. It isn't that difficult.

To make the task of learning the lines and spaces more manageable, drill can be confined to a neighborhood until it is securely learned. To illustrate, let's focus on the neighborhood around "third space C" of the treble clef. We can start our drill by including only that C and the pitches on the lines immediately above and below it. Point at and name these three locations, skipping from one to another in random order, gradually increasing your speed until you are no longer "figuring out" the names consciously. When these are secure, add the spaces immediately above and below those pitches. Drill these five pitches until your responses become automatic.

This procedure can be repeated in other neighborhoods until you have mastered the whole span of lines and spaces on both clefs. By learning the clefs in this manner, you will tend to think of them together as one continuous area of pitch, instead of thinking of the two clefs as merely "different."

Another important bit of information regarding drill is that it should be **paced** in order to get the best results. You may have noticed that after about fifteen seconds of intense drill, you begin to get confused and start making mistakes. At that point, stop the drill for five or ten seconds and think about something totally unrelated. When you resume the drill you will notice that you have "magically" improved in speed and accuracy.

pacing

Educators have known about this mysterious "gain-without-strain" principle for quite a long time. Recently, scientists have discovered the chemical activity in the brain that provides the basis for this phenomenon. Simply stated, during the rest periods between actively trying to make connections between stimuli and correct responses, a chemical flows into the new connections and strengthens them. That is why your performance is significantly improved when you resume the drill. Hopefully, knowing about this brain function will make your drill more productive and you less frustrated when the inevitable mistakes start appearing. Of course, the stronger your connections grow, the longer you will be able to sustain error-free drills. Enjoy!

## Reading Music

Have you ever watched an experienced musician perform complex music from notation that he or she had not previously seen? Did you think that the reader was attending to each note and individually translating its pitch and duration? If so, you will be pleased to know you are mistaken. The process is much easier than that.

When you read English, do you focus on each letter that passes your eye? You probably do not. Instead, you see configurations of letters and words that are so familiar that your perception scoops them up in large strokes of attention. The same thing happens when an experienced music reader views music notation.

This can be illustrated by looking at chords on the staff. Since chords in the major/minor system are usually constructed in thirds, and thirds consist of pitches two scale steps apart, and a staff uses lines and spaces (alternately) to 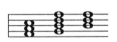 place consecutive scale steps, a chord in its fundamental position will appear on consecutive lines or consecutive spaces.

Therefore, a music reader does not need to look at each note in such a chord. Once it is clear that all the notes are on lines or all on spaces, one need only look at one pitch in the chord. Once that pitch is identified, the others are located in relation to it. If the reader is only concerned with theoretical analysis of the music, the lowest pitch in this configuration can be quickly recognized as the root. To perform those pitches on a keyboard, the player's hand simply assumes an appropriate shape for striking digitals spaced in the particular configuration, and the reader need only identify one pitch (usually the highest or lowest) in order to play the chord.

When seeing a scale fragment, a reader need not examine (or name) every pitch in the series. Only the beginning pitch and the ending pitch need be identified. The others simply fill out the scale steps between them. Often the rhythmic/metric setting helps the reader see such a fragment as a unified concept.

The more experience you have in music reading, the larger your vocabulary of chordal configurations will be, enabling you to interpret "shapes" in notation. Shortly, we will examine some of the more frequent pitch arrangements. With just a little practice, you will find that reading *groups* of pitches in context is much easier than reading the pitches individually.

## Accidentals

While the lines and spaces of the staff represent *letter names* of pitches, they do not necessarily represent the actual pitch or keyboard digital to be sounded. The lines and spaces correspond to the white digitals of the keyboard. Just as white-digital names are modified on the keyboard to represent other pitches in the major/minor system, the following symbols, or **accidentals,** are used to modify the meaning of a given line or space:

- A **sharp** sign (♯) placed on a line or space raises its pitch by a half step.

- A **flat** sign (♭) placed on a line or space lowers its pitch by a half step.

- A **double sharp** sign (𝄪) placed on a line or space raises its pitch by a whole step.

- A **double flat** sign (♭♭) placed on a line or space lowers its pitch by a whole step.

- A **cancel** (or **natural**) sign (♮) placed on a line or space causes it to revert to its original pitch.

A composer can use these symbols at any time to modify the pitch of a line or space. Usually, the effect of a symbol lasts only for the remaining duration of the measure in which it is placed. If a modification is intended to continue on the same line or space in successive measures, the accidental must reappear in each measure.

There seems to be a question among musicians regarding the octave effect of an inserted accidental. The issue is whether an accidental applies to all octaves of the affected letter name or whether it applies only to the specific line or space on which it appears. To be clear, it would seem wise to repeat an accidental in other octaves when those pitches are to be modified as well, and to place "courtesy" accidentals in cases where confusion might arise.

**half steps on the staff**

We noticed earlier that because the white digitals on the keyboard are equally spaced, there was some danger of assuming that the pitches played on those white digitals would be evenly spaced. We discovered that this was not the case. The same potential danger exists in the equal spacing of lines and spaces of the staff, and, in this case, there is no black-digital vacancy to provide a clue.

Keep in mind that a staff without a clef sign does not represent pitches. The illustration on p. 262 shows an abstract configuration of nameless chord members. Once a clef is placed on a staff, however, all the lines and spaces spring to life and represent specific pitches—not just letter names in general, but letter names in specific octaves. As you know, the lines and spaces of the G-clef staff represent different pitches with different names than the lines and spaces of an F-clef staff or a C-clef staff.

Once the letter names are designated by the clef sign, it is possible to locate the half steps. Since the lines and spaces represent pitches corresponding to the white digitals of the keyboard, they can, of course, be found between E and F and between B and C. On the treble staff, this occurs between the bottom line and the space above it, between the middle line and the space above it, and between the top space and the line above it. On the bass staff this occurs between the space below the middle line and the space below it and between the space above the middle line and the space above it. Others occur outside the staves between appropriate ledger lines and neighboring spaces.

Just as we use accidentals to move the half steps on the keyboard, we use accidentals on the staff to move the half steps. For example, adding a sharp to the lower pitch of a whole step will create a half step. Likewise, adding a sharp to the top pitch of a half step will create a whole step. Flats can be used similarly. When an established key includes a number of sharps or flats, the natural sign can effect the same kind of modification.

However, adding accidentals does not make the half steps any more evident on the staff. It all comes down to memorizing the "white-digital" half steps at the outset, and then becoming familiar with the various shapes of major and minor keys as they appear in the various clefs.

28

# Key Signatures

As you know, any pitch can serve as a tonal center. Since the shapes of major and minor scales are their "reason for being," those shapes need to be kept intact when changing to various tonics. Therefore, since unmodified lines and spaces only represent pitches on white digitals, certain lines and/or spaces must be modified (raised or lowered) for each key. Accidentals applied to appropriate lines and/or spaces cause them to represent scale members that do not occur on white digitals.

As we noted at the end of the previous chapter, the music reader must keep in mind that the same half steps that occur on the keyboard (between B and C and between E and F) are the same half steps that occur on the staff. This is true in all octaves, of course, just as on the keyboard. Also, as on white digitals of the keyboard, all other neighboring lines and spaces represent whole steps.

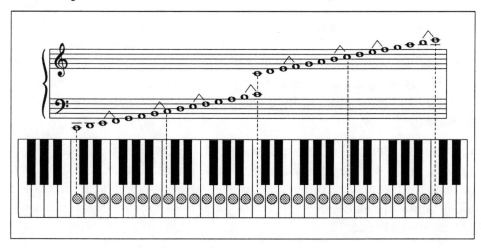

This being the case, the lines and spaces are ready to accommodate the key of C major with no modifications. Did you note the location of the E-F and B-C half steps on the staff as well as their relation to the keyboard? Did you find this graphic reminiscent of the "big picture" graphic on p. 260. Spending a few moments absorbing the information contained in this graphic will be beneficial to you, both in relating the staff to the keyboard and seeing the staff's limitations in communicating the shape of a major key.

## Major Mode Key Signatures

As you may remember, the key of G major requires that F be raised to F♯ in order to move the E-F half step to F♯-G, creating the leading tone to G and forming the F♯-C tritone that is the "power generator" for that tonality.

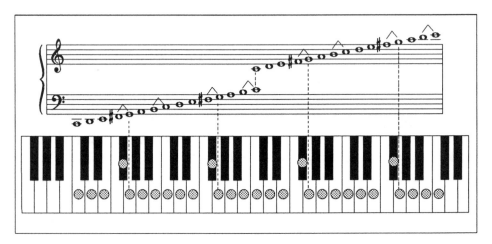

Notice the sharp *precedes* the affected note rather than follows it. Beginners frequently place accidentals to the right of a note, probably because we verbally refer to modified pitches with the accidental name coming *after* the letter name— as in "F *sharp*" or "B *flat.*"

Also, notice that the sharp is centered precisely on the line or space to the left of the note to which it applies. Beginners often place the sharp "somewhere in the vicinity," not realizing that the horizontal bars in the sharp specifically designate a line or space by surrounding it. When a single pitch in a chord is to be affected by a sharp, placing that sharp carelessly can confuse the reader.

In the above illustration, a sharp appears before every F in the continuum of pitches. In a key having many sharps, writing in all the individual sharps for each note affected would clutter the printed music. A practical device called a **key signature** makes this unnecessary and makes for a clean appearance of the printed music.

In the key signature for G major, only one F♯ is placed on each staff, which affects every F, no matter in which octave it might occur. The key signature for G major, then, is said to be "one sharp," and that sharp appears at the beginning of the staff (after the clef sign and before the meter signature) on the top line of the treble staff and on the line above the middle of the bass staff.

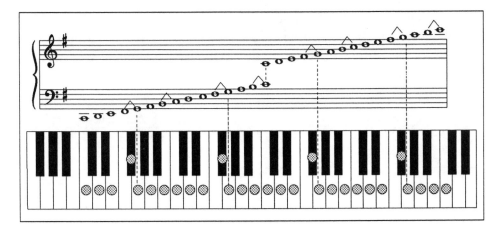

Notice that although the individual Fs on the staves are not prefixed by a sharp sign, all are played on an F♯ digital. This key signature, by changing all the F lines and spaces to F♯, designates the key as G major (provided the pitch patterns and chord structures in the music agree). All other key signatures work the same way. Sharps and flats appearing in a key signature affect the specified pitches in all octaves.

The keys signatures of G, D, A, E, B, F♯ and C♯ major are shown on the treble and bass staves below. The order and placement of the sharps on the staff are standard. Therefore, by learning the shape of the seven-sharp signature (C♯ major), you will have learned the shape of them all. The only thing left to do then is to memorize the *number* of sharps in each key.

Because the keys are related in perfect fifths, the addition of each new sharp (the "new" leading tone) in succeeding key signatures will, of course, occur in perfect fifths. (Remember that a fifth up is the same as a fourth down.) In general, the descending fourth alternates with the ascending fifth; however, there is one place where two consecutive descending fourths occur. We have a "down-up-down-down" pattern here instead of a symmetrical "down-up-down-up" pattern. The obvious reason for this asymmetrical pattern is to avoid placing a sharp on a ledger line in the treble clef signature, which should help you remember where it appears.

While each "new" sharp is placed up a fifth (or down a fourth) in sharp signatures, each "new" flat in flat signatures is placed down a fifth (or up a fourth). As you remember from our earlier look at key relationships, the key of F major begins the pattern with B♭ on its fourth step. That fourth step, since it is down a fifth from tonic, in turn becomes the tonic of the next key in order, and so on.

The flat signatures are more symmetrical than the sharp signatures, and therefore their shapes are easier to memorize. Notice that the "up-down-up-down" pattern is continuous, in contrast to the inconsistent "down-up-down-down" pattern of the sharps.

This quirk could have been avoided had tradition placed the first and third sharps one octave lower. The key signatures having seven sharps and seven flats would have mirrored each other.

Had this pattern been adopted, it would have demonstrated the symmetrical nature of key relations. Notice that the first sharp is on the same letter as the last flat, and the last sharp is the same as the first flat, and that the order of sharps is the reverse order of flats.

Unfortunately, the sharp-key signatures were not configured that way, and that probably is not going to change soon. Therefore, students new to music notation may not appreciate the symmetry of the system. Happily, you do.

**some handy tips**   Let's briefly look at some key-signature characteristics that can help you identify the major keys to which they belong. For example, the last sharp in a signature (the one at the far right) is the leading tone (scale step 7) of that key. Therefore, the major mode tonic is always a half step higher than the last sharp in any sharp key signature.

The last flat added to a major mode signature is scale step 4. That is not as helpful in quickly finding the tonic as is the leading tone, but there is another feature that is even more immediately helpful. The second to the last flat in the flat signature *is* the major mode tonic pitch. This information will not help you with the key of F major, since it has only one flat, but that signature is easily memorized.

If you use music notation frequently, eventually you will become so familiar with the signatures that you will recognize them at a glance by their shapes, and will no longer need these "last sharp" and "next-to-last flat" crutches. You won't even have to count the number of sharps and flats in order to realize the key they represent. If you would like to accelerate that process, simply drill them as you did the lines and spaces. This will free your conscious effort for more important functions.

Besides helping to define the key and keeping the printed music uncluttered, the use of a key signature makes it easy to see occasional accidentals inserted for temporary modifications. For example, when a modulation to a dominant key occurs, it is signalled by the appearance of a raised fourth scale step. If all normally sharped members of the prevailing key were marked on the music, the modified pitch would not stand out.

## Minor Mode Key Signatures

Earlier, we observed that the difference between major and minor modes essentially has to do with the major/minor quality of the tonic and subdominant chords. The scale of C minor, having a minor tonic chord, has a lowered third scale step, and having a minor subdominant chord, has a lowered sixth step. We also noted that the lowering of the sixth step also creates a step-and-a-half "gap" between it and scale step seven.

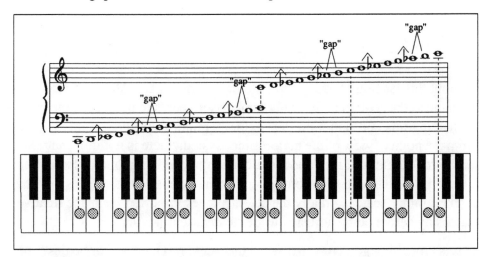

It would be logical for the minor-mode key signatures to contain the specific sharps or flats needed to identify their minor-mode scale members, as major-mode key signatures do. Unfortunately, that is not the case. Instead, a major key signature containing most of the needed sharps or flats is borrowed for the job. For example, the key signature for C minor should contain flats on E and A. The major-key signature that most resembles that configuration is the one that represents E♭ major. It contains the E♭ and the A♭, but brings with it an unnecessary B♭ on scale step 7. Therefore, this B♭ has to be canceled whenever the leading tone is needed. This happens frequently since the leading tone is needed whenever the dominant chord prevails, .

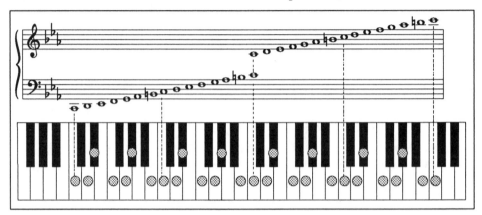

How did this awkwardness occur? Perhaps looking at the key of A minor will help to explain. Once scale steps 3 and 6 of the key of A major are lowered to produce the key of A minor, the result is a scale having all "naturals" except for leading tone G♯. The key signature nearest this configuration is the one belonging to C major (having no sharps or flats). As seen in the key of C minor above, the line or space representing the leading tone must be adjusted every time that pitch appears in the music.

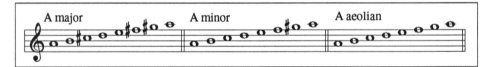

Without this leading-tone adjustment, the "all-natural" scale from A to A is the same as the aeolian mode. This comparison seems to have been the basis for naming this configuration the "natural" minor (or "pure" minor) scale. From the point of view of the major/minor system, there is nothing "natural" (or "pure") about it. It is a modal scale having no leading tone, therefore no functional tritone, and therefore no dominant seventh chord. The so-called "natural minor scale" is really the set of pitches imported from the relative major key before being adjusted to fit the *actual* minor scale.

This is probably a good time to review the sidebar "Three Minor Scales?" on p. 131 in which the traditional "natural," "harmonic" and "melodic" scales are described and discussed. The "natural" minor scale is the one that matches the "imported" key signature; the "harmonic" minor scale is the one that matches the actual basic minor scale; and the "melodic" minor scale is the one that supposedly repairs the melodic awkwardness caused by the step-and-a-half gap between the lowered submediant and the leading tone.

As stated there, the "harmonic" minor scale consists of the pitches derived from the three primary chords of the minor mode—a minor tonic triad, a minor subdominant triad, and a *major* dominant triad. Here is a comparison

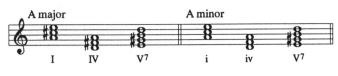

of the three primary chords in A major and minor and in C major and minor.

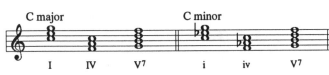

As you can see, sharped pitches adjusted to represent lowered steps 3 and 6 appear as natural pitches, and natural pitches adjusted to represent lowered steps 3 and 6 appear as flats. In both cases, these steps are "lowered" only in comparison to the major key having the same tonic.

The minor key signature automatically accomplishes this lowering process. Many musicians casually refer to the third and sixth steps of the minor mode as "flat 3" and "flat 6" even when the actual pitches would not literally be written as flats. While this colloquial use of terms is not precise and risks being misunderstood, it does show that musicians think of major and minor keys on the same tonic as intimately related.

## Two Major/Minor Relationships

The relationship of a major and a minor key sharing the same tonic pitch is said to be **parallel**. For example, the key of C minor is called the "parallel minor key" of C major. And inversely, the key of C major is called the "parallel major key" of C minor.

**parallel major/minor**

This terminology is potentially confusing for a number of reasons. *Parallel* usually means "continuing side by side," like railroad tracks. Parallel major and minor scales are not "side by side," rather they occupy the "same space." Also, major and minor scales don't follow the same course since their third and sixth steps are different. (A train riding on such tracks would surely be doomed.) Supposedly, what makes a pair of scales "parallel," is that they both "start" (a dangerous concept) on the same pitch. This also renders the term suspicious since geometrically parallel lines are not required to begin and/or end at any particular point. Nevertheless, this term is in standard use so you will want to be aware of it—confusing misapplication and all.

The parallel minor of D major, then, is D minor; the parallel major of E minor is E major; the parallel minor of E♭ major is E♭ minor, and so forth. The concept is simple; only its connection to the term "parallel" is confusing.

**relative major/minor**

Major and minor keys that share the same key signature are said to be **relative**. For example, C major is called the "relative major key" to A minor because both keys show no sharps or flats in their signatures. The terminology also works reciprocally, so the key of A minor is the "relative minor key" to C major. Relative keys are easy to find since their tonic pitches are always a step-and-a-half apart. (Theorists often express minor keys with lower case letters and major keys with upper case letters, as we have done here.)

| |
| --- |
| a - C |
| c - E♭ |
| e - G |
| d - F |

Since relative keys share the same set of pitches (almost), it is important to use the correct letter names. For example, the relative minor key to A major is F♯ minor, not G♭ minor (which has the same sound on the keyboard). Since the key signature used by both A major and F♯ minor has "three sharps" (F♯, C♯ and G♯), G♭ is not involved in either. You will stay out of trouble by thinking carefully in this regard.

Another way of thinking of relative tonics is to note that the tonic of a relative minor key is scale step 6 of its major key. Before you start counting *upward* to the sixth scale step of a major key, remember that counting down

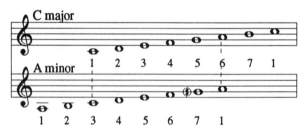

to scale step 6 is much closer, and therefore more convenient. From the minor scale point of view, the tonic pitch of a relative major key is scale step 3 of a minor key.

In contrast to the dubious term "parallel," the term "relative" is well-used here. The common pitches belonging to relative major and minor keys are like "one big family," first celebrating their allegiance to one "parent" and then to the other. Composers can conveniently modulate to and from relative major and minor keys. By raising the dominant pitch (5) of a major key, the leading tone (7) of its relative minor key is created. Likewise, by lowering the leading tone of a minor key, the dominant of its relative major key is created. Appropriate dominant harmony is required, of course, to make the shift convincing.

28-1

As with most relational theoretical concepts, these are better viewed and experienced than simply memorized. In this regard, you might keep in mind a "model" of the relative positions of the C major scale and the A minor scale as shown above. This will quickly dispel any doubts about "which way to count" or "how far to count." Eventually, you will learn and remember which major and minor keys are relatives simply by using them. If you would like to accelerate the process, you might find the classic "circle of fifths," showing standard key signatures related to both major and minor tonics, a helpful tool for drill.

This "circle of fifths" illustration shows relative major and minor keys and the number of sharps or flats in the signatures they share. Major keys are shown outside the circle in upper-case letters and minor keys are shown inside the circle in lower-case letters. As we noted earlier, keys with five or more sharps or flats can be notated two different ways since they sound the same on the keyboard.

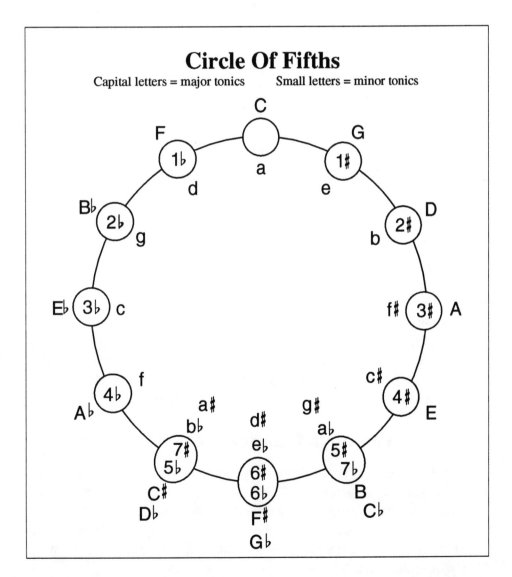

# The "Look" of Modality in Notation

Since both major and minor keys use the same signatures, you may be wondering how to determine which mode is being represented. For example, when the signature consists of two flats (B♭ and E♭), is the composition in B♭ major or G minor? For that matter, might this key signature also be used for G aeolian? How about C dorian?

First of all, any of the keys mentioned in the previous paragraph can use the two-flat key signature. Furthermore, you don't have to know what the tonality and modality are in order to *perform* the music. Mechanically translating standard notation into sound on an instrument is certainly possible without knowing the key or mode. As a matter of fact, translating symbols to sound often provides much aural information regarding modality and tonality.

Visually determining the tonality and modality of a piece is not very difficult once you know what to look for. For example, most compositions begin and end with tonic harmony, frequently with the melody ending on the tonic pitch. Therefore, if a piece with a two-flat key signature begins and ends on a B♭ major chord with the final melody note on B♭, you can be quite certain that the composition is in the key of B♭ major.

On the other hand, if the initial harmony in our two-flat example begins and ends on a G minor chord and its melody ends on G, you can be assured that the tonality is not B♭, but rather G. Its modality, however, is not yet certain. If you see a number of accidental F♯s (leading tones to G), you can assume that the mode is minor. If F♯s are not in evidence, and instead there are F naturals throughout, the mode is likely aeolian.

If our two-flat piece were in C dorian, the harmonic and melodic characteristics would lead us to that conclusion. For example, if Cs and Gs were plentiful, that would be a significant clue indicating C dorian. Any other mode using this set of seven pitches would have its own characteristics, leading the ear toward its tonic by plentiful use of pitches closely related to the tonic and by the location of the final melodic pitch.

# Twentieth Century Innovations

As we have seen, many twentieth-century composers have ignored the boundaries of traditional conventions. This penchant for the unusual includes key signatures. Charles Ives, and others, combined traditional signatures in unusual ways—for example, having all the female singers perform in one key and all the male singers perform in another. This excerpt is from his "Sixty-Seventh Psalm."

God be mer - ci - ful un - to us, and bless us;

Bela Bartok invented key signatures to fit his musical purposes. In this piano piece, "Crossed Hands," from *Mikrokosmos*, Vol. IV, he creates a separate custom signature for each clef. Note that the "one flat" is not on B, and the two sharps are not on F and C.

Atonal music, having no allegiance to a tonal center, has no use for a key signature. While every "black digital" pitch requires an accidental, either sharps or flats can be used arbitrarily since there is no requirement to spell configurations "correctly" in a chord or key. For the same reason, double sharps and double flats are unnecessary.

In this excerpt from the piano part of Schoenberg's song "O alter duft," notice that accidentals are explicit, even on pitches already modified within a measure and on pitches on which sharps would have been automatically canceled by the barline. The reason for this extra care is that it is difficult to keep track of which pitches have been modified since there is no tonality (or key signature) to keep in mind.

Imaginative compositions that include sounds unrelated to the twelve standard pitches represented by the traditional five-line staff require equally imaginative notational systems. These, while interesting, are beyond the scope of this book.

# Key Signature Wrap-Up

The use of standard key signatures contributes both clarity and neatness to music notation. Once signatures are memorized, a performer can interpret the lines and spaces accordingly, modifying specified pitches throughout a piece. Because sharped and flatted pitches belonging to the scale in current use are not shown throughout, occasional pitches modified by accidentals stand out, thereby more clearly indicating modulations and chromatic embellishments.

Since key signatures are shared by major, minor and other modes, they do not precisely indicate the tonality and modality of a composition. The reader must examine the music itself for significant clues. Beginning and ending harmony, final melodic pitch, leading tones appearing as accidentals, and extensive use of harmonically related pitches are significant in this regard.

Major and minor keys using the same key signature are said to be *relative*. Major and minor keys built on the same tonic pitch are said to be *parallel*. Being aware of these relationships is important to understanding the internal harmonic structure of a composition.

None of this applies to atonal music, which, of course, is not concerned with keys, modes or leading tones. However, some modern composers have used key signatures in nonstandard and creative ways to notate music that is some-what tonal, but unconventionally so.

# 29

# Intervals On The Keyboard

We use the term **interval** in music to refer to "the distance between two pitches." While "distance," when applied to *perception* of pitch relations, is troublesome, it nevertheless is a handy and practical concept for measuring intervals in terms of keyboard scales. Therefore, as you read this chapter, don't forget that the identifying perceptual characteristics of intervals depend less on distance than they do on harmonic relationships. Remember, an octave is a very consonant interval, while the interval a half-step smaller, a seventh, is very dissonant, yet the next smaller interval, a sixth, is quite consonant. Also, the "spaces" between standard intervals—in other words, pitches in the "cracks"—are even more dissonant. Do you remember the sliding pitch illustration (CD example 2-9)?

As you know, we have been dealing with intervals since the early chapters where we considered the acoustic partial series in relation to our perception of tonal relations. We called the "distance" from a tonic pitch up to a dominant pitch a "perfect fifth," in that it encompasses a certain configuration of five scale steps. We also called the "distance" from tonic up to mediant a "major third" in that it encompasses a certain configuration of three scale steps. If those concepts have faded, quickly review Chapter 8 (pp. 79-84).

If you recall, at the end of that chapter you were left on a cliffhanger as to why some intervals are called "perfect" and others "major" or "minor." Now that you understand major and minor keys, this and other matters can be discussed in a more systematic way. In this chapter, we will pick up the topic of intervals from the keyboard point of view. In the next chapter we will look at intervals as they appear on the staff.

Needless to say, you will want to have a keyboard handy while you read this chapter so you can hear (in tempered tuning, of course) the intervals and visualize them spacially. This will also help you clarify "sound alikes" *before* they can confuse you in notation.

**unison and octave**    Strictly speaking, two voices sounding on the same pitch do not create an "interval" since there is no pitch "distance" between them. In other words, two pitches on the same pitch are really the same pitch. Nevertheless, in order to preserve the systematic language of musical intervals, this circumstance is called a **unison**, a 1:1 ratio. A unison does not imply tonality. It has only to do with a single pitch out of musical context.

In the following series of illustrations, each gray dot represents a "voice," or sound source. Several examples of each type of interval will be given to

show how each appears in different keyboard locations. Here are five arbitrarily placed unisons, that is, five pairs of voices on five different pitches.

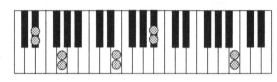

You already know that two pitches an octave apart are in a sense the "same pitch" (having the same name) and vibrating in a 1:2 ratio. As you also know,

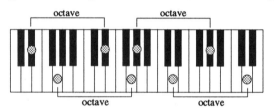

an octave (as with any musical interval) can be located in any position within the practical range of hearing. Again, don't assume that *octave* implies two tonic pitches. Octaves can occur

on any scale step in any key. Octaves—like unisons—do not in any way imply a tonality or mode.

**fifths  and fourths**    On the other hand, **perfect fifths** and **perfect fourths** *can* imply tonality, or at least suggest root function. These sturdy consonant intervals provide the structural "girders" of musical composition. They do not convey modal "flavors," however. That is the role of other less consonant intervals.

The acoustic nature of pitch relations, along with musical practices over the centuries, have conditioned us to hear one of the pitches as a root, even when these basic intervals are sounded without musical context. The lower pitch of a perfect fifth will be heard "naturally" as a root, and the higher pitch of a perfect fourth (the inversion of the perfect fifth) will be heard "naturally" as a root.

Because of the small "distance" difference and the small dissonance difference between the perfect fourth and perfect fifth, it is challenging to learn to

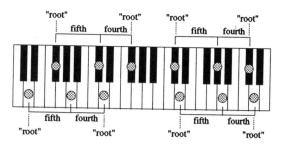

discriminate between them aurally. Therefore, it is very helpful to learn to hear and identify the pitch that sounds like the root.

Playing perfect fifths and fourths on the keyboard is quite simple. With one exception, both pitches of perfect fourths and fifths will occur either on white digitals or black digitals. Just lock your thumb and little finger in a five-digital position and drop them on any (almost any) white or black set of pitches and it will work. Can you hear the "root effect" of the lower pitch? Play each pitch separately going up, then down. The lower pitch sounds more "final".

The single exception to this is, of course, B and F, the tritone in the key of C major. If you happened to strike this fifth dur-

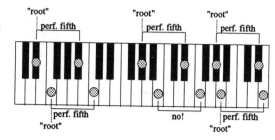

ing the exercise, you probably realized from its distinctive sound that this is the exception to the "white digital" rule of thumb regarding perfect fifths.

Now perform the exercise playing perfect fourths. This time use your thumb and ring finger (or your index and little finger), lock in the distance and play any combination of two white or two black digitals. Listen for the "root effect" in the *higher* pitch this time. All of them are perfect fourths except, again, a combination of F and B, the tritone.

This exercise reminds us that the tritone can be either a fifth or a fourth. Are they different sizes? Count the whole steps from F up to B. Now count the whole steps from B up to F. If you counted three whole steps both times, you were reminded why this unique interval has the nickname "tritone." It is the only interval in our tempered system that is the same size when inverted.

The acoustically tuned tritone is, of course, *not* the same size when inverted. You may be surprised to know that the acoustically-tuned tritone as a fourth is actually larger than the acoustically-tuned tritone as a fifth. A brain twister? Not really. Remember that the dominant seventh pitch—F in the key of C— is considerably lower than keyboard pitch. This moves it closer to the B below (a scalewise fifth away) and stretches it father from the B above (a scalewise fourth away).

So, if the tritone can be a fifth or fourth, but not a "perfect" fifth or fourth, what kind of fourth or fifth would this be? And what is this "perfect" business all about anyway? These are excellent questions, but at this point only the first is ready to be answered. The "perfect" question will have to wait just a bit longer.

**augmented and diminished fourths and fifths**

Here is the rule for identifying fourths and fifths that are not perfect: a fifth or fourth that is a half step smaller than perfect is said to be **diminished** and a fourth or fifth that is a half step larger than perfect is said to be **augmented**. These terms are easy to understand and apply, as they mean about the same in music as they do in general usage.

Because keyboard digitals can use two or three different letter names, the pitches will be specified in the following illustrations. Here are some augmented fifths. Note that the letter designations in each interval above are in a "fifth" relationship (EFGAB and DEFGA). "Adjustments" are accomplished by accidentals.

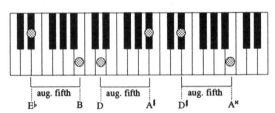

Here are some diminished fifths. Notice that the white-digital tritone, an augmented fourth when spelled F-B, is still a tritone when spelled here as a

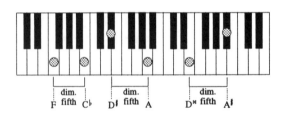

diminished fifth. The D♯-A diminished fifth reminds us that "raising" the lower pitch makes an interval a half-step smaller, as does lowering the top pitch. Finally, notice that the third diminished fifth, despite its complex "spelling," is the second example raised a half step. Modifying both pitches by the same increment does not change the size of the interval.

(Incidentally, music teachers and musicians use the term "spelling" —for better or worse—to refer to the letter names of the exact pitches that comprise intervals and chords. If you find this use of the term bothersome, we apologize, but the practice is not likely to change soon.)

Here are some augmented fourths. Notice that these appear on the same keyboard digitals as in the previous set. Are you beginning to realize that intervals that sound the same might not *be* the same?

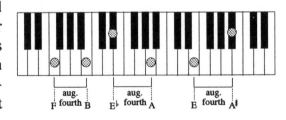

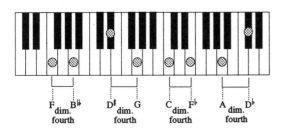

Here are some diminished fourths. Yes, you are correct. They look like and sound like major thirds on the keyboard. You are not likely to hear them as major thirds, however, in the harmonic contexts in which they appear.

As the illustrations show, it is very important to spell an interval accurately, otherwise it becomes a different interval. The augmented fifth from C up to G♯ should not be thought of as C up to A♭. Calling the top pitch A♭ would make this some kind of sixth which, of course, would need to be written differently on the staff. Pitches, intervals and chords that sound alike when played on the keyboard but are spelled differently are called **enharmonic equivalents**.

**enharmonic equivalency**

Intervals that sound alike but have different spellings are, in fact, different intervals. Knowing, as you do, that the keyboard cannot differentiate between acoustically tuned pitches, this information will come as no surprise. In any case, spelling intervals (and chords) correctly will make the function of their pitches clearer to the reader.

Occasionally, however, composers will purposely misspell pitches when it makes the music easier to read or play, particularly if the music's roots and tonality are already vague. It is important first to know which spelling is correct and then to use an alternate spelling only when it better suits the situation.

Keeping all this in mind, we will look now at some tritones spelled different ways and observe how spelling affects their function. Notice that the keyboard tritone from C up to the black digital between F and G can be spelled in different ways. When spelled with an F♯, the interval is an augmented fourth. It is a fourth because it encompasses four letter-names,

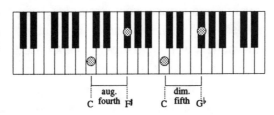

C-D-E-F. It is augmented in that it is a half step larger than the white-digital fourth from C up to F.

As you remember, there is only one tritone in any major key, and it occurs on scale steps 7 and 4. Therefore, reasoning inversely, any specific tritone (specified by its spelling) can only be in one major key. Since the key of G major is the only key that has both an F♯ and a C natural, this tritone belongs to the

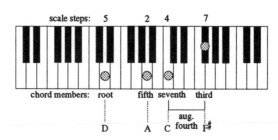

key of G major and no other. Notice that when spelled as an augmented fourth, the upper pitch functions as the leading tone (scale step 7), the third of the dominant chord, and the lower pitch functions as the seventh of the chord (step 4).

When this "same" keyboard tritone is spelled with a G♭, the interval is a diminished fifth. It is a fifth because it encompasses five letter-names, C-D-E-F-G. It is diminished in that it is a half step smaller than the white-digital fifth from C to G. The only major key that contains both a C and a G♭ is the key of D♭ major. In this case, the lower pitch functions as the leading tone and the upper pitch functions as the chord seventh.

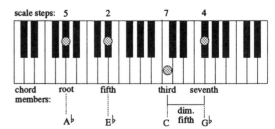

You can see that spelling intervals correctly provides very important information to the music reader, particularly when appropriate tuning adjustments can be made according to the context of the music. As it works out, making these adjustments is not very complicated. Generally, pitches that are raised—notated with a sharp, or with a natural in a flat key—will usually find acoustic tuning slightly higher than tempered tuning, and likewise, pitches that are lowered—notated with a flat, or with a natural in a sharp key—will usually find acoustic tuning slightly lower than tempered tuning.

One reason this generalization works is that the majority of accidentals (pitches not in the prevailing key) are either the leading tone or the chord seventh in a tritone. (For examples, see pp. 87-88.) Also, other accidentals are generally spelled in such a way that proper tuning is implied. For example, chromatic lower auxiliaries (neighbors) are normally written as raised versions of the scale step below, and chromatic upper auxiliaries are normally written as lowered versions of the scale step above. In each case, the auxiliary pitch leans in the direction of the chord tone, making the "half step" very small. (See sidebar "Can The Human Ear Hear Ratios?", p.31.)

The concept of enharmonic equivalency, then, is truly a keyboard idea. While a G♯ and an A♭ are sounded by the same digital on a keyboard, the pitch of an acoustically tuned G♯ is somewhat higher than an acoustically tuned A♭. However, even keyboard music should be spelled properly to reflect the music's harmonic sense.

Thus far, we have discussed unisons, octaves, fifths and fourths, all of which are called "perfect" when in the proper configuration. The remaining intervals (within an octave) are seconds, thirds, sixths and sevenths, none of which can ever be described as "perfect." Is this simply discrimination or is there a logical reason for the difference? The answers are "no" and "yes," respectively. The "why" will soon become clear.

**major and minor intervals**

Thirds and sixths are less consonant than perfect fifths and fourths. Their role, in general, is to provide warmth and sometimes modal color. Seconds and sevenths are considerably more dissonant, and tend to create conflict or restlessness.

Earlier we noted the size of the third from tonic (scale step 1) up to mediant (scale step 3) in the major scale is two whole steps (in keyboard language), and the size of the third from mediant to dominant (scale step 5) in the major mode is a step and a half. We also noted the two-whole-step third is called a major third and the step-and-a-half third is called a minor third.

Those interval designations hold true even when the two pitches are not on scale steps 1-3 or 3-5. In fact, a major third occurs when any two pitches on any scale steps, or in no key at all, are two whole steps apart and are spelled with the high and low letter-names of a three-letter sequence (for example, F to A in F-G-A).

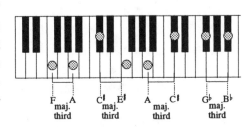

Likewise, a minor third occurs when any two pitches are a step-and-a-half apart, provided they are spelled using the high and low letter-names of a three letter sequence (as above). In other words, an interval is called a third when it uses appropriate letters, and is designated as major or minor when it configures to the appropriate size.

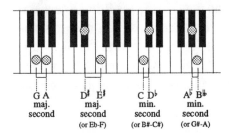

Seconds are similar to thirds in that a large one—specifically a whole step—is called a major second and a small one—specifically a half step—is called a minor second. Again, double-check your spelling to ensure that you are designating the correct interval.

The pitch a major sixth above C is A. The pitch a major seventh above C is B. Each of these major intervals can be modified to minor intervals by making them a half step smaller. While this information may work well in a familiar key like C major, it does not always help in learning to identify major and minor sixths and sevenths in strange locations.

While seconds and thirds are instantly identifiable, due to their keyboard sizes, sixths and sevenths are not. The number of whole and half steps in sixths and sevenths is not something most of us can perceive instantly. We probably would need to do some counting, which is just as inefficient here as it is in learning lines and spaces.

Actually, probably very few experienced musicians readily know or care how many steps or half steps there are in major and minor sixths and sevenths. There are better ways to identify them. We will explore them separately.

**major and minor intervals relative to tonic**

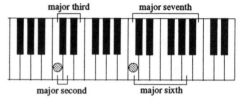

You may have noticed during the preceding discussion that pitches in the major scale a second, third, sixth and seventh above tonic pitch all constitute major intervals.

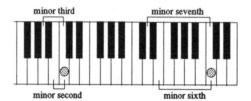

An interesting feature of the major scale is that pitches in the major scale a second, third, sixth and seventh *below* a tonic pitch all constitute minor intervals.

Thus, in a major key, the interval from tonic to the scale step a third above it is a major third, while the interval from tonic to the scale step a third below it is a minor third. Notice that the major third has two whole steps and the minor third has one and a half steps. Likewise, tonic up to scale step 2 is a major second (a whole step) and tonic down to scale step 7 is a minor second (a half step).

This information will help you readily identify major and minor sixths and sevenths. When the lower pitch of a major third is moved up an octave, the resulting interval is a minor sixth. When the higher pitch of a minor third is moved down an octave, the resulting interval is a major sixth. When the lower pitch of a major second is moved up an octave, the resulting interval is a minor seventh. When the higher pitch of a minor second is moved down an octave, the resulting interval is a major seventh. So, by temporarily converting the larger intervals to their smaller reciprocals, their sizes can be determined easily and accurately. This process, called **inversion**, is discussed in more detail below.

Here is another way to determine, easily and without counting, whether sixths and sevenths are major or minor. By comparing the size of a sixth or

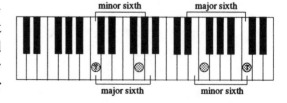

seventh to a perfect fifth or octave, both of which are relatively easy to identify, one can quickly determine its major or minor quality. A major sixth is a whole step larger than a perfect fifth and a minor sixth is a half step larger than a perfect fifth.

Identifying the size of sevenths as major or minor is also very simple. A major seventh is a half step smaller than an octave and a minor seventh is a whole step smaller than an octave. Like the fifth/sixth comparison above, this can be visualized both upward and downward.

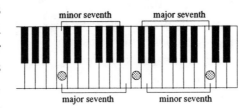

One of the benefits of visualizing major and minor intervals in the context of a major key is that this is where they regularly occur in music. Just as it is more interesting and informative to study animals in their natural habitats, it is more meaningful to study intervals by viewing them in the places they frequent. Too often, students think of a minor third as a "major third made smaller," for example, by lowering the third of a major triad. They then are confused by the third on scale steps 6-1, which is not *made* smaller. It just *is* smaller.

We noted earlier that fifths and fourths are the "same" harmonic relationship turned over—or inverted. Just above, we saw that sixths are harmonically the same as thirds and seconds are harmonically the same as sevenths. Stated another way, thirds invert to sixths and vice versa, and seconds invert to sevenths and vice versa.

**inversion of major and minor intervals**

In contrast to fourth/fifths, the "quality" description changes with inversion of third/sixths and second/sevenths. That is, a major third inverts to a minor sixth and a minor third inverts to a major sixth. Likewise, a major second inverts to a minor seventh and a major second inverts to a minor seventh. These reciprocal pairs can be seen in this illustration.

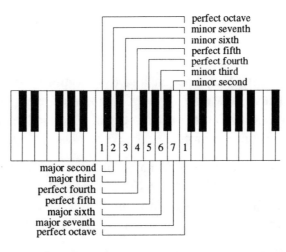

To further test this principle of major/minor inversion, we will lower the top pitch of the major second, major third, major sixth and major seventh in the context of the major mode and note the effect on the respective inversions.

The intervals we made minor by reducing their sizes now invert to major intervals measured down from tonic. Interestingly, most of the intervals in this chart are commonly used in these locations in the minor mode. Scale steps 3 and 6, as you know, are lowered (in comparison to major) to make the tonic and subdominant chords

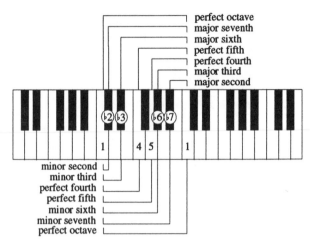

minor, and scale step 7 is sometimes lowered for melodic purposes. Even scale step 2 is occasionally lowered in the minor mode, creating a major II chord.

This view of the minor mode is a strong argument for seeing it as the singular alternate "color" reflection of the major mode, rather than merely an offspring of the aeolian church mode, a position many music educators seem to assume. To make up your own mind, you will want to consider both points of view. You may encounter selections that are difficult to categorize as distinctly minor or aeolian. Hopefully, this discussion will help you relate to this issue with more insight than might otherwise have been the case.

One other matter should be mentioned before leaving this topic. It is important to realize that the terms "major" and "minor" when applied to intervals do not imply a modal feeling. Since a major third and a minor sixth are reciprocal inversions, it follows that they cannot by themselves consistently convey a major-mode flavor or a minor-mode flavor. Also, a major triad contains *both* a major third (root to third) and a minor third (third to fifth). Likewise, a minor triad also contains a major third (third to fifth) and a minor third (root to third). Clearly, isolated intervals do not necessarily connote a major or minor context in the same sense as do scales and chords.

**major/minor vs. perfect**  Now that you realize major/minor intervals change from major to minor, or vice versa, when inverted, while perfect ones do not, we are ready to answer the question, "Why are some intervals perfect and others are not?" The distinction may seem arbitrary, but you will soon see that it is not.

Perhaps you already have realized that if fourths and fifths were called "major," the system of intervals we are describing here simply could not work. Did you notice that the higher pitch in major intervals is always in the major key of the lower pitch, while the lower pitch is never in the major key of the higher pitch? Conversely, in minor intervals, the lower pitch is always in the major key of the upper pitch, while the upper pitch is never in the major key of the lower pitch. If those concepts are still unclear you, apply them to familiar intervals and you will see that they are *always* true.

By contrast, *both* pitches in perfect intervals are in each other's major key. *That* is why these intervals are called "perfect." The same is true, of course, when perfect intervals are inverted—they still are in each other's key. (Perhaps you already figured that out.)

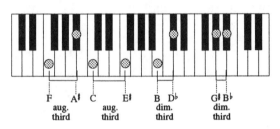

F    A♯    C    E♯    B    D♭    G♯ B♭
aug.      aug.       dim.      dim.
third     third      third     third

Just as perfect intervals are called "augmented" when made a half step larger and called "diminished" when made a half-step smaller, major/minor intervals can also be so designated. Of course, in this case,

**augmented and diminished third/sixths and second/sevenths**

there is already a half-step difference between major and minor sizes. Therefore, it is major intervals that become augmented when made a half step larger and it is minor intervals that become diminished when made a half step smaller. Therefore, a diminished third is a *whole* step smaller than a major third.

There is a progression in half steps, then, from larger to smaller in the designations "augmented," "major," "minor" and "diminished." Notice that the letter names in this illustration do not change from one interval to the next. The differences are expressed only by the accidentals.

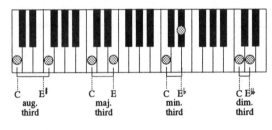

C    E♯    C    E    C    E♭    C E♭♭
aug.      maj.       min.      dim.
third     third      third     third

Remember that spelling is important. Notice that the augmented third in this illustration uses the same digitals used by the C-F perfect fourth. When one of the two pitches in any interval is spelled differently, the numeric interval changes, even though the sound does not (at least not on the keyboard). So, be careful to use correct spellings. It does make a difference.

We have seen that perfect intervals invert to perfect intervals and that major intervals invert to minor intervals and vice versa. The same is true of augmented and diminished intervals, regardless whether they are fifth/fourth types or major/minor types. We noticed earlier that the interval B-F, a diminished-fifth tritone, becomes an augmented-fourth tritone when inverted to F-B. This relationship exists between all tritone invertible pairs.

**inversion of augmented and diminished intervals**

Similarly, all augmented third/ sixths and second/sevenths invert to diminished intervals when spelled with the same pitch names. Here are a few examples. As mentioned earlier, these intervals are enharmonic equivalents of major, minor and

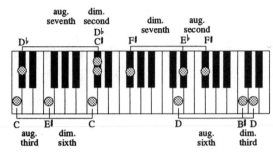

perfect intervals, so don't be misled by their apparent consonant sounds when played on the keyboard. They don't necessarily sound like this when tuned acoustically in a musical context.

This system of classifying intervals is remarkably rational and balanced. There are no loose ends. There are no issues open to debate and there is no room for improvement (although its misleading terminology should be replaced—the use of "major" and "minor," for example). This is yet another musical example of a logically "closed system."

# 30

# Intervals On The Staff

The musical staff is well-designed for perceiving intervals at a glance. Notice how quickly your eye picks up thirds. Thirds are always expressed on neighboring lines or neighboring spaces.

Fifths are also readily perceivable in that both notes appear on lines with an empty line between or on spaces with an empty space between.

Sevenths are also expressed with both pitches on lines or both on spaces. They are similarly iden-tifiable by the two empty lines or spaces between.

Seconds, fourths, sixths and octaves are expressed with one pitch on a space and the other on a line. Because seconds are so close together, one of the two pitches is displaced to the side.

Fourths are placed with one empty line/space set between the two pitches.

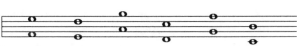

Sixths have two empty line/space sets between pitches.

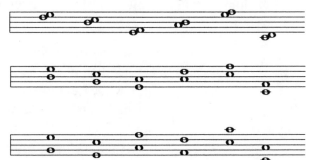

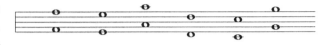

Octaves are also easy to recognize, since the distance between their pitches is approximately equal to the vertical size of the staff.

With just a little drill, you can learn to identify all the intervals at sight—instantly and WITHOUT COUNTING. Counting lines and spaces is a needless waste of time. If you must, do it once per interval just to make sure you understand the descriptions above. If you persist in counting, be warned that you will only delay your own progress.

Determining the numerical size of an interval on the staff—third, fifth, sixth, etc.—is the easy part. Determining the qualitative size—major, minor, diminished, etc.—is the challenge. To master it, you must know where the half steps are located. No doubt, you remember that they occur between every B and C and every E and F in every octave.

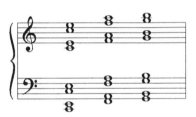

It also helps to have memorized where the three white-digital major thirds occur on the staff. This feature, like the half step, is easy to see on the keyboard (having two black digitals between) but not on the staff. You already know that these are located at every C-E, F-A, and G-B.

Relating the half-step and major-third images will help you transform the featureless lines and spaces into a meaningful "shape." For example, you can use the half step information to quickly locate the major thirds. Logically, "white" major thirds will not include a "white" half step between its two pitches since it is composed of two whole steps; therefore, any "white" third not containing a "white" half step is major. Of course, the flip side of the same logic is that a "white" third that *does* contain a "white" half step is a minor third.

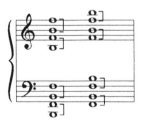

Knowing where the "white" half steps are also reminds you of the location of the "white" tritone. The "white" diminished fifth (B up to F) contains both half-step locations, while the "white" augmented fourth (F up to B) contains neither. This will help you avoid inadvertently calling it "perfect." (All the other "white" fifths *are* perfect.)

# Using the system

As you view intervals on the staff, translate them (in imagination or reality) to the keyboard. This will help eliminate "abstract" errors and also help you relate the language of intervals to the real sounds of music. Engaging in a puzzle of disconnected intellectual exercises will not help you learn how music really works.

There are many ways to analyze a notated interval: (1) view it as having the lower pitch on tonic, (2) view it as having the upper pitch as tonic, (3) invert it to view it as a more convenient smaller interval and then reinvert the result, (4) transpose both pitches up or down a half step to a simpler key, (5) modify an unusual interval by a half step or so until it is recognizable and then logically adjust names back to the original form. Deciding which method to use depends on the interval and the way it strikes you. Actually, it is probably a good idea to use at least two methods in order to double check your analysis.

To demonstrate, here are a few "problems" to solve. Let's start with a fairly obvious one. Analyze this interval. Since the letter names here (A and C) occur in a minor-third location, the "raised" top pitch makes it a major third. You might also consider that when viewed in the key of A major, C♯ is the third scale step, being two whole steps above tonic. That leaves no doubt that this interval is a major third.

 Try this one. In this case, we can't use the lower pitch as a tonic since there is no key of G♯ major. We can use the upper pitch as tonic since there *is* a key of E major, having a key signature of four sharps, one of which is G♯. Since the lower pitch is in the key of the upper pitch, the interval is a minor sixth.

To double check, we might use a number of methods. We can invert it to a third which would show us two whole steps and then invert that major third to a minor sixth. Or, we can temporarily suspend the sharp, note that E is in the key of G major, making it a major sixth, then replace the sharp, making the interval a half step smaller—a minor sixth.

Fifths and fourths are quite easy. There are no keys of D♯ or A♯ major, so viewing this interval in one of these keys is not possible. Actually, we don't need to think about keys here at all. Ignoring both sharps lowers this interval intact to white digitals, therefore verifying that it is a perfect fifth (since it is not B-F). When any fourth or fifth (except B-F) has the same accidental on both pitches, it is perfect. Now, how's that for easy?

Let's look at one more interval. Inverting this sixth to a third is unwieldy because of the B♯. Nevertheless, you might like to do it just to notice that it results in  what appears on the keyboard to be a whole step. As a third, this "whole step" is a half step smaller than a minor third, and is therefore diminished. Reinverting this diminished third results in an augmented sixth.

An easier method is to temporarily ignore the sharp and note that B is in the key of D major, having two sharps, F♯ and C♯. Since B is not one of them, D up to B is a major sixth. Replacing the sharp makes the interval a half step larger than major—an augmented sixth.

As you can see, analyzing intervals can be an intellectual challenge. If you enjoy puzzles, you might even find analyzing intervals entertaining. In any case, your success in recognizing intervals depends on how well you understand both staff notation and the interval system.

# Interval Wrap-Up

Interval terminology is very systematic. It not only "measures" the distance between two pitches, it offers practical clues to their melodic and harmonic meanings. There are two categories of intervals: perfect and major/minor. Perfect intervals are so named because the two pitches are in each other's key, while in major/minor intervals one pitch is in the other's major key but not vice versa.

In both categories, it is possible to modify intervals by using accidentals to make them larger or smaller. Perfect intervals become augmented when they are made a half step larger and diminished when they are made a half step smaller. A major interval made a half step larger is augmented, made a half step smaller is minor, and made a whole step smaller is diminished. A minor interval made a half step larger is major, made a whole step larger is augmented and made a half step smaller is diminished.

Intervals can be categorized in three reciprocally invertible pairs. Perfect fifths and fourths invert to each other and provide harmonic stability due to their strong consonance. Major and minor thirds and sixths invert to each other and provide warmth and color due to their moderate consonance. Major and minor seconds and sevenths invert to each other and provide conflict and restlessness due to their dissonance.

Since most augmented and diminished intervals are enharmonic spellings of perfect, major and minor intervals, they have no consonance/dissonance sound quality of their own (particularly on a keyboard). Composers have consistently treated these intervals as dissonances, however, and their acoustic tunings are dissimilar to their more consonant enharmonic equivalents. The exceptions are the augmented fourth and its inversion the diminished fifth (tritones), which are very recognizeable and distinctive.

The names of intervals apply without regard for their position or function in a musical context or key. Names simply designate the size of the interval. Therefore, the terms "major" and "minor" when applied to intervals should not be understood to imply a quality of sound, as in "major key" or "minor chord." Perhaps a better choice of terminology would be "standard," "large," "small," "dinky," and "gigantic." However, new terms are not likely to be adopted, so just keep in mind that a "minor sixth" is simply a "major third" upside down and can imply either a "major" or "minor" flavor, depending on perceptual disposition and/or musical context.

On the following page is an excerpt of a chorus from G. F. Handel's famous **practical drill** oratorio, "Messiah." You might like to use it to exercise your ability to identify intervals in a musical context. The vocal lines provide practice of melodic intervals (notes in succession) and the piano reduction of the orchestra score provides practice of harmonic intervals (simultaneous notes). Don't forget to consider the key signature when identifying pitches. You will know you are correct when you get the same result using two methods of analysis. If you have difficulty, review the discussion above. Play fragments on the keyboard to hear them. (Measure numbers are included to facilitate classroom discussion.)

# And With His Stripes We Are Healed - excerpt

You might enjoy analyzing other aspects of this music as well. What is the first tonality in this excerpt? What other keys are visited? Does repetition of a melody in other voices help you find that answer? Are tritones involved in any modulations? Is there imitation between voices? Do sequences occur? Are any melodic patterns inverted? Are any melodic fragments "displaced" metrically to create rhythmic meaning?

31

# Intervals In The Major/Minor System

A practical way to learn the language of intervals, both theoretically and aurally, is to become familiar with where they appear in the major/minor system. We have already described how to do this to some extent in earlier discussions; however, now that you understand the terminology and know how to use the system, you are better prepared to benefit from a comprehensive overview.

If you previously thought intervals are always "measured" up from tonic, you might want to read the sidebar "A Little Knowledge *Is* A Dangerous Thing " on p. 298. This will minimize any confusion you might experience if or when you find things where you don't expect them to be, or vise versa.

In the illustrations on the following page, all the perfect, major and minor intervals, plus the tritone, are shown where they occur in the primary chords of the key of C, in both major and minor modes. Browse through each chord, playing and singing the intervals. Take your time.

Notice pairs of intervals in reciprocal inversions. Notice similarities and differences between intervals in different chords. Play chord roots and sing the other chord members in acoustic tuning, particularly noticing the smaller size of the 6:7 "minor" third in the dominant seventh chord.

The addition of the chord seventh creates many more intervals in the dominant seventh chord. The ones that occur in the major-mode tonic and subdominant triads are there, of course. With the addition of the seventh (scale step 4) we get the "blue" sounding seventh and second, a smaller minor third and larger major sixth, as well as the two distinct tritones.

## Major Tonic

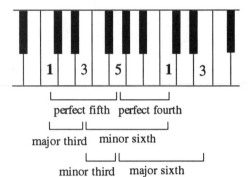

## Minor Tonic

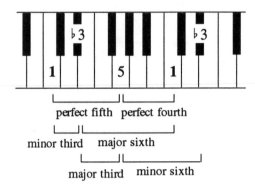

## Major Subdominant

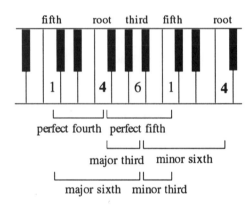

## Minor Subdominant

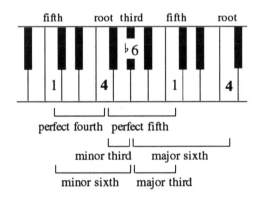

## Dominant Seventh

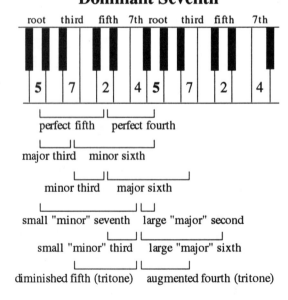

Our sense of tonic plays a major part in identifying intervals at work. For example, the minor third between scale steps 3 and 5 (major mode) sounds different than the 6-1 minor third, the former sounding in the context of the major tonic triad and the latter sounding in the context of the major subdominant triad. Both minor thirds (5:6 ratios) function as the 3rd and 5th of their respective harmonies, yet the influence of the tonic as the fifth of the subdominant triad creates a significantly different flavor. Play and sing them. What do you think?

The 6-1 minor third can also be tuned as a 13:16 ratio in the context of a tonic root, but this relationship may be too obscure for a beginner to perceive. The 6-1 minor third is much easier to hear in the context of subdominant harmony in its simpler 5:6 ratio. When A and C are sounded without context, we tend to imagine an F root. One would suspect this is caused by the acoustical properties of a major triad, in which 5:6 is the ratio between the third and fifth of that chord. Thus, we have a "minor" interval implying a "major" harmony. (Remember, the names of intervals do not imply modal "flavors.")

The 1-♭3 minor third is perceived as different from the 3-5 minor third. Even though the acoustical ratio appears to be 5:6 in both cases, the sense of root created by the presence of the fifth and the flavor of the minor triad makes these two minor thirds sound different. In the major triad, the minor third does not contain the root, and in the minor triad, it does. Also, the *upper* pitch of the minor third in the major chord (5) is more stable, and in the other, the *lower* pitch (1) is more stable.

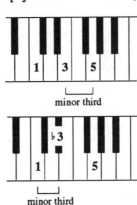

Another way to compare the sound of the minor third in the context of major and minor triads is to hold constant the pitches of the minor third and change the pitch that completes the triad. Notice that E and G, the third and fifth of the C major triad, also serve as the root and third of the E minor triad. By alternately playing (or singing) C or B with E and G, you can hear the difference in the perceptual effect, particularly when all pitches are sung or played acoustically. When C is sounding, the perfect fifth (or fourth) between C and G causes C to be heard as the root. When B is sounding, the perfect fourth (or fifth) between B and E causes E to be heard as the root.

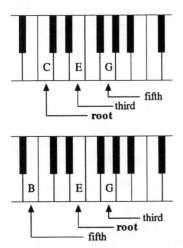

# A Little Knowledge *Is* a Dangerous Thing

Current music teaching largely ignores the influence of musical context on interval perception. The common procedure of measuring all intervals up from a tonic pitch seems based on the erroneous idea that intervals are simply "distances" and that learning to hear an interval up from tonic will prepare a student to hear that same interval in any musical context. Needless to say, this approach produces a lot of confused and frustrated music students.

Even worse, students are given interval sound models without regard for the harmonic context of the example. For example, the opening of "My Bonnie Lies Over The Ocean" is often used as an example of a major sixth

(correctly) without the information that its opening scale steps are 5 up to 3, not 1 up to 6. The tonic pitch falls on the word "lies," not on the first syllable "My." The underlying harmony in the opening of the phrase is the tonic chord.

Practicing the major sixth up from tonic will prevent hearing this interval in its most common context. If you learn this interval as 1-6, you are probably "hearing" this interval as the fifth and third of a subdominant chord. By not realizing that, aural and theoretical confusion is inevitable.

Another interval frequently "taught" out of its common musical context is the tritone. To teach that the "tritone" between scale steps 1 and ♯4 is the same interval as between 7 and 4 is irresponsible. When the melodic tritone appears in its natural habitat, as scale steps 4-7 or 7-4, it functions and tunes as part of a dominant seventh chord. When it appears in another context, it will have some other purpose. Its tuning will depend on its harmonic and melodic setting.

Since songs usually begin with the harmonic stability of a tonic chord which establishes the tonal center, there are few, if any, songs that begin with a tritone in its common dominant context. This being the case, teachers frequently resort to Bernstein's "Maria" as a sound model for the tritone. The supporting harmonic background for the

opening of this phrase is tonic, therefore the structural melodic interval here is the perfect 5th—1-5. The ♯4 is simply a chromatic appoggiatura (a non-chord tone) that relates as a lower neighbor to 5. *Maria* serves absolutely no purpose as a sound model for a

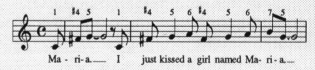

functional tritone. In fact, when presented as such, this melody is actually "lying." A functional tritone doesn't sound like this. More specifically, it doesn't tune like this.

Under some circumstances, even the melodic scale steps 4-7 do not constitute a dominant-function tritone. Here, the 4-7 melodic interval is not a functional tritone. The 7 is an embellishment to 1 (it happens four times here),

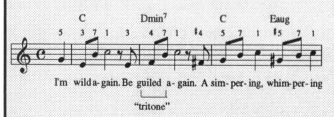

while 4 is performing a *subdominant* function in a chromatic scalewise line which then continues upward to ♯4, 5, ♯5 etc. The harmony underlying this "tritone" is a ii⁷ chord, which performs a subdominant function. Therefore, this example, even though it uses scale steps 4-7, is not a good model for learning the sound of the "real" tritone.

Using sound models to develop a functional vocabulary of melodic intervals can be an excellent educational tool. However, it is very important—indeed critical—that the models selected are ones that accurately represent the aural concepts to be learned.

As you sing the C or B, be sure to find the tuning that "locks." Do you hear C's tonal firmness as compared to B's "wandering spirit"? When you sing the E, does its pitch seem to move slightly when the chords change or does it remain constant? If you sense a change in perception, might it be caused by root effect (or lack of it)? When you sing the G, does its tuning tend to move when you change chords or does it remain constant? Is a change in perception caused by the different role G plays in these two chords? Whether tuning changes or not, the aural perception of the minor third certainly does.

## Sound Models Versus Context

Some people find it helpful to associate specific intervals with the opening pitches of familiar melodic phrases while developing a sound vocabulary of intervals. Others work more "abstractly," hearing the intervals directly in their functional locations in the major/minor system.

If you choose to collect sound models from melodic phrases, be sure to identify the musical context of the models you adopt. For example, If you choose to include "Here Comes The Bride" as your model for a perfect fourth, be sure to think of it as 5-1, not 1-4. Also, don't expect one example of an interval to represent all others. For example, the opening interval of "Brahms' Lullaby" is a good choice to represent the 3-5 minor third, but you should find another model to represent the 1-♭3 minor third. Also, it is important to select phrases from songs you know well so the sounds of the intervals being modeled are immediately available to you.

Eventually, you will find that always thinking of intervals in terms of sound models is rather cumbersome. As in learning to read lines and spaces, you will want to be able to recognize and produce intervals in a more immediate way. Being able to hear intervals in their functional harmonic environments is an important step toward realizing that goal.

The ear-training improvisation charts included in earlier chapters will help you meet that challenge. As you sing around the charts, identify intervals (in mind) as you sing them. Take your time. Repeat intervals melodically to reinforce their characteristic sounds within harmonic context. Sing to a sustained root in order to ensure accurate tuning.

Compare the "same" intervals in different harmonies. We discussed the difference in the perception of the 3-5 minor third when heard in the tonic and mediant (iii) chords. Also, listen to the difference in sound of the 1-3 major third when heard in the tonic and submediant (vi) chords. Find other intervals that appear in more than one chord and notice the effect of context as you compare them.

Of particular importance is hearing the different sounds of the 2-4 minor third in the supertonic chord and the 2-4 "small" minor third in the dominant seventh chord. It is essential to hear these pitches when the chords are tuned carefully to their sounding roots.

Remember, frequent short drills are better than infrequent long ones. Fresh ears are more likely to hear with precision than ears saturated with sounds. Alternate your singing drills with silent theoretical ones. Better yet, simply gaze out the window from time to time and think about something else—or about nothing at all.

Hopefully, this discussion has demonstrated that intervals sound different when heard in various musical contexts. This information should help you avoid aural confusion and to escape the naive view of thinking of an interval as having a single perceptual quality. Learning your way around interval sounds and connecting everything to a label cannot be accomplished overnight, but at least you now have a realistic view of what is involved in the challenge.

# 32

# Chords

We have been discussing chords from the beginning—even before describing intervals. Let's take a systematic look now at the terminology used to describe chords.

We defined the term **chord** as the "simultaneous sounding of three or more pitches," as opposed to **harmony**, which is the "simultaneous sounding of pitches" (in general). Some musicologists hold that *two* simultaneous pitches constitute a chord, and there are reasonable arguments to support this point of view. However, considering two-pitch sonorities to be *intervals* seems an important and convenient distinction, particularly when used in the abstract, and without a specific context.

The type of harmony most commonly used in the major/minor system is called **tertial** (ter-shul), referring to the practice of constructing chords (theoretically, at least) in stacks of thirds. Other types, such as **quartal** (built in fourths) or **quintal** (built in fifths), are found in twentieth century music; however, compositions that use them exclusively are rare. More frequently, when quartal or quintal chords are used they are incorporated, for contrast, into a largely tertial composition.

Although quartal chords offer a distinctively modern "steel and glass" sound, they often can be analyzed in terms of traditional tertial theory. Consider this quartal chord sounding in the key of C major. Its quartal flavor is the result

 of its voicing (arrangement), since these same pitches can be revoiced into what is called a **cluster** chord. Both the quartal and cluster versions can be analyzed as a C major triad with a sixth and ninth added.

In the remainder of this chapter, we will focus on terminology that applies to tertial harmony, by far the most common type of harmony in current use.

There are at least three different systems of terms used to describe chords, and we have been using words from all of them. There is a system that describes the **quality** of a chord (such as major or minor) and one that describes the **function** of a chord (such as tonic or dominant). Unfortunately, the system of terms we commonly use for designating the **number** of pitches "stacked" in thirds is rather illogical. Also, a term from one system is often used colloquially as if it belonged to another.

We will attempt to unravel the twisted threads in this "body of knowledge" and present them logically. However, even though you will see and understand the problem, you will still have to use these common terms as they are likely to be understood by others.

# Triads, etc.

As you know, chords in the major/minor system are normally constructed from a fundamental pitch—or root. Chord members are added above the root in multiple intervals of a third. Theoretically, there is no limit to how many pitches might be added, but from a practical and perceptual point of view, three to five is the norm. The terms we use to describe these constructs seem to be derived from two different systems. The terms not in common use are crossed out.

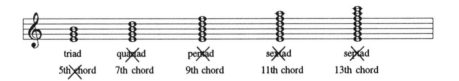

| triad | ~~quadad~~ | ~~pentad~~ | ~~sextad~~ | ~~septad~~ |
|---|---|---|---|---|
| ~~5th chord~~ | 7th chord | 9th chord | 11th chord | 13th chord |

# Voicing

In practice, pitches in a chord can be sounded in almost any configuration, with member pitches sounding both above and/or below a root. The arrangement of chord members—called **voicing**—generally follows a number of well-established principles (most of which are beyond the scope of this book) which are based on historical practice and acoustical common sense.

When pitches in a chord (usually not including the bass voice) are positioned as close as possible, the chord is said to be expressed in "close" voicing. When the pitches are spread apart, leaving open spaces where chord members might have been sounded, the chord is said to be expressed in "open" voicing.

Here are some common voicings of the C major triad and the G seventh chord.

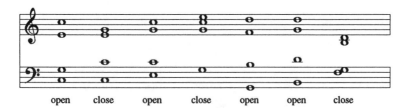

open    close    open    close    open    open    close

# Inversion

A chord is said to be in **root position** when its root is sounded as the lowest pitch. A chord is said to be **inverted** when a member other than the root is sounded as the lowest pitch. The number of possible inversions depends on

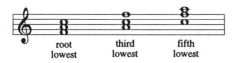

root     third     fifth
lowest   lowest    lowest

how many pitches are in a chord. A triad can have two. When its third is the lowest sounding pitch, a triad is said to be in **first inversion**, and when its fifth is the lowest sounding pitch, a triad is said to be in **second inversion**.

A seventh chord, having four-pitches, can be expressed in root position plus three inversions. The **third inversion** places the chord seventh as the lowest sounding pitch.

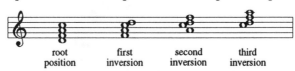

root        first        second       third
position    inversion    inversion    inversion

A ninth chord theoretically affords four inversions. However, common practice indicates that the ninth of a chord is seldom used as the lowest sounding pitch, therefore only root position and three inversions are usually used.

In the above illustrations, all the chords are in close voicing. As you can see, each inversion is visually easy to recognize. When open voicings are used, inversions are harder to distinguish (although experienced eyes usually can see them at a glance). Nevertheless, determining the inversion still depends on which chord member is the lowest-sounding.

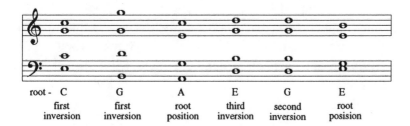

root - C      G            A            E            G            E
first         first        root         third        second       root
inversion     inversion    position     inversion    inversion    posision

Unlike "voicings," there is no generic term that includes all the options regarding "root position" and "inversions." This deficiency results in some strange use of language. For example, the answer to the question "In what inversion is this chord?" may be, "Root position." Of course, one could answer, "None," but that doesn't really compensate for the lack of a generic term.

It would be more logical to use the term "position" for this purpose. This would make possible the designations "root position," "third position," fifth position," etc., indicating the chord member voiced lowest in each case. On the other hand, some theorists use similar terminology to refer to the *highest* voiced chord member. Perhaps "first position," "second position," "third position," etc. for each configuration, in turn, would work.

It seems unlikely that either system will be adopted, but perhaps these speculations have helped clarify for you the language of inversion.

## "Tall" Chords

When a chord includes more than four or five pitches stacked in thirds above a root, for example, "eleventh" and "thirteenth" chords, composers frequently omit one or more pitches to keep the sound from getting too dense. According to some music theorists, even the root can be omitted.

D eleventh          E thirteenth          G ninth

Recently, certain theorists have suggested other ways of analyzing such chords. For example, instead of designating the above as a thirteenth chord, some prefer to call the C♯ in the highest voice a "substitute" for the chord fifth, B. There is value to this argument, as it simplifies an otherwise complex analysis.

However, to experienced keyboardists and guitarists, a thirteenth chord is just a name, a label, that calls for a specific chord with voicing learned and memorized. (See **Chord Symbols** below.) The "simpler" analysis might have to be explained to them. (Sometimes "progress" is difficult to achieve.)

# Chord Quality

The only requirement for membership in the tertial system of harmony is that a chord be spelled with letter names corresponding to alternating white digitals. The size (major, minor, etc.) of its "thirds" is not a criterion. For example, the pitches C-E♯-G♭ would constitute a triad, but the quality of this triad would not have a name because it does not conform to a standard pattern. There are, however, a number of chord shapes that are common enough to have standard names. These names are used to refer to a chord's **quality**, or **sonority**.

We have already described and named the four standard triads—"major," "minor," "diminished" and "augmented"—as they are found in their major/minor-mode habitats (see p. 99). Now we will observe and compare them built on a common root.

**triads**

First, a few observations might help. Notice that only the major and minor triads contain a perfect fifth. Only major and minor triads contain both a major

major    minor    augmented    diminished

third and a minor third. Also, notice that the augmented triad consists of two major thirds (one above the other) and the diminished triad consists of two minor thirds. This "closed system" view of triads is another symmetrical and logical construct in traditional music theory.

Four-pitch chords, commonly called seventh chords, present a more complex challenge because not only must the basic triad be described but the quality of the chord's seventh as well. Although the descriptive terminology is not as standard as the chords themselves, it is fairly logical, so you should have little problem understanding the variations.

**seventh chords**

The designation "major-major seventh" specifies the triad and the chord seventh individually. The designation "major seventh" indicates that the adjective applies to *both* the triad and the chord seventh. One system is more efficient, the other more specific. You can decide for yourself which terminology is more practical.

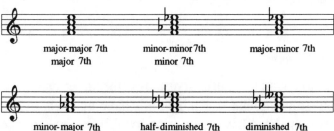

major-major 7th      minor-minor 7th      major-minor 7th
major 7th            minor 7th

minor-major 7th      half-diminished 7th      diminished 7th

The two seventh chords having a diminished fifth have one distinguishing characteristic which tells them apart. The diminished seventh chord is constructed entirely of minor thirds and the half diminished seventh chord contains a major third between its fifth and seventh.

Other combinations of triad and seventh are possible—an augmented-minor seventh, for example—however, the ones shown above are the most frequently encountered. The terminology describing the components of ninth chords and other "tall" chords is not as standardized as that of triads and seventh chords, however it is likely that similar language when applied to ninths would be understood. (Major-minor-major, for example).

With practice and experience, you can learn to aurally identify all the chord qualities illustrated above, even when heard out of context. Chord qualities can be heard as a *single perceptual entity*, as opposed to hearing intervallic components individually and then combining them. Even the differences between triads, seventh chords, ninth chords, and others have a single identifiable sound quality. This is a good example of a *Gestalt* being something more than the sum of its parts.

# Chord Function

You already know what is meant by **chord function**. The terms "tonic," "dominant" and "subdominant" are by now old friends. The charts on p. 99 identified the sonority, or chord quality, that occurs on each functional triad.

Here, we will identify sonorities that perform seventh chord functions in the major and minor modes. The triads we examined earlier are still here, of course. This exercise is simply a matter of adding a chord seventh by noting the scale step on which it would logically fall. Here are the seventh chords that occur in the major mode. Their quality is shown here using "M" and "m" to indicate "major" and "minor" elements.

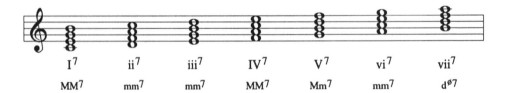

Although all three primary triads in the major mode are major, only the tonic and subdominant seventh chords have major-major quality. The dominant seventh chord has major-minor quality because of the tritone. All three of the secondary seventh chords in the major mode (ii7, iii7 and vi7) are minor-minor sevenths. The leading-tone seventh chord in the major mode has half-diminished quality.

The seventh chords in the minor mode are not nearly so symmetrical. Lowering the third and sixth scale step creates a few awkward characteristics and composers have learned to work around them. Here are the seventh chord sonorities occurring on the seven scale steps of the minor mode.

Because the leading tone (scale step 7) is often replaced by the subtonic (♭7), the tonic seventh chord appears here as two different sonorities. The same is true of the mediant seventh chord, although the one using the leading tone is rare. Major-major sevenths occur only on ♭III[7] and ♭VI[7]. Minor-minor sevenths occur on i[7] and iv[7]. The half-diminished seventh that appears on vii[7] in the relative major mode appears here on ii[7]. The leading-tone seventh chord in the minor mode is fully diminished due to the "lowered" sixth scale step.

The leading tone seventh chord warrants special consideration in that many music theorists regard it as a "non chord," due to the lack of a perfect fifth above the root. According to these authorities, the vii[7] chord is an "incomplete" dominant ninth chord in which the absent root still exercises its tonal influence. This view has great merit, reflecting the strong influence of the tritone toward resolving the dissonances in these chords. In the minor mode, there are, in fact, two tritones (between 7-4 and 2-♭6) that drive its resolution.

Composers do not consider the major and minor modes mutually exclusive, especially regarding scale step 6. They have used either the major or minor position of this versatile member as it served their artistic intent. As a result, the fully diminished seventh chord (vii°7) is almost as plentiful in the major mode as it is in the minor mode. On the other hand, there are far fewer half-diminished chords on vii found in the minor mode.

One final point should be mentioned here. The term "dominant seventh chord," a functional term, is frequently used to mean "major-minor seventh," a qualitative term. The reason why this illogical usage has become almost standard is that the dominant seventh chord is unique in sound quality as well as in harmonic function—thus the invitation to imprecise terminology.

# Chord Symbols

There is no universal method of symbolically representing chords in sheet music and instrumental part scores. However, a few systems are fairly common. Using Roman numerals, as we have, is standard among music theorists. Nashville studio musicians prefer Arabic numerals. In commercial sheet music, roots are shown by letter name and quality is shown by abbreviations and numbers.

Using **Roman numerals** to represent chords is very efficient as it shows both function and quality with a minimum of symbols. As you have observed, the numeric value identifies the scale step on which the chord is constructed. Major triads are shown with upper case (capital) numerals and minor triads are shown with lower case (small) numerals. For augmented triads, a plus sign is appended to an upper case numeral. For diminished triads, a small circle is appended to a lower case numeral.

Added chord members, such as sevenths and ninths, are shown by a superscript (sometimes subscript) Arabic numeral after the Roman numeral. The quality, or specific size, of the seventh or ninth is not always indicated in the symbol but usually is understood by the music's modal context. Chord inversions are shown by a numbers system inherited from a seventeenth century practice of musical shorthand called "figured bass." If you continue a formal study of common harmonic practice, you inevitably will encounter this system, and if you then leave academia there is a good chance you may never encounter it again.

The **Nashville system** of indicating chords is quite practical in that studio musicians using it can quickly jot down the harmonic structure of a song they are about to record. The system seems to have developed as singer/songwriters would come to the studio without their songs written in music notation. After announcing that "it goes like this," the artist(s) would perform their pieces, usually strumming the harmonies on a guitar, and the recording session musicians would jot down the chords as they were played.

Like the Roman numeral system, the Nashville system uses numbers to indicate the scale step on which a chord is constructed, but in this case the numbers are Arabic. A sharp or flat following a number indicates that the root of that chord is out of the scale a half step higher or lower. Chord quality other than major is indicated by a superscript symbol following the number—"m" for minor, "A" or "Aug" for augmented, and "d" or "dim" for diminished. Added chord members are indicated by superscript numbers—"7" for seventh, "9" for ninth, etc. A major-major seventh chord requires "M" or "MA" to distinguish it from the more common major-minor "dominant" seventh.

In this illustration, the barlines indicate measures of four beats. A forward slash places divides beats between two chords. A backward slash indicates a chord to be played with a different bass pitch—in this case, a tonic chord played with scale step 5 in the bass.

$$| \quad 1 \ / \ 4 \ | \ 1^7 \ | \ 2m^7 \ / \ 5 \ | \ 1 \ / \ 6^\flat \ | \ 1\backslash5 \ / \ 5^7 \ | \ 3^7 \ | \quad |$$

This system is convenient for studio use, since it is based on scale steps and not specific pitches, therefore allowing the players to easily transpose the music up or down.

In contrast, most **commercial** sheet music and "fake" book publications represent chords by using specific letter names of roots. In this case, the chord's scale-step function is not indicated. Therefore, transposition requires writing out the series of chords in the new key. Traditionally, West coast and New York recording studios have used this system for writing keyboard and guitar parts, since much of the music recorded there has been arranged and written out in a specific key. However, with the explosion of rock and other popular music styles, the number of improvised sessions has greatly increased.

The commercial system of indicating chords consists of identifying roots by letter name and then, similar to the Nashville method, adding suffixes to indicate chord quality and added pitches. A letter by itself indicates a major triad. For example "D" represents D-F♯-A. "Dm" means D-F-A. Because the dominant (major-minor) seventh chord is by far the most frequently used of all the seventh chords, it requires only the root name and the number 7, for example, "$A^7$" (A-C♯-E-G) All other seventh chords require additional suffixes, for example "$Am^7$" (A-C-E-G) or "$Amaj^7$" (A-C♯-E-G♯).

This illustration shows the same chords in the Nashville illustration above, this time in commercial notation in the key of C major. In this system, the *forward* slash indicates a chord played with a different bass pitch. Two chords in the same measure are assumed to sound for two beats each.

$$| \quad C \quad F \ | \ C^7 \ | \ Dm^7 \ \ G^7 \ | \ C \quad A^\flat \ | \ C/G \ \ G^7 \ | \ E^7 \ | \quad |$$

Symbols vary from user to user, and studio musicians working in this system are obliged to learn the variations. The symbol for "minor" is variously "m," "mi," "min," or "-". The symbol "-" can also indicate that an added pitch is to be lowered a half step. Therefore, while "Dm9" indicates the sounding of D-F-A-C-E, the symbol "D-9" is somewhat ambiguous, leaving the player to decide whether the triad is minor or the ninth is lowered. Parentheses are often included for clarity, such as "D-9" (D-F-A-C-E) or "D(-9)" (D-F♯-A-C-E♭). Similarly, a flat or sharp sign is used both to identify the pitch of the root and to modify an added pitch. Here, too, parentheses can clarify symbols, such as "D(♭6) (D-F♯-A-B♭) as opposed to "D♭6" (D♭-F-A♭-B♭).

Learning to use commercial chord notation does not help you understand how music works. Like standard notation on staves, using commercial chord notation is simply an associative process of reading symbols and producing the appropriate pitches without regard for their function. While this system helps students to make music quickly and "efficiently," users tend not to understand the musical meaning of the chords they are playing. This is not to say that sensitive and intelligent players will not intuit this over time by paying attention to the relationships of the sounds they are playing. Of course, learning standard functional vocabulary is another matter.

Our description of these three systems was abbreviated. While knowing they exist may be of general interest to many readers, the detailed information required to use them probably is not. If you would like to investigate any of them further, you should be able to find many excellent publications that provide practical and detailed information.

33

# Other Notational Tools

We have looked at notation that represents the temporal and pitch aspects of music. Methods of representing other aspects of music have been developed and we will examine them in the following four chapters.

We noted earlier that the speed at which a composition is played can be a part of its meaning. *Changes* in speed are also sometimes significant. It is important to understand clearly the separate concepts called *meter*, *tempo* and *pace*—meter being the configurations of pulse ratios, tempo being the speed of the primary pulse, and pace being the general speed of musical events within the tempo. Meter and pace are shown within standard notation, but tempo is not. It is indicated separately.

Since repetition is an important aspect of musical design, the same music is often intended to be played more than once. When a repetition is exactly the same, it need not be written out again. The reader needs only to know what music to perform a second and perhaps a third time and when to do so. A number of very efficient devices have been developed to communicate this information.

While a series of notes on paper may *look* alike, the series of sounds intended by the composer might not *be* alike. A standard system of markings alerts the reader to special performance characteristics. When the sounds are to be smooth and connected, certain markings can be inserted in the notation to indicate that style. When the sounds are to be delivered with other characteristics, those can be indicated as well.

Since the seventeenth century, loudness has been an important aspect of music. The markings used to indicate loudness are not at all precise. A performer has to use practical judgment in making dynamic contrasts. Also, "loud" in one era may not be the same as "loud" in another. In fact, the same music may require more or less decibels of sound when performed in different venues.

Performing convincingly from notation is not a mechanical process. This is often painfully obvious when comparing a performance of the same piece played by a beginner and by a seasoned professional. Notation provides an abstract blueprint and the performer (at any level of achievement) provides an expression of it based on his or her sensitivity and experience.

# 34

# Tempo Indicators

Before the seventeenth century, most art music was vocal and its formal structure generally followed the shape of the lyric. The sections in a Renaissance madrigal, for example, reflected the succession of topics expressed in the poem or story. A single phrase might be passed from voice to voice within the conventional polyphonic texture, creating a formal section lasting from a few seconds to perhaps a half-minute. The second phrase of the lyric might be set to a new melodic idea and/or the texture changed in order to reflect the meaning of those words.

During the seventeenth century, music began to be composed specifically for instruments. The development of the violin allowed for musical flights of fancy that were beyond the capabilities of the human voice (although vocal virtuosity later developed to a degree that would challenge that notion). The invention of new instruments and the improvement of old ones led to the formation of orchestras and chamber groups that played music without lyrics. Formal design, then, depended on purely musical considerations.

## Movements

Formal structure in early instrumental music consisted largely of the most obvious means for creating continuity and contrast—loudness and tempo. Changes in loudness were achieved by contrasting larger groups of instruments with smaller groups of instruments, thus the concerto (soloist with orchestra) and concerto grosso (small group of soloists with orchestra) were born. Tempo changes were accomplished by dividing a composition into sections—usually in the pattern fast-slow-fast. Eventually, these sections were split into separate "compositions," each standing independently.

These individual compositions within a composition were called **movements**, referring to their contrasting tempos. This term is still used today, and refers to any portion of a larger work that can be performed separately as a "stand alone" unit. When a multi-movement composition is performed in concert, it is important that the performer or conductor control the length of the pause between movements in such a way that the energy of the movement just completed is not allowed to dissipate before the following movement is begun. Attention to the length of this silent "connection" helps to preserve the aesthetic continuity of the composition. For this reason, experienced concert goers usually refrain from applause until the last movement of a work is completed.

The convention of pausing between movements is sometimes confusing to novice concert goers who are embarrassed when caught applauding alone between movements, and then having learned their lesson, remain silent and perplexed as a sophisticated audience explodes into applause between movements when an extraordinary performance has moved them to do so. Only experience as a concert goer will provide a sense of when suspending the "no applause between movements" convention is appropriate.

The fast-slow-fast pattern of movements continued into and through the eighteenth century, sometimes interpolating an additional dance-like movement before the final one. Beethoven, as a nineteenth-century romantic, was one of the first composers to break this tradition and begin a symphony with a slow movement. Also, many nineteenth-century composers preferred to incorporate a variety of tempos within a sizable uninterrupted single "movement" called a **symphonic poem** (or **tone poem**). Nevertheless, the tradition of composing large instrumental works in separate movements with contrasting tempos continues to the present day.

# Tempo Markings

The speed of the primary beats in a musical performance is referred to as **tempo**. While the final decision in this regard must be made by the performer, the composer generally has some input in the matter. To that end, a composer usually will indicate the general character or speed of the music in language or as a metronome mark, or both, at the beginning of the printed music. Sometimes just the title—"Nocturne," "Minuet in G," "Flight of the Bumble-bee"—will indicate the tempo.

Traditionally, tempo and style indications have been in Italian, which for centuries was considered the universal language of music. More recently, composers have turned to the local language for this purpose. Here are some of the more frequently used terms.

| Italian | English | German | French |
|---|---|---|---|
| grave | very slowly | schwer | lourd |
| largo | broadly | breit | large |
| lento | slowly | langsam | lent |
| adagio | rather slowly | langsam | getragen |
| andante | walking speed | gehend | allant |
| moderate | moderately | mässig | modéré |
| allegretto | rather fast | bewegt | animé |
| allegro | fast, cheerful | rasch, schnell | vif |
| presto | very fast | geschwind | vite |
| prestissimo | extremely fast | lebhaft | rapide |

There are many other descriptive words commonly encountered in scores. In learning any vocabulary, experience is the best teacher. Owning a pocket music dictionary is certainly advisable if you intend to pore over historical or foreign scores.

**the metronome**

As with many other perceptual modes, humans do not have an absolute sense of tempo. Just as we use watches and clocks to regulate our daily comings and goings, we often use a **metronome** to more accurately specify tempos in terms of beats per minute. The original metronome was invented by Dietrich Nikolaus Winkel of Amsterdam in 1812, but is named after Johannes N. Maelzel, the man who subsequently marketed the device, giving the impression that it was his creation.

A few decades ago, the Maelzel metronome was largely replaced by an electronic quartz metronome that offers a silent flashing light as well as an audible click. Very recently, there appeared the "Tempo Watch," a device looking very much like a pocket watch, which indicates to a conductor, even while in concert, the tempo he or she is currently beating.

Some musicians, particularly conductors and percussionists, can establish tempos that are very close to "clock time," usually by associating tempos with specific pieces of music. A tempo of 120 beats per minute is fairly easy to identify since it is the tempo of a brisk march. By memorizing metronome speeds for such pieces as *Largo* from Dvořák's New World Symphony or the third movement from the Haydn trumpet concerto, one can accumulate a library of reference pieces by which to determine specific tempos.

Another useful method is to create related reference points by which to estimate tempos by comparison. We noted above that the common march tempo is 120 beats per minute. A tempo half as fast, 60 beats per minute, can be arrived at quickly by attending to the grouping pulse of the march tempo. A blazing 240 beats can be quite accurately created by attending to the duple division pulse of the march tempo. Other tempos can be estimated from these fairly secure ones.

All of the foregoing considered, metronomic precision of tempo is not nearly so important as perceptual *impression* of tempo. In an acoustically "live" hall the tempo of a normally fast piece will likely be played slower so as not to blur its details. On the other hand, in an acoustically "dead" hall, a piece will likely be played faster to avoid sounding dull and lifeless. The bottom line, then, is that a tempo needs to be "right" for the character of the music and for the performance conditions. Subjective considerations are ultimately more important here than objective information.

Interestingly, famous and revered conductors often widely disagree on the "correct" tempo for specific pieces and movements. It seems that one person's "moderato" is another's "andante." Can both be right? What do you think?

# 35

# Formal Directional Signs

Several conventions have been developed to help the reader reconstruct musical form from notation. This includes markings that show which sections are to be repeated, how many times the repetition is to be performed, and when the piece has come to an end.

## Double bars

Formal sections of an extended composition are usually shown in notation by means of the **double bar**. The name and appearance of the double bar suggests that it has something to do with the single barline used to designate metric measures—that perhaps it performs a large "metric grouping" function. That is not the case. As a matter of fact, double bars sometimes appear within single measures. A double bar simply indicates that a formal section of a composition has been completed and another section is about to begin. It has nothing to do with meter.

Composers and arrangers have not always been careful to place double bars accurately, however, and this can make the precise point of beginnings and endings of formal sections ambiguous. This is certainly understandable when sections overlap, but the ambiguity is often unnecessary. In the following illustration, the same fragment is notated two ways. In the first, the double bar is placed correctly before the first syllable of the refrain. In the second, the double bar is placed incorrectly on a nearby barline.

be for-got, and days of auld lang syne?   For auld— lang— syne, my dear, For

be for-got, and days of auld lang syne?  For auld— lang— syne, my dear, For

A double bar does not indicate the end of a measure, therefore, it can be placed at any point within a measure. Its only function is to show that the reader is leaving one formal section and entering another.

Music publishers usually try to finish formal sections at the end of a printed line, even when it splits a measure. In such cases, appropriate metric value is contained in a partial measure completing the line and the balance of the value is contained in a partial measure at the beginning of the next line.

Should auld ac-quain-tance be for-got, and  days of auld lang syne?

For    auld—— lang—— syne, my dear, For auld—— lang—— syne;

**"the end"**     The double bar that signifies the end of a composition consists of a thin line and a heavy line. It, too, has nothing to do with meter or measures, with one exception. When a short composition, a song for example, begins with "pickup" values (the final beat or so from an incomplete measure), it is customary to exclude those values from the final measure. The practical reason for doing this is to accommodate a graceful return to the beginning of the song without breaking the flow of the metric scheme. The refrain of "Auld Lang Syne" finishes with a dotted half note (three quarter-note beats).

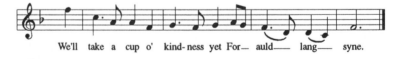

We'll   take a cup o' kind-ness yet For— auld—— lang—— syne.

The beginning of the second verse begins with a single quarter-note beat, completing the four beats of the notationally disconnected 4/4 measure.

And here's a hand, my   trust-y frien', And gie's a hand o'   thine;

When there is no reason to place an ending double bar within a measure or after an incomplete measure, it usually is placed at the end of a complete measure, sometimes providing rests to fill the space after the sound stops. Occasionally, this principle calls for the addition of empty measures in order to fill out a formal section to a symmetrical eight, sixteen or thirty-two measures.

## Repeating Material

When a composer or arranger wants a portion of music to be repeated exactly, several options are available. The music can be written out a second time, or "repeat" indications of various types can be used, or words or symbols can be inserted to direct the performer to the material to be repeated. The choice will be affected by the amount of music to be repeated, the number of times it is to be repeated, and whether there is intervening music between the repetitions.

The most common symbol for indicating repeated material is a pair of double **repeat signs** bars with two dots, which work like a bracket. The music reader, passing the first sign of the pair, notes its location and then expects a second sign. When it is found, the reader goes from that point, immediately and in tempo (unless indicated otherwise), back to the first sign and repeats all of the music between the two signs. Notice that the dots in each symbol face the music to be repeated.

If the reader comes upon a "go back" repeat sign (having dots on the left side of the double bar) but has not previously passed a "remember this location" repeat sign (having dots on the right side), the music is repeated from the beginning.

If the music is to be repeated more than once, it is usually indicated at the beginning of the section. Instructions such as "play three times" or simply "3X" are common. An instruction to "vamp until ready" is frequently seen in show music, where stage business often takes varying amounts of time, so the music is repeated until the show is ready to proceed.

Like double bars, repeat signs have nothing to do with barlines. Repeat signs can appear within a measure or between measures. In order to maintain a continuous flow of meter, however, it is important to place both signs at corresponding locations in their respective measures. If the first sign appears before the last beat of a four-beat measure, and the second sign appears at the end of a four-beat measure, the result will be a five-beat measure.

There can be any number of measures between a pair of repeat signs—from one measure to hundreds of measures. The writer must decide whether it is easier (and/or clearer) to write out repeated patterns or to use repeat signs. If the material is simple and can be expressed in a few notes, it is more practical to write out repeats. If the material is complex and requires many notes, it is more practical to use repeat signs. From the reader's standpoint, knowing that a complex passage is the same as the one just played is certainly an advantage over struggling through "written out" music not knowing whether there are going to be changes in what *appears* to be identical material.

Another way to indicate one- or two-measure repeats is with the "repeat previous measure" sign. If the repeating pattern is one measure long, the sign

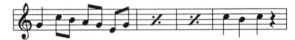

appears in as many measures as the pattern repeats. If the repeating pattern is two measures long, a sign with a double slash and the number 2 above is placed on

the barline between pairs of measures as many times as the pattern repeats.

This device is commonly used in percussion music, where a pattern is often repeated for a number of measures. To help the player keep track, the measures are often numbered.

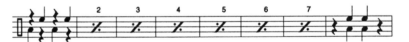

**endings**   Repeat signs can be used with modified endings. This example is short enough to be written out, however, it conveniently demonstrates the device.

While a repeated section having *two* different endings (as just shown) is the most common, there is no limit to how many repetitions might be called for. Each repetition may have a different ending or may share an ending, which is indicated by consecutive numbers placed under the appropriate bracket.

As you can imagine, this can get complicated, particularly if some of the endings also apply to repetitions that occur after intervening sections are performed. Of course, confusion can always be avoided by writing out some of the repetitions. These are typical decisions a composer or arranger must make to achieve balance between efficiency and clarity.

Since the advent of computer notation, some of these efficiency problems are easily solved. With a few clicks of a mouse, whole sections of music can be copied to other locations where they can be given new endings or otherwise modified as it suits the situation. But whether written out by hand or by computer, representing the music in the clearest possible way is the primary purpose of notation.

Another way to indicate literal repetition is to place verbal "directions" at **"road signs"** strategic points, usually done with standard Italian words (or abbreviations). The most commonly used expressions are:

- Da Capo (or D.C.) — "go back to the beginning"

- Dal Segno (or D.S.) — "go back to the sign (%)"

- al Coda (or ⊕ ) — "jump to the coda" (which is identified by the same sign or by the word "Coda")

- al fine — "play to the end or until the word 'fine' appears"

- fine — "the end"

Normally, when repeating material after responding to a D.C. or D.S., it is standard procedure to ignore first endings and proceed directly to second endings. If that is not the intent, the composer is obliged to so indicate.

These word cues often are used in combination with other devices, all of which are designed to provide a clear "road map" for the music reader. Can you follow the "signs" in the example on the next page? (The letters represent the music contained in those measures. See if you can arrange them in order of performance.)

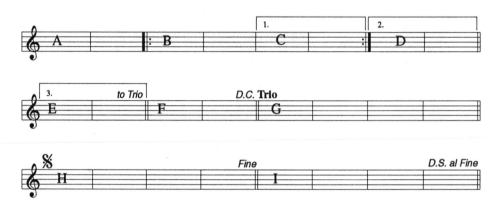

If you read this map as A-B-C-B-D-F-A-B-E-G-H-I-H, you are correct. Notice that there is no repeat sign in the second ending, indicating that the music proceeds ahead (skipping over the third ending). If you got lost, you might want to consult the preceding paragraphs to find out where you took the wrong turn.

# 36

# Phrasing, Articulation And Dynamics

Sounding a series of pitches in rhythm without infusing them with expressive character might be compared to a robot reading Shakespeare. In such a stilted performance, every note or word would be delivered with the same loudness and inflection. There would be no eloquent shape to the phrases, no provocative or evocative import conveyed. Would you find such a representation truly "meaningful"?

In contrast, an accomplished and sensitive performer can take a naked series of notes and "clothe" them expressively—not just in one, but in many different ways. Each new way adds special character and meaning to the music. Taking into consideration the compositional style, a skilled performer will strive to express a creative and personal, yet appropriate, "interpretation" of the signs and symbols contained in printed music.

Personalized emoting is less appropriate in some musical styles than in others. In the music of J. S. Bach and his contemporaries, where the meaning is largely contained in the configurations of pitches and rhythms, it is generally inappropriate to interfere with the steady flow of the music. To do so would obscure the clarity of the melodic shapes. On the other hand, a performance of certain Schubert songs would be quite lifeless if performed without the personal "shapings" of a talented singer.

This is not to say that well-placed dynamic accents that enhance the shape of a Bach phrase would be out of place. Nor should it be implied that a singer is free to turn a Schubert verse into a gushing of tasteless emotion. Musical sensitivity and a feel for what is appropriate cannot be acquired quickly; they are learned over a lifetime of musical involvement.

Over the last two or three centuries, composers have become increasingly more specific when notating musical phrasing. As a result, a number of standard symbols have emerged that indicate a composer's intentions in this regard.

When a series of notes is to be performed in a smooth and connected way, the word **legato** can be placed in the score, or a phrase mark (a curved line) can be placed over or under the notes to be played this way.

When a series of notes is to be performed with a distinct separation between them, the word **staccato** can be placed in the score, or a dot can be placed over the affected notes.

When a mixture of connected and detached notes is to be performed within a phrase, symbols can be applied as appropriate. When the curved line is applied to only a few notes, it is usually called a **slur**.

When a series of notes is to be played in an accented manner (dynamically), the word **marcato** can be placed in the score, or an accent mark can be placed above or below each affected note.

A note that is to be slightly stressed durationally can be designated by a **tenuto** mark.

Marks are sometimes combined, for example *tenuto* and *staccato*, indicating that designated notes are to be stressed *and* separated.

There are many more markings used to indicate styles and phrasing details, some of which are specific to certain instruments. Those shown here are the most common and will give you an idea of how performance details are communicated from composer to performer.

Again, notation cannot express every subtle nuance of meaning that will bring a piece of written music to life. Only continued listening and performing can provide the sensitivity that transforms sound into art. Nevertheless, carefully used notational devices can communicate much to the reader that will help him or her craft a meaningful performance.

# Dynamic markings

While the Italian terms for tempo have fallen out of universal use, the Italian terms for degrees of loudness have not. The terms **fortissimo, forte, mezzo forte, mezzo piano, piano** and **pianissimo** remain standard for designating stations on a continuous progression from loud to quiet. Their corresponding symbols—*ff*, *f*, *mf*, *mp*, *p* and *pp*— usually appear in musical scores rather than the words themselves.

When the loudness of a series of notes is to be *gradually* increased or decreased, the words **crescendo** or **decrescendo** (also **diminuendo**), respectively, can be inserted into the score. An alternative is to place a crescendo or decrescendo symbol under or over the series of notes affected. When crescendo and decre-

scendo marks are used together, as in this illustration, the combination is sometimes referred to as a **swell**.

While tempos are frequently "objectified" in terms of beats per minute, dynamics information is never given in terms of decibels. The meaning of a dynamic marking is considered in relation to the performance medium, the general style of the music, the acoustics of the venue, and ultimately, to the judgment of the performer.

# Miscellaneous Markings

The fermata sign ( ⌒ ), sometimes called a "hold," placed over or under a note indicates a cessation of the pulse for an indefinite amount of time. A cesura (seh-zhur-uh) marking ( // ) indicates a complete silence for an indefinite amount of time. The performer is responsible for artistically determining these durations. The marking *a tempo* instructs the performer to resume the original tempo. A sforzando marking ( *sfz* ) calls for a very strong dynamic accent. Forte-piano ( *fp* ) means to begin a note loudly and then continue it softly. For other markings, consult your music dictionary.

# Meanderings

37

# Musical Scores

Music represented in notation is called a **score**. While the slang expression "knows the score," meaning "aware," is often thought to connote "score of a game," the expression is actually quite applicable, perhaps more so, to this kind of "score." Since a musical score is a spacial graphic, it offers the reader the opportunity to "be aware of" all of a composition's parts at once (provided the score fits a practical field of vision).

There are different formats used for scores, depending on the musical media for which they are created. Scores can consist of one line of music or dozens of lines proceeding simultaneously. Here are descriptions of some of the most common types.

## Lead Sheet

The most concise method of notating a song is to place the melody on a single treble-clef staff, with lyrics, and represent the harmony (if any) in chord symbols above the staff. This simple type of score, called a **lead sheet**, is commonly used by performers of popular music for several reasons. Perhaps chief among them is that hundreds of songs can be easily transported in a single volume, making it possible to grant requests of many a party guest and club patron without having to say "Sorry, we don't know that one."

Showing harmony by chord symbols (rather than specific pitches), allows the performer to create a custom accompaniment for a song according to his or her own taste and ability. Frequently, a talented artist will ignore the published chords and embellish the song harmonically in a personal and creative way.

Because a lead sheet is notated in a specific key, a reader who is not adept at transposition is more or less limited to performing a given song in the key in which it appears. Lead sheets seldom contain relative chord symbols such as I-IV-V-I.

A few decades ago, lead sheets of popular songs were often compiled in "fake books" without permission from the publishers and sold illegally to professional entertainers. Today, major publishers market legal fake books containing thousands of songs, from oldies to recent hits, greatly diminishing the demand for "unofficial" compilations.

Incidentally, the term "fake book" is somewhat a misnomer. When musicians are asked to play a song for which they do not know all of the chords, they are sometimes asked to "fake it," suggesting they improvise chords for the song. By using a fake book, musicians no longer need to "fake" the chords" since they are provided. Perhaps fake books should be called "no-need-to-fake books."

## Piano Score

Piano music is written on the grand staff, the treble and bass staves combined and connected by a curved brace. In general, the right hand plays the music contained in the upper staff and the left hand plays the music contained in the lower staff. Usually the upper staff uses the treble clef and the lower staff uses the bass clef, however, many instances can be found in which the lower staff uses the treble clef and/or the upper staff uses the bass clef.

On occasion, music for one hand or the other will appear in the staff usually used for the other. Crossed-hand passages are not uncommon in virtuosic piano music. Incidentally, the C moveable clef has no practical purpose in piano music and is not used.

Chord symbols seldom appear in piano music, probably because most music in this genre is to be played literally—that is, note for note. That is unfortunate, perhaps, because chordal information sometimes would be helpful in reading piano music. It also might help novice players understand the harmonic structure of a piece and perhaps influence the way they perform it. (Can you "see" the harmonic structure in the example above?)

## Piano-Vocal Score

Probably the most widely-used format today is the **piano-vocal score**. Almost every popular song is published in this format to enable fans to play and/or sing their favorites. Art songs are commonly composed with piano accompaniment. Full operas are often published in this format to facilitate study and informal performance, even though staged performances are nearly always accompanied by orchestra.

The clef of the vocal staff is treble unless specifically intended for a baritone or bass singer. The clefs of the piano staves are as described above. The piano staves are defined by a curved bracket. (When written for organ, with its pedalboard, there are frequently three staves included in the bracket.)

In the commercial music world, piano-vocal scores are generally referred to as "sheet music" (as opposed to "lead sheet"). Popular sheet music usually contains chord symbols as well as a written-out accompaniment, making it possible for both note readers and chord readers to perform it. This format is seldom used by professional entertainers in that the printed music is far more bulky than lead sheets in a fake book.

## Choral Score

When a choral arrangement is fairly simple, it can be notated in a format similar to a piano score. The four voice parts usually share the two staves, the soprano and alto lines appearing on the treble staff and the tenor and bass lines appearing on the bass staff. When voices on the same staff perform the same rhythms, their notes can share common stems (shown in the first two

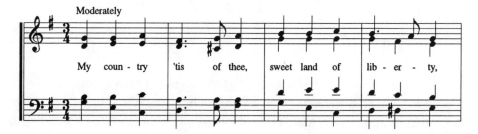

measures in this illustration). When their rhythms are different, however, different stem directions indicate which notes and rhythms are to be sung by which part (shown in the last two measures). Stem direction is also helpful when voices sharing a staff cross each other, for example, a soprano note lower than an alto note.

(The excerpt above contains two brief modulations, one to the dominant key and the other to the relative minor key. Can you find them?)

There is no single standard for handling stems in a two-stave choral score. Some publishers place stems up *and* down on every syllable, even when the sharing voices are singing the same pitches at the same time. Other publishers dispense with the up/down stems when a unison line of pitches and rhythms is shared by the two voices. In either case, if one of the voices drops out, rests will appear for that voice and stems on notes to be sung by the active voice will be in the appropriate direction.

Choral arrangements containing more than four voice-parts, or containing considerable melodic and rhythmic independence between parts, are generally notated on scores with more than two staves, called **open score**. The standard open score for a choir of mixed voices contains four staves, providing a separate staff on which to notate music to be sung by the sopranos, altos, tenors and basses. If there is a keyboard accompaniment, its bracketed staves are placed below the four vocal staves.

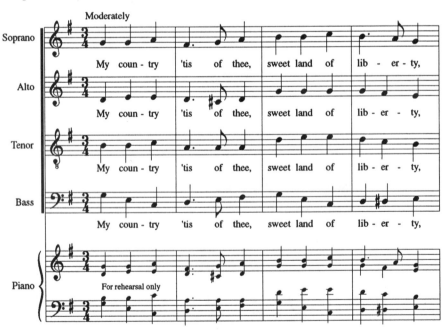

You may have noticed that the tenor staff in this score uses a treble clef with an 8 under it. The 8 indicates that these pitches actually sound one octave lower than in the regular treble clef. This very practical clef came into use to accommodate the pitches usually sung by tenors that would appear on ledger lines if written in the bass clef. Since most music-reading tenors are familiar with the treble clef but not the C clef (which also would have solved the problem), this solution is more practical.

Generally, when all voices sing the same pitches in unison (or in octave unison) the notes appear in every staff of the open score. However, some publishers choose to reduce the number of staves for such passages, if of sufficient duration, and designate the new location of each voice by name.

When an *a cappella* (unaccompanied) choral composition is notated in open score, it is customary to provide a keyboard "reduction" of the voice parts. Usually, the size of the notes in the keyboard part is smaller than normal, indicating that it is provided for rehearsal purposes only (see above graphic). Unfortunately, this practice often leads to out-of-tune performances, the singers having "learned their notes" from a tempered-tuned keyboard. On the other hand, judicious use of a keyboard reduction can at times be practical, particularly when singers already know how to sing in tune.

## Instrumental Scores

Scoring for instruments is similar to open scoring for voices. One significant difference is that the music for some instruments is written in a different key than others. This is not to say that the instruments will *sound* in different keys; rather, it has to do with the way those instruments are constructed.

The basic key of a woodwind instrument is determined, more or less, by the pitch produced when all of its holes are covered. The basic key of a brass instrument is determined by the overtone series produced when no valves are activated or slides moved. In most cases, when an instrument is playing in its basic key, the player is reading in the key of "C." In a sense, that is its "white digital" key. In other words, an instrument constructed in B♭ will sound B♭ when the player reads "C." However, there are many exceptions.

Perhaps the best illustration of the practical reason for building instruments in different keys is the saxophone family. Saxophones are built to sound in different pitch ranges, smaller instruments sounding higher pitches and larger instruments sounding lower pitches. The family includes soprano, alto, tenor, baritone and bass saxophones. The soprano, tenor and bass saxes are built in the key of B♭ and the alto and baritone saxes are built in E♭. However, all saxes are played with the same fingerings, so when a player reads "middle C" from the treble clef, the instrument produces its "low" B♭ or E♭ (according to its basic key) in an octave appropriate to its size. Therefore, with a bit of practice, a player who plays one sax can play them all.

Other woodwinds—flutes, clarinets, oboes and bassoons—also come in a variety of sizes and keys. Some are built in one key and play in another. There is no consistency here, only tradition. Brass instruments—trumpets, trombones, horns and tubas—also are built in a variety of sizes and keys. Interestingly, both the trumpet and trombone are built in Bb, however trumpet music is transposed and trombone music is not. (If you are looking for systematic logic here you are not likely to find very much.)

In this score for woodwind quintet, all the instruments are playing the same melody in various octaves. Notice that the transposing instruments are written in a different key than the others. Because of the way these instruments are constructed, as well as the way music is traditionally written for them, it all works out in the sound.

Yes, you are correct. The french horn (no capital needed) is not a woodwind. It's a brass instrument. So, what is it doing in a woodwind quintet?...Tradition!

In larger instrumental scores, instrument groups are connected by brackets and by common barlines. This helps the reader's eye to see at a glance where music for groups of instruments appears in the score.

In the jazz band score on the following page, the staves for the saxes, the trumpets, and the trombones are grouped. The piano staves are grouped as usual. The guitar, bass and drums are each on single staves at the bottom. The "concert key" (the one played by non-transposing instruments) is Bb major. Therefore, the players of Bb instruments are reading in the key of C, thus their sounds will come out in Bb. Yes, the players of Eb instruments are reading in the key of G. Notice that the drum staff includes a neutral clef sign and has no key signature since drums do not play in a key. The bass sounds an octave lower than written. The guitar part shows the rhythm on the middle line, however the pitches are determined as the player voices the chords indicated by the symbols.

The expression "score and parts" is often seen in publisher's catalogues. In this context, the word *score* refers to the conductor's music—the score that contains the music for the entire ensemble. The music each player reads contains only the music his or her particular instrument is responsible to perform, and is referred to as a "part." When an error is suspected in one of the parts, the phrase "Let's check the score" is usually heard, and in this context is understood to mean the "full score."

The word *score* is also used as a verb. To "score a movie" means to compose music for it. A piece to be played by violins, violas, cellos, and double basses is said to be "scored for strings."

As our discussion suggests, composing for instruments is quite specialized and sometimes complex. We probably have raised more questions here than we have answered, however, our purpose is simply to provide a brief overview of the subject. If you are interested in a more in-depth study, there are many volumes of excellent information available that will guide you through the intricacies of orchestration.

# Coda

While this book must come to an end, your exploration of the topics discussed need not. There is still much to be learned about how we perceive music and about the principles that shape its meaning and significance in our lives. Also, considerably more information exists regarding the representation of music in notation than we have had time or space to include. Of course, you have the remainder of your years to contemplate the importance of music in our lives and the ways we are affected by it.

Hopefully, your concepts of what music is are sharpened, your understanding of how it works is expanded, and your ability to read, write and hear it is in a promising state of progress. If you decided along the way that some of your previous concepts needed revising or replacement, a major goal of this book has been reached. The most gratifying outcome would be that your ideas about music are now more systematic and practical and that this book has contributed to your progress toward the goals that caused you to read it.

One of the most important rewards an author can receive is to know that his or her efforts have been helpful. If you have enjoyed this book and found it of value, perhaps you would be kind enough to share your response. It would also be helpful to receive your suggestions for future improvement, in the event that revised editions are published. The best conversations are those that are conducted in both directions.

Finally, whatever your musical goals and ambitions, you surely will savor those moments of "arrival," but don't forget to enjoy the journey.

# Index

# OTHER STAGE 3 PUBLICATIONS

## LIES MY MUSIC TEACHER TOLD ME
### Music Theory For Grownups

It was the enthusiastic response from readers of "Lies" that inspired the writing of "Sounds." Now in its third printing, "Lies" continues to amuse and inform as it discusses a number of widely-accepted misconceptions about music. Although most of the theoretical topics in "Lies" are covered in "Sounds," you might enjoy the anecdotes. Also, it makes a great gift for your musical friends.

## MUSICAL EAR TRAINING
### Improvisation Charts

The charts contained in "Sounds" are available in durable lamination for individual drill and in projection transparencies for classroom use. The full set contains eight charts—seven for pitch drill and one for rhythm reading drill. Suggestions for use are included.

## COMPONENTS OF VOCAL BLEND

In response to requests by many choral directors and group singers who have experienced the "Eskelin sound," this informative and "plain talk" book will be available in Spring of 1999. The ideas and concepts are general and apply to any kind of choral singing: from opera chorus to madrigal group, from barbershop quartet to church choir. There is no suggestion to ask offenders to "sing softer." Instead, the book shows how to *solve* the problems, not simply cover them up. To be notified when available, check here_____, copy and mail, or e-mail.

## L.A. JAZZ CHOIR RECORDINGS

*From All Sides*  -  This album was nominated for a Grammy when released in 1986. Something for every taste.
*Rosemary Clooney with L.A. Jazz Choir Sings Rodgers, Hart & Hammerstein.* Other guest artists as well.
*Sweet Dreams* - L.A. Jazz Choir and the Mark Davidson Trio - John Pattituci on bass and Chuck Flores on drums.
*An Evening of Popular Classics* - VIDEO - the latest recording of the L.A. Jazz Choir. Very hot! Cool, too!

## Order Form
(Please photocopy this page)

____*The Sounds Of Music*, with CD ($37.50)       _____.____
____*Lies My Music Teacher Told Me*  ($14.95)     _____.____
____*Musical Ear Training Charts*  ($9.95)        _____.____
____*From All Sides* - cassette ($8.50)           _____.____
____*From All Sides* - CD ($14.50)                _____.____
____R. Clooney with LAJC - CD ($12.50)            _____.____
____*Sweet Dreams* - cassette ($6.50)             _____.____
____*Popular Classics* - video cassette ($19.50)  _____.____

Subtotal                                          _____.____
California orders add 8.25%                        _____.____
P&H: $3.50 first item, $1.00 each additional      _____.____
Enclosed check (or money order)                   _____.____
No credit cards, please.

Name:_____

Company or School:_____

Address:_____._____

City:_____State:_____

Zip:_____ Telephone:_____

**TEACHERS:** If you adopt a Stage 3 product for your class and order ten or more copies, we will refund the cost of your copy.

**BOOKSTORES:** Please inquire by phone regarding wholesale orders.

**YOUR SATISFACTION GUARANTEED!** If you choose to return your order FOR ANY REASON within thirty days, you will receive a full refund.

**Stage 3 Publishing**
**5759 Wallis Lane**
**Woodland Hills CA 91367**
**818/704-8657**

**e-mail:**
stg3music@earthlink.net
**URL:**
www.earthlink.net/~stg3music/